LEADING FIGURES IN THE HISTORY OF
OMEGA PSI PHI FRATERNITY, INC.

UNIVERSITY PRESS OF FLORIDA

Florida A&M University, Tallahassee
Florida Atlantic University, Boca Raton
Florida Gulf Coast University, Ft. Myers
Florida International University, Miami
Florida State University, Tallahassee
New College of Florida, Sarasota
University of Central Florida, Orlando
University of Florida, Gainesville
University of North Florida, Jacksonville
University of South Florida, Tampa
University of West Florida, Pensacola

LEADING FIGURES IN THE HISTORY OF OMEGA PSI PHI FRATERNITY, INC.

VOLUME 1

Edited by Judson L. Jeffries

UNIVERSITY PRESS OF FLORIDA

Gainesville/Tallahassee/Tampa/Boca Raton
Pensacola/Orlando/Miami/Jacksonville/Ft. Myers/Sarasota

Copyright 2025 by Judson L. Jeffries
All rights reserved
Published in the United States of America

30 29 28 27 26 25   6 5 4 3 2 1

Library of Congress Cataloging-in-Publication Data
Names: Jeffries, J. L. (Judson L.), 1965– editor.
Title: Leading figures in the history of Omega Psi Phi Fraternity, Inc. / edited by Judson L. Jeffries.
Description: 1. | Gainesville : University Press of Florida, 2025. | Includes bibliographical references and index. | Contents: Volume 1: Historical Prologue: The World into Which the Illustrious Omega Psi Phi Fraternity, Inc., was Born / Judson L. Jeffries—Introduction: Setting the Tone for Greatness / Judson L. Jeffries—I. In the World of Science—Viewing the World Through a Microscope Lens: The Life of Ernest E. Just / Theodore Walker Jr.—Percy Lavon Julian: His Exemplary Life, Academic Achievements, and Contributions to Society / Waweise Schmidt—II. Civil Rights Lawyers: Agitating with the System —Fred Gray and the Desegregation of Alabama's Public Schools / Derryn Moten—Oliver Hill, Spottswood Robinson, and Black Legal Activism in Jim Crow Virginia / Marvin Chiles—"Fighting the Good Fight": Legal Influences and Experiences of Oscar W. Adams Jr. Before and During the Second Reconstruction in Alabama, 1947 to 1967 / Bertis D. English— III. Sports Pioneers—Robert Lee Elder and the African American Golf Legacy / Marvin P. Dawkins and Jomills Henry Braddock, II—Clarence Gaines: An Athlete and Coach Who Made a "Big House" of the CIAA / Arthur Smith—IV. Music Geniuses—Count Basie: Red Bank's Soulful Original / Matthew Buttermann—Max Roach: Deeds, Not Words / Kevin C. McDonald —Roland Hayes: The Quiet Social Activist? / Christopher A. Brooks. |
Identifiers: LCCN 2024017600 (print) | LCCN 2024017601 (ebook) | ISBN 9780813079226 (v. 1; hardback) | ISBN 9780813080840 (v. 1 ; paperback) | ISBN 9780813079240 (v. 2 ; hardback) | ISBN 9780813080857 (v. 2 ; paperback) | ISBN 9780813070919 (v. 1 ; pdf) | ISBN 9780813073583 (v. 1 ; ebook) | ISBN 9780813070926 (v. 2 ; pdf) | ISBN 9780813073606 (v. 2 ; ebook) Subjects: LCSH: Omega Psi Phi Fraternity—History—20th century. | African American college students—Societies, etc.—History—20th century. | African American fraternal organizations—History—20th century. | African American Greek letter societies—History—20th century. | Greek letter societies—United States—History—20th century. | BISAC: HISTORY / African American & Black | SOCIAL SCIENCE / Ethnic Studies / American / African American & Black Studies
Classification: LCC LJ75.O55 L43 2025 (print) | LCC LJ75.O55 (ebook) | DDC 371.8/550973—dc23/eng/20240814 LC record available at https://lccn.loc.gov/2024017600 LC ebook record available at https://lccn.loc.gov/2024017601

The University Press of Florida is the scholarly publishing agency for the State University System of Florida, comprising Florida A&M University, Florida Atlantic University, Florida Gulf Coast University, Florida International University, Florida State University, New College of Florida, University of Central Florida, University of Florida, University of North Florida, University of South Florida, and University of West Florida.

University Press of Florida
2046 NE Waldo Road
Suite 2100
Gainesville, FL 32609
http://upress.ufl.edu

CONTENTS

List of Illustrations vii

Acknowledgments ix

Prologue: The World into Which the Illustrious Omega Psi Phi Fraternity, Inc., Was Born xi

Judson L. Jeffries

Introduction: Setting the Tone for Greatness 1

Judson L. Jeffries

I. In the World of Science

1. Viewing the World through a Microscope Lens (and Drama among Nazis): The Life of Ernest E. Just 35

   Theodore Walker Jr.

2. Percy Lavon Julian: His Exemplary Life, Academic Achievements, and Contributions to Society 57

   Waweise Schmidt

II. Civil Rights Lawyers: Agitating within the System

3. Fred Gray and the Desegregation of Alabama's Public Schools 81

   Derryn Moten

4. Oliver Hill, Spottswood Robinson III, and Black Legal Activism in Jim Crow Virginia 98

   Marvin Chiles

5. "Fighting the Good Fight": Legal Influences and Experiences of Oscar W. Adams Jr. before and during the Second Reconstruction in Alabama, 1947 to 1967 128

   Bertis D. English

III. Sports Pioneers

6. Robert Lee Elder and the African American Golf Legacy   157

   Marvin P. Dawkins and Jomills Henry Braddock II

7. Clarence Gaines: An Athlete and Coach Who Made a "Big House" of the Central Intercollegiate Athletic Association   179

   Arthur Smith

IV. Musical Geniuses

8. Count Basie: Red Bank's Soulful Original   203

   Matthew Buttermann

9. Max Roach: Deeds, Not Words   222

   Kevin C. McDonald

10. Roland Hayes: The Quiet Social Activist?   251

    Christopher A. Brooks

List of Contributors   281

Index   283

ILLUSTRATIONS

Figure

6.1. Systemic racism and Black participation in sports—a framework   158

Tables

6.1. The African American Golf Legacy: Some Key Actions by Year (1896–2019)   161
6.2. Lee Elder: Selected Golf Career Highlights   167

ACKNOWLEDGMENTS

This two-volume project is first and foremost dedicated to the memories of Ernest E. Just, PhD; Bishop Edgar A. Love, STB; Professor Frank C. Coleman, MS; and Oscar J. Cooper, MD. With this two-volume project, I have done what I think these distinguished gentlemen would have expected me to do given my position as a professor, scholar, and intellectual.

Second, this work would not have been possible were it not for Professors Herman Dreer, PhD, and Robert L. Gill, PhD, whose books on the fraternity's history laid the groundwork for scholars such as me to build on and perhaps go beyond what they set forth decades earlier. As impressive as Dreer's and Gill's works are they only scratch the surface, for there is much to unearth, study, learn, and examine when it comes to the illustrious Omega Psi Phi Fraternity, Inc., and the pathbreaking, trailblazing, and trendsetting figures that comprise its membership.

Third, other people to whom I owe a debt of gratitude include Sonja N. Woods, University Archivist in the Moorland-Spingarn Research Center at Howard University in Washington, DC, for providing much needed info on Love, Cooper, and Coleman during their years as students at Howard University. The registrars' offices at the University of Pennsylvania, University of Chicago, Boston University, and Dartmouth College also provided useful information.

Fourth I'd also like to thank Sian Hunter for recognizing the value and importance of this two-volume project and Zubin Meer for adding his editorial flair. Marthe Walters also proved helpful in the late stages of this project, and for that I am appreciative. I'm especially grateful to Molly Reinhoudt, PhD, for providing much needed logistic support at an important time during this project.

Finally, I give thanks to the Brothers of Eta Nu Nu (#982) of the illustrious Omega Psi Phi Fraternity, Inc., of Columbus, Ohio, who welcomed me with open arms after a decades-long absence from the fold. My quest to contribute to building a body of scholarship that places the illustrious Omega Psi Phi Fraternity, Inc., and its members in their appropriate place in history has been significantly enhanced through this association.

PROLOGUE

The World into Which the Illustrious
Omega Psi Phi Fraternity, Inc., Was Born

JUDSON L. JEFFRIES

The world into which the illustrious Omega Psi Phi Fraternity, Inc., was born was staunchly anti-Black—with America, by then already "a world power in fact as well as in name,"[1] seemingly leading the charge—and in many ways committed to keeping Blacks in their place. With all four of its founders being reared south of the Mason–Dixon line, they understood this, particularly Ernest Just, who spent part of his youth in the Deep South state of South Carolina, the Palmetto State, before leaving it as a teenager at the urging of his mother to enroll in a lily-white college prep school in New Hampshire.[2] Author Maurice S. Evans, an Englishman who made his home in South Africa, was so struck by race relations in the United States that he wrote in his 1916 book *Black and White in South East Africa* that conditions in the American South were "strikingly similar" to those of his homeland. "The separation of the races in all social matters," he wrote, "is as distinct in South Africa as in the Southern States [of the United States]."[3] Interestingly, the same month and year that the illustrious Omega Psi Phi Fraternity, Inc., was founded, so was the South African Party (SAP), also known as the South African National Party, established, in the aftermath of the 1910 Union of South Africa by various parties allied with Boer general Louis Botha and Jan Smuts, the country's minister of defense, mines and interior. SAP served as South Africa's governing party from its founding in 1911 until 1924 but is infamous for laying the foundation for apartheid.

Being students and members of the faculty at an historically Black university in the nation's capital did not shield the founders of the illustrious Omega Psi Phi Fraternity, Inc., from the harsh realities of racism and white supremacy about which Evans writes. As the yoke of oppression around the necks of many Blacks tightened in the decades following slavery, some within the African American[4] community began to forge partnerships and coalitions that sought to challenge the system in ways that eschewed the accommodationist and conciliatory tactics of those such as Booker T. Washington (the white-appointed leader of Black America), which so shaped the thinking and drove the actions of some Blacks. For those more activist-minded Blacks, progress was not only slow but also precarious—with losses accruing at a much greater rate than victories.

In 1866, hopes were raised with the passing of the nation's first civil rights bill. The Civil Rights Act of 1866 was the first federal law to affirm that all US citizens are equally protected under the law. It also defined citizenship and made it illegal to deny any person the rights of citizenship based on race. That was followed by the Civil Rights Act of 1875, also known as the Enforcement Act or the Force Act, which affirmed the "equality of all men before the law" and prohibited racial discrimination in public places such as buses, libraries, trains, restaurants, and hotels.

No sooner had the excitement exhibited by many Blacks reached its peak, that they saw what little progress they actually enjoyed from 1865 to 1877 come to an end, as the withdrawal of federal troops from the South culminated in Democrats consolidating control of state legislatures throughout the region, effectively bringing an end to the era known as Reconstruction. As the forces of white supremacy continued to mount a resurgence, the 1880s were not kind to Blacks and they were dealt an unsurprisingly crushing blow. In 1883, by an 8-1 decision, the Supreme Court ruled that the 1875 Civil Rights Act was unconstitutional. According to the court, neither the Thirteenth nor Fourteenth Amendments gave Congress the right to pass laws that prohibited racial discrimination in the private sector. According to C. Vann Woodward, interestingly, white and Black southerners interacted and mixed freely up to the 1880s, when state legislatures passed the first laws requiring railroads to provide separate cars for "Negro" or "colored" passengers.

This 1883 disappointment was followed by others, none bigger of course than the court ruling in *Plessy v. Ferguson* in 1896, where the US Supreme Court, led by Justice Henry B. Brown, held in a 7-1 decision that "separate but equal" facilities in the state of Louisiana did not violate the equal protection clause of the Fourteenth Amendment. The case stemmed from an 1892 incident in which Homer Plessy refused to sit in a train car in New Orleans (bound for Covington, Louisiana) reserved specifically for Black people. After refusing to leave the whites-only car at the conductor's insistence, Plessy was arrested and jailed. Curiously, the court maintained that separate treatment did not imply that Blacks were inferior and that "separate but equal" did indeed satisfy Fourteenth Amendment guarantees, thus giving legal sanction to Jim Crow segregation laws. As the lone dissenter, Justice John Marshall Harlan argued that the Constitution was colorblind and that the United States had no class system. Accordingly, all Americans should be afforded civil rights. Harlan's colleagues were unmoved.

One wonders the extent to which the justices' opinions on this matter were shaped by the prevalence of anti-Black racist thinking that contaminated every aspect of American life and was featured prominently in books, plays, and films, such as the case with Charles Carroll's *The Negro a Beast* (1900), Robert Shufeldt's *The Negro: A Menace to Civilization* (1907), and Thomas Dixon's *The Clansman* (1905), on which D. W. Griffith's film *Birth of a Nation* (1915) was based. And let's not forget the 1911 film *For Massa's Sake*, where a former slave is so enamored with his former master that he, sadly, sells himself back into slavery to help pay the white man's debts. The penultimate production was not just a film but a cultural happening. It framed the Reconstruction era, a period where whites witnessed a modicum of Black progress, with twenty Black congressmen and two Black senators acting as public servants from the South, as an assault on white Christian-nationalist fundamentalism. As a cinematic sensation, *For Massa's Sake* was for all intents and purposes the nation's first blockbuster, with an impact on the white psyche that was both immeasurable and undeniable.[5]

If Black peoples' confidence in the system had not already been totally shattered, two cases in particular during the first decade of the twentieth century—one in 1903 and one in 1906—should have convinced them of the imaginative lengths to which some whites in power were willing to go in order to keep Blacks from fully participating in American society. In *Giles v. Harris* (Alabama), the court refused to compel the board of registrars to register an African American to vote, claiming that unless it could actually supervise elections it was unable to force white Alabamians to allow Blacks to vote. The decision in *Hodges v. United States* was equally dumbfounding, as the court reversed a conviction against whites who had summarily ejected "citizens of the United States, of African descent" from their places of employment; naturally the decision narrowed the congressional civil rights authority under the Thirteenth Amendment.

It was against this backdrop that organizations of varying kinds committed to uplifting the Black race began sprouting up everywhere. T. Thomas Fortune headed one such organization. In 1890, he established the first major civil rights organization in the form of the National Afro-American League (NAAL). Much of its efforts included targeting the South where it waged war against discrimination and the weakening of the Fourteenth and Fifteenth Amendments, which ostensibly afforded Blacks citizenship while granting only Black men the right to vote. By the early 1900s, however, the NAAL had disappeared, as it failed to attract sufficient numbers of members, not to mention financial supporters. During the abolitionist period and into the early twentieth century, some Black activists and their groups were dependent upon the financial and political support of white philanthropists, corporate boards, and white foundations. And in some cases, Blacks were trapped into these alliances as dependent clients, which meant they had to rely on white liberals or moderates to articulate their agendas in order to garner wide support. In the late 1880s and through the 1890s the Knights of Labor was one such exception, as it practiced a policy of building a mutually beneficial biracial organization, as Black workers were approximately 15 percent of its 600,000 membership. Fortune's later project, the National Afro-American Council (NAACL) experienced a level of success never enjoyed by the NAAL. In fact, it was, for a short time considered the nation's premier Black organization. That it had the ear of President William McKinley until his death in 1901 only enhanced its reputation. Ironically, both Washington and W.E.B. Du Bois, who were considered bitter political rivals, were members. NAACL gatherings were so high profile that they were covered extensively by both Black newspapers and mainstream dailies.

In electoral politics, at the national level, a group of Black independents and former Republicans founded the National Democratic League in 1900 and actively attempted to foster among Blacks a new electoral loyalty to white Democrats, prompting some Blacks to support the Democratic candidate for president. At the time, many thought Woodrow Wilson a reasonable alternative. In his 1921 book *Woodrow Wilson As I Know Him*, Joseph P. Tumulty, Wilson's closest adviser, described Wilson as the warmest-hearted man he ever met. Furthermore, Tumulty offered, "I could not have been associated with him all these years, witnessing the great heart in action, without having full faith in what I say now." "No man of all my acquaintances . . . was more responsive, more sympathetic, and more inclined to pity and help than Woodrow Wilson, his eyes would fill with tears at the tale of some unfortunate man or woman in distress."[6] The man that Tumulty describes is one whose acquaintance African Americans never had the pleasure of making. In fact, Woodrow Wilson thanked Blacks for their support by putting in place the most egregious racial segregation policies that had ever existed in the federal government. The idea that Blacks might be able to win concessions from the Democratic Party proved delusional. Proof of that is that not one single Black delegate was ever spotted at a national Democratic convention until 1936, during the presidency of Franklin D. Roosevelt.

While Black men's fight for full citizenship has historically saturated the pages of most history books, it should be noted that during this time, Black women were equally active, with Black women's clubs playing an important role in Black peoples' uplift. In fact, in 1892, the Colored Women's League (CWL) was established in the nation's capital. Four years later, in 1896, the CWL, recognizing the formidable forces that opposed Black liberation, joined with the National Federation of Afro-American Women to form the National Association of Colored Women's Clubs (NACWC) under the leadership of Harriet Tubman and Helen Appo Cook, with the venerable Mary Church Terrell serving as its first president. The NACWC viewed its work in terms of uplifting Black women, men, and children. Simply put, the group's members saw the struggle to secure the right to vote for not only women but also Black men who continued to be disfranchised in both the North and the South by way of creative and illegal political maneuverings on the part of whites. Scholars often forget that the northern states were out front where the development and promulgation of white supremacy as a permanent feature of local, state policy was of concern. In the end, the merger enabled the NACWC to serve as a national umbrella group for local and regional Black women's organizations.

As the 1880s ended, things were so bad that a fair number of Blacks moved to Canada[7]; still a new century was dawning, and activist work of varying kind and in various places picked up steam. With the assistance of millionaires Andrew Carnegie and Collis P. Huntington, Booker T. Washington founded the National Negro Business League for the purpose of promoting Black entrepreneurship. This venture meshed nicely with Washington's thinking about the importance of economic independence as well as Blacks' struggle for racial equality. In 1905, the Niagara Movement—of whom some of its members were among the vanguard of African American lawyers in the country, led by W.E.B. Du Bois, PhD, and William Monroe Trotter— held its first meeting at the Erie Beach Hotel in Ft. Erie, Ontario, Canada. The group's philosophy contrasted sharply with the conciliatory approach of Washington, who preached patience and cooperation over militancy and disruption. Washington drew the ire of some Blacks who figured Washington to be the white man's Negro. In their minds he went along to get along. A good example of what rubbed some Blacks the wrong way about Washington is reflected in a 1912 speech he delivered before an audience of white college presidents. Washington offered: "We are trying to instil [sic] into the Negro mind that if education does not make the Negro humble, simple, and of service to the community, then it will not be encouraged."

Of Washington's critics, Du Bois was unquestionably the most outspoken, advocating full integration and militant protest against white supremacy. The franchise was something that Du Bois was adamant that Blacks fight for whereas Washington discouraged Blacks from doing so lest they alienate whites even further. Du Bois and others believed that such advice only played into the white man's hands. Du Bois and Trotter also saw the courts as a means for redress. Washington did, too, but his support was done out of public view—sometimes funneling monies to lawyers in support of civil rights litigation. Du Bois was more direct and public with his admonition of the system and those whites that helped sustain it. Du Bois and Trotter, as spokespersons for the Niagara Movement, exhorted Blacks to demonstrate, protest, and pursue litigation in response to injustice. Du Bois also stressed a liberal arts education for Blacks, which was diametrically opposed to Washington's fixation on vocational and industrial training for Blacks, especially those Blacks who lived in the South where such skills, Washington believed, could be put to good use. In time, both men proved to be right, but their opposed personalities and perhaps egos prevented any semblance of an alliance.

Eventually, the Niagara Movement joined with white reformers and formed the National Association for the Advancement of Colored People (NAACP) in 1909, eventually becoming the nation's leading civil rights organization. The following year, George Edmund Harris, PhD, and Ruth Standish Baldwin, a white New York City philanthropist, founded the Urban League, focusing its efforts on such things as finding adequate and affordable housing and getting Blacks jobs. In some ways, the founding of the illustrious Omega Psi Phi Fraternity, Inc., by three college students and their adviser was in keeping with the kinds of efforts described above. In the minds of some young folks, the struggle for racial equality would not be waged by older and more established Black men and women alone; college students also had a role to play. And while the illustrious Omega Psi Phi Fraternity, Inc., was not founded in direct response to the trials and tribulations that prompted the founding of those Black-oriented organizations already mentioned, the purpose of its founding was, in the main, to identify men whose potential for leadership was not only great but also (when actualized) something to be put to good use on behalf of the Black world.

While no mention of W.E.B. Du Bois as an inspiration for the founding of the illustrious Omega Psi Phi Fraternity, Inc., can be found in the writings or remarks of the fraternity's founders, given Du Bois's prominence at the time and the attention his works *The Souls of Black Folk* (1903),[8] "The Talented Tenth" (1903),[9] and *The Study of the Negro Problems* (1898)[10] garnered in progressive circles, it is not a reach to assume that Du Bois's call for an intellectual Black vanguard called—the "Talented Tenth"—that would lead the fight for racial and social justice—may have resonated with the three college students Edgar A. Love, Oscar J. Cooper, and Frank C. Coleman. Du Bois's conception of the Talented Tenth, a term coined by Henry Lyman Morehouse, a white New York Baptist minister, was one that maintained "that morality, culture, refinement, and education were prerequisites for this leadership class."[11] Simply put, Du Bois believed "the cultured aristocracy should be held accountable for elevating and educating the masses in order to advance the race."[12] Alexander Crummell thought similarly and may have been even more pointed and eloquent than Du Bois about the role of the formally educated Black. Crummell wrote, "In all great revolutions, and in all great reforms ... scholars have been conspicuous; in the reconstruction of society"[13] Crummell envisioned the scholarly among the Black race employing knowledge to enlighten the masses: "the leader, the creative and organizing mind, is the master-need in all societies of man."[14] Crummell went on to say that "if the scholarly are not inspired with the notion of leadership and duty, then with all their Latin and Greek and science they are but pedants, trimmers, opportunists." "For all true and lofty scholarship is weighty with the burdens and responsibilities of life and humanity."[15]

When contextualizing the opposition posed by the average white citizen and sanctioned by white officials at the local, state, and federal levels against Black Americans, it is important to proceed similarly with Blacks in Africa. One could make the argument without much strain that Blacks in Africa were significantly worse-off than their brothers and sisters in the United States. As the twentieth century began, only two African countries, Liberia and Ethiopia, had independent regimes; the remaining countries were run by European governments and companies. This was the result of the partitioning of Africa that began in earnest with the Berlin Conference of 1884–1885. These colonizers brought with them teachers of lies, so-called Christian missionaries, and settlers, resulting in unprecedented levels of wealth for Europe. The colonialists also came with military force. And contrary to popular belief, Africans did not acquiesce but rather put up strong resistance, thus prompting the Europeans to seek allies among Black emirs, kings, and chiefs who viewed the lucrative result of cooperation to be more satisfying than loyalty to one's homeland. Some areas were obtained by making deals with selfish, money-grubbing African leaders, others by force, and still others by duping indigenous leaders to sign contracts written in European languages the natives could not speak or read.

Between 1885 and 1900, the Portuguese annexed large domains in Angola and Mozambique. The Italians commandeered over two barren tracts, Italian Somaliland, and Eritrea on the Red Sea. Then they moved inland, in search of more extravagant possessions, to conquer Ethiopia and the headwaters of the Nile. Approximately 80,000 Ethiopians, however, slaughtered and beat back some 20,000 Italians in pitched battle at Adowa in 1896. It marked one of the first times that native Africans successfully defended themselves against white poachers, and it discouraged would-be invaders of Ethiopia by the Italians and other Europeans for 40 years.

Over the course of two decades, materials such as ivory, copper, cocoa, tobacco, rubber, and finally, gold, were identified and extracted from Africa leaving many countries depleted of some of its most valuable resources. By 1914, 90 percent of Africa had been divided among seven European countries—Germany, France, Great Britain, the Netherlands, Belgium, Portugal, and Spain. The Berlin Conference's objective was to ensure that each European country that staked possession over whatever African area that interested it agreed to bring civilization there in the form of Christianity and to initiate commercial trade to each area that it planned to occupy. Also, a country's claim to a territory was only legally recognized if it informed the other European players of its intentions and put in place some level of military ground force.

Given the state of the Black world, the illustrious Omega Psi Phi Fraternity's founding could not have been timelier, as it followed the end of American slavery by less than six decades and the partitioning of Africa by a quarter century, and it endured the inhospitable environs of the Jim Crow era for nearly the combined length of both. While there were a few victories here and there, which at times offered a glimmer of hope, such as the ruling in the 1911 case of *Bailey v. State of Alabama*, invalidating a law that facilitated a form of involuntary servitude known as "debt peonage"; life, as written in the poem "Mother To Son" by the esteemed Langston Hughes, himself an Omega man, was no crystal stair: "it's had tacks in it, and splinters, and boards torn up, and places with no carpet on the floor ... Bare." As already referenced, Blacks could not count on either local or state officials to spearhead any sustained efforts intended to champion racial equality. Blacks were naive if they expected anything different from the executive branch. To say that the White House could not be counted on to support Blacks and their right to full citizenship is an understatement, as the presidential administrations between 1876 and 1900 opted not to challenge laws designed to subjugate African Americans, such as grandfather clauses, poll taxes, white primaries, literacy tests, and most importantly, lynching. In fact, between 1900 and 1914, approximately 1,000 American Blacks were lynched.

As Blacks became more literate and a college education became more accessible, by way of the Morrill Acts of 1862 and 1890 and resulting in the establishment of land-grant institutions,[16] Blacks began to explore new avenues for uplift. Realizing that the assault on white injustice had to be fought on several fronts, Blacks began to establish in earnest, certain kinds of enterprises, some of which for the first time. The most notable were banks, realty companies, and insurance firms.[17] Other examples include the fraternal orders such as the Masons, Odd Fellows, and the Knights of Pythias, along with Black Greek-letter fraternities and sororities on America's college campuses. Alpha Kappa Nu (1903), Pi Gamma Omicron (1905), Gamma Phi (1905),[18] Alpha Phi Alpha (1906), and Alpha Kappa Alpha (1908) rounded out the first group. Kappa Alpha Psi[19] and the illustrious Omega Psi Phi Fraternity, Inc., followed three years later in 1911,[20] with Delta Sigma Theta coming in 1913. Phi Beta Sigma (1914), Zeta Phi Beta (1920) and Sigma Gamma Rho (1922) followed. Anything less than a collective effort on the part of Black America was needed, if it had any hopes of experiencing the full measure of what it meant to be an American citizen.

If anyone thought he or she had reason to place one's faith in any of the presidents of that era, such a decision would, again, prove misguided. Again, neither Democrat nor Republican could be counted among the Negroes' allies. The election of Teddy Roosevelt, a Republican, in 1904, ushered into office arguably the first presidential administration that openly opposed civil rights and suffrage for African Americans.[21] To give an example of the extent to which Roosevelt was anti-Black, consider that he turned a blind eye after whites massacred Blacks in Atlanta in 1906 and he attributed the lynchings of Black men to their supposed lust for white women. History has recorded Roosevelt, after being in office for nary a month, inviting Tuskegee Institute's Booker T. Washington to the White House for dinner, the first such honor for an African American. However, Roosevelt's entreaty was not motivated by benevolence; instead, the purpose of the invitation was to discourage Blacks from striving for racial equality. It was not Washington's intention to quarrel with the president; rather, he sought the opportunity to ingratiate himself with Roosevelt for the purpose of currying political favor. Moreover, the story that Roosevelt extended to Washington a dinner invitation is slightly exaggerated. Roosevelt arranged to meet with Washington at the White House, but by the end of the meeting Roosevelt felt that things had gone so well that he then asked Washington if he'd like to stay for dinner and Washington accepted. When news of this development broke, many Blacks found reason to rejoice; many whites, on the other hand, were outraged, prompting some of them to question the president's mental acuity. Over time, some whites feared that Washington was positioning himself to dictate White House policy. Their fears lacked any semblance of common sense.

For all his rhetoric about fairness and equality, Roosevelt believed firmly in the existence of a racial hierarchy, which not surprisingly shaped his attitudes on race relations, land rights, American imperialism, and the emerging—and utterly disturbing—science of eugenics. In his book *Theodore Roosevelt and the Idea of Race,* Thomas G. Dyer wrote, "The force of race in history occupied a singularly important place in Roosevelt's broad intellectual outlook."[22] Roosevelt subscribed to the widely held belief that African Americans were intellectually inferior, so much so that he set out to decrease the number of federal appointments to African Americans and promised white southerners that he would appoint local federal officials who would not upset the tenor of the South and the North. "As a race and in the mass they [blacks] are altogether inferior to whites," Roosevelt admitted to a colleague in a 1906 letter.[23] Almost a decade later, he told Senator Henry Cabot Lodge of Massachusetts that "the great majority of Negroes in the South are wholly unfit for the suffrage" and that giving them voting rights could "reduce parts of the South to the level of Haiti."[24] Roosevelt believed wholeheartedly that American greatness stemmed from its rule by racially superior men of European descent.

Elected in 1908, William Howard Taft, Roosevelt's successor, proved to be no friend of the Negro either. He claimed to oppose racial discrimination and said that Blacks should vote, but he did not interfere in the domestic affairs of the southern states, where voting proved to be most difficult for Blacks. Taft was at best paternalistic and at worst racist. With an eye on the presidency Taft appealed to southern whites to break the Democratic Party's grip on the "Solid South," writing that the Jim Crow laws were not harmful to Blacks because Blacks were not ready to use the vote well anyway. In Taft's words, "When a class of persons is so ignorant and so subject to oppression and misleading that they are merely children, not having the mental stature of manhood, then it can hardly be said that their voice in the government secures any benefit to them."[25]

Picking up where Roosevelt left off, Taft also met with Booker T. Washington, but not over dinner, and in the strongest possible terms conveyed to him that Blacks should not expect the president to enforce the Fifteenth Amendment that granted Black men the right to vote but that instead they should concentrate on obtaining an education. This idea aligned perfectly with Washington's philosophy on Blacks and the struggle for racial equality, which some Blacks considered practical, while others such as Du Bois and Monroe Trotter considered limiting, accommodating, and played directly into the white man's hands. Some within the African American community were so put off by Taft's administration where Blacks were concerned that they publicly condemned his presidency. Among them was Du Bois, who was steadfast in his criticism, calling for new leadership.

The situation worsened with the election of Woodrow Wilson in 1912, despite promising Blacks justice—"not mere grudging justice, but justice executed with liberality and cordial good feeling."[26] Wilson was nothing more than a wolf in sheep's clothing. Some naively believed that Wilson had abandoned his racist ways that saw him prohibit the admission of Blacks to Princeton University years earlier when he served as its president. Wilson, formerly the governor of New Jersey and president of Princeton University, showed his true colors early on when he encouraged the introduction and passage of discriminatory legislation, such as a bill passed by the House of Representatives that made interracial marriage in the District of Columbia a felony. Wilson's ascendency to the presidency was fortuitous, as he benefited greatly from the split in the Republican Party caused by former president Theodore Roosevelt's attempted return to the White House via the Bull Moose Party. Some Blacks were willing to sign on to this new party if they could receive assurances that this new party would stand unequivocally for full citizenship for African Americans. NAACP officials (the primary author being Du Bois) crafted a carefully worded statement to be placed in the Progressive Republican platform. The statement called for the repeal of unfair discriminatory laws and for the universal enfranchisement of Black Americans. It was then hustled off to Chicago by Joel Spingarn[27] and advocated for by Henry Moskowitz[28] and Jane Addams.[29] Roosevelt wouldn't hear of it. Not only did he have the unmitigated gall to allow the southern white delegates to have their way in excluding the statement from the platform and in prohibiting some of the Black delegates from the convention, but he also counseled Spingarn that he should be "careful of that Du Bois," who was in Roosevelt's estimation a "dangerous" man.[30] With that, Blacks realized that the Bull Moose Party was nothing more than a mirage, and decided, in an unprecedent move, to cast their lot with Wilson, the Democrat, whom they saw as the lesser of the three evils. Apparently, what some may or may not have fully understood is that the lesser of three evils is still evil.

In his book *United States since 1865*, John A. Krout maintains that Wilson brought "a strong sense of right and wrong" to the presidency, a point on which many Blacks would disagree.[31] For example, upon taking office, much to the chagrin of Blacks, one of Wilson's priorities was making it a requirement to include a photograph with any application for a federal position to ensure the exclusion of African Americans from government posts. Wilson also pushed for the segregation of federal workers as well as for the methodical and systematic demotion of African American civil servants. What's more, he claimed unabashedly that any effort designed to improve Black peoples' lot was futile. In his demented mind, Blacks were beyond help. In his well-received five-volume *History of the American People*, Wilson glorified the Confederacy, inexplicably describing the peculiar institution of slavery as a gentle patrician affair and castigating Reconstruction efforts to improve the lives of the formerly enslaved.[32] What Du Bois saw in Wilson that prompted him to throw his support behind his presidential campaign is a great mystery. As an Alpha man, one wonders whether Du Bois's ill-advised endorsement of Wilson was his only regret in life.

African Americans—ever since Abraham Lincoln signed the Emancipation Proclamation—had expected some measure of equity from the federal government, more specifically the president. Yet the sense of neglect and, dare I say, betrayal, ran deep. Despite the odds stacked against many of the organizations, Black or white, that sought to lift up the Black race, the impact made by such groups during the late nineteenth and early twentieth century, no matter how small, was not, contrary to what some may argue, inconsequential. The illustrious Omega Psi Phi Fraternity, Inc., was no exception. Indeed, there are few areas of human endeavor that have not been touched by the men of Omega. These men have left an indelible mark on both the country and the world.[33]

Notes

1 Arthur S. Link, *American Epoch: A History of the United States since the 1890s* (New York: Alfred A. Knopf, 1958).
2 Just's mother read about Kimball Union Academy in Meriden, New Hampshire, in the *Christian Endeavor World* and urged him to apply. Just was accepted and enrolled in 1900, after working his way north aboard a ship. See Jan Onofrio, *South Carolina Biographical Dictionary*, vol. 2 (St. Clair Shores, MI: Somerset, 2000), 421.
3 Maurice S. Evans, *Black and White in South East Africa: A Study in Sociology* (London: Longmans, Green, 1916).
4 The words "African American," "Black," "Black American," and "Negro" are used interchangeably throughout this book according to sound and context as well as to avoid redundancy.
5 Joshua Myers, *Cedric Robinson: The Time of the Black Radical Tradition* (Boston: Polity Press, 2021).

6   Joseph P. Tumulty, *Woodrow Wilson As I Know Him* (Garden City, NJ: Doubleday, Page, 1921), 473.
7   Clifford Mason, *Macbeth in Harlem: Black Theater in America from the Beginning to "Raisin in the Sun"* (New Brunswick, NJ: Rutgers University Press, 2020), 63.
8   W.E.B. Du Bois, *The Souls of Black Folk* (Chicago: A. C. McClurg, 1903).
9   W.E.B. Du Bois's essay "The Talented Tenth" is published in Booker T. Washington's *The Negro Problem* (New York: J. Pott, 1903).
10 W.E.B. Du Bois, "The Study of the Negro Problems." *Annals of the American Political and Social Science* 11 (January 1898): 1–23.
11 Christopher Cameron, *Black Freethinkers: A History of African American Secularism* (Evanston, IL: Northwestern University Press, 2019), 112.
12 D. S. Green, "W.E. B. Du Bois' Talented Tenth: A Strategy for Racial Advancement." *Journal of Negro Education* 46 (Summer 1977): 358–366.
13 Alexander Crummell, "Civilization: The Primal Need of the Race," in *American Negro Academy, Occasional Papers No. 3* (Washington, DC: The Academy, 1897), 3–7.
14 Crummell, "Civilization."
15 Crummell.
16 The Morrill Act of 1890 gave rise to Alabama A&M, Alcorn State University, Central State University, Delaware State University, Florida A&M University, Fort Valley State University, Kentucky State University, Langston University, Lincoln University, North Carolina A&T University, Prairie View A&M University, South Carolina State University, Southern University and A&M College, Tennessee State University, West Virginia State College, and the University of the District of Columbia,
17 Despite the misguided ideas of people such as Wall Street financier Russell Sage, who believed that riches were the reward for superior intelligence, honesty, and thrift, race featured prominently in one's ability to accumulate wealth, then and now. Professor William Graham Sumner of Yale University, who was tone deaf to the deleterious effects of race as it relates to the acquisition of property and income, claimed heartlessly that economic inequality was not only inevitable but also violated no "law of nature, religion, ethics, or the State." Quoted in Eric Foner's *The Story of American Freedom* (New York: Norton), 139.
18 Gamma Phi, founded at Wilberforce University, is the first known Black fraternity founded at an HBCU. That same year, Pi Gamma Omicron was founded at the Ohio State University, a predominantly white institution. According to a Wisconsin newspaper article in the *Janesville Daily* dated Monday, October 12, 1903, Alpha Kappa Nu Greek Society was founded in 1903, on Indiana University's Richmond campus, but was short-lived due to the low number of African American men enrolled at the school. This means that Alpha Phi Alpha Fraternity, Inc., was not the first Black Greek letter fraternity founded on a college campus.
19 Interestingly, two of Kappa Alpha Psi's founders were former students at Howard University.
20 Contrary to conventional wisdom or a lack thereof, the illustrious Omega Psi Phi Fraternity, Inc., unlike Alpha Phi Alpha and Kappa Alpha Psi, was not founded due to Black exclusion from white fraternities and other clubs. After all, Howard University is an HBCU.

21 That Lt. Col. Theodore Roosevelt of the First Volunteer Cavalry Regiment could turn his back on Blacks upon becoming president after the Buffalo Soldiers (a force that included 1,250 Black troops of the Ninth and Tenth Cavalry in Brig. Gen. Samuel F. Sumner's Cavalry Division and the Twenty-Fourth Infantry in Brig. General Jacob F. Kent's First Division), which saved his hide during the Battle of San Juan Heights in Cuba on July 1, 1898, is indicative of the psychopathology of antiblack racism, then and now. See Edward Van Zile Scott, *The Unwept: Black American Soldiers and the Spanish-American War* (Montgomery, AL: Black Belt Press, 1996).

22 Thomas G. Dyer, *Theodore Roosevelt and the Idea of Race* (Baton Rouge: Louisiana State University Press, 1992)

23 Dyer, *Theodore Roosevelt*. Some Black leaders had become so disgusted with Roosevelt that by 1908 they cast their ballots for Democrats for the first time in their lives, opting to vote for William Jennings Bryan, who many Black leaders considered to be an "avowed enemy" to their "false friends" in the Republican Party. See Michael J. Klarman, *Unfinished Business: Racial Equality in American History* (New York: Oxford University Press, 2007), 94

24 Dyer, *Theodore Roosevelt*. One incident that should have told Blacks everything they needed to know about Roosevelt occurred that same year (1906), on August 14, in Brownsville, Texas. It involved a group of Black soldiers from nearby Ft. Brown, a dead white bartender, and a wounded police officer wounded. None of the alleged perpetrators was ever positively identified; nor did anyone come forward and confess to the crimes. None of the Black soldiers was ever brought before a court of law, military or civil. Yet Roosevelt, in an unprecedented breach of authority, punished three companies of Black troops with unusual severity, ordering the three companies "discharged without honor . . . and forever barred from re-enlistment." Of the 160 or more Black soldiers dismissed, several were near retirement and six had won the Medal of Honor in campaigns against Native Americans, Spaniards, or Filipino insurrectionists. Although the order was signed on November 5, Roosevelt withheld its release until after the congressional elections the following day, presumably to lessen its political impact. According to the *New York Herald,* a shift in the Black vote would have reduced the Republican majority in the House of Representatives from 59 to 14, and the *Washington Post* pointed out that a switch of one half of the Black votes in Cincinnati could have defeated Roosevelt's son-in-law, Representative Nicholas Longworth. For more detail, see William Henry Harbaugh, *Power and Responsibility: The Life and Times of Theodore Roosevelt* (New York: Farrar, Straus and Giroux, 1961), 304.

25 Dyer, *Theodore Roosevelt*.

26 Klarman, *Unfinished Business*, 98.

27 Formerly a professor of comparative literature at Columbia University from 1899 to 1911, Spingarn, a white liberal Republican (b. 1875), was instrumental in building the NAACP and served as its second president from 1930 until his death in 1939. In 1916, Spingarn, the holder of a Columbia PhD, enlisted in the US Army and served as a major during World War I. He was instrumental in seeing that a training camp for Black officers was established, resulting in the commissioning of approximately a thousand Black officers. He also donated uniforms for Howard University students who enlisted.

See "Joel Spingarn (1875–1939)," Jewish Virtual Library: A Project of AICE, accessed February 6, 2022, www.jewishvirtuallibrary.org/joel-spingarn.
28 Born in 1880 and died in 1936, Henry Moskowitz, a PhD in philosophy, was a Jewish civil rights activist and cofounder of the NAACP.
29 Jane Addams (1860–1935) was a cofounder of the American Civil Liberties Union and cofounder of Chicago's Hull House, one of America's most famous settlement houses. Addams was known as one of America's leading public philosophers.
30 W.E.B. Du Bois, *The Autobiography of W.E.B. Du Bois* (New York: International, 1968), 126.
31 John A. Krout, *United States since 1865* (New York: Barnes and Noble), 124.
32 In the end, Wilson was not only a racist but also a self-absorbed opportunist and someone from whom extracting the truth often proved somewhat difficult. Let us not forget that during his run for the presidency Wilson promised to keep the United States out of the war.
33 E.g., since the prestigious Spingarn Award was created in 1915, twenty-four of its recipients have been men of Omega.

Introduction

Setting the Tone for Greatness

JUDSON L. JEFFRIES

Until the Civil War (1861–1865), most Blacks lived below the Mason–Dixon line, where opportunities to pursue a college education were severely limited. W.E.B Du Bois spoke to this very issue when he wrote, "The South believed an educated Negro to be a dangerous Negro. And the South was not wholly wrong; for education among all kinds of men always has had, and always will have, an element of danger and revolution, of dissatisfaction and discontent."[1] Before 1860, less than 30 Blacks had earned a college degree. That number dropped even more during the Civil War, as many colleges were forced to shut down, making access to a college education even more difficult, not only for Blacks but everyone. However, between 1865, the start of Reconstruction, and three years following the end of Reconstruction, in 1880, college attendance among Blacks increased as scores of institutions of higher learning were founded, specifically to educate the growing numbers of Black students wanting to further their education. Howard University, founded in 1867, was among them. Interestingly, the university's founding coincided with the migration of free Blacks into the nation's capital on the heels of emancipation and the Missionary Society of the First Congregational Church's response to the education and training needs of these new northern transplants.[2]

As the numbers of Blacks enrolled in college increased, so did the number of graduates, totaling 208 by 1876. Steadily, more and more African Americans began to pursue higher education in the years following Reconstruction. In fact, some 20 odd years later, Blacks accounted for 1,336 of America's college graduates.[3] As the Black college student population continued to grow, Black students began establishing organizations that spoke specifically to their interests, fostered camaraderie and featured the idea of uplift as well as promoting excellence in and outside the classroom.

At the time of the founding of Howard University, named in honor of Civil War general Oliver O. Howard, who was commissioner of the Freedman's Bureau, the university's student body was relatively small but larger than most others' due to the rapidly growing size of the district's Black population. At the time of its founding Howard received more than $500,000 from the Freedman's Bureau to purchase a classroom building, two buildings for dormitories, and a medical building. Thus, Howard's campus was more developed than those of many other Black schools, making it more appealing to some aspiring college students.[4] What's more, in 1900 there were 72 cities with 5,000 black residents or more, with Washington, DC, leading the way with nearly 90,000 Black residents.[5] By the 1910s, with the southern economy struggling mightily, making farming[6] precarious at best, and with the resurgence of the Ku Klux Klan, not surprisingly, many Blacks fled north, and they did so at a rate of 19,000 per year.[7] Over the next ten years or so, 500,000 southern Blacks left the region. The North may not have represented the promise of freedom as it once did to escaping slaves many years earlier on the Underground Railroad, but its major cities did hold (real or imagined) the hope of a better life. The *Chicago Defender* was just one of several Black newspapers that urged southern Blacks to pick up their stakes and venture north. One callout read:

> "To die from the bite of frost is far more glorious than at the hands of a mob. I beg you, my brother, to leave the benighted land."[8] The biblical imagery, tightly woven into slave lore, reappeared when the new migrants compared their exodus north to the "flight out of Egypt" and "going to Canaan." In fact a group of Black migrants traveling from Mississippi to Illinois stopped their watches, fell on their knees, and, at the top of their lungs, sang the hymn "I Done Come Out of the Land of Egypt with the Good News" as they crossed Over the Ohio River.[9]

While many hopped off the train in Chicago and started new lives there, others found the mid-Atlantic and northeast states more to their liking. Washington, DC, was, as already alluded to, one such destination. And as was the case with many Black colleges and universities, Howard University's student body, in the early years, consisted mostly of students who lived in proximity or hailed from the neighboring states of Maryland and Virginia. Because interstate travel was not yet commonplace, the student body consisted of comparatively few students from faraway places. What's more, among Howard's majority-male entering class were several white female students, a few of whom were the daughters of two of the school's cofounders.

Initially Howard along with members of the First Congregational Society joined together to create a college to teach theology to African American clergymen, but in no time at all the university expanded into the area of liberal arts and medicine. Oliver O. Howard served as president from 1869 to 1874. Although the school was originally conceived in 1866, it was actually chartered as a university in 1867 by an act of the US Congress; the only HBCU to hold such a distinction. In the years following the founding of the Omega Psi Phi Fraternity, Inc., on November 17, 1911, at Howard University, campus life at colleges and universities wherever there was Omega, was forever changed. Said Frank Coleman: "I with Oscar Cooper and Edgar Love envisioned a land down in the valley that was purple and gold. The light we saw shined from beyond time itself. We took our light to Dr. Ernest Everett Just who assisted us in giving our foster mother life. The four of us combined gave all our love, peace, and happiness to Omega."[10]

The illustrious Omega Psi Phi Fraternity, Inc., was founded during Wilbur Patterson Thirkield's administration. Thirkield, a white man, was Howard University's eighth president, serving from 1906 to 1912. Born on September 25, 1854, in Warren County, Ohio, in the tiny town of Franklin, with a population of no more than 1,000 residents, Thirkield had virtually no experience interacting with Blacks as a youth. A highly educated man, naturally, Thirkield earned a BA degree from Ohio Wesleyan in 1876, a bachelor of sacred theology from Boston University in 1881 as well as a doctor of divinity from that same institution. A seasoned administrator, Thirkield had been president of Gammon Theological Seminary in Atlanta, Georgia, from 1883 to 1900. He had also been a member of the board of trustees of historically Black Meharry Medical College and Clark University in Atlanta, Georgia. For several years he resided in Cincinnati, where he was the general secretary of the Freedman's Aid Society of the Methodist Episcopal Church.

To fully appreciate the story of the illustrious Omega Psi Phi Fraternity, Inc., and the men who constitute its membership, it is imperative readers acquaint themselves with the organization's founders, especially Love, Cooper, and Coleman. It is true that Ernest Just is as important as the three undergraduates with whom he teamed up, but it was from the three college students that this idea originated. What's more, Just is known the world over, as books, scholarly articles, and popular writings about him are easily accessible and in no short supply, making the highly accomplished scientist a household name among those who study African American history. What readers may or may not know about Just, Theodore Walker Jr.'s chapter (chapter 1) is likely to fill in those gaps. In the cases of Love, Cooper, and Coleman, among laypersons and, dare I say, even the college educated, these men's names are not as well known. This is due, in large part, because their stories are not taught in American classrooms, nor are there books or scholarly articles devoted to their lives. Hence the importance of soaking up, as a starting point, the biographical information that appears on the pages that follow. Perhaps the information below will inspire scholars and writers to embark on more expansive treatments of Love, Cooper, and Coleman.

Love, Cooper, and Coleman were all raised in the eastern region (mid-Atlantic, to be exact) of the country. An inquisitive child and high-achieving student, Frank Charles Coleman, a DC native, was ideally suited for Howard University. Born on July 11, 1889,[11] the precocious young Frank Coleman attended the famous M Street High School,[12] housed at the time Coleman was a student there in a building on M Street, near New York and New Jersey avenues, and so hence the name. The M Street High School was considered one of the nation's best public high schools for Blacks during the first half of the twentieth century. Some of the luminaries that attended the M Street High School include Nannie Helen Burroughs,[13] Benjamin O. Davis Sr.,[14] Georgiana R. Simpson,[15] and Jean Toomer.[16] In 1899, the students at the M Street High School scored higher on standardized tests in English and other general subjects than the students at the city's white high schools.[17] Historian Rayford Logan, a 1913 graduate of the M Street High School, once bragged that

> the classical or college preparatory curriculum at M Street was superior to that of the first two years of some colleges and universities, regardless of geographical location, in 1972. It included, for instance, two years of Greek, three years of French, four years of Latin: grammar the first year, *Caesar's Gallic Wars* the second year, *Cicero's Orations* the third year, and *Virgil's Aeneid* the fourth year. Our courses in mathematics included geometry, trigonometry, and higher algebra. In English classes we read not only *Silas Marner* and some of the Plays and Sonnets of Shakespeare but also William H. Prescott's *The Conquest of Mexico* and *the Conquest of Peru*, Dickens's *Tale of Two Cities*, for instance.[18]

The number of students M Street High School sent to the nation's most prestigious colleges is impressive. For example, Edwin French Tyson (class of 1903) was the first Black M Street High School graduate to attend Harvard College.[19] Other graduates were admitted to such schools as Amherst, Bowdoin, Brown, Dartmouth, and Yale universities, to name a few.[20] The school also had an outstanding faculty. Among its teachers were Carter G. Woodson,[21] Jessie Fauset,[22] and Christian Fleetwood, the Black soldier who was awarded the Medal of Honor for his actions during the Civil War. At one point, the great Dr. Anna Julia Haywood Cooper[23] also taught there, mainly in the areas of Latin, mathematics, and science, while serving as the school's principal.

While at the M Street High School, Coleman developed an interest in physics and "conducted many an experiment to discover some new secret nature."[24] For him, every day was an opportunity to discover something new. Aside from his studies, being a high school cadet took up much of his time.[25] After graduating in 1908, Coleman carried his love of science to Howard one year later where he majored in physics.[26] While there Coleman wrote for the student newspaper, the *Howard Journal,* and like Love was a member of the Kappa Sigma Debating Society. After graduating cum laude in 1913 with a BS degree in physics, school officials offered him a full-time faculty position. Although flattered by the offer, Coleman was never tempted to accept a position as a full-time faculty member at that moment, for he believed that additional training was necessary if one were to take seriously the responsibility of being a college professor. Instead, Coleman took a teaching job at the Joseph K. Brick Agricultural Industrial and Normal School,[27] near Enfield, North Carolina. After a short stint there, Coleman returned to DC and secured employment at Armstrong Manual Training School.[28]

Eventually, on the recommendation of Professor Just, Coleman enrolled in graduate school at the University of Chicago on June 19, 1915.[29] However, the outbreak of World War I interrupted Coleman's graduate work,[30] as did his insufferable schedule, which included heading the Physics Department.[31] It is for these reasons that it wasn't until September 1922 that Coleman finally completed the MS in Physics at the University of Chicago.[32] With so many responsibilities to juggle, it seems implausible that Coleman would have had time to pursue a doctorate at the University of Pennsylvania,[33] but he did. Unfortunately, Coleman never finished, in part because his duties as head of the Physics Department took precedence, making it difficult to take a leave of absence. As evidence of Coleman's commitment, under his stewardship, the Physics Department became one of the university's strongest academic units.[34]

Upon being commissioned as an officer at Ft. Des Moines[35] in Iowa, Coleman was among numerous Howard University graduates in the ranks of the army's commissioned officers. He served with the American Expeditionary Forces in France and several defensive sectors, carrying out his responsibilities with honor and valor.[36] He was an exemplary role model for both Black and white soldiers. Upon returning to the states, First Lt. Coleman of the 368th US Infantry, then stationed at Camp Meade (now Ft. Meade) in nearby Maryland, married fellow Howard alumnus, Mary Edna Brown (a founder of Delta Sigma Theta) on May 25, 1918. Mary's father, the Rev. S. N. Brown[37] performed the ceremony.[38] After being discharged from the army, Coleman returned to Howard where he remained until retirement.

Coleman led a life characterized by faith and a strong sense of community. And his civic activities extended far beyond the fraternity. He was a member of the Boys' Committee of the YMCA as well as a Prince Hall Mason. Coleman was also a charter member and past commander of the James E. Walker Post 26 of the American Legion in Washington, DC, as well as a member of the American Society of Physics Teachers. From the outset, Coleman's commitment to Omega was steadfast and unwavering throughout his life. He served as the fraternity's first Grand Keeper of Seal (national treasurer). His loyalty to and love for Omega Psi Phi were matched by few who have worn the royal purple and old gold. Coleman entered Omega chapter on February 24, 1967.[39]

Like Coleman, Oscar James Cooper was also a DC native and attended M Street High School.[40] As a youngster he was quiet and studious—a voracious reader and lover of books, which explains the expansive library that stood out at his W. Jefferson Street residence, years later. Raised to be humble, reserved, and meticulous in appearance, Cooper was also a gentleman. The summer after graduating from high school in 1909, Cooper left home to find work to help pay for college. After amassing an unspecified sum of money, Cooper enrolled at Howard University. Cooper's love of science led him to excel in biology. Burning the midnight oil was not atypical for Cooper. His colleagues were therefore not surprised when he worked just as diligently to bring the illustrious Omega Psi Phi Fraternity, Inc., into being. For his efforts, he was made the fraternity's first Grand Keeper of Records (national secretary). In the fraternity's second year of existence, Cooper served as its Grand Basileus (national president). Cooper graduated in 1913 with a bachelor's degree (AB) from Howard University's College of Arts and Sciences.[41]

Cooper's penchant for hard work paid dividends as he entered medical school. Cooper's upbringing and his tutelage under Just formed the basis of his relentless pursuit of scientific inquiry. Rather than go to medical school elsewhere, Cooper remained at Howard University. So, determined and driven to earn an MD, he completed medical school in due course, finishing in 1918,[42] just two years after Ernest Just, his mentor, earned his PhD at the University of Chicago. That he was able to achieve such a lofty goal at a time when Blacks were often discouraged, and at times blocked from pursuing occupations traditionally reserved for whites, is a testament to his will and fortitude.

Upon earning his MD, Cooper moved to the City of Brotherly Love, where he interned at Mercy Philadelphia on the city's westside, which opened in the summer of 1918 as Misericordia Hospital. Philadelphia seemed like an ideal landing spot for Cooper, for it was just 140 miles from his hometown of Washington, DC, and his arrival occurred at a time when Blacks were starting to make their presence felt there, with the Black population growing by leaps and bounds. Due mainly to the Pennsylvania Railroad's policy of free transportation north to southern Blacks interested in working for the railroad, from 1910 to 1920, the city's Black population soared from 84,000 to 134,000. And by 1930, Blacks numbered 219,000. The numbers continued to climb, reaching 250,000 in 1940, 375,000 in 1950 and 655,000 by 1970.[43]

By the time Cooper settled in Philadelphia, Blacks were, figuratively and literally, on the move. For example, by 1920, E. C. Brown had founded the Dunbar Theatre while Major R.R. Wright established the Citizens & Southern Bank, its motto being "The Bank of Personal Service."[44] What's more, the strong and tight-knit community of Black churches,[45] for which Philadelphia was and continues to be known, along with the Christian Street YMCA and Catherine Street YWCA, were on hand to help ease the transition of new arrivals into the city. Black leaders teamed up with progressive whites to create the Negro Migration Committee, which figured prominently in job placement, healthcare, and vocational training. Other organizations emerged such as the Protection of Colored People to keep Black residents safe from potential harassment from whites. On a more positive note, it needs to be noted that in Philadelphia, Blacks were afforded a greater opportunity for home ownership than existed in many other major northern cities.[46] By 1930, more homes were owned by Blacks in Philadelphia than in any other city north of the Mason–Dixon line.[47]

Cooper practiced medicine in Philadelphia for 48 years.[48] His niece, Phyliss Crump remembers, "His office was always busy, it occupied a space on the second floor of the three-story house in which he and his wife, my Aunt Willa Mae lived . . . he was always taking care of someone . . . he had Saturday hours too . . . plus he made house calls."[49] Cooper is said to have had one of the most successful and well-respected medical practices in Philadelphia. Sadly, Cooper entered Omega chapter on Monday, October 9, 1972, leaving behind a huge void in the city's Black community, but an even bigger imprint.[50] Herman Dreer, author of the illustrious Omega Psi Phi Fraternity's first history book, maintained that Cooper's practice "exhibited the democratic spirit and the love of the humanitarian."[51] Cooper was held in high esteem by those who knew him. On a fall morning in October 2021, shortly after 11 a.m., in the city of Philadelphia, where he impacted so many lives, throngs of people gathered and crowded a street in North Philadelphia to witness the unveiling of a historical marker in honor of Cooper and the renaming of West Jefferson Street, between Sixteenth and Seventeenth Streets, to Dr. Oscar J. Cooper Way. A fitting tribute to a man who meant so much to so many.[52]

Born in rural Virginia on September 10, 1891, Edgar Amos Love spent his early years in small-town Harrisonburg, Virginia, in the state's beautiful Shenandoah Valley.[53] Both Love's parents were Methodist ministers, and thus he was reared in a household where religion played a prominent role in all that he did. A good student, Love was educated in the public schools of Maryland and Virginia. After graduating from the Normal and Industrial Academy of Morgan College, a college preparatory school in Baltimore in 1909, he enrolled in the college that many east coast Blacks longed to attend: Howard University. While there he played football and was on the debate team. In 1913, he graduated cum laude, with a bachelor's degree (AB) from the school's College of Arts and Sciences. That same year he was elected Grand Basileus for the second time at the Washington, DC, grand conclave. Herman Dreer said of Love, "It was Rev. Edgar Love in the germ, the stripling in his teens, the youth of promise and vision who helped organize the Omega Psi Phi Fraternity and start it on its pioneering way."[54] In 1916, he completed a second undergraduate degree, a bachelor of divinity, also, at Howard University. Love endeavored to further his education, but the outbreak of the war proved to be an impediment, at least temporarily.

When the call was issued for men to serve in France, Love entered the Officer's Training School at Ft. Des Moines, in Des Moines, Iowa, in June 1917. Upon receiving his commission, Love was put in charge of 3,000 men. His most important responsibility came when he was assigned as chaplain to the 368th Infantry, which saw action in the Vosges mountains in eastern France and the Argonne Forest, considered part of what became known as the Meuse-Argonne Offensive, the last battle of World War I. Lt. Love displayed tremendous courage under fire, especially during what has become known as the "great offensive," which lasted eight days and during which Love and his men were gassed. Aside from tending to soldiers' spiritual needs, Love helped organize a school for soldiers who were considered functional illiterates in the 809th Pioneer Infantry. The school's curriculum included subjects as wide-ranging as reading, writing, philosophy, and automotive repair.

As soon as he was able to return to his studies, Love did so and earned a third degree—a bachelor of sacred theology from Boston University, in 1918, and was promptly hired as pastor of the Mount Washington United Methodist Church in Baltimore. In *The Omega Psi Phi Fraternity and the Men Who Made Its History: A Concise History*, Robert L. Gill[55] writes that Love was honorably discharged from the military in 1919 with the rank of captain, at which time, he was hired by Morgan College in Baltimore as a professor of biblical studies and history.[56] In addition to his full-time teaching duties, he took on added responsibilities, serving as the school's athletic director. In the fall of

1919, Love served as a delegate to the first American Legion Convention held in Minneapolis, Minnesota, representing the state of Maryland. Possessed with an insatiable thirst for knowledge, Love enrolled in graduate school at the University of Chicago during the summer of 1920, but according to the registrar's office stayed for just one quarter.[57] The following year he was hired on as principal of the Academy of Morgan College and remained in that position for two years. In June 1923, Love, still only in his early 30s, made one of the best decisions of his young life when he took Virginia Louise Ross[58] as his wife.

Love's interests extended well beyond the illustrious Omega Psi Phi Fraternity, Inc., He was a devout member of the NAACP, the Elks Club, Frontiers of America Club, and Freemasons (as a 33rd degree Mason), as well as a founding member of the Corinthian Lodge No. 18 of the Prince Hall Free Masons in DC.[59] Love pastored at several churches throughout the mid-Atlantic area, as well as in West Virginia and Pennsylvania. However, he earned wide acclaim as director of the famous John Wesley UMC church in West Baltimore. Love's work in disadvantaged communities impacted the lives of thousands of residents in Maryland, Virginia, Washington, DC, West Virginia, Pennsylvania, and New York. In 1933, Love was appointed a church superintendent. Morgan College was so impressed with Love's accomplishments that in 1935 officials there conferred upon him the honorary degree of doctor of divinity.[60] Around that same time, he was serving as district superintendent of the Washington Annual Conference of the Methodist Episcopal Church. In 1940, following the appointment of Dr. William Alfred Carroll Hughes Sr. to the bishopric of the Methodist Board of Missions, Love was chosen as his successor. Also, during this time Love worked with Mary McLeod Bethune[61] on the Methodist Federation for Social Services Executive Committee. These experiences springboarded his election in June 1952, as bishop of the segregated Central Conference (Baltimore area) of the United Methodist Church. The Central Conference spanned from Delaware to North Carolina. Love served in that capacity for twelve years and retired in 1964, the year that white and Black jurisdictions in the Washington area merged, but was lured out of retirement where he served as the bishop of the Atlantic Coast Area of the Central Jurisdiction in Alabama, Florida, Georgia, and Mississippi from November 1966 to June 1967.[62]

Love was a fine example of a social engineer. At a time when racial conflict between Black and whites was on the rise, Maryland governor Albert C. Ritchie[63] appointed him to the Maryland Interracial Commission. Not one to shy away from conflict, Love agitated for civil rights on more than one occasion. For example, Love carried petitions to the White House in opposition to the anticommunist McCarran Act as well as to Annapolis, Maryland, protesting state civil defense expenditures. When Bishop Love entered Omega chapter on May 1, 1974, the ecumenical world suffered a great loss.[64] As a civic and religious leader, Love "made the church, wherever he was, function as a community center for the purpose of the neighborhood, as well as a temple of worship for the Most High God."[65] In 2015, the Virginia Department of Historic Resources approved a highway marker outside of John Wesley United Methodist church in Harrisonburg, Virginia, honoring Love.

For readers unfamiliar with the history of the illustrious Omega Psi Phi Fraternity, Inc., having some sense of how these men's lives unfolded after graduating from Howard University gives one a glimpse into their sense of determination, the life they envisioned for themselves, and their commitment to enhancing other peoples' life chances. One day early in the Fall semester of 1911, as the winds of war continued to swirl in a faraway backdrop, and the possibility of World War I had not yet registered on the radars of many Americans, Edgar A. Love and Oscar J. Cooper, by now fixtures at Howard University, stood on the steps of the main building, as their eyes scanned the campus. Panning the landscape as their schoolmates walked about while others stood around chatting, the two paid particular attention to men for the purpose of identifying those they believed were of like mind. Love and Cooper had come to a decision, a decision that would not only change their lives but also those of the men who endeavored to join them.

Love and Cooper had agreed that the time had come for the creation of a fraternal organization of young Negro men (as they were called then), united by shared ideals and common interests for the purpose of leadership development. The fraternity they had in mind would be uniquely different from the one that already occupied a place on Howard University's campus. The way Love saw it, the other fraternity was reserved solely for "men who had money to spend or who had great family backings or even color consciousness." In Love's words, spoken 60 years after the founding of Omega, the other fraternity "did not represent what . . . a fraternity ought to represent."[66] To the impartial observer, Love's observation seems unusually harsh. However, in a book edited by T. L. Brown and others, when Howard University students Watson Diggs and Byron Armstrong were approached about becoming members of Alpha Phi Alpha during the 1909–1910 academic school year, the two men respectfully declined due to "the attitudes and actions of certain members."[67] Diggs and Armstrong transferred to Indiana University where they helped founded Kappa Alpha Psi.

At any rate, Love and Cooper set up meetings to discuss the idea further. Some Omegas, now in their late 80s and early to mid-90s, remember hearing stories about the founders' initial meetings. Some believe the young men began seriously talking about the formation of a Black Greek-letter fraternity at a Saturday, November 11, meeting. It appears that this date sticks out in the minds of some older members of the fraternity because of the severe tornadoes that swept across the Midwest, stemming from a frigid cold front that overtook that region. Dramatic events, particularly calamities, often serve to mark time and space for some people. They know exactly where they were when they heard the news about the burning and pillaging of Black Wall Street in Tulsa, Oklahoma, or the bombing of Pearl Harbor in 1941 or the 1900 Galveston, Texas, hurricane that killed 12,000 people and destroyed 3,600 homes or the terrorist attacks on American soil, on September 11, 2001.

Although Washington, DC, and other east coast and mid-Atlantic cities were largely unaffected by the tornadoes, news of this natural disaster saturated the press. DC residents witnessed residual effects from the tornadoes, as the city experienced a downpour of rain that evening. At any rate, on this day, Frank C. Coleman joined Love and Coleman, and upon being abreast of the goings-on, found the idea of a Black fraternity to his liking. A subsequent meeting occurred the following week on Wednesday, November 15 in the office of Professor Ernest E. Just, a young professor of biology of only 28 years of age himself. By then, Just had been there just a few years, having come to Howard directly from Dartmouth College,[68] where he graduated in 1907.[69] Rumor has it that Just was sought after by other Black colleges, Morehouse College in particular. The all-male institution offered young Black men a superb undergraduate education while Howard University provided its students with both an outstanding undergraduate and graduate education in many academic disciplines—as well as professional fields such as law, medicine, and dentistry—for Black men and women from every corner of the country. Moreover, Howard was in Washington, DC, where Jim Crow practices were considered gentile. Morehouse College, on the other hand, is in the Deep South, in Atlanta, where Jim Crow was not only accepted but also thrived.[70] Just's choice of Howard proved to be the right one, and a fortuitous one for Love, Cooper and Coleman.

At any rate, not unaware of the young men's preoccupation with this venture of theirs, Just was kind enough to grant them an audience at 9 p.m., when most faculty members are home with their families preparing for the next workday. Love, Cooper, and Coleman were present at this meeting. Thoughts were tossed about, and ideas floated well into the night, as the men grappled with conceptualizing what exactly they had in mind. Just was patient with the young men as they hashed out one idea after another. As the hours passed, the men agreed to adjourn and start fresh later that week.

Two days later, on Friday, November 17, 1911, with raindrops, again, pelting the streets of the nation's capital and temperatures hovering in the mid-40s by nightfall, the three nattily dressed young men, once again made a beeline to Science Hall where they descended upon Professor Just's office. While their schoolmates busied themselves preparing for the type of weekend festivities that normally occur on a college campus, such as the regularly scheduled Saturday football game, Love, Cooper, and Coleman had other priorities. The objective of said meeting with Just was to finally work out the kinks and start putting in motion what the young men couldn't seem to stop talking or thinking about.

Love, Cooper, and Coleman were budding young scholars whose potential was great but not yet actualized. Yes, they excelled in the classroom and were fairly well known on campus for their involvement in extracurricular activities; however, they were only beginning to realize, that with the right tutelage, the sky was the limit. Love[71] had his eye on the ministry, Cooper endeavored to become a physician, and Coleman displayed a knack for physics. Known as the three musketeers,[72] a reference to Alexandre Dumas's 1844 novel of the same name, the three men were close friends, inseparable even. But more importantly, they were industrious and persistent, inviting (or cajoling, depending on one's perspective) Professor Just to join them in an official capacity, as their faculty adviser in their grand effort to bring the illustrious Omega Psi Phi Fraternity, Inc., into being. That Just accepted the young men's entreaty despite his rather hectic schedule was both commendable and selfless, especially given that in addition to his professorial duties the young professor had just started his doctoral studies at the University of Chicago in late July of that year.[73]

Just proved to be an excellent and logical choice, for several reasons. First, that he minored in Greek and history as an undergraduate, was sure to be of help to the three enterprising young men. In fact, at first, Just thought seriously about majoring in Greek due to his interest in the Greek philosopher-stateman Demosthenes, but changed his mind when he discovered that the man had already been the subject of much scholarship, leaving little room for an original contribution.[74] Second, at age 28 he was young enough that Love, Cooper, and Coleman found him relatable. Third, Just had been a member of the all-male Philadelphia Club from his days as a younger man at Kimball Union Academy,[75] and thus he understood the value of having a social group for Black men.[76] Fourth, despite not yet having his PhD (which he earned in 1916[77]), he still engendered a level of respect and esteem normally afforded older and more established faculty members, of which Howard University was chock full.[78]

By 1910, Just had moved away from English and rhetoric, the courses for which he was hired to teach, and given the title assistant professor of biology. The next year he was promoted to associate professor of biology in the college of arts and sciences and professor of physiology in the medical school.[79] In 1912, he was promoted yet again to full professor of biology and full professor of physiology in the medical school.[80] His stature was growing, as he was exerting his influence on science education at Howard that caught the attention of many. Fifth, and perhaps unknown to Love, Cooper, and Coleman, Just had been president of the debating team while in high school in New Hampshire.

Thus, his persuasive oratory skills would surely come in handy were the men to encounter opposition from faculty and administrators, which they obviously did. Sixth, Just had a reputation as a tough but fair-minded instructor. This reputation proved to be a blessing and a curse. The more his popularity grew, the more was asked of him. The more that was asked of him, the more students were exposed to him. At one point Just was put in charge of 500 pre-med students.[81] The more students were exposed to him, the larger his following grew. Given the manner in which students took to Just, by his own admission, he preferred the company of his students over that of his colleagues. He often spent his free time offering students advice and guidance, even those who hadn't taken classes with him. On the weekends, one might find Just, who exhibited boundless amounts of energy, squaring off against a student on the tennis court or holding his own against another in the swimming pool.[82]

By 1910, when the new science building opened, Just (along with Richard E. Schuh) was, at the behest of Howard's president, charged with building up the sciences at Howard, an appointment that required a much greater commitment than did the typical faculty position.[83] In the Department of Biology and Geology, Just was responsible for zoology and Schuh botany and geology. Before moving full-time into science, again, Just had been teaching English courses and such.[84] Just taught a range of courses, from "Narration and Description" to "Exposition." Students were captivated by Just's teaching style. According to Kenneth Manning, "He had a sensitive and adept mind and a talent for description and narration and could turn the most banal narrative into one of marvelous intrigue."[85] Just was believed to be a "superb" teacher who "awakened the enthusiasm of his pupils."[86] To say Just was a student-centered professor would not do him justice. One of Just's favorite students was Oscar J. Cooper. Cooper ingratiated himself with Just by exhibiting a love of science, stopping by Just's office at every opportunity and taking his studies seriously. Impressed with the younger man's drive and intellectual acuity, Just offered Cooper a position as his lab assistant. It is not a stretch to suggest that despite the closeness in age, Just had become a mentor to Cooper.

With so many responsibilities, including playing an integral role in starting a drama society, and with throngs of students vying for the professor's attention, it is a wonder Just found time to have a love life. Seven months after the illustrious Omega Psi Phi Fraternity was founded, however, Just took time out of his hectic schedule to make the strikingly beautiful and incredibly talented Ethel Highwarden,[87] a graduate of "The" Ohio State University and a fellow professor, his wife.[88]

At any rate, with Just now signed on as the faculty adviser, the idea of a Black fraternity had now materialized into something more tangible. From the initials of the Greek phrase meaning "Friendship is essential to the Soul," the name of Omega Psi Phi Fraternity was derived and the expression selected as the fraternity's motto. Given the bond that had developed between the three undergraduates and that which formed between Cooper and Love, which eventually grew to include all four men, "Friendship is essential to the Soul" was indeed an appropriate motto. Manhood, Scholarship, Perseverance, and Uplift were adopted as cardinal principles.[89] Before the meeting was adjourned, a decision was made regarding the design for the pin and emblem, thus giving rise to one of the most striking and recognizable shields among all Greek-letter organizations.

A follow-up meeting occurred on November 23, days before Thanksgiving break. At that meeting it was decided that Edgar A. Love, the youngest of the three young men would be the first Grand Basileus (national president). Cooper and Coleman took on the positions of Grand Keeper of Records (national secretary) and Grand Keeper of Seals (national treasurer), respectively. Between December 2 when school resumed and the fourteenth, according to Robert L. Gill, 11 undergraduate men were selected as charter members, culminating in the establishment of Alpha Chapter with a total of 14 members, on December 15, 1911.[90] Including the founders were William Gilbert, Charles Y. Harris, Clarence A. Hayes, Benjamin A. Jones, Clarence O. Lewis, William H. Pleasants, Charles B. Washington, Edward P. Westmoreland, Frank Wimberly, and of course the Love brothers—Julius H. and William A., thus the Loves becoming the "first family" of Omega. As was the case with most of Howard University's student body in the first few years of the school's existence, most of the young men hailed from neighboring states such as Virginia and Maryland, except for Gilbert, Jones, Westmoreland, Washington, and Wimberly whose hometowns were New York City, Indianapolis, Atlanta, Lovejoy, Illinois, and Tarboro, North Carolina. Months later, four more men were initiated into Omega—James Raymond Johnson (Owensboro, Kentucky), William B. Jason (Coatesville, Pennsylvania), Moses T. Clayborne

(Boone Mill, Virginia) and Christopher C. Cook (Richmond, Virginia). With that, Omega Psi Phi was officially born—or was it?

From the outset, the men of Omega Psi Phi Fraternity ran into opposition, most notably from President William P. Thirkield. A stalwart in the Methodist Church, Thirkield's opposition to the young men is not easily explainable, especially because the United Methodist Church has a long history of concern for social equality, standing up in the face of injustice of any kind, advocating for equal rights, and fighting against racial discrimination. John Wesley, the founder of Methodism, was well known for his public opposition to slavery, printing a pamphlet in 1773 titled "Thoughts upon Slavery," in which he decried the evils of the system and implored slave traders and owners to set their slaves free and repent. Twelve years later, the church's *Book of Discipline* denounced slavery and made the freeing of slaves within a two-year period a condition upon membership in the denomination. In a move that many Blacks found disappointing, the Methodists bishops repealed the edict months after it was written. The Methodist Church would not adopt a strong stance against slavery again until their General Conference of 1858, less than two weeks before President Abraham Lincoln's a "House Divided" speech.[91] Until that time, slavery was commonplace among so-called Methodists, most notably those in the antebellum South. Be that as it may, Wesley remained a public critic of slavery, maintaining that "liberty is the right of every creature . . . and no human law can deprive him of that right."[92]

First, Thirkield scoffed at the idea of Coleman, Love, Just, and Cooper attempting to launch a fraternity without going through the appropriate university channels. Second, his stance only began to soften when he thought he could sell the young men on the idea of confining the fraternity to local status, rather than being a national organization that was the young men's preference. Third, there was a sense on the part of some administrators, Thirkield included, that fraternities were subversive and their members incorrigible. On the first point, President Thirkield was on solid footing. The idea that Love, Just, Cooper, and Coleman could bring into existence a campus organization, let alone a fraternity, without going through certain protocols was both naive and misguided. One can only surmise that the three musketeers must have proceeded without informing Just of their plans to sidestep the administration. It is possible, however, that going around the administration was done inadvertently—that the young men were simply unaware of the channels through which they were required to go in order to establish a college fraternity. Possible, but unlikely.

As far as points number 2 and 3 go, neither holds up well under scrutiny. For example, there is no evidence that Thirkield was ill at ease with the arrival of Alpha Phi Alpha Fraternity, Inc., on campus. Although founded at Cornell University in 1906, by the following year Alpha Phi Alpha had established a chapter on Howard University's campus and expanded into Canada, making it international in scope. One year after that, Howard University administrators witnessed the founding of the Alpha Kappa Alpha Sorority, Inc., on campus. If there was any pushback on the part of the president and his administration to either the Alphas or the AKAs, documents to that effect are hard to locate. Also, the argument that fraternities were havens for dissidents is lacking in substance as there is little to no evidence of fraternities spearheading or participating in any subversive activity on or off campus during that period in American history. Any claims to the contrary are greatly exaggerated.

Previously unvetted theories may help explain President Thirkield's initial resistance to the idea of Omega. Again, by 1907, Alpha Phi Alpha had established a presence on Howard University's campus. Is it possible that the presence of members of that fraternity were the source of the president's obstinacy, with Thirkield, fearing that the presence of Omega Psi Phi would siphon recruits away from Alpha Phi Alpha? Such a theory is not far-fetched, as one of Howard's most powerful figures and administrators was Kelly Miller, dean of the university's college of arts and sciences and an Alpha man, as was Jesse E. Moorland, who succeeded Bishop Benjamin F. Lee of the African Methodist Episcopal Church on the university's board of trustees. Both Kelly and Moreland enjoyed a strong relationship with Thirkield. Kelly believed that the "race" would not progress unless its educated leaders recognized their "racial responsibility and duty" and assumed their "rightful place in race leadership which their culture calls for and which the situation demands."[93] Whether Kelly and possibly Mooreland thought such a responsibility rested solely with the men of Alpha Phi Alpha is unclear.

On the matter of the university's board of trustees, when one peruses its roster, one name stands out—Booker T. Washington. An accommodationist, Washington urged Blacks to go out of their way to avoid alienating whites. He steered Blacks away from electoral politics, arguing that whites were not yet ready to allow Blacks to participate in civic affairs. Washington's most vocal critic, W.E.B. Du Bois, argued that Washington's approach was a tacit acceptance of the inferiority of the Negro. As Du Bois saw it, per historian Benjamin Quarles, in *The Negro in the Making of America,* Washington was asking the Negroes to give up political action and civil rights agitation and instead to "concentrate all their energies on industrial education, the accumulation of wealth, and the conciliation of the South."[94] In other words, advocating going along to get along. Du Bois's colleague, Monroe Trotter, was even more scathing, calling Washington a traitor to the race.[95]

Washington's appointment to the board did not go unnoticed. Some believed Washington to be a capitalist and did not think such an appointment reflected well on a private liberal arts university. W.E.B. Du Bois accused Washington of being hostile to Black liberal arts colleges, prompting some to wonder if there were any truth to Du Bois's charge. Why would Washington be invited to the board, and more importantly, why he would accept such an entreaty to begin with? There were those who couldn't help but think that Washington's presence on the board was about political maneuvering, which meant that as a board member Washington envisioned himself swaying Howard in the direction of the Hampton Institute/Tuskegee Institute model.

Washington wasn't the only high-profile personality who thought Howard University would benefit from the Hampton/Tuskegee model. William Patton, who served as president of Howard University from 1877 to 1889, believed like Washington, that Blacks should cast down their buckets where they were and take advantage of the jobs and occupations that whites were comfortable with Blacks occupying; thus Patton advocated an agricultural and industrial training in blacksmithing, stonecutting, carpentry, bookkeeping, and the like. He even proposed to create a department of "mechanical training," to no avail, since Howard's Black students and their parents, along with faculty and other stakeholders, scoffed at the idea of students working with their hands, a reminder of an earlier period when many Blacks were viewed as white peoples' personal property and worked from sunup to sundown without remuneration.[96]

At any rate, whatever Washington's motive for agreeing to serve on the board, Thirkield came across as man with a mind of his own and thus it was unlikely that Washington's influence would extend that far. For instance, when Washington shared with a Howard University administrator that "it was contrary to the history and policy of the Federal Government to contribute buildings to private institutions," Thirkield ignored the naysayers, and reached out to Congress anyway with a request to secure $100,000, for a new science building.[97] Thirkield had accomplished what Washington didn't think was possible.

Still, some were leery of Washington's association with Howard and stood firmly against the manner in which he thought Blacks should go about getting ahead. At a Morgan College commencement exercise in 1908, its president, J. O. Morgan, both reamed the Hampton/Tuskegee model and its progenitor, and lauded the school's board of trustees, exclaiming that "we must stand absolutely for the best possible education, and this is what Morgan College stands for. Though there are many who stand for the cheapening or lowering of intellectual training, it can be said to the credit of our trustees that they have stood for the best. I do not believe with those who declare that the race is being overeducated."[98] At any rate, Washington may or may not have thought the idea of a Black fraternity to be a threat to white peoples' sensibilities.

While it is tempting to place Washington at the center of this discussion, it is not well founded for the following reason: wouldn't Washington have been just as concerned about Alpha Phi Alpha's presence on campus? The answer is yes, unless of course, the establishment of an Alpha chapter preceded Washington's appointment to the board. According to Rayford Logan's *Howard University: The First Hundred Years 1867 1967*, Washington's election to the board occurred on May 28, 1907, the same year that a chapter of Alpha Phi Alpha was established at Howard. However, Alpha Phi Alpha arrived in December of that year, a full seven months after Washington's appointment. There is also something else to consider—that is, the financial support HBCUs received from white donors, corporations, and foundations. In other words, some white funders were happy to funnel large sums of money to Black schools as long as the schools stuck to a certain kind of curriculum. For example, Robert C. Ogden, president of the board of trustees of Hampton Institute as well as the General Education Board (1894–1913), a private organization established in 1903 by the philanthropist John D. Rockefeller to support and promote higher education among poor whites and Blacks in the southern states, went on record wanting to "attach the Negro to the soil and prevent his exodus from the country to the city." William H. Baldwin, an early supporter of Black schools, wrote unabashedly in an 1899 edition of the Hampton Institute's periodical, *Southern Workman*, that Black students should "avoid social questions; leave politics alone; continue to be patient; live moral lives." Furthermore, he said, with conviction, "the South already treated Blacks far better than in any other section of the country."[99] Given the emphasis fraternities and sororities placed on uplift—i.e., not allowing oneself to be consigned to an inferior place in society and understanding the importance of learning one's history—some Black Howard administrators may have believed the advent of Black sororities and fraternities off-putting to whites. Baldwin and Ogden's comments certainly suggest so.

Finally, if Thirkield and his administration were concerned that the founding of fraternities would lead to social activism, they should have known that the kind of dissonance that worried them would not be limited to members of fraternities and sororities. Students and members of Black Greek organizations alike, as well as Howard University professors and administrators, were engaged in public acts of politics as early as the 1920s when several participated in the Pan-African congresses, including those in Europe.[100] Bishop John Hurst, a member of Howard's board of trustees from 1917 to 1918 participated in the 1921 Pan-African Congress in Brussels and Paris, as did Howard alumnus, William Stuart Nelson (AB, 1920).[101] Faculty members Channing H. Tobias,[102] E. Franklin Frazier,[103] and Rayford Logan[104] were also present at the Paris session. The 1921 congress, which included 41 delegates from Africa, 35 Blacks from America and seven West Indians, issued a challenge to white colonialism. "The absolute equality of races, physical, political and social is the founding-stone of world and human advancement," the delegates declared.[105]

During that same era, student activism led to the appointment of Mordecai Johnson in 1926. Until Johnson's appointment, all Howard's presidents had been white. Students and some faculty members established an even greater presence in the following years, as they protested segregation and job discrimination by department stores in downtown Washington, DC. One of the most noteworthy acts of defiance was a sit-in led by the militant Pauli Murray[106] at a United Cigar store on Pennsylvania Avenue, which ultimately led to her arrest and the women who accompanied her. In the 1950s, law professors and various Howard alumni argued NAACP cases that were instrumental in dismantling Jim Crow laws. And in the 1960s, students went south to participate in the modern civil rights movement. In addition to the role that Howard students and alumni played in the modern civil rights movement, other alumni like Eugene Davidson[107] remained in DC where he thought he might be more effective. As head of the local NAACP chapter, Davidson led a high-profile fight against police brutality, which served as a template for other activists in other major cities.[108] These acts of defiance fostered a long tradition of activism among Howard University students that continues today.

Despite the reticence on the part of Thirkield and his administration, the Brothers of Omega Psi Phi won over the opposition by (1) standing up for what they believed, despite risking possible expulsion; (2) reminding the president and members of his administration that they took scholarship seriously, as evident by the fact that they were among the student body's most high-achieving students; (3) reminding the administration that they had always represented Howard well, both on and off campus; (4) using logic that was both persuasive and difficult to counter (as a few of the young men were adept at debating, especially Love, who been president of the debating team); and (5) insisting that the goals and objectives of the fraternity aligned with the university's mission—that is, to uplift its students by way of intellectual enlightenment and personal development. Thirkield resigned in 1912 to become a Methodist bishop, the same year that things seemed to fall into place for the men of Omega. Whether his departure cleared the way for certain developments to occur cannot be known for sure. But at the same time, that should not be summarily dismissed. Paula Giddings writes *In Search of Sisterhood: Delta Sigma Theta and the Challenge of the Black Sorority Movement,* "There was change in the air in 1912."[109] Although Giddings does not elaborate, that March saw the opening of the first Alpha chapter house at 1907 Third Street, northwestern Washington, DC. Operating without formal approval for three years, under the presidency of Dr. Stephen Morrell Newman, on October 28, 1914, everything finally came together as the fraternity was incorporated under the laws of the District of Columbia with Edgar A. Love as grand basileus, Oscar J. Cooper as grand keeper of records, and Frank C. Coleman as grand keeper of seals. That same year Beta chapter at prestigious Lincoln University in Pennsylvania was chartered.

The courage and defiance exhibited by the founders of the Omega Psi Phi Fraternity in 1911 in the face of such adversity reflected the spirit described above. And that spirit of change and uplift is ingrained in all who cross the burning sands and enter the Kingdom of Omega. In these two volumes, readers will learn about some of the twentieth and twenty-first centuries' most accomplished figures (some of whom are unheralded) and the impact they have had not only on their chosen fields of endeavor but also the country generally. That each of the subjects happens to be a member of the illustrious Omega Psi Phi Fraternity, Inc., is by no means a coincidence.

These notable figures entered Omega at various times in their lives, some as college students, while others were pursuing advanced study. Still others entered the Kingdom of Omega later in life as accomplished professionals in their respective fields and others were bestowed "elected active" or honorary status for their immense talent and unique contributions in such areas as the arts, science, sport, politics, civil rights, education, and the US Armed Forces.

It is difficult to ascertain the extent to which the illustrious Omega Psi Phi Fraternity, Inc., impacted the luminaries about whom these authors have written. Determining the extent to which the fraternity benefited by having them as members is also not an exact science, but each of the subjects featured in this work brought great honor to the fraternity. For those whose membership in the fraternity was well known, any major accomplishment surely reflected well on the illustrious Omega Psi Phi Fraternity, Inc.

For many the lifeworks of those featured in this two-volume project involved improving Black peoples' lot in one way or another. Some were on the front lines, while others operated in less conspicuous ways but whose impact is still evident.

The struggle for racial equality in Virginia and Alabama, for example, cannot be written without placing attorneys Oliver Hill and Spottswood Robinson III, Fred Gray, and Oscar Adams at the center of analysis. As initiates of Alpha and Alpha Omega (Washington, DC) chapters in 1927 and 1961, respectively, Hill and Robinson were responsible for breaking down some of the most formidable barriers erected to keep segregation firmly entrenched in public places, not only in Virginia but throughout the South.[110] Few African American lawyers were more widely known across Virginia than that dynamic duo who, for decades worked very closely on several important cases. Both Adam's and Gray's achievements are vast as well; both worked with Dr. King, but few Alabama lawyers worked as closely with him and other civil rights leaders as Fred Gray. Where Rosa Parks and the Montgomery bus boycott were concerned, Gray was the attorney of note. Initiated in the fall of 1949 at what is now Alabama State University (Gamma Sigma), Gray is one of the country's oldest and most accomplished African American civil rights attorneys. Adams, a Gamma Psi initiate at Talladega College who seemingly had his hand in every important case in his neck of the woods is as interwoven in the fabric of Alabama's political struggles, particularly Birmingham, as Hill and Robinson are to Richmond, Virginia.[111] Emory O. Jackson, an Alpha Phi initiate (January 1939), used his journalism skills and his well-received newspaper to fight racial injustice as well as elevate Black peoples' social and political consciousness.

While the courts played an important role in the success of the modern civil rights movement, so did those activists who challenged the system in an array of unconventional ways such as Bayard Rustin (Upsilon, fall 1932),[112] Dr. T.R.M. Howard (Sigma Omega, fall 1955),[113] Lawrence Guyot (Rho Upsilon, fall 1959),[114] and the Rev. Jesse Louis Jackson (Pi Psi, spring 1960).[115] Rustin was a key adviser to Dr. King and the principal architect behind the historic 1963 March on Washington for Jobs and Freedom. His activism goes back to the early days of the movement, long before people like Dr. King arrived on the scene. About Howard, a dignified and pull-no-punches kind of man, his work with the Black poor as both a physician and entrepreneur in both Mississippi and later Chicago is unparalleled. Howard is one of the movement's unsung heroes.

Guyot and Jackson, young foot soldiers of the modern civil rights movement who spent much of their time marching, demonstrating, and registering people to vote as members of the Student Nonviolent Coordinating Committee (SNCC) and the Southern Christian Leadership Conference (SCLC), respectively were just two of the many beams of light in a constellation of civil rights activists that shined brightly. Decades later Jackson shocked many by running for president in 1984 and again in 1988, and although he didn't win, his massive voter registration campaign mobilized voters throughout the country, led to unprecedented numbers of Blacks and other people of color running for and being elected to public office in the following years.

In the area of education, Dr. Benjamin Mays, the legendary president of Morehouse College and mentor to Dr. King and summer 1919 initiate of Gamma[116] chapter, was known for his unwavering commitment to the modern civil rights movement and his innovative work as a college administrator. Any history of the most effective HBCU presidents of the twentieth century that doesn't include Mays would be inadequate. Speaking of Mays and Morehouse College, Dr. King is easily the college's most famous graduate, and not surprisingly, one of the most written about African Americans of the past one hundred years. And no one has produced more scholarly works in the form of books, journal articles, and book chapters on Dr. King than Vanderbilt University emeritus professor Lewis V. Baldwin, a spring 1972 initiate of Theta Omicron in Rochester, New York. Baldwin's work has shaped the way an entire generation views and studies the man known as the apostle of nonviolence. And few scholars rival Dr. Asa Hilliard III, a fall 1958 initiate of Pi Chi in San Francisco, in developing African centered curriculum and devising creative ways to better educate Black children.

In the arts, the fraternity boasts three of the most accomplished figures in their respective fields, in big band leader Count Basie (1961), drummer Max Roach (1995), and lyric tenor Roland Hayes (1919), all of whom came to the fraternity later in life as "elected active" or honorary members. Other men in this book who were bestowed "elected active" or honorary status include the venerable Brigadier General Charles Young (1912), the US Army's first Black colonel, founder Dr. Ernest E. Just (1912), and trailblazing golfer Lee Elder (2004).[117]

Although legendary scientist Percy Julian[118] and basketball Hall of Fame coach Clarence "Big House" Gaines, a spring 1947 Psi Phi (Winston-Salem, NC) initiate, were not directly involved in the movement per se, both worked diligently to avail opportunities to young Blacks in both science and athletics that otherwise would not have been available. Finally, no substantive discussions of the illustrious Omega Psi Phi Fraternity, Inc., can be had without acknowledging Charlotte "Lottie" B. Wilson, affectionately known by some as the fraternity's only female member, and whose support of the young men at Lincoln University in Pennsylvania was instrumental in helping them establish Beta chapter. For more details see page 13 in the March 1956 issue of the *Oracle*, the official publication of the Omega Psi Phi Fraternity, Inc. Wilson has also been called Omega Psi Phi Fraternity's First Lady and Beta chapter's foster mother.

The rich history of the illustrious Omega Psi Phi Fraternity, Inc., is owing to those whose stories tell of struggle, accomplishment, triumph, and uplift. While this is not a history of the fraternity per se, the subjects contained in the chapters therein provide readers with a glimpse into the history-making events and characters that make up this great fraternity.

Notes

1 W.E.B. Du Bois, *W.E.B. Du Bois: Writings*, ed. Nathan Huggins (New York: Library of America, 1986), 29.
2 Walter Dyson, "The Founding of Howard University," *Howard University Studies in History* 1, no. 1 (June 1921). Available at https://dh.howard.edu/hush/vol1/iss1/5
3 C. Johnson, *The Negro College Graduate* (Chapel Hill: University of North Carolina Press, 1938).
4 M. H. Parker, "Some Educational Activities of the Freedmen's Bureau," *Journal of Negro Education* 23 (Winter 1954): 9–21.
5 John Hope Franklin, *From Slavery to Freedom: A History of Negro Americans* (New York: Vintage, 1969).
6 One element that really impacted farming was the presence of the infamous boll weevil that ate its way through the South, from Texas in 1901 to North Carolina in 1921. The weevil decimated southern cotton fields, driving thousands of Black and white tenants and sharecroppers off the land or at the very least making their very existence a living nightmare.
7 David R. Goldfield and Blaine A. Brownell, *Urban America: A History* (Boston: Houghton Mifflin, 1990), 224.
8 Quoted in Gilbert Osofsky, ed., *The Burden of Race: A Documentary History of Negro-White Relations in America* (New York: Harper and Row, 1967), 263.
9 As told in Allan H. Spear, *Black Chicago: The Making of a Negro Ghetto, 1890–1920* (Chicago: University of Chicago Press, 1967), 137.
10 www.vsu.edu/students/organization/omega/private_private/coleman.htm (defunct URL).
11 Many of the fraternity's documents as well as chapter web pages have Coleman's birth year listed as 1890, but his headstone in the cemetery in which he is buried (Lincoln Memorial Cemetery in Suitland, Maryland) reads 1889, as do records at the registrar's office at the University of Chicago (July 11, 1889). Yet Student Registration and Financial Services at the University of Pennsylvania lists his birthdate as July 11, 1890. This writer is prone to agree with that which appears on his headstone, for which his family and relatives would have been solely responsible.

12 The M Street school was founded in 1870, initially, as the Preparatory High School for Colored Youth. From 1891 to 1961, it was known as M Street High School. In 1916, the M Street High School's name was changed to Paul Laurence Dunbar High School, Dunbar High School for short.

13 Nannie Helen Burroughs (born in Orange, Virginia, in 1879, and died in 1961) was one of the most important educators, suffragists, and religious leaders of the twentieth century. At the 1900 National Baptist Convention (NBC), Burroughs delivered a speech called "How the Sisters Are Hindered from Helping," which discussed the injustices women faced within the Black Baptist Church. The speech helped to build her national reputation and paved the way for a greater role for women in the church. This speech also led to her cofounding (along with Mary Virginia Cook-Parrish) the Women's Auxiliary of the NBC.

14 Benjamin O. Davis Sr. (1877–1970) was the first black general in the US Army specifically and US Armed Forces generally.

15 Georgiana R. Simpson is reported to be the first Black woman to earn a PhD in the United States, receiving her doctorate in German Romanticism at the University of Chicago on June 14, 1921, one day before Sadie Tanner received hers from the University of Pennsylvania and eight days before Eva B. Dykes completed her doctorate at Radcliffe College on June 22, 1921. Simpson's dissertation is titled "Herder's Conception of 'Das Volk.'" She was in her 50s when the degree was conferred. See Max Witynski, "100 Years Ago, Georgiana Simpson Made History as the First Black Woman to graduate with a PhD," UChicago News, June 10, 2021, https://news.uchicago.edu/story/100-years-ago-georgiana-simpson-made-history-first-black-woman-graduate-phd

16 Jean Toomer (1894–1967), a poet and playwright and author of *Cane* (1923), which was hailed by reviewers for its literary experimentation and portrayal of Black characters and culture. Toomer is the grandson of P.B.S. Pinchback (1837–1921), who was a former Union army soldier during the Civil War and the nation's first Black governor. Previously Louisiana's Lt. Governor, Pinchback was elevated to the governorship from December 9, 1872, to January 13, 1873, during the impeachment trial of Governor Henry Warmoth.

17 Constance McLaughlin Green, *The Secret City: A History of Race Relations in the Nation's Capital* (Princeton, NJ: Princeton University Press, 1967), 137.

18 Seventy-fifth Anniversary of the Birthday of Professor Rayford W. Logan, Department of History, Howard University, January 7, 1972, Vertical File, Rayford Logan, MSRC; transcript, Dr. Rayford Logan, September 20, 1977, in the library of the Columbia Historical Society.

19 Henry S. Robinson, "The M Street High School, 1891–1916," *Records of the Columbia Historical Society, Washington, D.C.* v 51 (1984): 119–143.

20 Robinson, "M Street High School," 119–143.

21 Carter G. Woodson (1875–1950) was the second African American to earn a PhD at Harvard University, after W.E.B. Du Bois. He founded what is now known as the Association for the Study of Negro Life and History, the *Journal of Negro History*, and Negro History Week. At M Street High School, he taught French, Spanish, English, and history.

22 Jessie Fauset, a 1905 Phi Beta Kappa graduate of Cornell University, was an extraordinary writer who taught French.
23 Anna Julia Cooper (1858–1964), an 1884 graduate of Oberlin championed both Black and women's rights. A noteworthy author, she is best known for her first book, *A Voice from the South by a Black Woman of the South* (Xenia, Ohio: Aldine Printing House, 1892). Cooper helped found the Colored Women's League in 1982 and joined the executive committee of the first Pan-African Conference in 1900. Also, since the YMCA and YWCA were not open to Black members, Cooper created "colored" branches to provide support for Black southern migrants moving to Washington, DC. She earned a doctor of philosophy from the Sorbonne in 1925.
24 Herman Dreer, *The History of the Omega Psi Phi Fraternity* (Washington, DC: Omega Psi Phi Fraternity, 1940), 7.
25 Vernon Steve Weakley, *The History of Omega Psi Phi Fraternity Inc: An Update for the Period 1960 to 2008* (Omega Psi Phi Fraternity and Zworldnet), 29.
26 Otis Alexander, "Frank Charles Coleman (1890–1967)," BlackPast, July 26, 2023, Blackpast.org/African-American-history/frank-charles-coleman-1890-1967/
27 The Brick School was a private boarding school for Blacks from 1895 to 1933. Founded by the American Missionary Association, the land and money came from Julia Brick, a well-off Brooklyn widow who named the school in honor of her husband. Thomas Sewell Inborden, the school's principal, opened its doors on October 1, 1895, to serve the large numbers of rural Blacks in the eastern counties of North Carolina.
28 Also referred to as Armstrong High School.
29 The University of Chicago's history of accepting Black students is noteworthy, with its first Black student graduating in 1896 (Cora B. Jackson). Eleven Black undergraduate alumni followed over the next 14 years. The first seven Black graduate student alumni were Monroe Nathan Work (graduating in 1902), Richard Robert Wright Jr. (1901), Charles H. Turner (1907), Dudley Weldon Woodard (1906), Carter G. Woodson (1908), Julian H. Lewis (1915), and Ernest E. Just (1916). For more detail, see "Integrating the Life of the Mind: African Americans at the University of Chicago, 1870–1940," UChicagoLibrary, accessed January 11, 2022, www.lib.uchicago.edu/collex/exhibits/integrating-life-mind/
30 Coleman was one of approximately 380,000 Black men who served in the armed forces during World War I. During the early part of World War I, the United States, during President Wilson's administration, tried to adopt a position of neutrality. However, public sympathy with the Allies and opposition to German activities eventually nudged America into the war.
31 Coleman headed the Physics Department at Howard University from 1916 to 1956.
32 Coleman's thesis is titled "Band Spectra and the Quantum Theory."
33 Records in the registrar's office at the University of Pennsylvania show that Coleman enrolled in the doctoral program in physics in the summer of 1924. Coleman also took classes there during the summers of 1927 and 1929 as well as that fall, spending an entire semester at the University of Pennsylvania. His last date of enrollment was in the summer of 1930, from July 3 to August 16. There is no evidence according to the school's registrar, however, that Coleman had achieved all-but-dissertation status.

34 Rayford W. Logan, *Howard University: The First Hundred Years 1867–1967* (New York: University Press, 1969), 155.
35 Pressure from Howard University Black college students who formed the Central Committee of Negro College Men for the purpose of forcing the government to train Black officers resulted in the War Department setting up the nation's first officer training school for Blacks, the Seventeenth Provisional Training Camp in Des Moines, Iowa. Black students from Lincoln, Harvard, Columbia, Brown, and Yale universities joined the effort. Approximately 200 students, faculty members and administrators were trained at the camp, with 95 of them receiving commissions. All told, 1,250 men were trained at the base and more than 600 received commissions. See Lopez D. Matthews, *Howard University in the World Wars: Men and Woman Serving in the Nation* (Charleston, SC: History Press, 2018).
36 Coleman performed admirably in the Argonne Forest. In that fire fight he led his platoon in a most impressive manner and personally accounted for killing one German officer. According to p. 18 in the June 1919 issue of the *Oracle,* Coleman, "naturally quiet and unassuming, . . . surprised his friends by conspicuous action both in the Vosges and the Argonne, and brought credit not only to himself, but to his entire organization."
37 The Rev. Sterling Nelson Brown (1858–1929) was also the father of Sterling A. Brown (1901–1989). He was a professor, teaching a bible introductory course and biblical history, and the director of Extension Work and Correspondence Study at Howard University's School of Religion.
38 Mary Edna Brown graduated from Howard in 1913 as valedictorian and class president. "Negro Officer Takes Bride," *Washington Post,* May 26, 1918, 19. Edna Brown Coleman died while giving birth, sixteen months after getting married.
39 Frank Charles Coleman died in Freedmen's Hospital in Washington, DC, after a long illness. At the time of his death, he lived with his wife Mabel Coleman at 1232 Girard Street, in northeastern Washington, DC. Services for Coleman were held on Tuesday morning on February 28, 1967, at Rankin Chapel on the campus of Howard University.
40 Cooper's birthdate is not clear. Numerous sources within the illustrious Omega Psi Phi Fraternity, Inc., cite his birthdate as May 20, 1888, while his headstone (a seemingly much more reliable source) at White Marsh Memorial Park in Ambler, Pennsylvania, reads 1890 as the year of his birth. Compounding the problem, his niece, Mrs. Phyllis Crump, by marriage, graciously sent me a photo of the funeral program that has 1880 as his birth year, which is undoubtedly incorrect. If that isn't enough confusion, a June 13, 1900, census cites Cooper's birthdate as May 1885, information likely provided by his parents. The day is written in a way that is illegible. There is less ambiguity about the year in which he died, which is 1972. Specifically, Cooper died on Monday, October 9, 1972, at Lankenau Hospital. That was Columbus Day, in fact. A news clipping cites Cooper's age as 82 at the time of his death, which would make 1890 the year he was born.
41 Information taken from the program for the Forty-Fourth Annual Commencement at Howard University, 1913. Wednesday, June 4, 4:30 p.m., Washington, DC.

42 Many documents that have been put out by the Illustrious Omega Psi Phi Fraternity, Inc. cite 1917 as the year Cooper earned his MD. Many of the fraternity's chapter web pages do likewise, but that year is incorrect. See sources: (a) Directory of Graduates of Howard University, 1870–1963, compiled by University Registrar F. D. Wilkinson, 1918–1919 and (b) Catalog of Officers and Students of Howard University. The 1918–1919 catalogue lists Dr. Cooper as a 1918 graduate of the medical college. See catalog, p. 303, which is Digital Howard page 305: https://dh.howard.edu/cgi/viewcontent.cgi?Article=1049&context=hucatalogs (defunct URL).

43 Charles Hardy III, "The Great Migration: A City Transformed (Historical Overview)." Greatmigrationphl.org (defunct URL), accessed on January 18, 2022.

44 Hardy, "Great Migration."

45 One such church was the East Cavalry Methodist Church where Rev. Charles Albert Tindley was so gregarious that he was known to shake the hands of thousands of people every Sunday. It has been said that Tindley's song "I'll Overcome Some Day," written in 1901, served as the basis for the modern civil rights movement's theme song "We Shall Overcome." "Charles Albert Tindley," Hymnology Archive, accessed January 18, 2022, www.hymnologyarchive.com/charles-albert-tindley?rq=Charles%20Albert%20Tindley

46 "Charles Albert Tindley."

47 "Charles Albert Tindley."

48 His office was located at 1621 W. Jefferson. According to a video presentation titled "Unveiling Recap" by the illustrious Omega Psi Phi Fraternity, Inc., Cooper once headed the Mudgett Hospital and Training School for Nurses, located at 2028 N. Thirteenth Street, in Philadelphia. He also served as treasurer to the National Medical Association.

49 Conversation with Phyliss Crump, January 17, 2022.

50 Cooper was also one of the founders of the Pyramid Club in 1937. In the Pyramid Club, the city's Black professionals were afforded opportunities for social, civic, and cultural enrichment. He was also a cofounder of the Mu Omega chapter (Philadelphia) in 1920, the city's first chapter of the illustrious Omega Psi Phi Fraternity, Inc. According to an obituary that appeared in the Thursday, October 12, 1972, edition of the *Philadelphia Inquirer*, Cooper died of cancer at Lankenau Hospital on Monday, October 9, 1972. His services were held at 11:00 a.m. on Saturday, October 14, 1972, at the First African Baptist Church on Sixteenth and Christian streets. At the time of his death Cooper lived at 1621 W. Jefferson Street, which is also where his office was located.

51 Dreer, *History of the Omega Psi Phi Fraternity*.

52 Valerie Russ, "In Honor of Philly's Dr. Oscar James Cooper, a Street Was Renamed, and a Historical Marker Erected," *Philadelphia Inquirer*, October 2, 2021, www.inquirer.com/news/oscar-cooper-omega-psi-phi-historical-marker-philadelphia-20211002.html

53 Many sources erroneously have Love being born in Harrisburg, Virginia, a mistake that this writer committed in past writings. A conversation with Love's only son confirmed it was the town of Harrisonburg.

54 Dreer, *History of the Omega Psi Phi Fraternity*, 3.

55 Robert L. Gill was a longtime faculty member in the Department of History and Political Science at Morgan State College (now Morgan State University), and an Omega man.
56 Robert L. Gill, *The Omega Psi Phi Fraternity and the Men Who Made Its History: A Concise History* (Washington, DC: Omega Psi Phi Fraternity, Inc., 1963).
57 On various chapters' web pages of the illustrious Omega Psi Fraternity, Inc., Love is credited by members of the fraternity with attending the University of Chicago for two semesters or two sessions, which is incorrect. The university was on a quarter system. According to the Assistant University Registrar John J. W. Plampin, Love was there for one quarter only in the summer of 1920.
58 According to Howard University's directory of graduates, she earned a BS at Miner Teachers College in 1938 and a MA in religious education in 1942 at Howard University. Her master's thesis is titled "A Study of the Graded Press Literature for the Primary Department of the Church School." Virginia Louise Ross Love was also a member of Delta Sigma Theta.
59 Minutes of the One Hundred Ninetieth Annual Session of the Baltimore Annual Conference of The United Methodist Church. Legislative Sessions held in Catonsville, Epworth Chapel, Mount Olive and Wesley Memorial United Methodist Churches on May 18, 1974; plenary sessions held in Morris A. Mechanic Theatre, Baltimore, Maryland, May 29 through June 1, 1974, p. 396, accessed January 13, 2022, Catalog.gcah.org. General Commission on Archives and History.
60 According to Love's obituary printed in the *Baltimore Sun* on 3 May 1974, p. 19, Boston University also gave him an honorary doctor of divinity degree in 1956.
61 Mary McLeod Bethune (1875–1955) is best known for founding a private school for Black students in Daytona Beach, Florida, that is now known as Bethune-Cookman University. Little known, but equally important, is the role she played along with others as part of the US delegation that created the United Nations charter.
62 Bishop Edgar A. Love, 84; "Led East Coast Methodists," *News Journal*, 4 May 1974, 19
63 A democrat, Ritchie was Maryland's longest serving governor (1920–1935).
64 Love died on Wednesday, May 1, 1974, at West Baltimore's Provident Hospital after a brief illness. At the time of his death, he lived with his wife at the 2416 block of Montebello Terrace in northeastern Baltimore. His services were held on Wednesday, May 8, 1974, at 11:00 a.m. at the Sharp street Memorial United Methodist Church at 1206 Etting Street. The interment was held at Mt. Auburn Cemetery, also in Baltimore.
65 Dreer, *History of the Omega Psi Phi Fraternity*, 3.
66 "History of Omega Psi Phi" by Bishop Love (a recorded lecture that was transcribed by Lewis Anderson in 1972).
67 T. L. Brown, G. S. Parks, and C. M. Phillips, eds., *African American Fraternities and Sororities: The legacy and the Vision* (Lexington: University Press of Kentucky, 2005), 187.
68 Dartmouth College is one of America's eight Ivy League colleges and universities.
69 Just won a scholarship to Dartmouth College in Hanover, New Hampshire, where he received his AB in zoology. He was the only Black student in a class of 287. He graduated magna cum laude and was inducted into Phi Beta Kappa.

70 Kenneth Manning, *Black Apollo of Science: The Life of Ernest Everett Just* (New York: Oxford University Press, 1983).
71 Many writings about the founders, including two authorized history books, have cited Coleman and Cooper as juniors and Love as a sophomore; yet records with the registrar's office at Howard University show that all three men were freshmen during the 1909–1910 academic year, sophomores during the 1910–1911 academic year, juniors during the 1911–1912 academic year, and seniors during the 1912–1913 academic year. Therefore, it is likely that all three students were juniors during the fall of 1911.
72 In Dumas's novel, the three musketeers are Athos, Porthos, and Aramis. The three men have little in common with Love, Cooper, and Coleman except that they were devoted friends who would eventually become soldiers.
73 According to University of Chicago's Assistant University Registrar John J. W. Plampin, Just embarked on his doctoral studies on Wednesday, July 26, 1911.
74 Aaron E. Klein, *The Hidden Contributors: Black Scientists and Inventors in America* (New York: Doubleday, 1971).
75 Kimball Union Academy is one of the oldest private boarding schools in America (est. 1813), located in Plainfield, New Hampshire. Just is a graduate of the class of 1903.
76 Manning, *Black Apollo of Science*.
77 According to the University of Chicago's Assistant University Registrar John J. W. Plampin, Just earned his PhD in zoology (primary department) and physiology (secondary department) on June 6, 1916. "Studies of Fertilization in Platynereis Megalops" is the title of his dissertation.
78 Examples of Black professors who were highly respected on campus included George Cook, Perry Blaine Perkins, and Lewis B. Moore.
79 Just was an associate professor, not professor, as noted in Robert L. Gill, *A History of the Omega Psi Phi Fraternity, Inc.* (Washington, DC: Omega Psi Phi Fraternity, Inc., 1963), 1.
80 Manning, *Black Apollo of Science*, 40.
81 Shelby Graham, "The Greatest Problem in American Biology," *Dartmouth Alumni Magazine*, November 1983, 25.
82 Manning, *Black Apollo of Science*.
83 Other sources have Just heading the newly formed Zoology Department.
84 Contrary to what appears in the two authorized history books by Drs. Herman Dreer (1940) and Robert L. Gill (1963), Just was not initially hired to teach biology or any other science course but rather English and rhetoric.
85 Manning, *Black Apollo of Science*, 38.
86 Wilbur P. Thirkield, "Doctor Just," Washington Afro-American, June 16, 193(?), in the E.E. Just file, Moorland-Spingarn Research Center, Howard University.
87 Ethel Highwarden Just, of Ripley, Ohio, entered the Ohio State University in 1902 and earned her BA in 1906 and a master's degree from Boston University in 1936. Her master's thesis is titled "Negro American Folk-Plays of Paul Green with Special Reference to Their Sociological Value." After her divorce from Just in 1939, she led a team of translators (code breakers) at the Arlington Hall Station during World War II and later became dean of women at South Carolina State College. See Kim O'Connell, "The Black Women Code Breakers of Arlington Hall Station," *Arlington Magazine*, June 7, 2021,

www.arlingtonmagazine.com/the-black-women-code-breakers-of-arlington-hall-station/

88 Just and Highwarden were married on June 26, 1912, at the home of Ethel's parents. That same year Just began serving as Professor of physiology in the medical school until 1920. Highwarden taught German at Howard University.

89 Although this is the order in which the fraternity's four cardinal principles appear in print (in both Dreer's and Gill's history books) and are articulated by its members, on p. 4 of the June 1919 issue of the *Oracle,* the year this publication was founded, the cardinal principles are listed in the following order: Scholarship, Manhood, Uplift, and Perseverance. The principles also appear this way on p. 11. Further study reveals a slightly different order on several different pages in the August 1921 issue of the *Oracle*. E.g., on p. 4 in the *Annual Message* by Grand Basileus Harold H. Thomas, the cardinal principles appear like so: Manhood, Scholarship, Uplift, and Perseverance. The same order appears on p. 6. Three pages later they appear as Scholarship, Manhood, Uplift, and Perseverance in an article under the heading "Subordinate Chapters." Nearly one year later, in a May 1922 *Oracle,* one finds the article "Some Fraternity Problems" by Charles A. Chandler of the Yale University School of Law, with the cardinal principles cited as Manhood, Scholarship, Perseverance, and Uplift. It may be that the order of the cardinal principles published in the 1919 edition of the *Oracle* represents the original intent of the founders. How the reordering occurred, as well as why and when, is unclear.

90 In the two authorized history books about the history of the Omega Psi Phi Fraternity, both Drs. Herman Dreer and Robert L. Gill cite fourteen initial members of the Alpha chapter of the Omega Psi Phi Fraternity, Inc. However, this number is at odds with statements made by Bishop Edgar Amos Love, who in a speech, "The History of Omega Psi Phi Fraternity" (transcribed by the organization's Grand Keeper of Record and Seal, Brother Lewis Anderson) claims that he and the other founders brought in 14 other men. Whether this was a slip of the tongue or a case of Brother Love simply misremembering remains unclear. For more details, see iotachapterques.org/content.aspx?page_id=22&club_id=66506&module_id=282320

91 The Methodist Church on Slavery, June 6, 1958 (a pamphlet).

92 John Wesley, *Thoughts upon Slavery* (London: Printed by Joseph Crukshank, 1774).

93 Raymond Wolters, *The New Negro on Campus: Black College Rebellions of the 1920s* (Princeton, NJ: Princeton University Press, 1975), 88.

94 Benjamin Quarles, *The Negro in the Making of America* (New York: Collier Books, 1987), 173.

95 "Monroe Trotter Denounces Booker T. Washington as a Traitor to the Race" (editorial), *Boston Guardian*, December 20, 1902.

96 A copy of this discourse appears in the Negro Collections, Founders Library, filed under Patton, William V. The university received scant support from private foundations during the period 1867–1884. An appeal by the board on April 8, 1867, to the Peabody Education Fund was unsuccessful ("Minutes of the Board," May 6, 1867). The John Slater Fund contributed, in 1884, the sum of $1,663.92 for the support of the Industrial Department; see Dyson, "Founding of Howard University," 114. Patton is not the only

president who put forward ideas about the kind of curriculum Howard should offer. One of the reasons Dr. Carter G. Woodson's tenure at Howard lasted just one year was because he found President J. Stanley Durkee's (Howard's last white president, 1919–1926) lack of support for incorporating black history courses in the university's curriculum untenable. See Zachery Williams, *In Search of the Talented Tenth: Howard University Public Intellectuals and the Dilemmas of Race, 1926–1970* (Columbia: University of Missouri Press, 2010).

97 Logan, *Howard University*, 155.
98 Baltimore Afro-American, June 6, 1908.
99 As quoted in Barry Goldberg and Barbara Shubinski, "Black Education and Rockefeller Philanthropy from the Jim Crow South to the Civil Rights Era," RE:SOURCE, September 11, 2020, https://resource.rockarch.org/story/black-education-and-rockefeller-philanthropy-from-the-jim-crow-south-to-the-civil-rights-era/
100 David Nicholson, "Opinion: Why Howard University Exploded Last Week," *Washington Post*, March 12, 1989, www.washingtonpost.com/archive/opinions/1989/03/12/why-howard-university-exploded-last-week/947f6c27-f44c-432f-9699-b7274402a443/
101 William Stuart Nelson was an internationally known expert on nonviolence who corresponded with Dr. Martin Luther King Jr. regularly during the modern civil rights movement.
102 Channing Tobias was the senior secretary of the YMCA's Colored Work Department from 1924 to 1946. After 1946, Tobias became the first Black director of the Phelps-Stokes Fund, a philanthropic association that awarded funds to institutions that provided educational opportunities for Black children.
103 A 1916 graduate of Howard University, having been elected class president in both 1915 and 1916, Frazier became a well-known professor and prolific writer who was instrumental in establishing African Studies at Howard University.
104 Rayford Logan was an African American historian and Pan-Africanist. A highly regarded professor and well-respected scholar of Black history, Logan coordinated the 1921 Pan African Congress held in Paris. His most provocative work is his 1965 book, *The Betrayal of the Negro: From Rutherford B. Hayes to Woodrow Wilson*.
105 W.E.B Du Bois, "The American Negro Intelligentsia," *Presence Africaine* 5 (December 1955–January 1956): 34–51.
106 Pauli Murray was the first Black to earn a JSD (doctor of the science of law) degree from Yale Law School and a cofounder of the National Organization for Woman.
107 Eugene Davidson (1896–1976) was the president of the local NAACP chapter in Washington, DC, from 1952 to 1958. He gained early notoriety when he was named administrator of the New Negro Alliance in 1939.
108 Logan, *Howard University*, 568.
109 Paula Giddings, *In Search of Sisterhood* (New York: Perennial, 1984), 46.
110 The source for Hill's spring 1927 date of initiation into the Alpha chapter is the website belonging to Iota Iota Iota chapter in Salt Lake City, Utah, which contains a rather long profile of Brother Hill. By contrast, the fraternity's online directory has Hill's birth chapter as Phi Phi in Richmond, Virgina, but with no associated year.

111 Oscar Adams crossed the burning sands in the early 1940s, but the exact year is unclear. According to a chapter directory, he was basileus of Gamma Psi at Talladega in 1943. See p. 30 of the June 1943 issue of the *Oracle*. The fraternity's directory mistakenly identifies him as an Alpha Phi initiate.
112 Wilberforce University is home to Upsilon chapter.
113 Sigma Omega is a graduate chapter located in Chicago.
114 Tougaloo College in Mississippi is home to Rho Epsilon.
115 The University of Illinois, Urbana/Champaign, is home to Pi Psi.
116 At the time of Mays's initiation, he was an undergraduate at Bates College in Lewiston, Maine. He was 25 years old when he crossed the burning sands into the Kingdom of Omega. Mays was also one of the founders of Sigma Omega in Chicago.
117 According to the article "The Subordinate Chapters" by Luther O. Baumgardner in the June 1919 edition of the *Oracle*, Just and then Major Charles Young were elected as active members on February 28, 1912, in that order; hence, Just has the distinction of being first. However, according to Robert L. Gill's 1963 *History of the Omega Psi Phi Fraternity*, on p. 3, Young's election occurred on March 8, 1912, at the meeting of the Grand Council (composed of the national officers who acted as a board of directors, now called the Supreme Council). See also Gill, *History of the Omega Psi Phi Fraternity*, 15.
118 Percy Julian served as an inspiration to many aspiring Black scientists, having received more than 130 chemical patents, and he was the first African American chemist to be inducted into the National Academy of Sciences. Julian was once a member of Gamma chapter when he was a graduate student at Harvard University as well as Sigma Omega when he moved his family to Oak Park, Illinois, in 1950. Still, it is not entirely clear the year he became a member of the illustrious Omega Psi Phi Fraternity, Inc., or the chapter in which he was initiated. One can find his name in several of the early *Oracles*, so it is clear to this writer that he was a member of the illustrious Omega Psi Phi Fraternity, Inc., as early as the December 1922 issue of the *Oracle* that cites his time as a stellar student at DePauw University, in Indiana. The fraternity's directory has Sigma Omega (Chicago) as Julian's birth chapter, which seems curious given that an early issue of the *Oracle* has Julian as a member of Gamma chapter in Boston, specifically, and New England, generally, during his graduate studies at Harvard University. Even Dr. Julian's daughter, Faith Julian, is uncertain of the chapter and the year of her father's initiation. Based on conversations with relatives and others Ms. Julian believes her father was initiated in 1922 in Sigma chapter (initially chartered in Chicago) or 1923 when the chapter became Sigma Omega (still in Chicago).

I

In the World of Science

1

Viewing the World through a Microscope Lens (and Drama among Nazis)

The Life of Ernest E. Just

Theodore Walker Jr.

E. E. Just's Life and Work

Ernest Everett Just was born to Mary Mathews Cooper Just and Charles Fraser Just in Charleston, South Carolina, on August 14, 1883. He was the youngest of five children, of whom two died as infants, leaving Ernest with one brother, Hunter, and one sister, Inez. His father died in 1887. In 1892 the Just family moved to James Island, South Carolina, where Mary Just founded the town of Maryville and taught in a school she founded there. Educational and religious instruction from his mother enabled Ernest to write well. By the time he was 16, Ernest had written a poem that was published in a Washington, DC, newspaper, and he earned a license to teach from South Carolina State College in Orangeburg in 1899. In 1900 he went to study at a college preparatory school, Kimball Union Academy, in Meriden, New Hampshire. His mother died in 1901. After Kimball Union Academy, he studied English and biology at Dartmouth College, graduating magna cum laude in 1907.[1] While at Dartmouth he continued writing and publishing poetry, and in biology he "contributed to a chapter in Professor William Patten's classic biology text The Evolution of the Vertebrates and Their Kin."[2]

At Howard University in Washington, DC, starting in 1907, Just taught English literature. By 1909 he was teaching both English and biology, and he was doing summer research (as assistant to Frank Rattray Lillie) at the Marine Biology Laboratory (MBL) in Woods Hole, Massachusetts. He continued doing summer research at the MBL through the 1920s. In 1911 he was transferred to Howard University's Zoology Department and became an associate professor of biology. Also, in 1911 Just served as faculty adviser for the Alpha chapter that inaugurated the Omega Psi Phi Fraternity, Inc., and started work on a University of Chicago PhD. In 1912 he was elected Omega Psi Phi's first honorary member and married Ethel Highwarden, a bilingual (German/English) teacher of German language from Ripley, Ohio, and graduate of the Ohio State University. They had three children: Highwarden, Maribel, and Margret. And Just published his first scientific article, "The Relation of the First Cleavage Plane to the Entrance Point of the Sperm," that year.[3] In 1915, at a NAACP ceremony featuring a speech by W.E.B. Du Bois, Just was awarded the first Spingarn Medal for high achievement.[4] The following year Just earned a PhD in zoology and physiology from the University of Chicago.

In 1917 he advanced pioneering research on marine egg cell responses to sperm; by 1919 he was the recognized authority on correct methods of handling marine invertebrates and was known for rigorous experimental methods. He published four major articles in 1919–1920 and was elected to five highly prestigious scientific societies. Throughout the 1920s and 1930s, Just was an internationally recognized researcher, traveling to Stazione Zoologica in Naples, the Kaiser-Wilhelm-Institute in Berlin, and to the Sorbonne and the Station Biologique in France. By 1938 Just had published nearly 70 scientific articles and one book chapter. In 1939 he published two books: *The Biology of the Cell Surface* and *Basic Methods for Experiments on Eggs of Marine Animals*.

In April 1939 in Riga, Latvia, Just filed to divorce his wife. In August 1939, in France, he married his research collaborator Hedwig Schnetzler, PhD in philosophy, who had been researching and writing with Just since 1931. By 1932 Ernest and Hedwig were working on a book offering a "new theory of vital phenomena."[5] There are hints and fragments of this new theory in various articles,[6] and it is discussed briefly in *The Biology of the Cell Surface* and developed in a book-length manuscript titled "The Origin of Man's Ethical Behavior" that was not published until 2020.

In February 1996, the US Postal service issued a Black Heritage postage stamp honoring Ernest Everett Just for his contributions to biology.

Social Location and Research among Germans

We can better appreciate Just's contributions to biology by also appreciating his social location. We can easily imagine living from 1883 to 1941 and being an African American pursuing a PhD degree and a university career doing pure research. During that time (and continuing to the present), research-oriented African Americans in the United States valued, and were valued for, studying in Europe.

This research-oriented space (Black researcher goes from the United States to Europe) and time (1883 to 1941) is addressed almost exactly in "'Of the Coming of John [and Jane]': African American Intellectuals in Europe, 1888–1938" (2002) by Corey D. B. Walker. Herein C.D.B. Walker follows Charles H. Long and Paul Gilroy in being attentive to Black peoples in the "'North America-trans Atlantic Ocean-Europe' space they call 'the Black Atlantic.'"[7] C.D.B. Walker finds that, from 1888 to 1938, the Black Atlantic featured a "steady stream of African American intellectuals" traveling from the United States to Europe—and travel to Germany was rivaled only by travel to France—while others traveled to England and other European destinations. C.D.B. Walker's title refers to the 1903 essay "Of the Coming of John" in The Souls of Black Folk: Essays and Sketches by W.E.B. Du Bois.

Du Bois's self-referenced fictional character "John Jones" is an African American intellectual embracing "the life of the mind" and scientific research in the context of anti-Black racism in North American universities. Like John (and Jane), Du Bois was an African American intellectual with deep appreciation for German research and German scholarship, and he traveled to Germany to study. After much studying, in 1903, Du Bois's John Jones came to "'strongly'" suspect that the Germans were "'thieves and rascals, despite his text-books.'"[8] Thirty-three years later, in 1936, the year Jesse Owens won four Olympic gold medals in Berlin, Du Bois lamented the treatment of Jews in Germany. W.E.B. Du Bois's enthusiasm for Germans became lamentation.

Similarly, Just was an African American intellectual with enthusiasm for German research and scholarship, and (in addition to traveling to Italy and France) he traveled to Germany.[9] To be sure, starting from his college preparatory years at Kimball Union Academy and his undergraduate years at Dartmouth College, Just's "favorite theologian" had been Adolf von Harnack.[10] Harnack was a member of the Berlin Academy of Science and the 1911 president of the Kaiser-Wilhem-Institute. In 1930, when Just was on research leave from Howard University and doing research at the Kaiser-Wilhelm-Institute für Biologie in Berlin, he resided at Harnack House, where he and Harnack became friends. They spent "many evenings" sharing tea and discussing the need to bring "science and religion into greater harmony."[11] In the preface to his book *The Biology of the Cell Surface* Just acknowledged, "The conception upon which the book is built, though latent in my earlier researches, did not come fully awake until 1930 while I was enjoying the hospitality of the Kaiser-Wilhelm-Institut for Biologie at Berlin-Dahlem" and where "I fell under the inspiration of Adolf von Harnack's personality." He continued, "My work was influenced by the rich experience of personal contact with him."[12] Harnack's natural "scientific theology"[13] and much else from Germany were greatly appreciated by Just. Nevertheless, according to Kenneth R. Manning, Just finally came "to despise the Germans—a people whom he had so revered in the past."[14]

Drama among Nazis, 1940

When Just was researching and writing in France, in response to the German invasion of Czechoslovakia in March 1939, he offered to serve in the French military to fight Germans. The French military declined Just's offer because he was in very poor physical condition, "too old and ill and tired to be of much use to any army."[15] The Germans invaded Paris in June 1940. In August 1940, "the Nazis interned Just."[16] Kenneth R. Manning relates:

> . . . Hedwig [Hedwig Schnetzler Just, co-researcher and spouse] was several months pregnant. . . . In early August the Nazis interned Just in a camp, probably Chateaulin. When Hedwig's father found out he mobilized his Nazi contacts on the board of the Brown, Boveri Company, and an official was dispatched to France to obtain Just's release. . . .
>
> Americans were gravely worried about him. Lillie [University of Chicago-MBL biologist Frank Rattray Lillie] had been receiving constant inquiries, and so had Harrison [Yale-MBL biologist Ross G. Harrison]. They got together and decided to contact the American Red Cross and the State Department to see if anything could be done to locate him and send help if he was in trouble. . . .
>
> By this time Just and Hedwig were making their way out of France, down into Spain, and finally to Portugal. In early September they boarded the S.S. Exambion in Lisbon. . . . But their problems were not yet over. The captain told them that he would not let Hedwig make the crossing: he had had an unpleasant experience with a childbirth on a previous passage and did not want a repeat episode. After much pleading, Just and Hedwig changed his mind. At last they were on their way to America.[17]

This early August 1940 internment and release, followed by hide-and-seek escape through Nazi-occupied France, then through Spain and Portugal to the United States in September 1940[18] was referenced in an October 15, 1940, letter from Just at Howard University to W. C. Allee at the University of Chicago. In this letter, now preserved at the Moorland-Spingarn Research Center, E. E. Just reported "the complete collapse, moral and spiritual, of all the people to whom I talked," and that his "escape" from Nazi-occupied France was "strong stuff" and "plenty dramatic."[19]

Theoretical Work on Evolution

In this 15 October 1940 letter from Just to W. C. Allee, he also reported that, during the last year, he had been "taking a shot at the problem of social instincts," and that he had "worked as never before on this manuscript," and that this "writing and thinking together with some very nice work on my eggs kept me going and enjoying life in the last year as never before." Just anticipated that getting this manuscript into print could be difficult because 1940 was, he said, "a bad time with the world." Plus, he knew that publishers could be influenced by his North American colleagues who were resolutely not interested in his philosophical and theoretical work.[20] Just was being pressured to continue microscope observations and experiments at the MBL without doing theoretical work, such as work on theory of evolution. And there were other pressures, including Howard University pressuring him to return to classroom teaching, as well as the ever-present pressure to do practical work, such as medical practice or applied biology, instead of pure research. And of course, Just was needing to recover from posttraumatic stress and increasing physical illness. Hence, pessimistically, in his October 15, 1940, letter to Allee, in reference to getting "this manuscript" published, Just wrote, "Maybe I can't get it out." And in fact, Just did not "get it out." He tried and failed to persuade a publisher to print this manuscript. There is no doubt that, by trying again, and perhaps again, he would have succeeded if he had not become severely ill and died.

Fortunately for this unpublished manuscript, there are onion-skin copies of typed pages, plus various typed and handwritten pages, preserved among the many Collected Papers of Ernest Everett Just at the Moreland-Spingarn Research Center at Howard University. In 2018–2019 these pages were identified and transcribed, and in 2020 a 251-page archival transcription was published as The Origin of Man's Ethical Behavior (1941) by Ernest Everett Just and Hedwig Schnetzler Just. Against North American pressure to avoid theoretical work, "The Origin of Man's Ethical Behavior" was highly theoretical. Furthermore, Just and Just resisted being overwhelmed by the evils of 1941 (including anti-Black racism in the United States and Nazism in Germany) by expecting "farther evolution" in human ethical behavior.[21] To understand this counterfactual expectation, we need to better appreciate Just's fairly well-known contributions to biology and his relatively unknown (and then unwelcome) contributions to theory of evolution and theory of ethical behavior.

Contributions to Biology

Even if we have not seen the 1996 Black Heritage postage stamp honoring biologist Just (1883–1941), and even if we have not studied the award-winning biography Black Apollo: The Life of Ernest Everett Just (1983) by Kenneth R. Manning, all of us have learned biology from Just. All of us have seen images of egg cell fertilization by a single spermatozoan interacting with the egg cell surface, and a "wave of negativity" sweeping around the egg cell surface repulsing all other sperm. The idea that egg cells are interactive rather than totally passive (totally inert receptacles) was an important corrective departure from then prevailing male-oriented thinking in biology. Much of what we now know about egg cell fertilization and early embryo development was first advanced by Just, who observed marine egg cells interacting cooperatively (i.e., cooperating) with other cells and the environment.

During many of the 1909–1928 summers of research at the Marine Biological Laboratory, generations of MBL biologists learned observational and experimental methods from Just. His lab notes and various MBL writings culminated in his second 1939 publication—*Basic Methods for Experiments on Eggs of Marine Animals*. Just advanced "methods" that are rigorously attentive to the environments that are normal for living specimens. Until Just, marine biologists had been in the bad habit of working mostly with specimens extracted from their normal environments, often killed, dissected, and fixed. Just criticized and corrected findings derived from such faulty methods. He encouraged attention to development within normal environments. For fertilized marine eggs, Just's criterion for environmental normalcy was 100 percent flourishing, all eggs developing.[22] Just argued that biologists should avoid separating a living organism from its environment because organism and environment "form together one inter-acting system," and "we should not speak of the 'fitness of the environment' or the 'fitness of the organism'; rather, we should regard organism and environment as mutually adapted."[23] According to Just, "Environment and organism are one; neither can be separated from the other."[24]

During his day, Just would have been identified as a "cytologist" or "embryologist." Today, he is a "pioneering African-American embryologist,"[25] a contributor to the study of embryo morphogenesis, a "developmental biologist," a "pioneer in ecological development biology,"[26] and an early advocate of non-reductionist/holistic approaches to biology.[27] W. Malcolm Byrnes describes "ecological developmental biology" as focusing, like Just, "on development in its natural environmental context," and he says Just has "much in common with what is known today as integrative systems biology, in which a top-down view is just as important as a bottom-up view for understanding the system."[28] Just's contributions to biology included advancing cytology, embryology, embryo morphogenesis, developmental biology, ecological developmental biology (eco-devo biology), integrative systems biology, and "basic methods" and best practices for handling marine animals.

Contributions to Theory of Evolution and Theory of Ethical Behavior

Today, "The Origin of Man's Ethical Behavior" is much more than a very interesting historical artifact. It was difficult to publish in 1941 partly because it was far ahead of its time. By tying evolutionary biology to ethics in 1941, Just and Just were doing "evolutionary bioethics" before "bioethics" became a word in English. In 1970, the word "bioethics" was "invented" by Sargent Shriver while conversing with his wife Eunice Kennedy Shriver and Jesuit priest president of Georgetown University Andrée Hellegers about sponsoring "an institute for the application of moral philosophy to concrete medical dilemmas."[29] Also, independently, in 1970, the word "bioethics" was coined by Van Rensselaer Potter,[30] and perhaps the first book with the word "bioethics" in the title was Bioethics: Bridge to the Future by Van Rensselaer Potter, printed in 1971. For the Shrivers and Hellegers, bioethics was biomedical healthcare ethics. For Potter, the purpose of "bioethics" was "to contribute to the future of the human species by promoting the formation of a new discipline" able to bridge "'two cultures' . . . science and the humanities" (biological facts and ethical values); and "the test of the value system" is the "survival of the total ecosystem."[31]

In 1984, Potter called for "evolutionary bioethics."[32] In 1941, Just and Just were doing "evolutionary bioethics" 30 years before "bioethics" was coined in English,[33] and 43 years before the term "evolutionary bioethics" was introduced in 1984. To be sure, Just and Just were so very far ahead of their time that in our time their work can still advance contemporary theory of evolution and theory of ethical behavior. Elsewhere, concerning E. E. Just advancing contemporary biology, I argue the following:

> E. E. Just advanced the idea that co-operative behavior at the cellular level is essential to the origin, development, and evolution of life . . . . This advance came 77 to 79 years before Scientific American reported the surprising [re]discovery that microbes were co-operative team players, as indicated in "Team Players: Long thought mostly to compete with one another, microbes turn out to form partnerships that rule the planet" (November 2018) by Jeffrey Marlow and Rogier Braakman.

Here, in November 2018, we see science starting to catch up to ideas advanced by Just during the 1930s.[34]

In his 1939 book and coauthored 1941 manuscript, Just argued that, starting from cells, cooperative behavior is essential to the origin, development, and evolution of life. Seventy-seven to 79 years later, in 2018, Scientific American announced the surprising discovery that microbes are cooperative team players. Contemporary science is rediscovering what E. E. Just had already discovered.

Concerning development from egg cells and evolution from a "single cell ancestor,"[35] in my abstract to "Reviewing Ernest Everett Just's Biology of the Cell Surface (1939) and Related Literature," I argue the following:

> Abstract: The Biology of the Cell Surface (1939) by Ernest Everett Just is focused on marine egg cells and egg cell surfaces. By studying egg cells, and cell surface mediated cooperation with sperm and environment, E. E. Just advanced egg cell fertilization and developmental biology, including embryo morphogenesis, ecological developmental (eco-devo) biology, and theory of evolution. According to Just, from cells to humans, development and evolution require co-operative behavior. In developmental biology, Just observed that co-operative behavior is essential to animal development from a single egg cell. In evolutionary biology, Just reasoned that co-operative behavior is essential to evolution from our common unicellular ancestor. And in evolutionary bioethics, Just tied evolutionary biology to evolutionary ethics by reference to evolution from a common unicellular ancestor with cell surface mediated co-operative interactions with the environment. In accordance with the "law of environmental dependence," evolutionary bioethics must also be environmental bioethics. Even though E. E. Just may have overestimated cell surface influences, he correctly estimated the developmental potence and the evolutionary potence of the whole living cell interacting cooperatively with its life-inspiring environment.
>
> Key words: Stammzell, stem cell, common unicellular ancestor, egg cell, cell surface behavior, interaction, co-operation, social instinct, developmental biology, evolutionary biology, evolutionary ethics, evolutionary bioethics, law of environmental dependence, environmental bioethics.[36]

According to the cell-biology-informed theory of evolution advanced by Just and Just, like human and nonhuman animals that developed from a single egg cell that interacted cooperatively with the environment, human and nonhuman species evolved from a "single cell ancestor"[37] (a "unicellular organism,"[38] our common unicellular ancestor) that interacted cooperatively with the environment. Furthermore, for Just and Just, the unicellular origin and evolution of physiology is inseparably tied to the unicellular origin and evolution of cooperative behavior.

In "The Origin of Man's Ethical Behavior," Just and Just recognized that physiology and behavior are the physical and the spiritual aspects of life or "the state of being alive."[39] Just and Just conceived that physiology is matter-physical while behavior is "inspired" and "spiritual," and that "spirituality" is "intangible and refractory to analysis except as a behavior."[40] They argued that physiology and inspired behavior evolved together, and that "all of man, physical and spiritual, is the product of evolution."[41] Natural selection cannot be only selections from among random-chance mutations. Nature selects from among many various physical structures and behaviors; and cooperative behaviors are strongly favored over "always eat your neighbors and struggle against the environment." According to Just and Just, the overemphasis on competitive "struggle for existence" is an overemphasis advanced by followers of Darwin, by Darwinians, not by Darwin, who was speaking in metaphor.[42]

Contrary to the popular Darwinian idea that evolution is driven exclusively by competitive struggles against others and against the environment, in 1902, in Mutual Aid: A Factor of Evolution, Peter Kropotkin argued that "mutual aid" or "co-operation" is essential to evolution. Zoological field observations of animals cooperating were made by Kropotkin and others, including Darwin. For the sake of gathering evidence sufficient to Kropotkin's thesis, however, these zoological observations needed to be supplemented by microscope observations of cells cooperating.[43] Just provided this much needed essential supplement. And, according to Just and Just, by adding observations of cellular cooperation, the evolution of human ethical behavior is "carried farther back than heretofore," carried back (in parallel with the evolution of human physiology) to the "first link of the chain," to our common unicellular ancestor.[44]

Species evolution from our common unicellular ancestor is connected to animal development from a single egg cell in *The Biology of the Cell Surface*, where Just argues, "The history of the multicellular organism as it develops from the egg, a single cell, to the adult is very much like a synopsis of the history of the whole world of multicellular organisms, this has most probably evolved from *a single cell ancestor*."[45] Here, italics are added to emphasize development (from a single egg cell) being "very much like a synopsis" of evolution (from a single cell ancestor).

Stem Cells

Historically, both single egg cells and our single cell ancestor were once called "stem cells." In their 2007 article "On the Origin of the Term 'Stem Cell,'" Miguel Ramalho-Santos and Holger Willenbring report that in the scientific literature the term "stem cell" or "Stammzell" originated with work by the famous German biologist Ernst Haeckel, starting in the year 1868. As Ramalho-Stos and Willenbring argue,

> Haeckel, a major supporter of Darwin's theory of evolution, drew a number of phylogenetic trees to represent the evolution of organisms by descent from common ancestors and called these trees "Stammbäume" (German for family trees or "stem trees"). In this context, Haeckel used the term "Stammzelle" (German for stem cell) to describe the ancestor unicellular organism from which he presumed all multicellular organisms evolved. . . . . In the revised 3rd edition of his book Anthropogenie . . . , Haeckel made one of his characteristic leaps from evolution (phylogeny) to embryology (ontogeny) and proposed that the fertilized egg also be called stem cell.[46]

In other words, as Ramalho-Santos and Willenbring claim, "Haeckel used the term stem cell in two senses: as the unicellular ancestor of all multicellular organisms and as the fertilized egg that gives rise to all cells of the organism."[47]

Just studied and appreciated Haeckel's work, and he employed Haeckel's "clean description" as "the basis" for defining "the ectoplasm" in chapter 4, "'The Ectoplasm' in The Biology of the Cell Surface."[48] And somewhat like Haeckel "leaping" from evolution to embryology, Just recognized that development from a single fertilized egg cell can be "very much like a synopsis" of evolution from "the unicellular ancestor."[49] Nevertheless, Just did not employ the term "stem cell."

Law of Environmental Dependence

As indicated by a fertilized marine egg cell developing into a multicellular animal by cooperating with others and the environment, according to Just and Just, the surviving and evolving of species depend upon cooperating with others (especially within species) and the environment. Just and Just emphasized the necessity of cooperating with the environment by recognizing the "law of environmental dependence."[50] According to Just and Just, the "law of environmental dependence" applies to development, and to evolution; again, "all of man, physical and spiritual, is the product of evolution."[51] In 1941, seemingly without recognizing a present or future environmental crisis (pollution, climate change, global warming, or Arctic ice melting), Just and Just theorized that, "in accordance with the law of environmental dependence, the continuing evolution of humanity is dependent upon co-operating with others and with the environment."[52]

Seeing and Foreseeing beyond 1940

Recall that October 1940 was, wrote Just, "a bad time" for the world, a time with anti-Black racism in the United States and Nazism in Germany, a time so bad that Just anticipated little interest in the Just and Just manuscript and he wrote, pessimistically, "Maybe I can't get it out." As noted, he did not get it out (did not find a publisher). Nevertheless, the manuscript that Just "could not get out" included a witness against the facts of October 1940, a counterfactual expectation of "farther evolution" in human ethical behavior.[53] This optimistic counterfactual expectation derived from the Just and Just study of egg cells and from their egg cell biology-instructed theory of evolution and human ethical behavior. According to the Just and Just theory of evolution, biological evolution includes together the continuing evolution of physiology and the continuing evolution of cooperative behavior. Human cooperative behavior sometimes qualifies as "ethical behavior."[54] Hence, ethics or ethical behavior must evolve (or stagnate and devolve).

By focusing on development from egg cells and cell biology-instructed theory of evolution, Just and Just could see beyond October 1940, beyond anti-Black racism in the United States and beyond Nazism in Germany, and almost prophetically they could foresee the possible continuing evolution of human ethical behavior.

Seeing with Microscopes and Telescopes

Beyond foreseeing the possible continuing evolution of human ethical behavior, Just could see cosmological connections because "the egg cell also is a universe."[55] Connections between viewing egg cells and viewing the local universe, between viewing with microscopes and viewing with telescopes, were appreciated by Just. Concerning universe and egg cells, in *The Biology of the Cell Surface*, Just claimed:

> The universe, however much we fragment it, abstract it, ever retains its unity.

> The egg cell also is a universe. And if we could but know it we would feel in its minute confines the majesty and beauty which match the vast wonder of the world.⁵⁶

This view of "the universe" and "the egg cell" reminds me of a Mandelbrot Set fractal image (a universe) containing deep within an identical image (egg cell, also a universe). Concerning viewing with telescopes and viewing with microscopes, Just said:

> The lone watcher of the sky who in some distant high tower suddenly saw a new planet floating before his lens could not have been more enthralled than the first student who saw the spermatozoon preceded by a streaming bubble moving toward the egg-centre. And as every novitiate in astronomy must thrill at his first glance into the world of stars, so does the student to-day who first beholds this microcosm, the egg-cell.⁵⁷

Moreover, Just and Just said, "in every living cell 'the grand cosmic phenomena' are manifested."⁵⁸ Astronomy and biology are connected.⁵⁹ Evolution applies to both.

Astrobiology, starting in 1946, would confirm Just's 1939 intuition by showing that we are inspired and evolved stardust. The heavy elements, including our bodily carbon, were forged in previous generations of stars. Our solar system, including Earth and life on it, evolved from "stellar evolution" in a finely tuned expanding universe,⁶⁰ from "cosmic evolution."⁶¹ Life is a "cosmic phenomenon," and there is an evolutionary "cosmic biology."⁶² Sir Fred Hoyle, who started and lead the process of recognizing connections among biological evolution on Earth, stellar evolution, and cosmic evolution,⁶³ was forced by his own mathematical calculations to abandon his previously very his famous commitment to atheism. In astronomy and cosmology, the possibility of life depends upon the "coupling constants" of physics being chosen with enormous precision. Creating and sustaining such an enormously precise cosmic environment (today called cosmic fine-tuning) requires "all embracing intelligence."⁶⁴ In biology, Hoyle's mathematical calculations decisively disqualified the idea of life emerging from nonlife by random or chance assembly. The mathematical evidence from astronomy, cosmology, and biology (astrobiology and cosmic biology) converged in ways that affirm the necessary existence of God.⁶⁵

Evolution and God

Just and Just held that their theory of evolution is "not incompatible with belief in God."[66] This is minimally consistent with the religious influence of Just's mother, Mary Mathews Cooper Just, and with the natural "scientific theology" advanced by his favorite theologian Adolf von Harnack. Moreover, Just and Just embraced Alfred North Whitehead's historical claim that "faith in the possibility of science" derived from medieval theology's insistence that Nature is rationally ordered by God.[67] I find that the Just and Just theory of evolution is fully compatible with belief in God. The physical and the spiritual aspects of life together are essential to the Just and Just theory of evolution. Making life's spiritual aspect (which inspires observable behavior) essential to theory of evolution yields "a richer account of evolution"[68] that is fully compatible with natural theology.

Biology and Poetry

Recall that Just studied English and biology at Dartmouth College starting in the fall of 1903, that during his first year at Howard University in 1907 he taught English literature, that he taught both English literature and biology in 1909 and 1910 as an "Instructor in English and Biology," that he was moved from the English Department to the Zoology Department to teach biology in 1911, and that he wrote poems throughout his life. Therefore, it is not surprising to see that when Just was writing about biology he wrote with a poetic style. For example, the final chapter of Biology of the Cell Surface includes the following passages:

> The living thing is part of the natural world, it grows and lives on the stuff of which it is made and whence it came. Then living thing and outside world constitute on interdependent unity, as evolution teaches, as the development of an animal egg reveals. As the boundary, the living mobile limit of the cell, the ectoplasm, controls the integration between the living cell and all else external to it. The ectoplasm is the means of exchange for incoming and outgoing substances. It is keyed to the outside world as no other part of the cell. It stands guard over the peculiar form of the living substance, is buffer against the attacks of the surroundings and the means of communication with it.[69]
>
> Life is not only a struggle against the surroundings from which life came; it is also co-operation with them. The Kropotkin theory of mutual aid and co-operation may be a better explanation of the cause of evolution than the prevailing popular conception of Darwin's idea of

the struggle for existence. The means of co-operation and adjustment is the ectoplasm....⁷⁰

We feel the beauty of Nature because we are part of Nature and because we know that however much in our separate domains we abstract from the unity of Nature, this unity remains. Although we may deal with particulars, we return finally to the whole pattern woven out of these. So in our study of the animal egg though we resolve it into constituent parts the better to understand it, we hold it as an integrated thing, as a unified system in it life resides and in its moving surface life manifests itself.⁷¹

Just's concluding summary (of egg cell-surface-mediated interactivity with others and the environment) is beautifully worded. Not only is there poetry in his writings about biology, according to Just, life itself is musical and harmonious. "Life," says Just, "is exquisitely a time-thing, like music."⁷² Like music, life is a moving "harmonious organization of events, the resultant of a communion of structures and reactions."⁷³

Here again, concerning cellular cooperation and harmony, contemporary scientists are rediscovering what had already been discovered by Just. They are rediscovering that "every aspect of animal life—from morphology to physiology and behavior—requires the cooperation of thousands to billions of cells" and "cellular choreography,"⁷⁴ and that cells "coexist by cooperating."⁷⁵

Encouraging and Funding Pure Research

In addition to doing pioneering research at the MBL, at Italian, French, and German research facilities, and at Howard University, Just was an "administrative pioneer and fund-seeking pioneer."⁷⁶ Administratively, and as a mentor, Just encouraged women to do pure research. For example, he encouraged Hedwig Schnetzler to "put on a lab coat" and do laboratory research, plus library and museum research. And he encouraged Roger Arliner Young to help with preparing microscope slides, and to do pure laboratory research at the MBL.⁷⁷ Consequently, Young became the first African American woman to conduct research at the MBL and the first to earn a PhD in zoology (from the University of Pennsylvania).⁷⁸ In fund-seeking, Just was among the first African American scientists to solicit and receive major foundation grants to fund pure research.⁷⁹

The Continuing Legacy of E. E. Just

Just did pioneering research in marine egg cell fertilization and early embryo development biology (celebrated with a 1996 Black Heritage postage stamp). He is best known for calling attention to the biology of the egg cell surface, and discovering the "wave of negativity," fast and slow blocks to polyspermy, and relations between adhesive properties of cells and stages of embryo development, and for emphasizing the importance of normal environments. Moreover, teaching MBL and the world "basic methods" for doing embryology is a hugely important and perhaps everlasting scientific legacy, as Just himself recognized, saying that "this knowledge" is "the sine qua non of all experimental work in embryology."[80] Demonstrating that egg cells are interactive, rather than totally passive (totally inert receptacles), was an important advance against male chauvinist biology. Furthermore, with a female researcher, he coauthored a book advancing a new theory of evolution and ethics. According to the Just and Just theory of evolution, biological evolution is evolution of physiology (the physical aspect of life, encompassing form/structure and function) together with evolution of cooperative behavior (the spiritual aspect of life inspires behavior), including cooperating with the environment; this is the origin of human ethical behavior.

Advancing pure research among African Americans, women, and underrepresented minorities is essential to continuing legacy of Just. In South Carolina, where Just was born, the Medical University of South Carolina sponsors an annual E. E. Just Program and Symposium directed by Titus Reeves. At Dartmouth College, the Department of Biological Sciences has an endowed chair in his name, the E. E. Just Professorship, and there is there an E. E. Just Program for supporting students who are underrepresented in science, technology, engineering, and mathematics (STEM). At the University of Chicago, each year, UChicago Biosciences "invites a distinguished member of a group underrepresented in science to deliver a lecture to honor the legacy of Dr. Just."[81] At Howard University's College of Medicine, in the Department of Biochemistry and Molecular Biology, biochemist Walton Malcolm Byrnes has published more articles than anyone else appreciating the scientific legacy of E. E. Just, and he and co–principal investigator cell biologist Stuart Newman, at the New York Medical College in Valhalla, New York, were awarded a National Science Foundation symposium grant for "From Cells to Developmental Systems and Beyond: A Symposium Honoring Ernest Everett Just" [Award No. IOS-0830114] with symposium papers in a Special Issue of Molecular Reproduction and Development (October 2009). Also at Howard University, the Collected Papers of E. E. Just are available to researchers at the Moorland-

Spingarn Research Center. Plus, there is the Ernest Everett Just Foundation, Inc. (EEJFI), "for the Advancement of Science, Technology, Engineering and Mathematics among Minority Youth." In his February 24, 2021, lecture "Why is Dr. Ernest Everett Just So Important to Black History Month?"[82] EEJFI president Wesley Jarmon, reports that the foundation helped with establishing in 2002 the Ernest Everett Just Middle School in Mitchellville, Maryland, to promote education of STEM students, and that the foundation placed a life-size statue of E. E. Just on the school's campus in August 2010. Jarmon's lecture (sponsored by the Woods Hole Diversity Advisory Committee, the Woods Hole Oceanographic Institution, and others) was the fortieth Black History Month lecture at the Marine Biological Laboratory (MBL). Kenneth R. Manning was the first Black History Month lecturer. The MBL and related research communities are continually inspired to increase ethnic and gender diversity in biology by the memory of E. E. Just, who was the first African American researcher at the MBL, and by the memory of Roger Arliner Young, who was the second African American and the first African American female researcher at the MBL.

For the sake of Just's research legacy, it is important to look beyond the "Black Atlantic" and appreciate connections to research in India. In 1954, in the Journal of the Zoological Society of India, in a 38-page article on "The Significance of the Cell Surface," Cedric Dover argued that, in India, "we have preserved in biology a view of life as process, as interrelatedness, as a totality of subtle harmonies rather than a Darwinian war,." and that "Asian biologists" (including Calcutta zoologists Nelson Annandale and Sunder Lal Hora) emphasize "living things in their natural milieu." Accordingly, Just "belongs to their company" because "his philosophy, like theirs, was a unitary one."[83] Beyond the "Black Atlantic," on philosophical grounds, Dover argued that Just belongs in the company of Asian biologists.[84] Also, embryology everywhere has been directly or indirectly instructed by E. E. Just.

Finally, it is important to recall and emphasize that E. E. Just studied both English literature and biology at Dartmouth College, that he was "Instructor in English and Biology" during his first two years at Howard University, that he wrote poetry throughout his life, that he encouraged fine arts appreciation on campus, that illustrations from his microscope slides were artistically rendered, and that his scientific findings were sometimes poetically expressed.[85] Hence, the full legacy of Just includes both STEM (science, technology, engineering, mathematics) and art. In the life and work of E. E. Just, science and art developed and evolved together.

Notes

1. Kenneth R. Manning, *Black Apollo of Science: The Life of Ernest Everett Just* (Oxford: Oxford University Press, 1983). See also Lillie R. Jenkins, "Black Apollo of Science: The Life of Ernest Everett Just—Summarizing Timeline, Sumitography and Concept Poster," SMU Scholar: A Digital Repository for SMU's Research and Achievements, May 9, 2021, https://scholar.smu.edu/theology_research/27
2. Mélina Mangal, *The Vast Wonder of the World: Biologist Ernest Everett Just*, illustrations by Luisa Uribe (Minneapolis: Millbrook Press, 2018), 31.
3. Ernest Everett Just, "The Relation of the First Cleavage Plane to the Entrance Point of the Sperm," *Biological Bulletin* 22, no. 4 (1912): 239–252.
4. Mangal, *Vast Wonder of the World*, 33–35.
5. Manning, *Black Apollo of Science*, 240, and also pp. 327 and 385.
6. See "On the Origin of Mutations," *American Naturalist* 66, no. 702 (1932): 61–74; "Cortical Cytoplasm and Evolution," *American Naturalist* 67, no. 708 (1933), 20–29; and "Unsolved Problems of General Biology," *Physiological Zoology* 13, no. 2 (April 1940): 123–42, all by Ernest Everett Just.
7. See Paul Gilroy, *The Black Atlantic: Modernity and Double Consciousness* (Cambridge, MA: Harvard University Press, 1993). See also Sharon J. Grant, "A Brief Historiography of Methodism and the Black Atlantic Worldview," in *Rebaptism Calmly Consider: Christian Initiation and Resistance in the Early A.M.E. Church of Jamaica* (Eugene, OR: Pickwick, 2019), 6–13, and Abraham Smith, "Black Atlantic Studies," in *Black/Africana Studies and Black/Africana Biblical Studies* (Leiden: Brill, 2021), 9–10.
8. Corey D. B. Walker, "'Of the Coming of John [and Jane]': African American Intellectuals in Europe, 1888–1938," *Amerikastudien/American Studies* 47, no. 1 (2002): 7.
9. Walker, "'Of the Coming of John,'" 16.
10. Manning, *Black Apollo of Science,* 23
11. Manning, *Black Apollo of Science*, 189–191. See also pp. 23, 186, 199, 310, 318.
12. Ernest Everett Just, *The Biology of the Cell Surface* (Philadelphia: P. Blakiston, 1939), ix.
13. Adolf von Harnack, "Fifteen Questions to the Despisers of Scientific Theology" (1923) and "Stages of Scientific Knowledge" (1930 [1929]), in *Adolf von Harnack: Liberal Theology at Its Height*, ed. Martin Rumscheidt (New York: Collins, 1989).
14. Manning, *Black Apollo of Science*, 324.
15. Manning, 324.
16. Manning, 324.
17. Manning, 324.
18. Stephen Kimmel, "The Escape of Ernest Everett Just from a German Internment Camp in 1940" (unpublished research paper, Summer 2021, Southern Methodist University, Perkins School of Theology) is a follow-up to Kenneth R. Manning's account of Just's August 1940 internment, release, and travels through France, Spain, and Portugal and on to the United States in September 1940. While in *Black Apollo of Science* Manning claims "the Nazis interned Just in a camp, probably Chateaulin" (324), Kimmel argues that "Chateaulin seems improbable since it was primarily listed as an internment camp during the first World War under French control" (1), and that "Ilag Rouen which was one of the camps located in northwestern France and the closest to Roscoff seems a

more probable detention location," and another more probable detention location is "the camp at Vittel ... located north of Paris and specifically mentioned as including 'a number of North-American families and women'" (2).

19. A photocopy of the 15 October 1940 letter from E. E. Just to W. C. Allee appears in Theodore Walker Jr., "Bioethics in the Work of Ernest Everett Just: + Missing - some 400 typed pages," SMU Scholar: A Digital Repository for SMU's Research and Achievements, January 28, 2017, https://scholar.smu.edu/theology_research/9/
20. Manning, *Black Apollo of Science*, 206–207, 239, 253, 263, 274–279, 282–283, 289.
21. Ernest Everett Just and Hedwig A. Schnetzler Just, *The Origin of Man's Ethical Behavior* (2020 [originally 1941]), 176.
22. Just, *Biology of the Cell Surface*, 22–24; Manning, *Black Apollo of Science*, 111, 78–84, 110–112.
23. Just, *Biology of the Cell Surface*, 356–357.
24. Ernest Everett Just, "Cortical Cytoplasm and Evolution," *American Naturalist* 67, no. 708 (1933): 23.
25. See "Ernest Everett Just, Johannes Holtfreter, and the Origin of Certain Concepts in Embryo Morphogenesis," *Molecular Reproduction and Development* 76, no. 10 (2009): 912–921; and Malcolm W. Byrnes, "The Genius of Ernest Everett Just," *Howard University Graduate School (HUGS) Research Magazine and Graduate School Research Archive*, no. 2 (December 2013): 1–6.
26. See W. Malcolm Byrnes and William R. Eckberg, "Ernest Everett Just (1883–1941)—An Early Ecological Developmental Biologist," *Developmental Biology* 296, no. 1 (2006): 1–11; Stuart A. Newman, "E. E. Just's 'Independent Irritability' Revisited: The Activated Egg as Excitable Soft Matter," *Molecular Reproduction and Development* 76, no. 10 (2009): 966–974 (2009); Stuart A. Newman, "Evolution Is Not Mainly a Matter of Genes," in *Genetic Explanations: Sense and Nonsense*, ed. Sheldon Krimsky and Jeremy Gruber (Cambridge, MA: Harvard University Press, 2013), 26–33; Katelyn M. Williams, Bryan A. Wilson, Wendi G. O'Connor, and Monte S. Willis "Ernest Everett Just, PhD: Pioneer in Ecological Developmental (Eco-Devo) Biology," *Journal of the South Carolina Academy of Science* 11, no. 1 (2013), 18–22; W. Malcolm Byrnes and Stuart A. Newman, "Ernest Everett Just: Egg and Embryo as Excitable Systems," *Journal of Experimental Zoology, Part B, Molecular and Developmental Evolution* 322, no. 4 (2014): 191–201; and W. Malcolm Byrnes, "E. E. Just's Broad, yet Hidden, Influence on Modern Cell and Developmental Biology," *Molecular Reproduction and Development* (2019): 380–391.
27. James F. Crow, "Just and Unjust: E. E. Just (1883–1941)," *Genetics* 179, no. 4 (2008): 1735–1740.
28. W. Malcolm. Byrnes, "Ernest Everett Just: Experimental Biologist Par Excellence." *ASBMB Today (American Society for Biochemistry and Molecular Biology)* (February 2010): 22–25.
29. Robert Martensen, "The History of Bioethics: An Essay Review," *Journal of the History of Medicine and Allied Sciences* 56, no. 2 (2001): 168–175. See also Albert R. Jonsen, *Birth of Bioethics* (New York: Oxford University Press, 1998) and Jonsen, *Short History of Medical Ethics* (Oxford University Press, 2000).

30 Van Rensselaer Potter, *Global Bioethics: Building on the Leopold Legacy* (East Lansing: Michigan State University Press, 1988), 2.
31 Van Rensselaer Potter, *Bioethics: Bridge to the Future*, ed. Carl P Swanson (Englewood Cliffs, NJ: Prentice-Hall Biological Science Series, 1971), vii–viii.
32 Van Rensselaer Potter, "Bioethics and the Human Prospect," in *The Culture of Biomedicine: Studies in Science and Culture*, vol. 1, edited by D. Heyward Brock (Newark: University of Delaware Press, 1984), 124–137, citing p. 135.
33 While "bio-ethics" or "bioethics" was first spoken of in English in 1970–1971, in German in 1927 there was the (translated) Fritz Jahr, "Bio-Ethics: A Review of the Ethical Relationships of Humans to Animals and Plants"; see Hans-Martin Sass, "Fritz Jahr's 1927 Concept of Bioethics," *Kennedy Institute of Ethics Journal* 17, no. 4 (2007): 279–295, doi: 10.1353/ken.2008.0006
34 Theodore Walker Jr., "Reviewing Ernest Everett Just's Biology of the Cell Surface (1939) and Related Literature, Plus Annotated References, Hereby Advancing Evolutionary Biology and Evolutionary Bioethics," *SCIREA: Journal of Health* 5, no. 6 (2021): 123–144, doi: 10.54647/pmh33179
35 Just, Biology of the Cell Surface, 36.
36 T. Walker, "Reviewing Ernest Everett Just's Biology." Also by T. Walker: "The Bioethical Significance of 'The Origin of Man's Ethical Behavior' (October 1941, unpublished) by Ernest Everett Just and Hedwig Anna Schnetzler Just," *Journal of the South Carolina Academy of Science* 18, no. 1 (2020): 12–14; and "Ernest Everett Just (1883–1941): Hero in Cell Biology and in Evolutionary Bioethics," *Journal of Health Care for the Poor and Underserved* 31, no. 1 (2020): 4–10, doi: 10.1353/hpu.2020.0002
37 Just, *Biology of the Cell Surface*, 36.
38 Just, 354.
39 According to Ernest Everett Just and Hedwig A. Schnetzler Just, *The Origin of Man's Ethical Behavior* (2020, originally 1941), both physiology and behavior are essential to the "state of being alive" (72, 128, 131–132, 137, 140, 163). This is consistent with "The Physical and the Spiritual," in Charles Hartshorne, *Omnipotence and Other Theological Mistakes* (Albany: State University of New York Press, 1984), 51–64; Karen Baker-Fletcher, "To Live as People of Dust and Spirit," in *Sisters of Dust, Sisters of Spirit: Womanist Wordings on God and Creation* (Minneapolis: Fortress Press, 1988), 15–20; and Charles H. Long, "Matter and Spirit: A Reorientation" [1991], in *Ellipsis . . . The Collected Writings of Charles H. Long* (New York: Bloomsbury, 2018), 345–347.
40 Ernest Everett Just and Hedwig A. Schnetzler Just, "The Origin of Man's Ethical Behavior" (unpublished 1941 book manuscript, archival transcription published in 2020), 8.
41 Just and Just, "Origin of Man's Ethical Behavior," 16.
42 Just and Just, 108, 110, 119, 240.
43 Without such observations, "evidence is insufficient to warrant the hypothesis that sociality parallels the course of evolution"; Just and Just, 240.
44 Just and Just, 248, 251.
45 Just, *Biology of the Cell Surface*, 36, 354.
46 Miguel Ramalho-Santos and Holger Willenbring, "On the Origin of the Term 'Stem Cell,'" *Cell Stem Cell* 1, no. 1 (2007): 35–38 citing p. 35, https://doi.org/10.1016/j.stem.2007.05.013

47 Ramalho-Santos and Willenbring, "On the Origin of the Term 'Stem Cell.'"
48 Just, *Biology of the Cell Surface*, 75, 88–89.
49 Just, 36.
50 Just and Just, "Origin of Man's Ethical Behavior," 5, 157–168, 174.
51 Just and Just, 16.
52 Similarly, in "Evolution" (chapter 2, pp. 44–65), in *The Liberation of Life: From the Cell to the Community* (Cambridge: Cambridge University Press, 1981), John B. Cobb Jr. and Charles Birch hold that "ecology and evolution belong together" and a "species co-evolves with its environment" (64–65).
53 Just and Just, "Origin of Man's Ethical Behavior," 176.
54 Here I correct myself. Previously, I sometimes incorrectly used "co-operative behavior" and "ethical behavior" interchangeably. Correctively, I hereby note that Kropotkin and E. E. Just used the terms "mutual aid" and "co-operation" or "co-operative behavior" for describing all animal cooperation (including cooperation among microbes) and they used the terms "ethics" or "ethical behavior" for describing some human animal cooperation. Accordingly, human "ethical behavior" evolved from prehuman "co-operative behavior" (not from prehuman "ethical behavior").
55 Just, *Biology of the Cell Surface*, 368.
56 Just.
57 Just.
58 Just and Just, "Origin of Man's Ethical Behavior," 108.
59 Fred Hoyle, *The Relation of Biology to Astronomy* (Cardiff, UK: University College Cardiff Press, 1980).
60 Fred Hoyle, "Stellar Evolution and the Expanding Universe." Nature 163 (1949): 196–198.
61 Neil de Grasse Tyson and Donald Goldsmith, *Origins: Fourteen Billion Years of Cosmic Evolution* (New York: Norton, 2004).
62 Concerning cosmic biology, see Fred Hoyle and N. C. Wickramasinghe, "The Case for Life as a Cosmic Phenomenon," *Nature* 322, no. 6079 (1986): 509–511, and Chandra Wickramasinghe, ed., *Vindication of Cosmic Biology: Tribute to Sir Fred Hoyle (1915–2001)* (Hackensack, NJ: World Scientific, 2015).
63 Concerning stellar and cosmic evolution, see Fred Hoyle, "The Chemical Composition of the Stars," *Monthly Notices of the Royal Astronomical Society* 106, no. 4 (1946): 255–259; Fred Hoyle, "On the Formation of Heavy Elements in Stars," *Proceedings of the Physical Society* 59, no. 6 (1947): 972–978; Fred Hoyle, "Stellar Evolution and the Expanding Universe," *Nature* 163 (1949): 196–198; and E. Margaret Burbidge, Geoffrey R. Burbidge, William A. Fowler, and Fred Hoyle, "Synthesis of the Elements in Stars," *Review of Modern Physics* 29, no. 4 (1957): 547–650. Among astronomers "Synthesis of the Elements in Stars" is famously signified by author initials as "B2FH" because it was "a turning point in our knowledge of how the universe works"; see Tyson and Goldsmith, *Origins*, 165.
64 Fred Hoyle, *The Intelligent Universe: A New View of Creation and Evolution* (1983; New York: Holt, Rinehard and Winston, 1984), 215.
65 See "Convergence to God" (chapter 9), in Fred Hoyle and N. Chandra Wickramasinghe, *Evolution from Space: A Theory of Cosmic Creationism* (New York: Simon and Schuster, 1981).

66 Just and Just, "Origin of Man's Ethical Behavior," 10.
67 Alfred North Whitehead, Science and the Modern World, Lowell Lectures, 1925 (New York: Macmillan; Free Press, 1967), 25; Just and Just, "Origin of Man's Ethical Behavior," 145.
68 See John B. Cobb Jr., ed., *Back to Darwin: A Richer Account of Evolution* (Grand Rapids, MI: William B. Eerdmans, 2008). See also Theodore Walker Jr., *Evolutionary Bioethics: A Richer Account of Evolution: Beyond Darwin, Ernest Everett Just Ties Evolutionary Biology to Evolutionary Ethics* (n.p., 2020).
69 Just, *Biology of the Cell Surface*, 366.
70 Just, 367.
71 Just, 369.
72 Just, 2.
73 Just, 7.
74 See Nicole King, "The Unicellular Ancestry of Animal Development," *Developmental Cell* 7 (2004): 313–325; Thibaut Brunet and Nicole King, "The Origin of Animal Multicellularity and Cell Differentiation," *Developmental Cell* 43, no. 2 (2017): 124–140; and Thibaut Brunet and Nicole King, "The Single-Celled Ancestors of Animals: A History of Hypotheses," in *The Evolution of Multicellularity* (CRC Press, 2022), 251–278.
75 Athena Aktipis, "Malignant Cheaters: Cells Coexist by Cooperating. When Some Break the Rules, Cancers Result," *Scientific American* 324, no. 1 (2021): 62–67.
76 Jenkins, "Summarizing Timeline." [Alternative Title—E. E. Just: Administrative and Fund-seeking Pioneer].
77 In *Black Apollo of Science* Manning reports that in 1930, while at the Kaiser-Wilhelm-Institute for Biology, "some of Just's time was spent poring over a large group of slides he had brought with him from America. These slides were the result of the ultraviolet work on Nereis limbate that he and Roger Young had begun at Woods Hole. . . . Several scientists . . . were so impressed . . . that they loaned Just the service of their artists and technicians for several hours a day. Up to ten people might be studying the slides at any one time, drawing painstaking diagrams and making careful measurements" (188). In "Attempt to Locate Microscope Slides Prepared by E. E. Just with Help from Roger Arliner Young" (unpublished research paper, Summer 2021, Southern Methodist University, Perkins School of Theology), William Keck indicates that today, these slides and diagrams are probably not at Woods Hole nor at the Kaiser-Wilhelm-Institute, but perhaps at the Archives of the Max Planck Society or Station Biologique de Roscoff—CNRS—at the Sorbonne University. Other possibilities include the attic of a descendant or a neglected laboratory space at Howard University. Consider Keck's conclusion: "Overall, I think it is likely that the slides and diagrams are still out there. However, I think it will require time and manpower to locate them. It will likely require a certain group of passionate people who know exactly what they are looking for" to find them (4).
78 Sara P. Diaz, "Roger Arliner Young (1889–1964)," BlackPast, March 7, 2007, www.blackpast.org/african-american-history/young-roger-arliner-1889-1964/
79 See also Kenneth R. Manning, "Ernest Everett Just: The Role of Foundation Support for Black Scientists 1920–1929," in the *"Racial" Economy of Science: Toward a Democratic Future*, ed. by Sandra Harding (Bloomington: Indiana University Press, 1993);

and see Kenneth R. Manning, "Reflections on E. E. Just, Black Apollo of Science, and the Experiences of African American Scientists," *Molecular Reproduction and Development: Incorporating Gamete Research* 76, no. 10 (2009): 897–902.

80 Ernest Everett Just, *Basic Methods for Experiments on Eggs of Marine Animals* (Philadelphia: P. Blakiston, 1939), 10.

81 Angela Wells O'Connor, "Just Tribute: Honoring the Legacy of Pioneering Biologist Ernest Everett Just, PhD 1916," UChicago Biosciences, April 19, 2018, https://biosciences.uchicago.edu/diversity/ee-just

82 Wesley Jarmon, "Why Is Dr. Ernest Everett Just So Important to Black History Month?" [To commemorate 24 February 2021, the fortieth Black History Month lecture at the Marine Biological Laboratory at Woods Hole, sponsored by Woods Hole Diversity Advisory Committee.] Posted March 10, 2021, YouTube video, 58:59, www.youtube.com/watch?v=gTAsocnzMAQ&t=2058s

83 Cedric Dover, "The Significance of the Cell Surface (The Work of EE Just)," *Journal of the Zoological Society of India* 6, no. 1 (1954): 3–4.

84 Indian appreciation for E. E. Just exemplifies why, in Black/Africana Studies and Black/Africana Biblical Studies (see n. 159), Abraham Smith finds that connecting Black people to a given ocean such as "the Black Atlantic" is inadequate, asking "Why not speak as well about a Black Mediterranean or a Black Indian Ocean?" (10). And because "Black Studies" too often means study of Black Americans in the United States, Smith prefers the term "Black/Africana Studies."

85 Both art and science are appreciated in Manning's *Black Apollo of Science*, in Jenkins, "Black Apollo of Science," and in Mangal, *Vast Wonder of the World* (beautifully illustrated by Luisa Urbe).

2

Percy Lavon Julian

His Exemplary Life, Academic Achievements, and Contributions to Society

WAWEISE SCHMIDT

The Early Years

Percy Lavon Julian was born on April 11, 1899, in Montgomery, Alabama, the eldest of six children, to Elizabeth Lena Adams and James Sumner Julian, a railway mail clerk. In addition to their own six children, the Julians also cared for four of Elizabeth's orphaned siblings, and "Elizabeth Adams Julian, ... played the major role in rearing the children according to the rules she and her husband embraced."[1] The Julian family lived in what many considered the ancestral heart of the Confederacy yet held a better economic position than held by many Black[2] people during the Jim Crow period.

When the US Civil War ended, on April 9, 1865, there followed a lengthy period of strife even after the ratification of the Thirteenth Amendment, abolishing slavery. Black codes were established by most states, effectively or legally controlling the lives of formerly enslaved people. Laws and policies determined where and how Black people lived, where they worked, how they were educated, and what professional organizations they could join, and methods were devised to deny them the ability to vote. Despite the disparity between the rights of Black citizens in comparison with their White southern counterparts, the Julians appeared to thrive, as both of Percy's parents were educated and were graduates of a school that would later become Alabama State University,[3] and his father was a federal employee. The Julians were interested in not only the improvement of their economic standing but also in the cultivation of their children's minds and strived to maintain high educational standards within the home. David Taylor reflected that "the Julians saved to create a family library for the children to use, and Percy worked hard."[4] Having a personal library was unusual for the era and probably aided in educating the Julian children in both academic expectations and in nurturing cultural paradigms.

Regardless of the educational expectations of the Julians, Percy, like many Black children of that time, attended a segregated elementary school and afterward attended the State Normal School in Montgomery, Alabama, for two years. In the early 1900s, public education for Black children in many southern cities frequently ended with the eighth grade. While it appeared that southern states thought little of the education of Black people, education and maintenance of high standards were important to the Julian family as was noted by the actions of James Julian, Percy's father. When Percy "proudly brought home a math test with a grade of 80," his father responded, "a son of mine must not be satisfied with mediocrity. After this make it 100!"[5]

In 1916, despite the educational constraints forced upon him due to his race, Percy gained admission to DePauw University, in Greencastle, Indiana, as a subfreshman. In the fall of 1916, when a 17-year-old Percy Julian boarded a train for Indiana, to begin his schooling, two generations of the Julian family, including his father were there to send him off. Edward Jenkins described the scene like this:

> His diminutive grandmother waved to him with hands that once picked a record 350 pounds of cotton in one day. His grandfather waved with fingers missing from one hand because his slave owner cut them off upon discovering the Black man had learned to read and write. His mother, with tears brimming.[6]

Due to the deficits in his early education, Percy had to attend remedial classes at a nearby high school while also attending his regular college classes, and because he lacked a scholarship he had to find a job to pay for his education at DePauw. David Taylor asserted that though

> DePauw University in Greencastle, Indiana, had been educating black students since the Civil War, they were still segregated from many parts of university. Unlike his white classmates, Julian received no dorm assignment. Instead, he was given a room away from campus with few furnishings and a slop jar for a toilet. His landlady told him she didn't have to provide him with meals.[7]

Black codes meant that Percy Julian could not stay in the dormitories on campus, so not only did he have to pay for school, but he also had to find a place to live and a job to pay for it. So because of his desire to learn and achieve, he shined shoes at a local barbershop until he accepted an offer to work at a campus fraternity house. There he waited tables . . . his compensation included meals, and a room in the attic. On weekends, Percy played with a music group . . . during the summers, Percy worked as a ditch digger on various construction projects.[8]

Percy started DePauw University scholastically disadvantaged, but he was a determined, self-directed learner.[9] So during the four years he attended, he earned the best average in chemistry, was class valedictorian, and earned membership into two prestigious honor societies, Phi Beta Kappa[10] and Sigma Xi.[11] Therefore, he carried on the family tradition of pursuing excellence in education, and by achieving his goal he served as an example to his siblings and other Blacks. In addition, during Percy's time at DePauw, the entire Julian family moved to Greencastle, Indiana, allowing all the Julian children the opportunity for a better education. They all entered DePauw and two of Percy's brothers became physicians while three of his sisters earned masters' degrees.

While Percy pursued his degree, moral support was freely given from his family during his time at DePauw, but his choice to enter the field of chemistry was not to his father's liking, according to William M. Cobb:

> His father . . . wanted Percy to study medicine. When Percy insisted, he wanted to be a chemist his father nearly had a heart attack. "You mean then that you want to be a teacher, for that's all your becoming a chemist can mean. And that in totality means you're going to starve to death."[12]

Percy's father was alluding to the commonplace idea that Black people were not able to pursue a career in research in the field of chemistry, and so most were relegated to teaching within Black colleges or high schools. The practice of medicine was a field that Black people were able to participate in within the Black community and earn a reasonable salary to subsist on.

After Percy received his AB degree in 1920 from DePauw University, he wanted to continue his education at the graduate level but was unable to gain admittance into graduate school. David Taylor noted that when he attended DePauw, "Julian attracted the notice of chemistry professor William Blanchard, whose enthusiasm allowed Julian to envision for himself a future in research."[13] Unlike his classmates, and regardless of the awards earned during his undergraduate years, Percy was not offered a scholarship or any other funding to continue his graduate education at DePauw and consulted with Blanchard, who in turn "contacted many schools on Julian's behalf and recommended him highly. He received only negative responses."[14]

According to William M. Cobb, his main professor called Percy into his office and showed him letters from prominent university chemists that said in effect:

> Discourage your bright colored lad. We couldn't get him a job when he's done, and it'll only mean frustration. In industry, research demands co-work, and white boys would so sabotage his work that an industrial leader would go crazy! And, of course, we couldn't find him a job as a teacher in a white university.[15]

During the 1920s, like previous eras, academic communities tended to follow larger societal patterns and had little tolerance for an African Americans who attempted to advance their knowledge or pursue a position in research in the field of chemistry outside the Black scientific community. So, with his AB degree from DePauw, Blanchard suggested that Percy pursue a career at a Black college, and he was hired at Fisk University to teach chemistry, which he did from 1920 until 1922. A less determined person could have been discouraged and been content with his position as an academician at the historically black college; however, Percy continued to endeavor to achieve a higher education, perhaps due to the family compulsion for learning or because of the example set by other scientists such as Saint Elmo Brady, who, in 1922, became the only African American in the United States to earn a doctoral degree in chemistry.

In 1922, with the help of his former teacher, Professor William Blanchard, Percy applied for, and won an Austin Fellowship in biophysics and organic chemistry at Harvard University, in Cambridge, Massachusetts. Percy earned his master's degree from Harvard in 1923. When Julian "applied to Harvard University's PhD program, the leading chemists there said that there was no point. Nobody would hire a Black researcher." "Why don't you find him a teaching job in a Negro college in the South" they suggested to Blanchard. "He doesn't need a PhD for that."[16] Edward S. Jenkins insisted that Percy Julian's

> performance recommended him for a teaching fellowship that he coveted but Harvard turned down his application. University officials feared they might offend some white students were they to assign a Black instructor to teach them. Julian remained at Harvard two more years . . . Finally, in an effort to escape his impoverished condition, he accepted a faculty position at . . . West Virginia State College where he spent one year before he moved on to teach at Howard University, Washington, D.C.[17]

In 1928, when Percy Julian was hired as an associate professor and head of the Department of Chemistry at Howard University, William M. Cobb said that Percy viewed the post as a "tremendous opportunity . . . [and that] he was a magnetic lecturer and ignited in associates as well as students the flame of enthusiasm . . . [and that] he was always discussing research problems."[18] During his time at Howard, he was also responsible for designing the chemistry lab at the cost of $1 million. Even through several disappointing educational and career episodes Percy continued to express his love of chemistry and illustrated it by attempting to light the flame of appreciation within his students and colleagues. Edward S. Jenkins said that Julian "suggested that we should be sensitive to conditions in the environment that were detrimental to scientific aspiration . . . Yet he believed there would always be people of determination . . . who would emerge, rise above the froth, and make their contribution to the scientific world."[19] Percy responded to adversity, educational and career setbacks, by working harder, seeking short-term employment at Black universities, acquiring experience teaching, saving money toward continuing his pursuit of a doctoral degree, and applying himself to be the best in his field; thereby, he served as an inspiration for other developing scientists as well as members of the Black community.

In 1930, Percy won a General Education Board Fellowship sponsored by the Rockefeller Foundation providing him the financial support he needed to advance to doctoral studies at the University of Vienna in Austria. Percy took a leave of absence from Howard University and traveled to Vienna, where he worked under Dr. Ernst Späth, a prominent scientist in the field of natural products chemistry. While in Vienna, Percy studied alkaloids. Alkaloids were an unexplored chemical class that had the potential of containing potent natural components that could be used to form medicines like morphine and quinine or poisons such as nicotine and strychnine. Percy's study of natural plant products led to many of his important breakthroughs in the mass production of chemicals and medicines such as physostigmine[20] and hydrocortisone.[21]

During his studies in Vienna, Percy made friends with and impressed his fellow students, professors, and other artistic personalities, showing himself as an African American to be equal to if not superior to them in various scientific pursuits. He arrived in Vienna with

> large crates shipped to Späth's laboratory . . . the contents of which were marveled at by all the students . . . The boxes contained treasures of ground glass equipment . . . and other extravagances not known to

the average student. Percy's good humor and friendly personality conquered all hearts in no time.[22]

While Percy spent time with the various researchers and enlightened thinkers from various socioeconomic positions, they stimulated his interest in pursuing a career in research even more. It was during this time that he met Josef Pikl and Abraham Zlotnik, who would both play key roles later in Julian's life, by aiding in his success as an independent researcher and the development of his own research laboratory. Bernhard Witkop remarked that

> Percy impressed his Viennese fellow students . . . with his passion for hard work and study, his profound chemical knowledge, and his astounding memory. Professor Ernst Späth, a critical . . . teacher who ignored lazy or untalented students, characterized Percy . . . "[as a]n extraordinary student, his like I have not seen before in my career as a teacher."[23]

The influence that Späth had on Percy during his years in Vienna was significant, as was illustrated by his actions when he learned of Späth's death. Percy flew to Vienna, paid for Späth's funeral, and commissioned a bust to be made, which was then placed in the foyer of the Faculty of Chemistry of the University of Vienna.

Percy's stay in Austria not only reinforced his desire for research but also appeared to enrich his cultural development and gave him a chance to experience racial equality, according to Pikl:

> The time spent in Austria had a great influence in developing the personality of Julian. For the first time in his life, he was completely at ease, no open or hidden barriers, really an equal among equals. He may have even enjoyed a standing a few notches higher than his friends.[24]

While in Vienna Percy wrote home that "for the first time in my life . . . I recognize that publications and research will be, for me, as natural a thing as going to bed and eating a meal,"[25] further emphasizing his desire for a career in research.

Through his academic interactions Percy provided a great example of the capabilities of African Americans in the academic side and he did it on an international scale. Percy was not only a member of the student body, but he integrated into the culture by having learned to speak German and Viennese fluently, having learned to play piano through the teachings of an associate's mother, having participated in their family outings and musical performances, having played tennis with them, having attended the opera, and having hosted parties in his apartment located in an upscale area in Vienna.

Upon earning his doctoral degree in 1931, Dr. Percy Julian returned to Howard; however, he became embroiled in scandals and was accused of making unflattering comments in letters written to colleagues while he was in Vienna. Percy chose to resign his position at Howard; however, all was not lost during this turbulent episode because it was during this time that he met Anna Roselle Johnson—soon to become his wife, as Anna Johnson Julian. It is often said that behind every great man there's a great woman,[26] much like the relationship between Dr. Percy Julian and Dr. Anna Julian.

Anna Roselle Johnson

The woman that captured the heart of Dr. Percy Julian, Anna Roselle Johnson—a sociology professor and civic activist, from a prominent African American family in Baltimore, Maryland—was born on November 24, 1903, as the fifth daughter of seven girls, to Adelaide Scott Johnson and Charles Speare Johnson (a chiropodist).[27] Anna contracted rheumatic fever as a child and was unable to begin school until the third grade and at twelve years of age, she moved to Philadelphia, to live with her aunt and uncle to attend an integrated high school with higher academic standards. Like Dr. Percy Julian's family, the Johnsons were also interested in education and community activism.

In 1919, Anna began her college studies at the University of Pennsylvania, in Philadelphia, and earned a bachelor of science degree in education in 1923. During her undergraduate studies she pledged Delta Sigma Theta, later serving as its fourth national president from 1929 to 1931. In 1924, Anna received a university scholarship in sociology and enrolled in the University of Pennsylvania's Graduate School of Arts and Sciences. In 1925, she continued her education at the University of Pennsylvania and earned her master's degree in sociology, after which she served in several positions, such as a case worker for the Family Service Association in Washington, DC, an instructor teaching in Bordentown, New Jersey, and a research assistant in the Public Schools of Washington's Department of Research (studying the factors that inhibited children's education), and an instructor teaching sociology at Miner Teachers College in the District of Columbia.

In 1931, Anna enrolled in the University of Pennsylvania's graduate school to continue her studies for her doctoral degree while she continued to work in Washington, DC. In 1934 she was awarded a Bloomfield Moore Fellowship in sociology for women who planned to become teachers to undertake research. In 1937, Anna Julian became the first African American woman at the University of Pennsylvania to earn a PhD in sociology. During her pursuit of her doctoral degree, she became the first African American woman at the university elected to Phi Beta Kappa honor society, comparable to her husband, Dr. Percy Julian, who in 1920 had been inducted into Phi Beta Kappa honor society. Before the completion of her doctoral degree, Anna and Percy Julian were married on December 24, 1935.

It should be noted that even while attending graduate school Dr. Anna Julian held the position of research assistant in the Department of Research of the Public Schools of Washington D.C. as well as served as an instructor in educational sociology at Miner College. The Julians had two children—Faith Roselle Julian and Percy Julian Jr.—and they also raised Anna's nephew, Leon "Rhoddy" Ellis. Dr. Anna Julian's life choices were similar to her husband's, and she was also a seeker of knowledge and a person of great determination; moreover, she not only supported her husband in his research efforts but also provided a role model for individuals who wished to pursue careers in teaching, social welfare, and sociology. There were numerous periods throughout her life where Dr. Anna Julian demonstrated her interest in education, child welfare, and social justice. In 1963, she was appointed to the Birth Control Commission in Illinois, which advised on the legal, social and moral aspects of state-sponsored birth control to women receiving state aid; she was also a delegate to the 1970 White House Conference on Children, served as chairman of the Women's Division of the Chicago Urban League and vice president of the Chicago YWCA, and with Percy founded the Chicago chapter of the NAACP's Legal and Educational Fund.

From Academia to Industry

After Dr. Percy Julian left Howard, in 1932, he returned to DePauw University, where he was hired as a research fellow in organic chemistry and continued researching natural products with Dr. Josef Pikl as his research partner. While at DePauw, Julian and Pikl researched natural plant products, with a focus on the production of physostigmine, previously found in the Calabar bean, used to treat glaucoma. The synthesis of physostigmine was known, but the ability to produce a large volume in the laboratory for medical applications was not known. So instead of practicing medicine, like his brothers, Dr. Julian advanced research in the processing of medicines. Unfortunately, Dr. Julian's choice to study the synthesis of physostigmine also placed him in competition with Sir Robert Robinson,[28] a well-known chemist of the day who was also attempting to synthesize physostigmine and was also widely published.

Dr. Julian and Dr. Pikl chose to approach the synthesis of physostigmine using a different technique than Robinson, and they published consecutive articles on the incomplete process. The next paper that Julian and Pikl wrote described their final method of physostigmine synthesis and alluded to an error discovered in Robinson's methodology. Writing a paper declaring errors in a well-known scientist's technique was risky and could have led to Dr. Julian and Dr. Pikl loosing employment and standing within the scientific community; however, Julian's triumph made him a major figure in chemistry research. Dr. Julian and Dr. Pikl's study was supported and their methodology for synthesis of physostigmine was confirmed in 1999.

During the four years that Dr. Julian was a research fellow at DePauw, his reputation grew and he was recommended for employment to a faculty position at the University of Minnesota, but according to William M. Cobb "his endorsers were told that the regents of the institution would not appoint a black man to the faculty."[29] After four years the grant money that supported Dr. Julian's research at DePauw ran out and his career was again insecure because while Dr. Julian was recommended by the president of the university for a professorial position, the trustees of the institution were not ready to appoint a Black man to the faculty. In 1936, regardless of his accomplishments in chemistry research, he did not get the position and was "forced to leave DePauw after local critics challenged the school for hiring him."[30] After several disappointing results from academic job applications, Dr. Julian decided to leave academia and pursued a career in research.

Dr. Julian applied for jobs in industry and "accepted a research position at the Institute of Paper Chemistry in Appleton, Wisconsin, only to learn that a statute in that city stated, 'No Negro should be bedded or boarded in Appleton overnight,'"[31] as it was a sundown town. Dr. Julian recounted that "every company . . . said it had never hired a black research chemist before and didn't know how to do it now."[32] Shortly, he was hired by the vice president of the Glidden Company in Chicago, to serve as the director of research for its new Soya Products Division and the Vegetable Oil, and Food Division, and as the manager of Fine Chemicals. The appointment of Dr. Julian to this position was a major accomplishment not only because the Glidden Company was one of the largest manufacturers of paints and varnishes in the nation but also because the position was a significant position for a Black scientist. William M. Cobb remarked that "for the first time a Negro was able to direct a modern industrial laboratory employing chemists of various ethnic origins,"[33] thereby, breaking down barriers for future scientists in underrepresented groups.

When Dr. Julian started working at the Glidden Company, he was charged with the development of a new process for the isolation and preparation of soya bean (soybean) protein to be used in the coating of paper in cold water paints and in textiles. Dr. Julian supervised the plant assemblage and proceeded to isolate soy protein to replace the more expensive milk casein that had been used in industrial sizing of paper, glue for making plywood, and the manufacturing of water-based paints. For the Glidden Company "the work was so successful that the company's profit from these products rose from $35,000 to $135,000 in one year."[34] Dr. Julian also isolated soybean derivatives that were used in the fire retardant "Aerofoam" used by the Navy in World War II to extinguish gasoline fires on aircraft carriers, and the soybean protein was also an important component in latex house paints, which made a substantial amount of money for the Glidden Company. Working for the Glidden Company brought Dr. Julian wealth, allowed him to conduct some research, and brought some appreciation of his genius outside academia.

Dr. Julian worked for the Glidden Company for 18 years, but his research interest changed direction in 1940 when he was able to produce 100 pounds of mixed soy sterols daily. Dr. Julian recalled how in Vienna, Austrian chemists had used soybeans for the preparation of male and female sex hormones and for the manufacture of physostigmine. He had investigated methods of producing physostigmine from the Calabar bean at Howard and completed his work at DePauw, and at Glidden he perfected a technique for extracting sterols from another plant product, soybean oil, which could then be used to form progesterone, testosterone, and estrogen, to be used as sex hormones. The sex hormones that Dr. Julian investigated facilitated the mass production of hormones that could be used in treatment of hormone deficiencies, regulating menstrual cycles, and supporting pregnancy. Furthermore, the production of these hormones in large quantities could lower the retail prices for clinical use of the hormones. At Glidden, Dr. Julian and his coworkers obtained patents for the key processes in the preparation of progesterone and testosterone from soybean plant sterols, previously held by European pharmaceutical companies, which kept the wholesale and retail prices high.

By 1950, Dr. Julian, working at Glidden, was also producing steroid compounds closely related to cortisone activity from soybean oil. The steroid called Reichstein's Substance S was not directly effective in treating rheumatoid arthritis; however, later experimentation in 1952 was able to convert the compound to cortisone or hydrocortisone. James Ravin and Eve Higginbotham stated that "Glidden wanted Julian to continue to concentrate on paint-related products rather than botanical compounds that really interested him,"[35] so in 1953 Julian left to start his own company.

Dr. Julian's success at the Glidden Company not only allowed him to pursue a career in research but also carried with it a substantial salary as well as opportunities to speak to larger and more diverse audiences concerning social justice causes and produce numerous scientific papers for major journals. This placed him in a position to earn many civic awards and allowed him to grow his family. Dr. Julian and his wife, Anna, had two children, a son, Percy Jr., who was born in 1940, and a daughter, Faith, who was born in 1944. In 1950, Dr. Julian purchased a house in the Chicago suburb of Oak Park, his family becoming the area's the first African American residents. Some residents welcomed them, others not so much. "As they prepared to move, Julian's wife and ten-year-old son arrived to find that someone had attempted to burn the house down. A homemade gasoline bomb had been planted by arsonists opposed to a black family in the all-white suburb."[36]

Despite a series of events orchestrated to encourage them to leave, Dr. Julian stated, "Anna and I felt we had no choice but to stay";[37] moreover, he wrote, "The right of a people to live where they want to, without fear, is more important than my science."[38] So even though Dr. Julian was a successful scientist and was well known within industry, he was still not able to live in the physically secure manner that most White Americans of that time enjoyed. Still, he refused to give in to the threat his family suffered on that Thanksgiving Day in 1950. The damage to the house was fixed. and the family moved in. The threats did not end after that arson attempt in 1950. When Dr. Julian and Anna left to attend Dr. Julian's father's funeral, June 1951, a stick of dynamite was thrown at their home, landing outside their children's bedroom, where it exploded. Fortunately, there were no injuries and little damage to their property; however, Percy Julian Jr. later related that during the time, he and his father kept watch over the family's property by sitting on the front porch with a shotgun.[39]

Like the life of most African Americans, racism was a continuous presence in the life of Dr. Julian. When he was invited to attend a luncheon in honor of a White scientist at the Union League Club in Chicago he was turned away. The club was off-limits to Blacks, and in Julian's mind this event linked to his overall treatment as an African American and to the bombing of his home. According to Ron Grossman, Dr. Julian told a *Chicago Tribune* reporter that "when individuals supposedly in high places behave as the Union League Club has behaved, ordinary citizens of lesser intelligence follow suit."[40] Dr. Julian further explained to the reporter that the reason he wanted to live in Oak Park was to prevent his children from experiencing the fear that he had grown up with in the Jim Crow South. As reported in the *Chicago Tribune*, Dr.

Julian commented, "But the other night, my little girl knew fear for the first time in her life."[41]

After the bombing of the Julian residence some members of the public expressed support for them, and William M. Cobb wrote about an editorial in the *Chicago Sun* that stated:

> Arsonists tried to burn down the newly purchased home of Dr. Percy Julian to keep him out of Oak Park because he is a Negro. We wonder whether these cowards whose mad prejudice drove them to commit a felony would refuse to use the lifesaving discoveries of Dr. Julian because they came from the hand and brain of a Negro ... No! The bigots welcome the discoveries of Dr. Julian the scientist, but they try to exclude Dr. Julian the human being.[42]

After the bombing of the Julian home, 46 citizens of Oak Park signed a letter of apology published in the *Sun Times* of July 3, 1951, and according to William M. Cobb the letter stated:

> We, as citizens of Oak Park, wish to express the dismay and indignation we feel regarding the further attack on the sanctity and security of Dr. Julian's home. We ask Dr. Julian and his family to accept our sincere apology that such un-American and bigoted action should occur in our village. We welcome them to Oak Park.[43]

While the sentiment may have been sincere, the reality was that little change was produced in the attitudes in Chicago as noted by the Cicero Riot on July 11, 1951,[44] over housing desegregation. One might wonder whether Dr. Julian, during his lifelong experiences of battling against racism and despite his successes in the academic and industrial realms, had not become disillusioned by the threats and mental and physical attacks that he had to overcome. Notable African Americans in science, technology, engineering, and mathematics (STEM) fields such as Thomas Burton, Charles R. Drew, Ernest Everett Just, and Daniel Hale Williams all appeared to utilize several methods as a means of maintaining a positive attitude during periods of strife such as continuously striving for excellence, speaking truth to false beliefs, relying on spirituality, seeking more amenable environments, and standing their ground by building communities of supporters. These same methods appeared to be used by Dr. Julian as well.

Even during his college years Dr. Julian had been a fighter against racism. William M. Cobb recalled how Dr. Julian was "in demand as a speaker for forums at Harvard in 1923 when he was working for the master's in chemistry.

His addresses published and unpublished, in the realm of social justice and human advancement are almost countless."[45]

On to Independent Ventures

During the 18 years he worked for the Glidden Company, developing numerous products related to derivatives of the soybean and possessing numerous patents, Dr. Julian was told that the Glidden Company would no longer be in the steroid-processing business. While the discovery of various steroids, their applications, and processing was of interest to Dr. Julian, for the Glidden Company it was relatively unprofitable despite the innovative work of Dr. Julian; therefore, the company sold some patents and ceased producing steroids, and Dr. Julian was left to pursue his own interest. After Dr. Julian left the Glidden Company in 1953, he decided to start his own company and opened Julian Laboratories, Inc., in Oak Park, Illinois, in 1954. With determination, previous experience in research, and managerial experience through his career with the Glidden Company, Dr. Julian retrofitted the rundown warehouse in Oak Park into a functional manufacturing plant.

The ascendency of Dr. Julian, from Glidden Company employee to the presidency of his own company, with his wife as vice president and bookkeeper, allowed him to continue to pursue his own path in natural products chemistry research; however, it was not without some roadblocks. During the first few years of the operation of Julian Laboratories he spent more of his time as a businessman, and very little of his time was devoted to any research other than steroid research focused on specific pharmaceutical clients such as Smith, Kline, and French Laboratories. As Dr. Julian stated in a letter to a friend, "Now that Julian Laboratories have become a success (. . . our sales for the first 10 months of our fiscal year ending August 31st, . . . show close to 1.5 million dollars), I am again able to turn back to some of the things which have interested me, of course most of my life."[46] Yet, even with the positive accounting of funds, other aspects of Julian Laboratories were in short supply such as personnel. Even though he had acquired some employees from the Glidden Company, they needed more individuals with PhDs, junior research assistants, and personal assistants as well as a plant manager to work at the laboratory.

Employees of Julian Laboratories in Oak Park were from a diversity of groups; however, it was particularly appealing for African Americans during the 1950s, when employment for Black chemists interested in research was difficult to find. Jim Letton, a chemist at Julian Laboratories remarked, "I looked for two years for a job. I had applications probably in 10 federal agencies. I had contacted probably 15 to 20 companies."[47] Letton noted "Julian Labs" was the "haven for black chemists."[48] Comments made by Peter Walton, an employee and lifelong family friend, supported the concept that Dr. Julian/Julian Labs was an incubator for Black chemists. Peter Walton stated that "Dr. Julian explained to me, one of his missions in life, in creating Julian Laboratories and its affiliates, was to offer decent employment to black chemists throughout the nation."[49] While serving as owner of the laboratory, Dr. Julian showed characteristics of a servant leader[50] (valuing people, humility, listening, trust, and caring, much like other esteemed STEM leaders Charles Richard Drew and Kelly Miller).

As was recounted to Susan K. Lewis, by Risher Watts, a friend and physician who was present at Julian's death:

> Percy Julian was a good man. He was learned. He was sympathetic when you needed him to be. He would push you sometimes harder than you thought you should have been pushed. But as a person, as a human being (it's what I admire the most about him) he helped the people who worked for him immensely.[51]

Therefore, while Dr. Julian was very dedicated to building his business, he also appeared determined to build a better future for other African Americans by supporting his employees.

Despite Dr. Julian's entrance into the industrial field, he still maintained currency in research and academia by not just application in industry but also by attending association meetings in chemical research. Unfortunately, regardless of his education, awards, journal articles, patents, and reputation within industry, he was still treated in an unjust manner in contrast to the treatment his White colleagues received. One such incident occurred in Dallas, Texas, in 1956, during the meeting of the American Chemical Society, during which Dr. Julian faced the obstacle of segregation in relation to hotel lodging. In a letter dated February 3, 1956, addressed to Dr. John C. Warner, president of the American Chemical Society, Dr. Julian wrote that when he looked at the hotel announcement for the spring meeting, he noticed at the bottom of the list that two unknown hotels had been listed for the chemists of color to find lodging. Dr. Julian expressed his ire by suggesting that

> the time has come . . . capable scientists enrolled in our Society can no longer close their eyes to the "oughtness" involved in a ridiculous American situation like this and acquiesce in the stupidity of the "is-

ness" of an apparent Southern determination to continue to make the American democracy a laughingstock for the rest of the world. I sincerely feel that there must be thousands of chemists in the ranks of our Society who—like the members of my staff of all races—will boycott such a meeting and refuse to participate in this insult to the individual dignity of their fellow Americans of color.[52]

Dr. Julian suggested that other societies had made resolutions and refused to host meetings in cities that denied equal hotel accommodations for persons due to race, color, or creed and that he hoped the next meeting in Miami, Florida, in 1957 would not be as disastrous with a recurrence of the earlier meetings-accommodation problems. Again, much like for most of Dr. Julian's life, he coped with his disappointment and anger at the behavior of the American Chemical Society's response to minority accommodations in Dallas, by writing to the entities responsible for scheduling and writing resolutions, by standing his ground and showing a high degree of moral resilience, by building communities of supporters, and by presenting to the society the possible results of not acknowledging and correcting the disparity in treatment of their diverse members.

When Dr. Julian focused his attention on building his business, he concentrated on producing steroid intermediates and landed contracts with Upjohn, Ciba, Pfizer, and Merck pharmaceutical companies to produce progesterone from soybeans, but to continue being competitive with the Mexican pharmaceutical company Syntex Laboratories he needed Mexican yams. In 1956, Dr. Julian decided to build a facility to process Mexican yams in Mexico; however, "Banks were reluctant to make industrial loans to people of color. So, he built Laboratorios de Julian de Mexico, just outside of Mexico City. Using his own savings, along with the assistance of friends and private investors."[53] Even with the successful funding for the laboratory, the project was still on shaky ground because after the factory was completed the Mexican government refused to grant permission to harvest yams in Mexico.

Rebecca J. Anderson remarked that

> In 1956, the US Senate held public hearings, investigating allegations that Syntex had used its influence with the Mexican government to maintain a monopoly on Mexican yams. Julian's company was one of several that claimed damages . . . As a result of pressure on the Mexican government, yams became readily available to any buyer.[54]

Before the judgment against Syntex and the Mexican government, Julian had been contacted by a former fellow student from Vienna, Abraham Zlotnik, who was familiar with Central American geography and believed that he could locate the yams in Guatemala. Moreover, Zlotnik led an expedition on behalf of Julian and found a stable supply of yams. So, by 1957, Dr. Julian had founded plantations in Guatemala and launched another processing facility for yams called Empress Agro-Quimica Guatemaleca.

Dr. Julian remarked that after the acquisition of the plantation and facility in Guatemala Julian Laboratories had "become very competitive, and the field a bit overcrowded, we have enjoyed a very good business, and are looking forward to double our sales for the coming year, now that our raw material supply is adequate."[55] Rebecca J. Anderson stated that "Julian's Oak Park chemists found a way to quadruple production of progesterone from yams. The breakthrough made Julian Laboratories one of the world's largest producers of drugs from yams."[56] Furthermore, Dr. Julian could have held on to huge profits but instead he chose to drop the "progesterone price 10-fold, from $4000 to $400 per kilograms."[57]

Dr. Julian was a businessman, "but when he negotiated with a buyer, he would often make an over-generous offer or concession. Later, he would tell his attorney, Benjamin Becker, 'I don't mind making a profit, but I want them to make one too.'"[58] Still Dr. Julian became a millionaire, and as his attorney Benjamin Becker said,

> It is often said that business is rough, tough, ruthless and heartless. Percy . . . proved the American dream from obscurity to astounding business greatness, but with heart. He helped employees with personal and financial problems . . . he never had a single lawsuit against his company.[59]

Dr. Julian ran Julian Laboratories until 1961, and then he "sold Julian Laboratories to Smith, Klein, and French for $2,338,000 ($20 million in today's currency), remaining as president at a generous salary. At the same time, Upjohn purchased the Guatemala factory."[60] During his time as president of Julian Laboratories under the ownership of Smith, Klein, and French, Dr. Julian stayed involved in research, coauthored more scientific papers, and participated in several civil rights groups. Civic obligations, which had always been important to Dr. Julian, continued to occupy his time. Even though he had reached what some people might have considered to be a high position in African American society, he did not waver from trying to improve the life of other Blacks. Julian recognized the barriers that many African Americans faced and the role that his family had played in supporting him during his education and career. According to Bernard Witkop, Julian said the hope I grew up with is missing in today's ghetto youth ... because of a breakdown in the family life ... I think as we resolve the breakdown of the black family, caused by slavery and continued by welfare, the problem will come closer to its solution.[61]

Dr. Julian recognized that the family was important in providing for financial needs, sustenance, positive role models, and moral support, but he also recognized that the community was also important in building a supportive environment for the development of youth. He aided the development of young scientists by providing familial support to his employees and colleagues, often by assuming the role of an extended family member, whether by helping financially or offering advice and he was active in church and other community activities.

In 1964, Dr. Julian founded Julian Associates, Inc., and Julian Research Institute, a nonprofit organization that was dedicated to training young research chemists. He served as the director there until his death. At the Julian Research Institute, he continued his pursuits as a chemical researcher and he acted as a consultant for some pharmaceutical companies. Even as he took on the role of director at the institute, Dr. Julian's struggle for parity in opportunities for minorities continued as he attended board of trustee meetings and engaged audiences in conversations on civil rights at many college campuses and academic society meetings. Dr. Julian embodied the American dream: he rose from a southern African American family just a generation short of being slaves to being a well-educated, exceptional businessman. During his lifetime the range of experiences and accolades awarded to Dr. Julian was extensive and more than can possibly be acknowledged in this chapter; however, Bernhard Witkop listed a number of his awards in his biographical memoir of Percy Julian.[62] The following list are an example of a few of his academic and civic honors awarded after 1961 found in articles by William M. Cobb,[63] Bernhard Witkop,[64] and Rebecca J. Anderson[65]:

Layman of the Year Award, Church Federation of Greater Chicago, 1964
Founder's Day Award, Loyola University, Chicago, 1967
Merit Award of the Chicago Technical Societies Council, Chicago, 1967
Recipient of the first McNaughton Medal from DePauw University, for meritorious public service, 1967
Chemical Pioneer Award, American Institute of Chemists, Atlanta, 1968
MacMurray College's Chemistry Building named the Percy Lavon Julian Hall of Chemistry, 1972

In addition to the multitude of civic awards earned during his life, Dr. Julian was the recipient of at least 15 honorary degrees from various universities and he also held positions as a member of several learned societies. The following list can also be found in articles by William M. Cobb,[66] Bernhard Witkop,[67] and Rebecca J. Anderson[68]:

Laureate, Lincoln Academy, Springfield, Illinois, 1972

National Academy of Sciences, where he became the second African American to be elected, 1973

fellow, American Institute of Chemists

fellow, Chemical Society of London

fellow, New York Academy of Science

inducted into the National Inventors Hall of Fame, 1990

member, American Association for the Advancement of Science

United States Postal Service, Percy Lavon Julian commemorative stamp, 1993

American Chemical Society designated the synthesis of physostigmine a National Historic Chemical Landmark, 1999

"In 1974, Julian began undergoing treatment for liver cancer. Although his family tried to restrict his activities, he continued to head Julian Associates and the Julian Research Institute."[69] In 1975, when Dr. Julian was becoming terminal, Risher Watts said,

> Dr. Julian's reaction to having cancer as far as I could determine, was that he never quite accepted it. . . . he still had plans . . . he would talk about the things that he needed to do . . . he did not accept the fact, that he was terminal and was gonna die. He just seemed to have other plans, and they seem to have been for this world.[70]

Percy Julian Jr. remarked that "my dad was father, scientist, humanitarian, teacher of many things—both scientific and moral—a good person who never reached his potential . . . who took advantage of the country's promise of equality but in some ways was undone by the country's failure to live up to the promise."[71]

Percy Julian Jr. also responded during the interview for the *Nova* special about his dad that

> he once said that he was a good chemist but he dreamed of being an even better chemist, and he felt that the failure of the country to deal with the issue of race blocked not just his opportunities, but all of the opportunities of people who were talented of his generation, whether in science or elsewhere.[72]

Despite his difficulties, Dr. Julian did not turn his back on society and continued to maintain his moral standing. Toward the end of his life, he said, "I have had one goal in my life ... that of playing some role in making life a little easier for the persons who come after me."[73] Percy Lavon Julian died on April 19, 1975, but his legacy lives and his avowed goal appears fulfilled.[74]

Notes

1. Edward S. Jenkins, "'Beyond the Seventh Fold': A Historical Account of a Natural Product Chemist," *Science and Education* 5 (1996): 32.
2. The words "Black" and "African American" are used interchangeably throughout the chapter to avoid repetition.
3. Alabama State University was founded in 1867 as the Lincoln Normal School of Marion. Normal schools were created to train teachers, educating them in the norms of pedagogy and curriculum. Instruction at these schools was generally at the high school level.
4. David Taylor, "Percy Julian: A Scientist Makes Inroads in Chemistry and Civil Rights," *Humanities* 28, no. 1 (2007): 4.
5. "Percy Lavon Julian," in *Encyclopedia of World Biography*. ed., S. M. Bourgoin, 18 (Detroit: Gale Group, 1998), para. 3.
6. Jenkins, "'Beyond the Seventh Fold,'" 35.
7. Taylor, "Percy Julian," 5.
8. Jenkins, "'Beyond the Seventh Fold,'" 35.
9. A more thorough explanation of the term "self-directed learner" can be found in Lucy Guglielmino, "Development of the Self-Directed Learning Readiness Scale" (PhD diss., University of Georgia, 1977).
10. Phi Beta Kappa, founded in 1776, is an invitation-only honor society that recognizes excellence in the arts and sciences.
11. Sigma Xi, founded in 1886, is a scientific research honor society.
12. William M. Cobb, "Percy Lavon Julian, Ph. D., Sc. D., LL. D., L. H. D., 1899." *Journal of the National Medical Association* 63, no. 2 (1971): 143.
13. Taylor, "Percy Julian," 5.
14. Jenkins, "'Beyond the Seventh Fold,'" 36.
15. Cobb, "Percy Lavon Julian," 144.
16. Taylor, "Percy Julian," 5.
17. Jenkins, "'Beyond the Seventh Fold,'" 37.
18. Cobb, "Percy Lavon Julian," 144.
19. Jenkins, "'Beyond the Seventh Fold,'" 46.
20. Physostigmine is a compound found in the Calabar bean and is anticholinergic in activity; it can be used in treatment of glaucoma.
21. Hydrocortisone is a steroid produced by the adrenal cortex and used for treatment of inflammation.

22 Bernhard Witkop, *Percy Lavon Julian 1899–1975: A Biographical Memoir*, (Washington, DC: National Academy Press, 1980), 10. Available at www.nasonline.org/publications/biographical-memoirs/memoir-pdfs/julian-percy.pdf
23 Witkop, *Percy Lavon Julian*, 13.
24 Witkop, 14.
25 Taylor, "Percy Julian," 6.
26 This phrase was thought to have been coined in February 1946 by the Port Arthur, Texas, newspaper in relation to an athlete (Meryll Frost—most courageous athlete of 1945).
27 A chiropodist is a podiatrist. Information for Anna R. Johnson was not as readily available as for Percy Julian. In addition to the information from the University of Pennsylvania's archive found at "Anna Johnson Julian 1901–1994," Penn Libraries, https://archives.upenn.edu/exhibits/penn-people/biography/anna-johnson-julian/, information on her can be found at "Anna Johnson Julian," Wikipedia, last modified February 20, 2022, 12:42, https://en.wikipedia.org/wiki/Anna_Johnson_Julian
28 Sir Robert Robinson was a British chemist and Nobel laureate for his research on alkaloids.
29 Cobb, "Percy Lavon Julian," 144.
30 Taylor, "Percy Julian," 4.
31 James Ravin and Eve Higginbotham, "The Story of Percy Lavon Julian," *Archives of Ophthalmology* 127, no. 5 (2009): 691.
32 Taylor, "Percy Julian," 4.
33 Cobb, "Percy Lavon Julian," 144–145.
34 Cobb, 145.
35 James and Higginbotham, "Story of Percy Lavon," 691.
36 Taylor, "Percy Julian," 9.
37 Taylor, 9.
38 Taylor, 9.
39 After the dynamite incidence at the Julian home, several sources, including the *Chicago Tribune*, Taylor, "Percy Julian," and Percy Julian Jr., related that both Dr. Julian and his son stood watch at their home with a shotgun in fear of another attempt to bomb their home.
40 Ron Grossman, "Chemist Percy Julian Pushed Past Racial Barriers—Amid Attacks on His Oak Park Home," *Chicago Tribune*, February 15, 2019, www.chicagotribune.com/2019/02/15/chemist-percy-julian-pushed-past-racial-barriers-amid-attacks-on-his-oak-park-
41 Grossman, "Chemist Percy Julian Pushed," 4.
42 Cobb, "Percy Lavon Julian," 145.
43 Cobb, 145.
44 The Cicero Riot of 1951 occurred on July 11–12, in Cicero, Illinois. Approximately 4,000 whites attacked an apartment building in an all-white neighborhood, because a black family moved into it.
45 Cobb, "Percy Lavon Julian," 145.
46 Witkop, *Percy Lavon Julian*, 22.

47 Susan K. Lewis, "[Percy Lewis:] Those Who Knew Him," NOVA, accessed April 22, 2014, www.pbs.org/wgbh/nova/julian/knew-text.html/, p.4 of transcript.
48 Lewis, "Those Who Knew Him," 3.
49 Lewis, "Those Who Knew Him," 5.
50 The definition of servant leadership and characteristics can be found at "What Is Servant Leadership?" Center for Servant Leadership, accessed April 22, 2014, www.greenleaf.org/what-is-servant-leadership/
51 Lewis, "Those Who Knew Him," 6.
52 Percy Julian Letter, February 3, 1956, to Dr. John C. Warner, president of the American Chemical Society, concerning treatment of Black scientists during their meeting in Dallas in 1956. Science History Institute Digital Collection, https://digital.sciencehistory.org/works/hx11x25t
53 Rebecca J. Anderson (2018), "The Extraordinary Percy Julian," *Pharmacologist* 60, no. 3 (2018):156.
54 Anderson, "Extraordinary Percy Julian," 157.
55 Witkop, *Percy Lavon Julian*, 23.
56 Anderson, "Extraordinary Percy Julian," 157.
57 Anderson, 157.
58 Anderson, 157.
59 Witkop, *Percy Lavon Julian*, 24.
60 Anderson, "Extraordinary Percy Julian," 157.
61 Witkop, *Percy Lavon Julian*, 6.
62 Witkop, 29–32.
63 Cobb, "Percy Lavon Julian," 145–146.
64 Witkop, *Percy Lavon Julian*, 29–32.
65 Anderson, "Extraordinary Percy Julian," 157–158.
66 Cobb, "Percy Lavon Julian," 145–146.
67 Witkop, *Percy Lavon Julian*, 29–32.
68 Anderson, "Extraordinary Percy Julian," 157–158.
69 Anderson, 157.
70 Lewis, "Those Who Knew Him," 6.
71 Lewis, 2.
72 Lewis, 3.
73 "Percy Lavon Julian," in *Encyclopedia of World Biography*, para. 16.
74 Faith Julian is currently trying to raise money to pay for repairs and back taxes on the Julian family home in Oak Park, Illinois, as discussed in Stacy Sheridan, "Back Taxes Have Percy Julian Home in Peril," Wednesday Journal, September 29, 2021, www.oakpark.com/2021/09/28/back-taxes-have-percy-julian-home-in-peril/

II

Civil Rights Lawyers

Agitating within the System

3

Fred Gray and the Desegregation of Alabama's Public Schools

DERRYN MOTEN

When Charles Hamilton Houston, associate dean of Howard University's School of Law, wrote his 1935 article "The Need for Negro Lawyers," Alabama had four Black lawyers in full-time practice servicing a Black population of 944,834. Two years later, the Alabama Bar admitted Birmingham attorney Arthur D. Shores, raising the number of Black lawyers in the state to five. Shores retained the dubious distinction for years as the Magic City's only Black lawyer. One year before the Supreme Court of the United States decided its 1954 landmark *Brown v. Board of Education,* making racially segregated schools a violation of the Fourteenth Amendment and overturning *Plessy v. Ferguson* (1896), Charles D. Lanford became the ninth licensed Black attorney in Alabama. Blacks in the state who wished to attend law school had to attend a law school out of state as so-called Jim Crow Scholars.[1] In 1953, there were ten such Black students from Alabama attending out-of-state law schools including Fred D. Gray, who attended Western Reserve University Law School. He graduated in 1954 and returned home to Montgomery, Alabama, to practice bringing the number of Black lawyers in Alabama to double digits. In 1958, the *Montgomery Advertiser* announced that C. C. (Charles Caffey) Pryor passed the Alabama State Bar Examination. Pryor graduated from Howard University School of Law. In 1958, he was one of 14 Black attorneys in Alabama and one of four Black attorneys in Montgomery, including fellow Howard Law graduates Solomon S. Seay Jr. and Charles Conley. Houston opined at the end of his article, "The great work of the Negro lawyer in the next generation must be in the South."[2]

Mahala Ashley Dickerson also graduated from Howard University School of Law, becoming Alabama's first Black female attorney in 1948. She moved to Indianapolis, Indiana, and Anchorage, Alaska, becoming the first Black female attorney in those states as well.[3]

Within his first year of practice, Gray would represent Rosa Parks, Martin Luther King Jr., Claudette Colvin, Mary Louise Smith, Susie McDonald, and Aurelia Browder, foot soldiers in the Montgomery bus protest. The latter four became plaintiffs in *Browder v. Gayle* (1956), the federal class-action lawsuit that outlawed the segregated seating laws in Montgomery, Alabama. Gray, a 1951 graduate of Alabama State College, became boycott counsel when he became the attorney for the Montgomery Improvement Association. Alabama's racial milieu epitomized "The Lost Cause" argument in that white rule became the principal right in which the state dared to defend. Segregation, disenfranchisement, and quasi-servitude became three legs of the New South stool. Alabama's Latin state motto, *Audemus jura nostra defendere,* is translated in English as "We dare defend our Rights," begging the question, Whose and what rights?

Fred Gray returned south determined to eradicate everything segregated that he found, and his legal career reflects his quest. This chapter will discuss attorney Gray's legal acumen and determination to quash Jim Crow by examining his litigation in *Lee v. Macon County Board of Education* (1963). This case showcases Fred Gray's work with the NAACP Legal Defense and Education Fund Inc. (LDF) and the US Department of Justice. NAACP LDF leaders such as Constance Baker Motley, Robert Carter, Thurgood Marshall, Derrick Bell Jr., and Leroy Clark helped Fred Gray litigate some of his and America's most important civil rights cases. The tandem desegregated the University of Alabama, Florence State College, and Auburn University. Fred Gray, Author Shores, Charles Langford, Orzell Billingsley, Solomon Seay Jr., and other early Black attorneys became the tip of the spear for the LDF. Together, they were, in Jack Greenberg's words, "Crusaders in the Courts."[4]

When the Southern Christian Leadership Conference (SCLC), established Project C (Confrontation) in Birmingham in 1963, Dr. King asserted that if segregation could be broken in "the most segregated city in America," segregation could be broken anywhere. The NAACP felt similarly about its legal work in the South. In the wake of James Meredith's 1962 integration of Ole Miss, University of Mississippi historian James Silver likened the Magnolia State to a "Closed Society." Many felt similarly about the other former Confederate states.

Lee became the paradigm for public school desegregation. An adroit Gray came up with a legal strategy to desegregate all Alabama public primary and secondary schools as well as the state's public-supported colleges in one court ruling as opposed to pursuing desegregation school district by school district. The idiom "the bigger they come, the harder they fall" certainly fit Alabama in the twentieth century. The 1958 gubernatorial contest between Alabama attorney general John M. Patterson and Third Circuit Court judge George C. Wallace fully displayed the politics of race. After losing, Wallace proclaimed, "John Patterson out-nigguhed me. And boys, I'm not goin' to be out-nigguhed again."[5]

Wallace's biographer, Marshall Frady described Wallace as "the most resourceful, durable, and unabashed of the Southern segregationist governors."[6] Wallace defenders argued that the populist governor's bigotry was sheer racial chicanery. Wallace vehemently denied being a racist. He told journalist Carl Rowan, "I'm one of the ones that advocated taking 'white supremacy' off the rooster that was the symbol of the Democratic party in this state."[7] Despite the governor's protestations, Frady countered, "Wallace once confided to a reporter in the lobby of a Cleveland, Ohio hotel, removing his cigar for a moment to whisper behind his hand, 'Let 'em call me a racist. It don't' [sic] make any difference. Whole heap of folks in this country feels the same way I do. Race is what's gonna win this thing for me.'"[8]

For his part, Governor-Elect John Patterson proved his racist bona fides disallowing Black marching bands to participate in his January 19, 1959, inauguration. Alabama's newly elected governor made his position on school integration clear in his inauguration speech: "I will oppose with every ounce of energy I possess and will use every power at my command to prevent any mixing of the white and Negro races in classrooms of this state . . . There can be no compromise in this fight. There is no such thing as a 'little integration.' The determine and ruthless purpose of the race agitators and organizations such as the NAACP is to bring about as fast as possible an amalgamation of our society."[9] Patterson accepted the endorsement of the Klan, whom *Montgomery Advertiser* editor Grover Hall called "that herd of albino swine."[10]

Patterson had "tossed the gauntlet" George Wallace would memorialize four years later as governor. As University of Leicester lecturer George Lewis noted about America's anti-miscegenation movement, "Positing the belief that school desegregation would lead . . . to interracial breeding and the destruction of the 'purity' of the white race was a staple of white supremacist discourse and formed an integral part of the Massive Resistance arsenal."[11]

At its sixth annual meeting in Birmingham, the Alabama State NAACP cited "planned legal attacks against education inequality" as one of its priorities at the 1951 meeting. America's most revered civil rights organization set up its southeastern regional headquarters in Birmingham, Alabama, under the supervision of Mrs. Ruby Hurley. Five years later, attorney Arthur D. Shores and the NAACP desegregated the University of Alabama when a Birmingham federal district court ordered the admission of Autherine Lucy in 1956. UA became the first southern white public university desegregated in the wake of *Brown v. Board of Education*. That same year saw the successful conclusion of the Montgomery bus boycott.

Convinced that the NAACP fomented both Lucy's admission and the Montgomery bus protest, Alabama attorney general John Patterson succeeded in banning the NAACP in Alabama. Montgomery Circuit Court judge Walter B. Jones issued an injunction preventing the NAACP from doing business in Alabama. He furthered ordered the NAACP to surrender its membership rolls and imposed a $100,000 fine when it did not.

Between 1956 and 1966, Fred Gray, assisted by the LDF, litigated civil rights cases that included *Dixon v. Alabama State Board of Education* (1961), *Franklin v. Parker* (1963), *Gomillion v. Lightfoot* (1960), *Williams v. Wallace* (1965), and *Lee v. Macon County Board of Education* (1963).[12]

The year 1963 marked the one-hundred-year anniversary of President Abraham Lincoln's Emancipation Proclamation making "freedom" the watchword for the NAACP and its members. Fred Gray filed his lawsuit in *Lee* in January 1963. He, Arthur Shores, and the LDF compelled the second desegregation of the University of Alabama in June 1963 with the admission of James Hood and Vivian Malone, and in June 1963, Gray and the LDF attorney Constance Baker Motley filed a lawsuit on behalf of Harold A. Franklin, who sought admission to the Auburn University Graduate School. Franklin, an Alabama State College graduate, became the first Black student to attend Auburn when he started classes in January 1964.

In a televised, statewide address on September 8, 1963, Gov. Wallace spoke to Alabama citizens about school segregation, "There is a Supreme Being and He made each and every one of us regardless of our color. . . . I believe that segregation of the school system in Alabama is an inherent right, that it is in the interest of Negro and white. I feel that in my heart and the overwhelming majority of the people in this state feel that in their heart and, therefore, there is nothing sinful or immoral or irreligious about a system we believe is in the best interest of all concerned."[13] The governor ignored the number of Alabamians, albeit Black, who protested segregated public schools, public parks, and public swimming pools. Gov. Wallace personified the tyranny of the majority. In his 1963 "Letter from Birmingham Jail," Martin Luther King Jr. reminded us that Reinhold Niebuhr said, "Groups tend to be more immoral than individuals."[14]

In his televised speech, the governor cited the expert witness testimony in the public school desegregation case in Savannah, Georgia. The federal judge in *Stell v. Savannah-Chatham Board of Education*, 220 F. Supp 667 (1963), allowed the school board's arguments of intellectual differences between the Negro and white pupils to be put in the record. The court opinion asserted, "The separation of Negro and white children in public schools was not determined solely based on race or color but rather upon racial traits of educational significance." *Stell*-like arguments were introduced in the Mobile, Alabama, school desegregation case but not in other state school desegregation cases. Perhaps the state decided to jettison racial-scientific arguments because the federal appellate courts viewed such reasoning with a jaundiced eye. Perhaps the state decided to skuttle this legal track because scientific organizations such as the committee of the American Association for the Advancement of Science lambasted these theories and their theorists. The American Anthropological Association refuted the idea that "Negroes are biologically inferior. . . . There is no scientifically established evidence to justify the exclusion of any race from the rights guaranteed by the Constitution of the United States."[15]

When Fred Gray entered his lawsuit for *Lee,* there was not a single public primary or secondary school in Alabama's 102 city and county school districts where Black and white students were taught in the same classroom. De jure segregation even consigned Black school teachers to Black-only schools.

In 1963, public school desegregation litigation in Alabama concurrently occurred in Mobile, Birmingham, Tuskegee, and Huntsville. Twenty-seven Black parents in Mobile signed a petition asking for the NAACP to help end segregation in the city's and Mobile County's public schools. Gov. Wallace used every unsavory scheme to justify racial segregation in public schools. Ultimately, segregation was predicated on white supremacy and white racism, defined as the belief that "race" accounts for differences in a person's ability.

In the Mobile school desegregation case *Davis v. Board of School Commissioners of Mobile County* (1963), US District Court judge Daniel H. Thomas, took the testimony of Dr. Wesley Critz George, a retired University of North Carolina professor of histology and embryology who argued the "Negro is less capable of abstract reasoning and hard intellectual functioning than whites." Dr. Frank C. K. McGurk, a sociology professor at the Alabama College in Montevallo, Alabama, argued that school integration would "harm educational opportunities for Negroes and white persons."[16]

In a letter to Professor Henry E. Garrett, one-time president of the American Psychological Association and chair of Columbia University's Department of Psychology, Dr. George explained why "Ralph Smith, a lawyer from Montgomery representing the governor [John Patterson] and the state of Alabama," sought Dr. George's expertise. "Alabama has escaped integration, but it is anticipated that in time they [*sic*] be the object of frontal attacks. They want to be prepared to meet that attack in the courts. They hope to base their case not only on legal precedent but on scientific evidence that will withstand the attacks of lawyers and other scientists. The Supreme Court in its 1954 decision disregarded legal precedents and based their decision on what they called scientific evidence that segregation does psychological harm to Negro children. Mr. Smith wants evaluation of that evidence and the 'authorities' cited."[17]

Governor John Patterson commissioned Dr. George in 1961 to produce a study proving the biological inferiority of Blacks in general and school-age Blacks in particular. Alabama taxpayers paid Dr. George $3,000 for his bogus study. The thinking of Dr. George fueled anti-miscegenation and racial integrity laws throughout the United States. Such codified laws became the bedrock of the American eugenics movement championed by politicians great and small. LDF lawyers Constance Baker Motley and Derrick Bell Jr. assailed Dr. George's study during their cross-examination in the Mobile school desegregation case, *Davis v. Board of School Commissioners*. Publicly, Dr. George eschewed discussions about Negro inferiority. The UNC professor claimed, "That expression—white race, intellectually, is superior to the Negro race—has never been used in any . . . discussions with the State of Alabama."[18] Dr. W. C. George did not testify in the Macon County school case.

In 1962, Detroit Lee, lead plaintiff in *Lee v. Macon County Board of Education*, wrote Dr. Charles Gomillion, professor of sociology at Tuskegee Institute and president of the Tuskegee Civic Association, revisiting the idea of desegregating the white Tuskegee High School. Charles Gomillion and Detroit Lee first discussed integrating Macon County public schools in 1956. Lee spoke with Fred Gray, who drew up the petition for a class-action suit demanding total desegregation of public schools in Macon County. Nine families consisting of 15 parents became plaintiffs in *Lee* and signed the petition. The Tuskegee Civic Association financed the case and presented the petition to the Macon Board of Education on September 12, 1962. These Black parents implored the board to "begin immediately operating the schools under your jurisdiction according to the principles laid down by the U.S. Supreme Court on May 17, 1954, in the case of *Brown v. Board of Education*."[19]

Fred Gray filed *Lee v. Macon County Board of Education* in January 1963. Joining their father and mother, Hattie M. Lee, were plaintiffs Anthony T. Lee and Henry A. Lee. The patriarch Lee was a member of the Tuskegee Civic Association and a founding member of the 3Ts; namely, the Tuskegee Institute Community Education Project, the Tuskegee Institute Summer Education Program, and the Tuskegee Institute Community Action Corps. Together, Tuskegee Institute students and Tuskegee adults tutored elementary and high school students, repaired homes in Macon County, and planted and harvested crops for those who needed help.

The densely Black populated–Macon County became well known in legal circles when in 1960, Fred Gray sued Tuskegee Mayor Phillip M. Lightfoot in

Gomillion v. Lightfoot. The Supreme Court of the United States overturned a gerrymandered 28-sided legislative district ostensibly designed to prevent the Black Macon County majority from elective offices in the City of Tuskegee. The case represented white hubris in its most brazen and basest form.

The future plaintiffs of Lee petitioned the Macon County School Board in September 1962 representing themselves as "residents of Macon County, Alabama, and members of the Negro race, and parents of school age children attending various schools located in Macon County." *Brown v. Board of Education* became the crux of the plaintiffs' argument for desegregation. It also became the bone of contention for Alabama defendants including various jurists who adjudicated school desegregation cases, begging the question, Does the Fourteenth Amendment merely forbid racial discrimination, or does it require enforced integration?[20]

LDF attorney Constance Baker Motley assisted Gray and his law partner, Solomon Seay Jr., in *Lee v. Macon County Board of Education*. Argued before US Middle District Court judge Frank M. Johnson Jr., Gray charged that Alabama operated a dual-race public school system in contravention of the May 1954 and May 1955 US Supreme Court landmark decision *Brown v. Board of Education*. In Civil Action 604-E, attorneys Gray and Motley et al. argued that "defendants maintain and operate a compulsory biracial school system by the use of dual school zone or attendance areas for white and Negro pupils. Under the dual attendance areas, defendants make initial assignments of students to the public schools under their control on the grounds of race and color. Principals, teachers, and other professional personnel . . . are likewise assigned to the schools on the basis of race and color."[21]

On August 22, 1963, Judge Johnson agreed and ordered the Macon County Board of Education to desegregate Tuskegee High School, the white public high school in the City of Tuskegee. Judge Johnson made the United States an amicus curiae or "friend" in the lawsuit, to assist in the enforcement of his desegregation orders. The US Supreme Court mandated in its 1955 *Brown v. Board of Education II* decision that the desegregation of public schools happen "with all deliberate speed." This enforcement order became the task and conundrum of federal district courts and federal appellate courts. Alabama's federal district courts became an important public education arbitrator. Deep South governors complained loudly about federal judicial overreach and the courts' misinterpretation of the Fourteenth Amendment. The Fifth Circuit Court of Appeals answered this question in *United States v. Jefferson City Board of Education*, 380 F. 2d 385 (1967), when it wrote, "If Negroes are to enter the mainstream of American life as school children, they must have equal educational opportunities with white children."[22]

On December 9, 1963, Judge Johnson ordered the Macon School Board to present a desegregation plan to the court no later than December 12, 1963. Judge Johnson clearly noted he expected a plan "under which Defendants make an immediate start in the desegregation of schools in Macon County, Alabama, to begin in January 1964 and that makes general use of the Alabama Pupil Placement Law without discrimination." The plan had to eliminate, once and for all, the dual school system.

In their "Plaintiffs' Objections to Defendant Macon County School Board's Proposed Plan for Desegregation," attorney Fred Gray and LDF attorney Jack Greenberg noted, "The Board's plan limits transfers [through the Alabama Pupil Placement Law] in the first year of its operation solely to pupils in grade 12 and would expand to further grades only on a year-by-year basis. Moreover, it fails to provide for the assignment of teachers or the transportation of pupils on a non-racial basis."[23] Using this formula, it would take 17 years to desegregate grades K–12 in Macon County public schools. The school board's plan was classic stall and delay used by southern politicians who opposed integration. Gray and Greenberg concluded, "The [February 28, 1964] plan does not attempt to, nor can it effect desegregation of the public schools of Macon County." Plaintiffs' attorneys also accused the defendants of dereliction failing to renew the accreditation of Tuskegee High School causing the school to lose it accreditation while maintaining the accreditation of the county's other white public schools. The Macon County School Board intentionally sabotaged the educational integrity and viability of Tuskegee High School.

The Alabama legislature passed the Alabama School Placement Law, also known as the Pupil Placement Law, in 1955 to thwart the US Supreme Court's *Brown v. Board of Education* decision. The law was held constitutional in *Shuttlesworth v. Birmingham Board of Education*, 162 F. Supp. 372. Civil rights leader Rev. Fred Shuttlesworth and three other Black parents became the first to inveigh the constitutionality of the Alabama law. The Placement School Law gave sole authority to school boards to assign pupils to public schools under their jurisdiction. School boards accounted for a student's "scholastic aptitude and relative intelligence." The law also stipulated, "No child shall be compelled to attend any school in which the races are commingled when a written objection of the parent . . . has been filed with the Board of Education."[24]

The Macon Board of Education initially decided to comply with the court's order and prepared for a smooth transition. Governor Wallace had other plans, however. On September 2, 1963, Wallace issued Executive Order No. 9, ordering the Macon Board of Education to delay opening Tuskegee High School for one week or until September 9, 1963, purportedly, "to allow the governor of the state to preserve the peace, maintain domestic tranquility, and to protect the lives and property of all citizens of the state."[25] As a sign of force and intimidation, Wallace deployed Alabama state troopers to Tuskegee. Approximately 200 troopers surrounded the high school.

Gov. Wallace's impetuous decision to close Tuskegee High School became the watershed moment Gray needed for the Macon school case. The governor's mercurial temperament made his order almost predictable. It was akin to Black students egging on Birmingham police commissioner Eugene "Bull" Connor in Kelly Ingram Park during Project C. Fred Gray reasoned that if Gov. Wallace used his state powers to close Tuskegee High School, overturning the decision and wish of the Macon County School Board, he had the state power to desegregate all state public schools. School desegregation cases had to be tried school district by school district, and the US attorney general did not have the constitutional authority to sue individual school districts in a discrimination lawsuit. This fact underscores the wisdom of Judge Frank M. Johnson Jr. adding the US government as a party to *Lee v. Macon*.

The motion written by attorney Gray and his legal staff petitioned the federal district court for the governor to show cause why he should not be a defendant and to show why the court should not compel Wallace to cease and desist from interfering with the court's desegregation orders. US attorney general Robert Kennedy and Department of Justice (DOJ), lawyers disagreed with the idea of a blanket order to desegregate schools statewide. Questions of federalism in the South were historically fraught with notions of interposition and nullification. DOJ would change its mind after Gov. Wallace's continued interference and disobedience of federal court orders.

In addition to Tuskegee High School, Gov. Wallace ordered public schools closed in Birmingham and Huntsville, Alabama. Two Black students quietly desegregated Murphy High School in Mobile, the state's largest high school. Richard Wasserstrom reported in a September 11, 1963, memo to "Mr. [Burke] Marshall: The Negro students entered Murphy High School without incident this morning. White students had gathered outside the school before classes began but went in when classes started."[26] School and law enforcement authorities in Mobile, Birmingham, and Huntsville beseeched the governor not to send Alabama state troopers to their cities and not to veto decisions made by their school boards to follow orders of the federal courts. *The Birmingham News* editorialized, "Wallace now not, defies federal courts, he defies the wishes of legally constituted local authorities. Alabamians had best awaken. George Wallace is not 'saving Alabama.' He is destroying self-government and the education system of the state."[27] A panel of five federal judges placed

Gov. Wallace under a temporary restraining order barring him from interfering with school desegregation efforts in Tuskegee, Birmingham, and Mobile. President John F. Kennedy had 100 National Guardsmen on standby if needed in Birmingham. Trucks from Ft. McClellan would transport the soldiers. Another force of 100 guardsmen had established a bivouac at the Tuskegee Armory, and in Mobile, 500 Ft. Bragg soldiers were on a 30-minute alert to be transported on C130s. Some observers had likened Tuskegee, Birmingham, and Mobile to another potential "Little Rock."

The closing of Tuskegee High School and the war of words between Governor Wallace and President John Kennedy was déjà vu for the White House. The president was prepared to issue a "cease and desist" order to the governor instructing the chief executive to obey the federal court rulings for public schools in Birmingham and Tuskegee. A "cease and desist" order was a prerequisite for President Kennedy to federalize the Alabama National Guard as he had done in the June 1963 University of Alabama integration by Vivian Malone and James Hood. In the September 1963 standoff, President Kennedy, asserted, "The U. S. government action regarding Alabama [public] schools will come only if Wallace compels it."

Based on Judge Frank M. Johnson Jr.'s August 22, 1963, order, 13 Black student plaintiffs were assigned to Tuskegee High School, but Alabama state troopers enforced Gov. George Wallace's September 2, 1963, order to delay its opening for one week. A week later, the federal government in the case, *United States of America, Plaintiff, v. George C. Wallace, et al, Defendants,* enjoined defendants, Governor George C. Wallace et al., from

> [i]nterfering with or obstructing the Macon County Board of Education . . . from operating the Macon County School System in compliance with the Order of the Court in the case of *Lee v. Macon County Board of Education* wherein this Court ordered the Macon County Board of Education to make an immediate start, to be effective for the school term commencing September 1963, in the desegregation of the schools of Macon County, Alabama, through the use of the Alabama Placement Law, without discrimination on the basis of race or color.

Tuskegee High School reopened with only its thirteen new Black students in attendance. All white students formerly enrolled at the school transferred to other all-white schools in Macon County. Gov. Wallace arranged for state troopers to ferry the former Tuskegee High white students in state police vehicles to Notasulga High School and Shorter High School where most of them transferred. The state board of education further ordered the Macon County School Board to provide county bus service for those same white students.

In January 1964, the Alabama State Board of Education passed a resolution to permanently close Tuskegee High School for insufficient enrollment and to remand the 13 Black students back to Tuskegee Institute High School, an all-Black school on the campus of Tuskegee Institute. In the same month, the Macon County Board of Education cited an opinion of Alabama attorney general Richmond Flowers acknowledging that the Alabama State Board of Education had the legal authority to close Tuskegee High School and that the Macon Board of Education was obligated to carry out the state board's order to do so. Judge Johnson ordered that the 12 Black students who attended the defunct Tuskegee High School be admitted to Notasulga and Shorter public high schools, six to each school. One of the original 13 Black students was withdrawn for disciplinary reasons. In an advisory opinion, the Alabama Supreme Court disagreed with Attorney General Flowers stating that only city and county school boards of education had the authority to close a city or county school.

In a February 3, 1964, brief filed by Fred Gray, Jack Greenberg, Constance Baker Motley, and Charles Jones, Gray and plaintiff's counsel noted that the *Lee* lawsuit was made "on behalf of other Negro children and their parents similarly situated residing in the various counties throughout the state of Alabama." The brief also asserted that the defendants "maintained and operated a compulsory biracial school systemin all of said counties in the State of Alabama by use of the dual school zones or attendance areas for white and Negro pupils."[28] Finally, Gray contended that since the state board of education had assumed statewide jurisdiction in ordering the closure of Tuskegee High School the state board should be required to comply with the US Supreme Court's 1954 decision removing race barriers at schools in all Alabama's 67 counties. This time, the US Department of Justice supported attorney Gray's request for a federal court statewide order desegregating all public schools in Alabama.

Supplementing his February 3, 1964, complaint, Fred Gray filed another brief on February 10, 1964. That brief noted a resolution passed by the Alabama State Board of Education on February 4, 1964, in which the board proclaimed, "The State Board of Education deplores the Order of Judge Johnson and pledges every resource at our command to . . . defeat said integration Orders and . . . to support every effort to maintain our way of life and high educational standards for all citizens of our State."[29] The complaints of February 3 and February 10 culminated in a two-day hearing before a panel of three federal judges.

At stake was whether Gov. George Wallace, as the ex officio chairman of the Alabama State Board of Education, and the latter, exercised control over

Alabama's public schools and if so, whether there was sufficient evidence to warrant a statewide desegregation order. If the three-judge panel agreed, attorney Gray would have accomplished what no other civil rights attorney had, and that is persuading a federal court to desegregate all state public schools in one fell swoop.

The panel of three federal judges Frank M. Johnson Jr., Richard T. Rives, and Hobart Grooms returned their verdict on July 13, 1964, finding that Gov. Wallace and the Alabama State Board of Education worked in concert to maintain a dual school system in Alabama based on race and color. The panel also ruled that the tuition-grants program was devised to assist white students and their families to attend private schools and therefore was unconstitutional. Fred Gray, LDF, and DOJ won a major battle, but they had not won the war. Despite the ruling, Gov. Wallace was undeterred, and he continued to interfere and meddle with the federal court desegregation school orders. More lawsuits against George Wallace filed by Fred Gray and DOJ followed. The same judicial trio heard renewed arguments for an order desegregating all Alabama public schools. That order came on March 22, 1967, mandating the desegregation of 98 school districts excluding school districts already under court supervision. *Lee v. Macon Board of Education* became the paradigm for DOJ's future statewide school desegregation efforts. As law professor Brian Landsberg notes, "No court had yet issued statewide relief in a school desegregation case . . ." The three-judge panel endorsed the Department of Health, Education, and Welfare (HEW). Freedom of Choice plans were approved by the judges for Alabama school systems covered by the March 22, 1967, order. However, HEW stated its dissatisfaction with that method of ending dual school systems in Alabama.

As a last gasp, the Alabama legislature passed an anti-guidelines bill that would establish Governor George Wallace and the legislature as a commission to negotiate with HEW officials as a proxy of local school boards. The new law also declared null and void all compliance forms signed by local school boards agreeing to the desegregation regulations enforced by the Department of Housing, Education, and Welfare. The governor called the HEW guidelines a "socialist plot." The law required the Alabama legislature to replace the $3.8 million in federal appropriations.[30] The Fifth Circuit Court eventually overturned the law.[31]

The Fifth Circuit Court cleared up any ambiguity about whether the US Constitution impels or compels public schools to desegregate or to integrate. Two judges wrote the majority opinion for the court concluding, "Negroes as a class must be free of the stigma of 'apartheid.' The U. S. Constitution requires that schools be integrated not merely desegregated."[32] The court also ordered lower federal courts to follow HEW guidelines when fashioning school desegregation plans.

Attorney Gray's efforts were facilitated by the passage of the Civil Rights Act of 1964, particularly Title VI of the CRA which barred federal agencies from giving federal funding to programs engaged in racial discrimination. Regulations under Title VI allowed the nascent Department of Health, Education, and Welfare to require school systems to submit desegregation plans to receive federal resources and to show that they complied with the regulations. Through the CRA of 1964, the US attorney general now had authority to initiate school discrimination lawsuits on behalf of any pupil denied equal protection by a school board if a parent sought redress through the US Department of Justice.

Lurleen Wallace succeeded Gov. George C. Wallace, her husband, as the forty-sixth governor of Alabama on January 16, 1967. Three months later, a three-judge federal court ordered Alabama to desegregate its public schools statewide except for school systems already under court-ordered desegregation plans. Gov. Lurleen Wallace railed about federal intrusion and asked the Alabama legislature to consider placing the state's public schools under her control.

Gov. Lurleen Wallace aired her grievances on a radio and television broadcast before a joint session of the Alabama legislature on March 30, 1967. The governor asserted that the order would compel white students "to go to all-Negro schools" and compel Black students "to go to predominantly white schools." Another mistruth was that the order would require the closing of every "Negro college, trade school, all-Negro elementary and secondary school in the state. . . . They have made their decree, now let them enforce it."[33]

The press lambasted and lampooned Gov. Lurleen Wallace. *The St. Louis Post-Dispatch* editorialized that defiance got the governors of Mississippi, Arkansas, and Virginia nowhere, summing up, "It's a strange way to become a hero or a martyr, but so far the politics of racism has not paid much attention to history."[34]

In the end, the US Supreme Court affirmed the March 22, 1967, decision in a one-paragraph opinion. The court ordered Governor Lurleen Wallace and Alabama state officials to "take affirmative action to disestablish all state-enforced public-school desegregation." It is ironic that Gov. Lurleen Wallace was tasked with desegregating public schools that her husband and former Alabama governor staked his political career and betted his political reputation on. The court further opined, "Alabama officials flouted every effort to make the 14th Amendment a meaningful reality to Negro school children in Alabama." A conversation Gov. George Wallace had with President John Kennedy underscored the governor's ignominy: "Kennedy coarsely asked Wallace, 'You think it would be horrifying to have a Negro attend the University of Alabama, governor?' Undeterred, Wallace retorted, 'Well, I think it's horrifying for the federal courts and the central government to rewrite all the laws and force upon the people what they don't want, yes . . . I will never myself submit voluntarily to any integration in a school system in Alabama.'"[35]

The lessons learned from public school desegregation litigation in Alabama were invaluable for future forays. Gray, LDF, and DOJ had to "keep their eyes on the prize;" they could not allow themselves to be distracted by the inane ploys of governors George or Lurleen Wallace. LDF director Thurgood Marshall use to say, "Lose your temper, lose your case."[36] Fred Gray had argued many cases before federal judge Frank M. Johnson Jr., giving Gray a familiarity not shared by some of the LDF and DOJ attorneys. A similar comfort existed between Fred Gray and Constance Baker Motley, perhaps the one NAACP lawyer that litigated more cases in Alabama with Gray than any other LDF lawyer. The LDF was pivotal to attorney Gray's legal victories. The Mach 1967 ruling ordering the statewide desegregation of public schools in Alabama did not finally and totally end segregation in public education in Alabama. If "the devil is in the details," there were a lot of details in the eradication of Jim Crow in Alabama's public schools. Additional federal court orders were necessary for Black teachers to receive equity in pay and school assignments. Gov. George Wallace threatened to use Alabama state troopers to prevent Black teachers from teaching in white schools or from teaching white students.

Fred Gray began his lawsuit against the Macon County School Board during the administration of President John F. Kennedy. Eleven months later Kennedy would be beatified by an assassin's bullet. The Department of Justice, under US attorney general Robert F. Kennedy, the president's brother, deployed DOJ attorneys and FBI agents to Alabama. Notable among them was the ubiquitous John Doar, deputy assistant attorney general. Doar became a familiar face and pivotal figure in Alabama's school desegregation battles. DOJ sent Doar into southern states embroiled by racial tension. He helped Fred Gray interview the parents and students who became plaintiffs in *Lee v. Macon County School Board*. He mediated for the latter and the Tuskegee Civic Association, the financial impetus behind *Lee*. He was in Tuscaloosa when Governor Wallace "stood in the schoolhouse door" at Foster Auditorium. He was attorney General Robert Kennedy's "eyes and ears." Local newspapers called him the federal government's "troubleshooter."[37] Doar flanked Harold Franklin during his first days on the Auburn University campus in January 1964.[38]

While Fred Gray argued the merits of desegregating public schools in Macon County, Alabama, social scientists were offering pseudoscientific evidence of Black intellectual inferiority in public school desegregation cases in Mobile, Alabama, Savannah, Georgia, and Charleston, South Carolina. Ralph Smith, the attorney whom Alabama governor John Patterson assigned to hire Dr. W. C. George said of Dr. George's study *The Biology of the Race Problem*, "Scientific data supports the contention that the white race, intellectually, is superior to the Negro, and that is the point we seek to make in this study."[39]

James Hood, the Black student who, with Vivian Malone, desegregated the University of Alabama for the second time in June 1963, revealed 35 years later that he was a subject of the Dr. W. C. George's study during his sojourn at the University of Alabama. The university expelled Hood for allegedly making disparaging remarks about Gov. George Wallace and UA administrators. According to Hood, "We were told at the time that the study was to compare our scholastic aptitude scores with those of white students.... 'Federal courts,' [Dr. George] indicated, should take special note of the study before ruling on integration cases.' I sent a 27-page research paper to Dr. George [refuting the researcher's race-based conclusions], and I got a letter back written on a napkin. And it said, 'As a Negro boy, you don't have the intellectual capacity to challenge a white scholar like myself.'"[40]

In the landmark, *Plessy v. Ferguson*, 163 U.S. 537 (1896), Chief Justice Henry Billings Brown opined that the US Constitution could not make Negroes equal to whites. The court argued, "Legislation is powerless to eradicate racial instincts, or to abolish distinctions based upon physical differences.... If one race be inferior to the other socially, the Constitution of the United States cannot put them upon the same plane" (26). The rationale of Justice Brown and the court's majority would become the catechism of white supremacy. It was the baby's milk of social scientists such as Dr. W. C. George. It was the mantra overturned by a latter US Supreme court in *Brown v. Board of Education* (1954).

Fred Gray and the NAACP did not seek Harold Franklin's admission to Auburn University or Vivian Malone's and James Hood's admission to the University of Alabama or Wendell Gunn's admission to Florence State College (now the University of North Alabama) because they believed white students and white teachers were more intelligent than Black students and Black teachers. Fred Gray and the NAACP sought the admission of Franklin, Gunn, Hood, and Malone because Fred Gray and the NAACP knew that if Auburn, the University of Alabama, and Florence State College remained "white," the notion of white superiority would remain a fallacy in the hearts and minds of Americans, white and Black.

Notes

1. "Jim Crow Scholars," *Alabama Citizen*, May 9, 1953.
2. Charles Houston, "The Need for Negro Lawyers," *Journal of Negro Education* 4, no. 49 (1935): 49–52.
3. Richard Bailey, "Magnet for Black Achievers," *Montgomery Advertiser*, February 11, 2011.
4. Jack Greenberg, *Crusaders in the Courts: How a Dedicated Band of Lawyers Fought for the Civil Rights Revolution* (New York: Basic Books, 1994).
5. Marshall Frady, *Wallace* (New York: Random House, 1996), 131.
6. Frady, *Wallace*, 8.
7. Carl T. Rowan, *Dream Makers, Dream Breakers: The World of Justice Thurgood Marshall* (Boston: Little Brown, 1993), 268.
8. Frady, *Wallace*, 9.
9. Fred Taylor and Hugh Sparrow, "No Segregation Compromise, Patterson Says," *Birmingham News*, January 19, 1959
10. Dan T. Carter, *The Politics of Rage: George Wallace, the Origins of the New Conservatism, and the Transformation of American Politics* (New York: Simon and Schuster, 1995), 94.
11. George Lewis, "'Scientific Certainty': Wesley Critz George, Racial Science and Organised White Resistance in North Carolina, 1954–1962," *Journal of American Studies* 38 (2004): 2, 227–247.
12. Fred D. Gray, *Bus Ride to Justice: The Life and Times of Fred D. Gray*, rev. ed. (Montgomery, AL: NewSouth Books, 2013).
13. US Department of Justice, "Racial Situation: School, Integrations Matters: Special Matters; Obstruction of Justice," Birmingham, Alabama, September 4, 1963.
14. James M. Washington, ed., *A Testament of Hope: The Essential Writings and Speeches of Martin Luther King, Jr.* (San Francisco: Harper San Francisco, 1986), 289–302.
15. W. D. Workman, "Savannah Case Holds Much Significance," *State*, May 13, 1963.
16. Associated Press, "Prof Claims Study Proves Negro Inferior," *Huntsville Times*, October 4, 1962.
17. "W. C. George Papers," UNC: University Libraries, Wilson Special Collections Library, University of North Carolina, https://finding-aids.lib.unc.edu/03822/#d1e511
18. "Race Study Plans," *Selma Times-Journal*, November 2, 1961.
19. Papers of the Tuskegee Civic Association, Tuskegee University.
20. David Lawrence, "School Desegregation Bill Introduced in Congress," *Troy Messenger*, February 18, 1963.
21. Fred Gray, Constance Baker Motley, Jack Greenberg, and Norman Amaker, Complaint, "In the United States District Court for the Middle District of Alabama Eastern Division," 2, Papers of George C. Wallace, Alabama Department of Archives and History.
22. UPI, "Desegregation Decision Implication Enormous," *Lincoln Journal*, April 2, 1967.
23. Fred D. Gray, Jack Greenberg, Constance Baker Motley, Charles H. Jones Jr., "Plaintiff's Objections to Defendant Macon County Board's Proposed Plan for Desegregation," Filed April 9, 1964, 3–4, Papers of George C. Wallace.

24 George Biggers III, "Some Public School Mixing Due in Four Alabama Areas this Fall," *Birmingham News,* August 16, 1963.
25 Arthur Osgood, "Over 100 State Police Turn Away Students," *Montgomery Advertiser,* September 3, 1963.
26 Papers of Burke Marshall, John F. Kennedy Library Archives.
27 "Don't' Let Wallace Seize the Schools," *Birmingham News,* September 3, 1963.
28 Fred Gray and Jack Greenberg, "In the United States District Court for the Middle District of Alabama, Eastern Division, Filed Feb 3, 1964, Civil Action No. 604-E," 5, Papers of George C. Wallace.
29 Fred D. Gray and Jack Greenberg, "In the United District Court for the Middle District of Alabama, Eastern Division, Filed Feb 10, 1964, Civil Action No. 604-E," 2.
30 UPI, "Alabama Set to Outlaw Integration," *Chicago Defender,* August 27, 1966
31 UPI, "The Anti-guidelines Law passed the Alabama Legislature in 1967: Judge Rives, U.S. Lawyer Don't Agree," *Alabama Journal,* February 3, 1967.
32 UPI, "5th U.S. Court Faces an Issue in School," *Alabama Journal,* February 20, 1967.
33 Lurleen Wallace, "Speech Prepared for Delivery by Lurleen B. Wallace, Governor of Alabama, Before the Legislature of Alabama in Joint Session Assembled First Special Session, 1967, Montgomery, Alabama, March 30, 1967," Papers of Lurleen B. Wallace, Alabama Department of Archives and History.
34 "State Superiority Again," *Sacramento Bee,* April 7, 1967.
35 Larry Tye, "RFK in the Heart of Dixie," *Anniston Star,* July 10, 2016
36 Gail Russell Chaddock, "Loretta Lynch Hearing: Why All Those Red Suits in the Crowd," *Christian Science Monitor,* January 29, 2015, www.csmonitor.com/USA/Politics/Decoder/2015/0129/Loretta-Lynch-hearing-Why-all-those-red-suits-in-the-crowd
37 "'I Am Not a Chamberlain; I Will Fight Like Churchill,'" *Dayton Daily News,* September 3, 1963.
38 "Auburn Negro Student Studies, Eats, on Previously All White Campus," *Greenville News,* January 7, 1964.
39 "Scientist Confirms Race Study Plans," *Selma Times-Journal,* November 2, 1961.
40 John Stewart, Director of Education, "The Struggle for Civil Rights—Session I," 04/28/1998. Boston: John F. Kennedy Library.

4

Oliver Hill, Spottswood Robinson III, and Black Legal Activism in Jim Crow Virginia

Marvin Chiles

Oliver White Hill and Spottswood William Robinson III were history-making black men. The civil rights attorneys from Richmond, Virginia, gained much of their notoriety from the contemporary public at the demise of the more recent "era of colorblindness."[1] Roughly two decades since their deaths (Robinson in 1998 and Hill in 2007), Virginia officials countered the Commonwealth's Lost Cause memory by renaming various streets and buildings as well as erecting historical markers in honor of accomplished black residents.[2] Hill and Robinson are two of the many black Virginians honored during this collective mentality shift. The most telling moves came in 2008 and 2020, with the erection of statues and historical markers in their honor.[3] These relics compelled Virginians to openly acknowledge and honor these men for their efforts to end racial segregation. Yet, as their legacy has been rightfully and more recently incorporated into Virginia's public memory, it has been tethered to the 9–0 US Supreme Court decision for the *Brown v. Board of Education* case, decided on May 17, 1954.

Recent memory and commemoration of Hill and Robinson has largely overshadowed their complete activist legacy and impact on Jim Crow Virginia. Many believe that Hill and Robinson connected the Commonwealth to the national "long civil rights movement" through suing Prince Edward County Public Schools in 1951.[4] The Supreme Court later consolidated this case with four others to form *Brown* (1954). The success of *Brown* (1954) is why many contemporary Virginians know of Hill and Robinson, and why current Virginia political leadership evoke their names to display their historical bona fides.[5] Less discussed and often ignored about these two men is that before *Davis* (1951) became a vital part of *Brown* (1954), Hill and Robinson spent the better part of two decades making Virginia more susceptible to the legal changes most associated with the long civil rights movement. It was these two decades that created the legal climate where *Davis* (1951) and *Brown* (1954) became possible. Thus, this chapter historicizes Hill's and Robinson's lesser discussed legal efforts before the 1950s. In the process, it expands their legacy beyond the confines of what is often called the "Big Bang" of *Brown* (1954), claiming that black Virginians, and especially their activist lawyers, were the prime engines of legal change in the Commonwealth during the mid-twentieth century.

Using newspaper articles, court cases, census data, and archival materials, I argue that Oliver Hill and Spottswood Robinson were the nexus that brought Virginia more in line with the trends associated with the long civil rights movement. Through legal campaigns for equal education and transportation in the World War II era (1935–1948), Hill and Robinson worked with middle-class black women to convert Virginia's black freedom struggle from sporadic mass mobilization efforts to a systematized legal push in the Jim Crow courts. With steady court victories, Hill and Robinson also aligned Virginia's strong black legal tradition with the broader trend of black lawyers assuming civil rights leadership through successful court campaigns.[6]

To date, the accomplished literature is heavily focused on the post-*Brown* era of massive resistance in the 1950s, passive resistance in the 1960s, and the antibusing activism of the 1970s. This focus reinforces the narrative that Virginia's main contribution to the black freedom struggle is *Brown* (1954).[7] Even Margaret Edds's monograph *We Face the Dawn* (2018) documents the lives of both Oliver Hill and Spottswood Robinson with *Brown* (1954) being the logical conclusion to decades of legal advocacy.[8] This chapter refocuses Virginia's civil rights narrative on the legal efforts before the 1950s. In doing so, it shows that black Virginians significantly contributed to the national civil rights movement well before *Brown* (1954), and that Hill and Robinson headed this patchwork effort through reinforcing black trust in constitutional and judicial law as well as the courts' ability to correct injustice through legal change. It was only after a generation of courtroom success did Hill, Robinson, and their supporters feel confident in seeking the complete end of racial segregation by the 1950s.

This legal history of Hill and Robinson's activism is timely because of more recent scholarly and popular emphasis on Virginia's place in the long civil rights movement. In terms of civil rights collective memory, the Commonwealth lies in the backdrop of states with more explosive episodes such as Georgia, Alabama, and Mississippi.[9] This dynamic comes from the belief in Virginia exceptionalism—the idea that Virginia's civil rights history is minimal because of the lack of large-scale racial violence between World War I and the end of World War II. Historians have corrected this issue since the 1990s, and this chapter ideologically fits well with works of that regard. As a historian once claimed, "No state [NAACP] conference in the nation did more than Virginia's, and n—law firm in Virginia did more than" the one ran by Hill and Robinson during the modern civil rights era.[10] This claim encapsulates this chapter's theme. Legal activism in Virginia fits well with the black freedom struggle given that Hill and Robinson filed and won more suits in Jim Crow Virginia than other attorneys did in other southern states.[11]

This chapter also seeks to establish Hill and Robinson as key contributors to the way scholars now understand race and law in contemporary American life. While legal scholars had long taken an interest in the intersection of race and law, it was not until the 1980s that historians seriously analyzed the relationship between the two, particularly in the South. The seminal *Ambivalent Legacy* (1984) argues that the South had been historically a legal backwater that was not in step with American law in general, because its codes violated the spirit of the US Constitution by openly benefiting the few at the behest of many. This scholarship largely ignored blacks as the actors of legal change, seeing them only as subject to the whims of oppressive regimes.[12]

Black legal histories—also known as "Black Bar Studies"—helped to correct this scholarly lacuna on black agency in American law. In aggregate, these works argue that black lawyers overtly professionalized and structuralized civil rights efforts through converting the direct-action protest and economic populism of the late nineteenth century into systemic legal pushes for equality by the mid-twentieth century.[13] This effort springboarded the sanitized and professionalized "traditional" civil rights movement for racial equality into the American consciousness after World War II. Thus, the notion of racial equality as a *legal right under law* long belied moral claims made by mass mobilization of the 1960s and electoral politics of the 1970s. While Charles Hamilton Houston, William Henry Hastie, and Thurgood Marshall are lauded as the legal minds of this generation of black lawyers, this chapter argues that Oliver Hill and Spottswood Robinson should be seen in a similar light given their efforts in Jim Crow Virginia.[14] Shaping Hill and Robinson's legal efforts was the ideological commitment that American law should be a progressive tool to benefit society, and especially the oppressed. This commitment, along with their savvy use of constitutional and judicial law to validate it, should put Hill and Robinson in the company of influential black legal minds of their age.

Becoming Black Virginia Lawyers in the Age of Jim Crow

The long civil rights movement put Hill and Robinson on the same path toward a shared legacy of legal activism. Paving this road was the radical transformation of the black legal profession just as they entered it. Hill and Robinson became black Virginia lawyers when black lawyering transitioned from an entrepreneurial avenue of racial uplift to securing racial equality through courtroom activism.[15]

While being born on separate sides of the track, Hill's and Robinson's backgrounds were more similar than they were different. Both were born in Richmond, Hill—originally named Charles B. White—in 1907, and Robinson in 1916. However, Hill was a child of the city's large black working class, while Robinson was a member of Richmond's small but prominent white-collar black middle class. Both had nurturing mothers who raised families while being married to alcoholic husbands. Hill's mother Olivia Lewis—a domestic worker—eventually divorced his biological father and printer William Henry White Jr. and remarried Joseph Cartwright, a federal employee from Washington, DC.[16] Robinson's mother Inez never divorced her successful entrepreneur and real estate attorney husband. Beyond affection, societal expectations had to have impacted Inez's decision. Middle-class blacks largely adhered to Victorian norms about marriage—namely that divorce brought shame upon the family. Thus, "proper" women shouldered the disproportionate burden of maintaining their family's reputation regardless of their husbands' misdeeds.[17] Both Hill and Robinson maintained a doggedness as lawyers because of their upbringing. Hill wished to overcome the burden of poverty. Robinson wanted to continue his familial legacy of white-collar professional employment.[18] Most importantly, both wanted to be better men than their fathers.

Hill and Robinson came of age in a Jim Crow city that was the microcosm of the state and region it rested in. By the 1910s, Hill and Robinson's hometown was a jewel in the New South crown. Richmond held the title of fifth largest southern city with a population of 85,000, an industrial economy worth $43,366,000, retail chains profiting $35 million annually, banks earning $165,901,000, residential real estate valued around $70 million, along with 75 sewer lines, and the nation's first ever electric streetcar system that transported over 7,000,000 passengers annually.[19] However, this economic prosperity was beyond the reach of most blacks, as they made up the majority of low-wage manufacturing and service labor.[20] While being home to large swaths of Virginia's black working poor, Richmond also had one of the nation's most prosperous black middle classes (in real estate, insurance, law, and banking)—a group that Robinson was born into.²¹ Uniting poor and well-off blacks was the rise of Jim Crow segregation. By the turn of the century, racial segregation and disenfranchisement was the law of the Southland. From Delaware to Texas, local, state, and private vendors segregated blacks into unequal public accommodations. Solidifying this reality were the courts, as they allowed disenfranchisement laws to bar blacks from ending Jim Crow via the ballot box.²²

Although they grew up on separate sides of the tracks in Richmond, Hill and Robinson found neutral footing upon matriculating at Howard University Law School. Black Virginian John Mercer Langston founded the program at a time when legal training became a prerequisite for admission to state bars. From the late nineteenth to the mid-twentieth century, Howard Law "bore a heavy responsibility," training nearly 80 percent of black American lawyers by the time Hill and Robinson attended in the 1930s.²³ Nearly every distinguished black lawyer in the two generations after the Civil War were Howard Law alums. For a long time, Howard Law was the only black law school in America.²⁴ This monopoly on black legal talent created an apathy that long prevented Howard Law from being an elite training ground. It was not until the hiring of Howard's first nonwhite president, Mordecai Johnson, and most importantly, his selection of Charles Hamilton Houston as law school dean in 1929, that Howard Law became a premiere program.²⁵

"When we started in 1930," the year after Hamilton took over, "Howard was not accredited by the American Bar Association and Association of American Law Schools," Oliver Hill later remembered correctly.²⁶ Until Johnson gave Houston control of Howard Law School, it was a subpar part-time program that accreditation agencies did not quite care for.²⁷ In seeking to make the program akin to his alma mater of Harvard Law School, Houston abolished Howard Law's night school, hired full-time black faculty, and taught rigorous legal theory courses. Because of this, Howard Law School gained full accreditation by 1931.²⁸

By the time Hill and Robinson matriculated at Howard Law, the program was in the vanguard of transforming the black legal profession into a respected institution in black life. Black lawyers, a group that began with the admission of Macon Bolling Allen to the Maine State Bar in 1844, were an endangered species by the time Houston took over Howard Law School.²⁹ There were only 1,230 black lawyers (many of whom being unbarred) and 159,735 white lawyers nationwide in 1930. "Negro lawyers today," complained Houston five years later, "are not sufficiently numerous or widely enough distributed to render the service desired."³⁰

The few black lawyers available were not desired by clients because of their limited formal legal training.[31] Oliver Hill once recalled in his memoir that white jurists often joked that they could tell an attorney was black by the amount of spelling and grammatical errors in their briefs.[32] Others were, as Houston once surmised, "the victim of subtle propaganda spread by the lower-class white lawyer to the effect that a Negro throws away his case in getting a Negro lawyer because a Negro lawyer has no influence with the Court."[33] For every black superstar litigator like A. T. Walden of Atlanta, Z. Alexander Looby of Nashville, or Perry Wilbon Howard Jr. of Jackson, Mississippi, for example, there were dozens of black attorneys who, because of their lack of training or the belief in the inferiority of black lawyers, had not garnered the respect of most black and white people.[34] Thus, many black lawyers served the black underclass in drafting wills, transferring deeds, conducting divorces, and in some cases, simply helping them read and sign contracts. This was the case until Houston assumed control of Howard Law School.

As Howard Law School transformed into a rigorous program, the reputation and competency of black lawyers drastically improved. Under Houston's leadership, Howard capitalized on its sheer monopoly on black legal talent by producing more competent black attorneys.[35] While the short inadequate supply of black lawyers was largely the result of American racism, it allowed Howard's curricular transformation to better impact the black legal profession. As will be discussed later in the chapter, Houston and Howard Law School faculty (through the NAACP Legal and Educational Defense Fund) also helped bolster the reputation of existing black attorneys by partnering with them on key civil rights cases between 1925 and 1935. This helped black communities view black lawyers as institutional pillars of morality and meritocratic competence.[36] Before Houston's transformation of Howard Law, William Hastie— friend, colleague, and fellow Harvard alumnus and future first black federal judge—admitted that "there were not ten Negro lawyers, competent and willing to handle substantial civil rights litigation" throughout the country.[37] After, however, black lawyers became the prime movers of the black freedom struggle.[38]

Undergirding the functional changes in the black legal profession was Howard Law's ideological commitment to making black attorneys into social engineers. By the time Houston got to Howard, many black people ideologically cast black lawyers as rugged businessmen. While some mischaracterized them as money-grubbing, dishonest grifters, others like historian Carter G. Woodson viewed them as more conservative entrepreneurs who embraced the Bookerite tradition of racial uplift through economic independence.[39]

In sum, many saw black lawyers as morally unfit to do civil rights work because of their concern over earning a living. Others like black legal scholar Fitzhugh Lee Styles were less skeptical, seeing black lawyers as wholly willing but inadequate in effectuating legal change in the courts.[40] Houston, however, believed that while pursuing profit within the industry, black lawyers had a moral obligation to use the courts to conform laws to black interests.[41] "It is where the pressure is greatest and racial antagonisms most acute," said Charles Houston "that the services of the Negro lawyer as a social engineer are needed." Black lawyers who practiced without an ideological commitment to social justice, Houston believed, were parasites who subjected their race to the bigoted judicial precedent of the past and present. "If a Negro law school is to make its full contribution to the social system," Houston once said in his call for more black lawyers, "it must train its students and send them into just such situations."[42] Houston's commitment and mission was a part of an early twentieth-century movement by some Harvard Law professors such as Felix Frankfurter and Roscoe Pound to undo injustice in American law by training socially conscious litigators.[43]

While Hill and Robinson's path *to* Howard could not have been any different, their path *through* Howard was remarkably similar. "The turning point in my life," said Spottswood Robinson years later, "was the day I put my foot in there [Howard Law School]."[44] Hill remembered that Houston often told enrollees to "look at the person on your left, look at the person on the right, 'cause one of you is not going to be here next year." Houston believed that black legal excellence required addition by subtraction. To churn out the most skilled black attorneys meant unsympathetically ejecting lesser students from the program. Houston's no-nonsense demeanor led to students like Hill and Robinson secretly calling the "strict disciplinarian" "Ironpants" and "Iron Shoes." Because they responded well to Houston's challenge, "we became his protégés," Hill later claimed about himself and Robinson. The best students became the closest to Houston, as they "would think in terms of how we were going to tackle *Plessy* right on through law school."[45]

Upon graduation and passing the Virginia Bar, Hill and Robinson became a part of the evolution of black esquires in Virginia and the South. Every former Confederate state had black lawyers by 1873.[46] By 1935, the region held 487 of America's 1,230 black lawyers, with only "100 Negro lawyers in the South devoting full time to practice." Southern black lawyers made less than half of the annual salary of a white teacher. Thus, despite Houston imploring his students to go south, he found that, "it has been extremely difficult to get the most promising law graduates to go South. Even students Southern born and bred are loathe to return."[47] Yet, Hill and Robinson went anyway, joining the tight-knit fraternity of black Virginia lawyers.

Black Virginia lawyering began with Howard Law School helping Wathal G. Wynn become the Commonwealth's first licensed black attorney in 1871.[48] Howard trained most of the second generation of black lawyers (1880s–1920s), namely political figures such as James H. Hayes (president of the National Negro Suffrage League), Alfred W. Harris (state legislator and founder of historically black Virginia State University), James A. Fields (state legislator), Andrew W.E. Bassette Jr. (assistant commonwealth attorney), J. Thomas Newsome (state legislator, newspaper editor, and attorney), and prominent legal practitioners B. F. Harris and Thomas Harris Reid of Portsmouth.[49] Despite the accomplishments of this bunch, black Virginians, particularly those of means, were like their economic counterparts around the nation in retaining white lawyers for their legal needs, especially if it involved civil rights.[50]

It was not until the legal success of NAACP attorneys and affiliates in the late 1920s that black Virginians began funneling their civil rights activism into the courts with black lawyers. In 1929 and 1930, Virginia native and Howard-trained lawyer Joseph Roland Pollard successfully litigated two pivotal anti-segregation and disenfranchisement cases in Richmond. These cases, heavily covered by black newspapers in Virginia and across the country, helped black Virginia communities gain faith that black lawyers would lead future fights for racial equality.[51] Pollard's untimely death in 1937 must have compelled Oliver Hill, Spottswood Robinson, and their associate Martin A. Martin to form the Hill, Martin, & Robinson firm and pick up where their fellow alumnus left off. Beyond the Richmond-based firm, they organized the Old Dominion Bar Association. Like the National Bar Association, the Old Dominion Bar Association (with Hill serving as longtime president) became a network of mostly Howard-trained attorneys in Virginia ensuring that black lawyers were abreast to the constant legal changes confronting their new civil rights agenda.[52] They did this because black lawyers in the South and nation were "uniformly excluded from the benefits of membership in [white] bar associations," Charles Houston once complained.[53] Black trust in more competent, socially conscious black lawyers was key because Virginia's freedom struggle was fully entrenched in the courts. By the time Hill and Robinson began their legal odyssey, blacks made up less than 1 percent of American attorneys and only 3 percent of litigators in Virginia.[54]

School Equalization in Virginia

Upon becoming licensed attorneys, Oliver Hill and Spottswood Robinson set out to "challenge the constitutionality of Virginia segregation laws."[55] Getting to this point, however, took some time for the Richmond duo. Hill was an admittedly underwhelming student who graduated from Howard Law in 1933 and passed the Virginia Bar shortly after.[56] In 1936, Robinson enrolled in Howard Law with a stellar undergraduate record from Virginia Union University in Richmond.[57] After graduation, Hill struggled mightily to establish himself as a Virginia lawyer while Robinson became a professor in Howard Law School because he earned the highest grades in school history to that point.[58] Robinson's rapid rise in the legal academe was rarely questioned. Fellow Howard Law student and future US District Court chief judge William B. Bryant said that Robinson "was probably the most serious student I'd seen," often working well into midnight, nearly every night.[59]

Because of Robinson's initial focus on teaching and scholarship, Hill took the lead in placing Virginia in the national civil rights movement through the school-equalization campaign of the mid-1930s. This movement was strongest in its advocacy for all-white local and state governments to pay black and white teachers the same. Because black legal activism shifted toward full racial integration by the 1950s, a historian once noted that, "the salary cases have been subsequently glossed over in the NAACP's history."[60] Many scholars overlook how the equalization movement reflected the marriage between black lawyers and grassroots activism during a time when integration was practically unfathomable. This marriage was ironically consummated in Southern courts, as this region-wide legal movement laid the foundation for what later became *Brown* (1954).

School equalization in the South began with the NAACP switching its legal strategy to include more black legal counsel. When the organization began litigating as early as 1910, their legal strategy reflected the sentiments of their mostly white founders and board members. That was to ensure court victories by contracting elite white lawyers such as Moorfield Storey (president of the American Bar Association), Arthur Spingarn, Louis Marshall, and others to litigate civil rights cases. By the mid-to-late 1920s, the NAACP opened its leadership ranks to more blacks (Walter White, Roy Wilkins, James Weldon Johnson, and others). It was from these men that the push to hire black attorneys came. This advocacy was not easy, as black lawyers were notorious for losing civil rights cases (mostly against segregation ordinances in the 1910s and 1920s) because of poor arguments, something that W.E.B Du Bois often complained about.[61] However, with the death of Marshall and Storey in

1929, black members advocated for and received $100,000 from the NAACP to fund more legal education for black attorneys—much of this taking place at Howard Law School. The NAACP also aided local black attorneys in presenting and winning key civil rights cases to help coax black communities into becoming members between 1925 and 1935. This strategy grew the organization by endearing it to Southern black communities through financing their lawyers to lead their legal civil rights movement. This strategy also debunked the common myth perpetuated by Southern white segregationists that civil rights suits were ploys by liberal northern whites to ruin the racial harmony of the South.[62]

Virginia was a part of the NAACP's membership growth in black southern communities. In the 1910s, the upstart NAACP eagerly expressed their desire to grow branches in Virginia's blackest cities. However, black Virginians, more so the urban bourgeoisie, maintained their independence from the "Radical New York Group" until the late 1920s.[63] One should not mistake this hesitancy to join the NAACP with a lack of activism. Black Virginians mobilized boycotts and legal challenges against disenfranchisement and segregation.[64] These efforts all failed while the NAACP won key desegregation (housing ordinances) victories across the South. This compelled black Virginians to create strong NAACP branches and align with the national attack on Jim Crow laws.[65] Aiding this alliance was the NAACP's financing of *Deans v. Richmond* (1929) and *West v. Bliley* (1930)—two voting-rights and housing-desegregation cases won by black Richmond attorney and Howard graduate Joseph Roland Pollard.[66]

When it became clear that the NAACP was fully invested in funding black lawyers' fight for civil rights in the Virginia courts, the black Virginia elite established solid branches in the blackest cities and counties between 1930 and 1934, around the same time black Virginia educators began their push for teacher-salary equalization.[67]

With black Virginians on board with the NAACP, they joined in the school-equalization movement. Yet this movement began outside the NAACP national orbit. Black Atlantans first pushed for school equalization during the World War I era—a time when the NAACP focused on undoing segregation ordinances, all-white primaries, and equal protection during criminal cases.[68] By 1931, white NAACP lawyer Nathan Ross Margold took notice of these independent movements and argued for an organizational shift toward suing southern school districts for their disparate investment in black and white education.[69] Adding teeth to this plan was Charles Houston, who enlisted his top Howard Law students to find black litigants and sue school boards in state and federal courts. Luckily, black southern lawyers were on solid legal ground. *Plessy* (1896)—separate but equal—relied on the equal protections clause in the Fourteenth Amendment. *Yick Wo v. Hopkins* (1886) and *McCabe v. Atchison, Topeka, & Santa Fe Railway Company* (1914) also aided the cause, as the US Supreme Court ruled that regardless of population size or need, the Fourteenth Amendment and *Plessy* (1896) required that separate facilities, and the policies governing them, had to be administered equally.[70]

Black Virginia educators enlisted their NAACP chapters to fight in the school-equalization movement. By the mid-1930s, the all-black Virginia Teachers Association (VTA)—a group of mostly black female tutors and teachers, along with male principals and college professors who raised hundreds of thousands of dollars to subsidize failing black schools—demanded that white Virginia leaders be held accountable for the *equal* portion of separate but equal.[71] VTA's internal studies unearthed that in sum, white Virginia teachers made nearly $900 a year while blacks made less than $500 with equal credentials.[72] Thus, at the 1934 annual meeting, VTA moved away from self-help and toward constitutional demands for equal rights and services under law. Over 3,500 black teachers (mostly members) and the black Virginia press (*Richmond Afro-American* and *Norfolk Journal and Guide*) donated to this cause by 1937. Therefore, hundreds of black teachers across Virginia (Chesterfield, Richmond, Sussex, Middlesex, Surry, Pulaski, Goochland, Allegheny, and Norfolk) began asking their all-white school boards to equalize their salaries by 1938 with the understanding that they would be fired.[73] As mass firings happened, the VTA engaged in legal action with the help of Oliver Hill.

Oliver Hill began his legal aid for school equalization in Norfolk. Black Norfolk was more assertive in its push for education equality than any other Virginia community. They had the most active VTA members, many of whom helped charter what later became Norfolk State University in 1935.[74] Three years later, the Norfolk Teachers Association (NTA—subsidiary of the Virginia Teachers Association formed in 1938) financed Aline Elizabeth Black's petition against the all-white Norfolk School Board to equalize teacher pay.[75] The Norfolk School Board and state courts denied the petition, claiming that black teachers waived their Fourteenth Amendment rights to equal protections by signing a legally binding contract. Black's case ended by the summer of 1938, as the school board refused to renew her contract before Hill appealed to the federal courts on her behalf.[76] The NTA paid Hill to file another case in the federal courts for Melvin Alston in 1939. Federal judge Luther B. Way ruled the same way as the Norfolk courts did with Black. However, the Fourth Circuit Court of Appeals in Richmond ruled in favor of Alston and Hill in June 1940. While upholding the binding nature of contractual agreements, the court opined that discrimination of pay based upon race was illegal because it violated the equal protections clause of the Fourteenth Amendment. More importantly, the courts ruled that no one can simply sign away their constitutional rights.[77]

The success in Norfolk followed Hill to Richmond, where he took a more subtle approach to equalize teacher wages. Unlike Norfolk, Richmond race relations relied heavily on paternalistic interracial cooperation between black and white elites.[78] However, this culture was not present in City Hall in the spring of 1941, when the Richmond Teachers Association (RTA—another subsidiary of the Virginia Teachers Association) retained Hill after more than a year of negotiating with the all-white Richmond school board to equalize teacher pay.[79] When RTA retained Hill, the school board flatly refused to negotiate with them any further, so Hill filed a petition against the board in November 1941 for black female teacher Antionette Bowler. She instructed Hill to push the case as far as the US Supreme Court with the understanding that her career was on the line.[80] After the school board ignored her petition, Hill filed *Bowler v. Richmond* (1941) in the federal courts by December 1941. The school board quickly reversed their decision, and by May 1942, they agreed to equalize black and white teacher pay.[81]

Hill's equalization work in Virginia was in lockstep with similar efforts throughout the South. Like in Virginia, the neglect of black Southern education writ large was based on the custom of white northern philanthropists financially supporting black schools because of the educational apartheid enforced by white southern officials.[82] Individually, white teachers earned around $1,000 a year while some black teachers earned as little as $200 annually.[83] Black Southern educators in sum earned nearly $600,000 less than their white counterparts annually in each state. In Florida, the aggregate disparity was $1.3 million. On average, across the South, black teachers earned 61 percent of what white teachers earned—the lowest being 38 percent in Mississippi. With the help of NAACP lawyers, black state teacher associations in Maryland, Delaware, Alabama, North Carolina, Louisiana, Tennessee, Mississippi, South Carolina, Kentucky, Arkansas, and Florida filed and won several equalization suits between 1935 and 1945.[84] In sum, the NAACP won 27 of the 31 equalization cases that entered the state and federal courts.[85]

Many white state leaders combated court-ordered equalization with firings and credentialling compensation metrics.[86] Maryland's William B. Gibbs—the first ever litigant for equalized Southern school spending—was fired after winning his case.[87] VTA Chairman Wesley D. Elam's and Principal Julia Pritchett's "connection[s] with the salary fight," said the *Norfolk Journal and Guide*, earned them pink slips from Alexandria City Public Schools in Virginia.[88] School boards in Norfolk County, Pulaski, and Newport News also dismissed black educators who were known supporters of the equalization movement.[89] School boards in Chesterfield, Fredericksburg, Newport News, King George, Surry, Arlington, and Gloucester also implemented competency (or IQ) testing, using disparate scores to avoid paying black teachers equally. Hill and Robinson consolidated these cases and won federal court victories by 1950.[90] Yet, all-white school boards' insistent evasion of educational equality compelled the black South to support desegregation litigation, later culminating in *Brown* (1954).[91]

Equalizing Transportation

As school-equalization cases made their way through the Virginia courts, another issue arose that specifically garnered Spottswood Robinson's attention. By 1944, Oliver Hill served in a noncombat army unit in France during World War II.[92] Thus, Robinson was alone running their newly formed law firm in Richmond when Miss Irene Morgan entered his office in the fall of that same year. In July 1944, the 27-year-old black Baltimorean boarded a Greyhound bus to head home after visiting family in Gloucester County, Virginia. When the bus stopped in the town of Saluda, the white bus driver demanded that Morgan surrender her seat to accommodate two oncoming white passengers. Morgan refused. Police responded by dragging her off the bus and arresting her for violating Virginia's Jim Crow transportation statute. Morgan retained Robinson to fight her unlawful arrest. A local judge added insult to injury by convicting Morgan in October 1944. Feeling that he had a chance to overturn the decision, Robinson quickly filed a motion to appeal in a superior court.

While some deem Morgan's incident as the prelude to the Rosa Parks incident in Montgomery, Alabama, over a decade later, it was, in fact, far from it.[93] Parks's protest spearheaded the mainstream mass mobilization efforts of the "Traditional" civil rights movement. Morgan's actions were not premeditated or planned by any civil rights organization. There were no organized boycotts or walking campaigns to protest the injustice inflicted upon her. Any attempts in that direction would not have worked. Thus, the seed money for Morgan's appeal came out of her own pocket, and her situation, while gaining some publicity, lived its full life behind the veil of the Virginia courts. Uniqueness defined Morgan's case, as it straddled the line between consumer and citizenship rights. Because of this, the skilled law professor Spottswood Robinson concocted the perfect legal case, helping Morgan etch her name in history as the woman who helped overturn *Plessy* (1896).

Robinson's agreeing to appeal Morgan's conviction helped fortify Virginia's anti–Jim Crow legal movement. "Transportation in the Southern states," said

Herman H. Long, president of the United Negro College Fund in 1954, "has [long] been characterized over the years by a consistent pattern of racial segregation and its attendant discrimination."[94] Historians have long argued that the codification of racially segregated travel began in the antebellum North. It was not until after the Civil War, however, that it became a southern problem. Pre-Reconstruction Southern governments imposed severe segregation restrictions on most common carriers. Although the Civil Rights Act of 1875 and subsequent state laws banned segregated accommodations, transit providers, southern legislators, and blacks were still embroiled in the cauldron of legal interpretation, as white providers and lawmakers continued imposing segregation rules. Blacks, on the other hand, used the courts to combat them.[95]

Morgan sought relief in the courts when southern blacks had a long contemptuous relationship with judicial interpretation and segregationists. In cases such as *Hall v. DeCuir* (1868), *Railroad Company v. Brown* (1873), *Cully v. Baltimore & Ohio R.R.* (1876), and *Chesapeake, Ohio & Southwestern Railroad v. Wells* (1887), *Heard v. Georgia* (1888), *State ex rel. Abbott v. Hicks* (1892), and others, blacks sued to end segregation on mass transit citing the equal protections clause in the Fourteenth Amendment of the US Constitution. Local, state, and US Supreme Courts jointly agreed that interstate travel came under congressional authority, and because of that racial segregation was not permitted. However, via the Civil Rights Cases of 1883, one of which being *Robinson v. Memphis & Charleston Railroad* (1883), the US Supreme Court overturned the Civil Rights Act of 1875, claiming that federal bans on segregated intrastate travel could not be based on the equal protections clause in the Fourteenth Amendment. Rather, it must be based on the commerce clause in the Tenth Amendment, as racial segregation impacted the efficiency of interstate commerce.

Legal loopholes allowed transit providers and Southern legislatures to segregate travel. Under the Tenth Amendment, state governments and transit providers had autonomous police powers in regulating travel. In some cases, as with *Green v. Bridgeton* (1879), the federal courts extended state and transit autonomy to interstate travel, allowing for racial segregation if the accommodations were "equal."[96] With the courts placing travel in the legal framework of the Tenth Amendment, legislatures and transit providers undercut the equal protections clause granted under the Fourteenth Amendment, which became the legal foundation for *Plessy* (1896). "It is clear," a legal historian argued, "that the Supreme Court was compelled [by popular sentiment and Southern custom] to distort cases before it could pollute the stream of the law with the 'separate but equal' doctrine."[97] Southern state governments and transit providers responded to *Plessy* (1896) by mandating segregated travel between 1898 and 1910.[98]

Segregated transportation generated the first phase of mass mobilization in the long civil rights movement. In Virginia, "acceptance by the whites of racial mingling on the railroads was encouraged" in the 1870s and 1880s, historian Charles Wynes found. While most Virginia transit carriers expected blacks and whites to segregate, they did not require it. In some cases, "well-dressed Negroes" traveled with whites and "poorly dressed whites were sometimes found in the Negro car." In all, Wynes concluded that "by the end of the nineteenth century, it was customary for the races to ride together on most of the railroads of Virginia without confinement to ... a Jim Crow car" on the part of blacks. By 1900, however, white Virginians clamored for their commonwealth to act like its neighboring southern states and enact more rigid segregation, especially in transit.[99] This call for racial apartheid did not go over quietly. Historians August Meier, Elliot Rudwick, and more recently Blair L. M. Kelley show that black Virginians protested segregated travel throughout Virginia. By 1906, the Virginia legislature ensured that segregated travel was the law of the land, and with *Plessy* (1896) no amount of protest would reverse it.[100]

Under the historical weight of both law and custom was a glimmer of hope for Irene Morgan's case. Strengthening Spottswood Robinson's appeal was the fact that every incremental legal gain in the fight against segregated travel had been made by black female litigants. Nearly 70 percent of antidiscrimination suits involving transportation between 1855 and 1914 involved black women.[101] They had the strongest legal cases because transit companies refused to provide them with accommodations (usually nonsmoking sections) equal with that of white women, even when they previously paid for them.

In 1868, Josephine DeCuir's (Louisiana) and Catherine Brown's (Virginia) suits established the precedent that segregated travel could not exist on interstate carriers.[102] Anne Williams (Wisconsin) in 1870, Milly Anderson (Texas) in 1876, Jane Brown (Tennessee) in 1880, anti-lynching advocate Ida B. Wells (Tennessee) in 1884, and Lola Houck (Texas) in 1888 compelled state and federal courts to establish that blacks had a right to travel on mass transit, and that transit providers must honor the tickets they sold to their patrons regardless of race. Furthermore, blacks who paid for first class accommodations must receive them.[103] This was important because black female litigants helped infuse the Tenth Amendment (commerce clause) with the spirit of the Fourteenth Amendment, ensuring that under law, black patrons must receive equal treatment with white patrons.[104] Thus, it was black women who first made the fight against segregated travel a legal one, and it was their legal fight that made the issue one of equal rights as a consumer and not rights as a citizen.

Robinson must have entered the Virginia courts extremely confident. Most black attorneys rooted civil rights cases in the equal protections clause of the Fourteenth Amendment, as was taught by Charles Houston and other law professors at Howard Law School. However, the US Supreme Court long separated the exercise of travel from equal protections. Robinson—the legal scholar—knew that the Tenth Amendment, while not being a child of Reconstruction like the Fourteenth Amendment, provided a slim ground for racial equality, and that that ground was based on consumer rights. Robinson's argument for Morgan's appeal was simple: Greyhound denied Morgan the accommodations she paid for on an interstate vessel. Under the Tenth Amendment, and subsequent cases involving segregated travel, blacks were entitled to receive the services they paid for. On those two grounds, Robinson argued, Morgan was not bound by Virginia's Jim Crow travel laws. Furthermore, she should never have been demanded to relinquish her seat for white passengers. The circuit and state appellate courts affirmed the conviction and fines, forcing Robinson and Morgan to appeal to the US Supreme Court.

By the summer of 1945, when the case was to be heard, Robinson had to sit at the counsel table as an aide and watch fellow NAACP attorneys and mentors Thurgood Marshall and William Hastie argue his case. While he rewrote the brief and perfecting the legal argument, Robinson was not yet eligible to argue in front of the US Supreme Court. To the amazement of many, the Supreme Court agreed with Robinson's argument as presented by Marshall and Hastie. They affirmed that states have flexibility in enforcing interstate travel laws that only Congress can make. Yet Congress made it crystal clear that racially segregated interstate travel was illegal. They also agreed that Morgan was unjustly denied the accommodation she paid for. Furthermore, in an 8–1 decision, the Supreme Court cracked the foundation of *Plessy* (1896) by siding with Morgan and Robinson.

Brown v. Board (1954): The Road to Legacy

The durability of Virginia's Jim Crow regime compelled Oliver Hill and Spottswood Robinson to make their legal activism more aggressive. White Virginia legislators took notice of the legal changes happening in the state and federal courts. Thus in 1946, the all-white legislature passed a law strengthening penalties against "disorderly conduct" on mass transportation, further empowering private vendors to eject riders who would not conform to their rules.[105] This shell game ensured that regardless of the changes in judicial law, blacks and whites continued receiving both separate and unequal treatment on mass transit in Virginia. The transportation issue was related directly to the education issue. Despite black and white teachers receiving pay equity in some parts of Virginia, public education spending remained separate and unequal, particularly regarding facilities and bus transportation. Between 1943 and 1950, Hill and Robinson pursued several cases to expand their equalization movement by suing for equal school resource funding and for the end of all segregation on mass transit.[106] While winning some of the cases, Hill and Robinson faced many defeats. The reason was that the case law they cited fundamentally argued for equalizing Jim Crow segregation, and not for fully dismantling it.[107]

With that in mind, Hill and Robinson, along with the NAACP national offices in New York City, entered the 1950s with a new legal strategy to dismantle Jim Crow segregation. Robinson led this charge, as he accepted the national and state NAACP task to document the disparate conditions in Virginia schools. Hill focused his attention on integrating schools in southwestern Virginia districts via judicial fiat. Hill's argument was that the black population in this area was so small, that these counties could not equally fund segregated schools. Aiding their various endeavors was a letter sent to Hill's and Robinson's law offices on April 24, 1951. In this short note, two black teenage schoolgirls from Prince Edward County, Virginia, named Carrie Stokes and Barbara Johns asked the famous legal duo for "help" with their "inadequate" facilities at their segregated Robert Russa Moton High School.[108]

The events in Prince Edward reflected the newest legal phase of the modern civil rights movement. Proceeding the letter, nearly 500 black students walked out of Robert Russa Moton High School in protest of their school conditions. This walkout was not spontaneous, but a result of years of black activism for newer school facilities. Because Prince Edward blacks pushed for newer segregated facilities, and not integrated schools, Hill and Robinson admittedly did not want to take their case to court. However, after local leaders and the potential plaintiffs agreed to be the test case for desegregated southern education, Hill and Robinson agreed to sue the school system. On May 23, 1951, Hill and Robinson filed the famous *Davis v. Prince Edward* (1951) in the Federal Eastern District Court of Virginia. By March 1954, the court connected *Davis* (1951) with four other cases to form *Brown* (1954). Along with a subsequent ruling for the enforcement of Brown (1954)—also known as *Brown II* (1955)—school segregation in the South was officially on borrowed time.

After *Brown* (1954) and *Brown II* (1956), Hill and Robinson faded from the spotlight of the modern civil rights movement. The 1960s is known as the age when sit-ins and marches took precedent over legal battles. Hill and Robinson welcomed this much. In a 1961 interview, Robinson, who resigned from the NAACP National Legal Committee and his own private practice to become the dean of Howard Law School and a member of President John F. Kennedy's US Civil Rights Commission, admitted that the "fight for full equality cannot be won in the courtroom alone." Robinson lamented the limitations of the legal movement he helped lead by saying, "Missionaries [activists] are needed to work among the people to remove misconceptions about solving the non-legal problems."[109] While serving on the Federal Housing Authority as a private contractor in the 1960s, Hill agreed with Robinson by saying that despite the legal gains they made, he would not "pretend that the situation [race relations] is ideal." He went on to say that he supported "the present wave of sit-ins, wade-ins, [and] kneel-ins," because his legal experience taught him that "segregationists [have a] disrespect for the normal processes of law."[110]

As the age of civil rights succumbed to the era of colorblindness, Hill's and Robinson's careers took them in opposite directions. The "meticulous jurist" Robinson left Howard Law to serve on the US Circuit Court of DC in 1964.[111] Two years later, he joined the DC Court of Appeals, a post he held until his retirement in 1989.[112] Hill continued practicing law privately while doing numerous speaking engagements about race and law until his health failed him in the late 1990s.[113]

As Hill and Robinson drifted further apart professionally, their legacies remained tethered together by the popular memory of *Brown* (1954).[114] Virginia' first (and to this date only) black governor, L. Douglas Wilder, claimed that he "would have never become governor had it not been for the efforts of . . . civil rights attorneys Spottswood Robinson, III., and Oliver Hill."[115] President William J. Clinton awarded the 92-year-old Hill the Presidential Medal of Freedom—the highest civilian honor. He was only the second Virginian to receive the honor behind James Farmer, founder of the Congress of Racial Equality. His namesake was also put on the NAACP Freedom Fighter Award, an accolade that he won upon its inception.[116] The Virginia legislature honored both men with statues on the capitol grounds in 2007, the year that both men were finally laid to rest.[117] The legislature also erected statues of black children who represented the students of Prince Edward County. The narrative of their lives and the reason they were honored centered on their participation in *Brown* (1954).[118]

Before *Brown* (1954), Oliver Hill and Spottswood Robinson rose above their humble beginnings and took part in the fundamental transformation of black lawyering in America and Virginia. Hill and Robinson enhanced the black legal profession—their cultural inheritance—by thrusting black Virginia's movement for racial equality into the Jim Crow courts. Their legal efforts, victories and defeats, set the foundation for desegregation efforts that proceeded them in the 1960s. They proved that a racist legal system could be a vehicle for racial progress, and that equality is an incremental game with incremental gains. Furthermore, while *Brown* (1954) was an important contribution to the movement for racial equality in America, Hill and Robinson's legacy should not be confined to it.

Notes

1 William Julius Wilson, *The Declining Significance of Race* (Chicago: University of Chicago Press, 1980); Eduardo Bonilla-Silva, *Racism without Racists: Color-Blind Racism and the Persistence of Racial Inequality in Contemporary America* (Lanham, MD: Rowman and Littlefield, 2003); and Tim Wise, *Colorblind: The Rise of Post Racial Politics and the Retreat from Racial Equity* (San Francisco: City Light, 2010).
2 Marvin T. Chiles, "An Honest Conversation about Race: Racial Reconciliation in Richmond, 1954–Present" (PhD diss., University of Georgia, 2020), 177–189.
3 "New Markers Honor Oliver Hill and Spottswood Robinson," 12 On Your Side, February 6, 2020, www.nbc12.com/2020/02/07/new-historic-markers-honor-oliver-hill-spottswood-robinson/
4 James T. Patterson, *Brown v. Board of Education: A Civil Rights Milestone and Its Troubled Legacy* (Oxford: Oxford University Press, 2001); Robert K. Poch, "Shaping Freedom's Course: Charles Hamilton Houston, Howard University, and Legal Instruction on US Civil Rights," *American Educational History Journal* 39, no. 2 (2012): 417–431. Popularized by historian Jaquelyn Dowd Hall in 2005, the "Long Civil Rights Movement" is a chronological and thematic concept arguing that black civil rights activism involved a *longue durée* for human rights that began around World War II. In feeling that the chronology is unjustly limited to the World War II era, this phrase will be employed throughout the chapter to encompass black activism since the early twentieth century.
5 "A Tribute to Oliver White Hill," statement made by Representative Bobby Scott at the Oliver White Hill Foundation, May 1, 2007, https://bobbyscott.house.gov/media-center/floor-statements/tribute-oliver-white-hill
6 August Meier and Elliott Rudwick, "Attorneys Black and White: A Case Study of Race Relations within the NAACP," *Journal of American History* 62, no. 4 (March 1976): 913–946.
7 Benjamin Muse, *Virginia's Massive Resistance* (Bloomington: University of Indiana Press, 1961); Robbins L. Gates, *The Making of Massive Resistance: Virginia's Politics*

of Public School Desegregation, 1954–1956 (Chapel Hill: University of North Carolina Press, 1964), 1–24; Robert A. Pratt, *The Color of Their Skin: Education and Race in Richmond, Virginia, 1954–89* (Charlottesville: University of Virginia Press, 1992); Matthew D. Lassiter and Andrew B. Lewis, eds., *The Moderates' Dilemma: Massive Resistance to School Desegregation in Virginia* (Charlottesville: University of Virginia Press, 1998); James R. Sweeney, "Southern Strategies," *Virginia Magazine of History and Biography* 106, no. 2 (Spring 1998): 165–200; Alexander S. Leidholdt, *Standing before the Shouting Mob: Lenoir Chambers and Virginia's Massive Resistance to Public School Integration* (Tuscaloosa: University of Alabama Press, 1997); Sara K. Eskridge, "Virginia's Pupil Placement Board and the Practical Applications of Massive Resistance, 1956–1966," *Virginia Magazine of History and Biography* 118, no. 3 (June 2010): 246–276; James R. Sweeney, ed., *Race, Reason, and Massive Resistance: The Diary of David J. Mays, 1954–1959* (Athens: University of Georgia Press, 2008); William P. Hustwit, *James J. Kilpatrick: Salesman for Segregation* (Chapel Hill: University of North Carolina Press, 2013); Jeffrey E. Littlejohn and Charles H. Ford, "Booker T. Washington High School, History, Identity, and Educational Equality in Norfolk, Virginia," *Virginia Magazine of History and Biography* 124, no.2 (Winter 2016): 134–162; Jeffrey E. Littlejohn and Charles H. Ford, *Elusive Equality: Desegregation and Resegregation in Norfolk's Public Schools* (Charlottesville: University of Virginia Press, 2012); Brian J. Daugherity, *Keep On Keeping On: The NAACP and the Implementation of Brown v. Board of Education in Virginia* (Charlottesville: University of Virginia Press, 2016); Jill Ogline Titus, *Brown's Battleground: Students, Segregationists, and the Struggle for Justice in Prince Edward County, Virginia* (Chapel Hill: University of North Carolina Press, 2011); Phillip Hamilton, "Race, Politics, and Education in Tidewater Virginia: Christopher Newport College and the Shoe Lane Controversy of 1960–63," *Virginia Magazine of History and Biography* 119, no. 3 (2011): 245–275; and Tamara Kennelly, "The Quiet Path of an Invisible Man: Irving Peddrew, III and Desegregation at Virginia Tech," *Virginia Magazine of History and Biography* 126, no. 4 (2018): 422–466.

8 Margaret Edds, *We Face the Dawn: Oliver Hill, Spottswood Robinson, III., and the Legal Team That Dismantled Jim Crow* (Charlottesville: University of Virginia Press, 2018).

9 Robert A. Pratt, "New Directions in Virginia's Civil Rights History," *Virginia Magazine of History and Biography* 104, no. 1 (Winter 1996): 149–151.

10 Edds, *We Face the Dawn*, 144.

11 "Civil Rights Lawyer Gets Honored," *Atlanta Daily World*, May 27, 1999, 2.

12 David J. Bodenhamer and James W. Ely Jr., eds., *Ambivalent Legacy: A Legal History of the South* (Jackson: University Press of Mississippi, 1984); W. Hamilton Bryson and E. Lee Shepard, "The Virginia Bar, 1870–1900," in *The New High Priests: Lawyers in Post-Civil War America*, ed. Gerard W. Gawalt (Westport, CT: Greenwood Press, 1984); and J. R. Oldfield, "A High and Honorable Calling: Black Lawyers in South Carolina, 1868–1915," *Journal of American Studies* 23, no. 3 (December 1989): 395–406. Much of the recent legal scholarship about the South resulted from the Legal History of the South Conference in 1983.

13 The key books that historicize civil rights litigation are Loren Miller, *The Petitioners: The Story of the Supreme Court and the Negro* (New York: Pantheon, 1966); Doug McAdam, *Political Process and the Development of Black Insurgency, 1930–1970* (Chicago:

University of Chicago Press, 1982), 133; Genna Rae McNeil, *Groundwork: Charles Hamilton Houston and the Struggle for Civil Rights* (Philadelphia: University of Pennsylvania Press, 1983); Mark Tushnet, *The NAACP Legal Strategy against Segregated Education, 1925-1950* (Chapel Hill: University of North Carolina Press, 1987); J. Clay Smith Jr., *Emancipation: The Making of the Black Lawyer, 1884-1994* (Philadelphia: University of Pennsylvania Press, 1993); Mark Tushnet, *Making Civil Rights Law: Thurgood Marshall and the Supreme Court, 1936-1961* (Oxford: Oxford University Press, 1996); Michael Klarman, *From Jim Crow to Civil Rights: The Supreme Court and The Struggle for Racial Equality* (Oxford: Oxford University Press, 2004), 95; Tomiko Brown-Nagin, *Courage to Dissent: Atlanta and the Long History of the Civil Rights Movement* (Oxford: Oxford University Press, 2011); Kenneth W. Mack, *Representing the Race: The Creation of the Civil Rights Lawyer* (Cambridge, MA: Harvard University Press, 2014); W. Lewis Burke, *All for Civil Rights: African American Lawyers in South Carolina, 1868-1968* (Athens: University of Georgia Press, 2017). Other key works are Fitzhugh Lee Styles, *Negroes and the Law* (Boston: Christopher Publishing House, 1937); Charles S. Magnum Jr., *The Legal Status of the Negro* (Chapel Hill: University of North Carolina Press, 1940); Walter J. Leonard, "The Development of the Black Bar," *Annals of the American Academy of Political and Social Science* 407, no. 1 (May 1973): 134-143; Will Sarvis, "Leaders in the Court and Community: Z. Alexander Looby, Avon N. Williams Jr., and the Legal Fight for Civil Rights in Tennessee, 1940-1970," *Journal of African American History* 88, no. 1 (Winter 2003): 42; Robert Jerome Glennon, "The Role of Rights Movement: The Montgomery Bus Boycott, 1955-1957," *Law and History Review* 9, no.1 (Spring 1991): 59-112; Randall Kennedy, "Martin Luther King's Constitution: A Legal History of the Montgomery Bus Boycott," *Yale Law Journal* 98, no. 6 (April 1989): 999-1067; Judith Kilpatrick, "(Extra)Ordinary Men: African-American Lawyers and Civil Rights in Arkansas before 1950," *Arkansas Law Review* 53, no.2 (2000): 299-399; Abraham L. Davis, "The Role of Black Colleges and Black Law Schools in the Training of Black Lawyers and Judges: 1960-1980," *Journal of Negro History* 70, no. 1/2 (Winter-Spring 1985): 24-34; Irvin C. Mollison, "Negro Lawyers in Mississippi," *Journal of Negro History* 15, no. 1 (January 1930): 38-71; Kenneth W. Mack, "Law and Mass Politics in the Making of the Civil Rights Lawyer, 1931-1941," *Journal of American History* 93, no.1 (June 2006): 37-62; Kenneth W. Mack, "Rethinking Civil Rights Lawyering and Politics in the Era before 'Brown,'" *Yale Law Journal* 115, no. 2 (November 2005): 256-354; Kenneth W. Mack, "Law and Mass Politics in the Making of the Civil Rights Lawyer, 1931-1941," *Journal of American History* 93, no. 1 (June 2006): 37-62; and Meier and Rudwick, "Attorneys Black and White," 913-946.

14 "National Bar Association Founders," accessed April 22, 2024, http://dsmpublicartfoundation.org/wp-content/uploads/2016/02/About-Founders.pdf
15 Mack, "Rethinking Civil Rights Lawyering," 278-279.
16 Oliver Hill Birth Certificate, May 1, 1907, Registration No. 24910, Virginia Department of Health, Virginia, Births, 1864-2016; US Federal Census 1920, Census Place: Washington, Washington, District of Columbia; Roll: T625-212; Page: 5B, Enumeration District: 303; Julian Bond and Oliver Hill, "Interview with Oliver W. Hill," *Virginia*

Quarterly Review, 80, no.1 (Winter 2004): 9–15; and Edds, *We Face the Dawn,* 18–23. Oliver Hill took his stepfather's last name and the masculine version of his mother's first name upon reaching adulthood.
17 US Federal Census 1900, Richmond, Monroe Ward, Richmond City, Virginia; Roll: 1738; Page: 4A; Enumeration District: 0073; FHL microfilm: 1241738; Edds, *We Face the Dawn,* 28–30; and Marvin Chiles, "Black Elites" and "Black Middle Class," in *World of Jim Crow: A Daily Life Encyclopedia,* ed. Steven A. Reich (Westport, CT: Greenwood Press, 2019), 253–259 and 332–336.
18 Edds, *We Face the Dawn,* 1–45.
19 James K. Sanford, ed., *Richmond: Her Triumphs, Tragedies, and Growth* (Richmond, VA: Richmond Chamber of Commerce, 1975), 90–92.
20 Stephen J. Hoffman, *Race, Class, and Power in the Building of Richmond, 1870-1920* (Jefferson, NC: McFarland Press, 2004), 4–26.
21 Raymond Gavins, "Urbanization and Segregation: Black Leadership Patterns in Richmond, Virginia, 1900-1920," *South Atlantic Quarterly* 79, no.3 (Summer, 1980): 258–261.
22 Charles E. Wynes, "The Evolution of Jim Crow Laws in Twentieth Century Virginia," *Phylon* 28, no. 4 (1967): 416–425.
23 Davis, "Role of Black Colleges," 26.
24 McNeil, *Groundwork,* 62; and Meier and Rudwick, "Attorneys White and Black," 918.
25 Okianer Christian Dark, "The Role of Howard University School of Law in *Brown v. Board of Education*," *Washington History* 16, no.2 (Fall/Winter 2004/2005): 83–85.
26 Oliver W. Hill Sr., *The Big Bang: Brown v. Board of Education and Beyond: The Autobiography of Oliver W. Hill, Sr.* (Geneva, IL: Grant House, 2007), 81.
27 Rayford W. Logan, *Howard University: The First Hundred Years, 1867-1967* (New York: New York University Press, 1969), 219–225; and W. E. B. Du Bois, "The Cultural Missions of Atlanta University," *Phylon* 3, no. 2 (1942): 105–115.
28 McNeil, *Groundwork,* 63–75.
29 Leonard, "Development of the Black Bar," 136.
30 Charles H. Houston, "The Need for Negro Lawyers," *Journal of Negro Education* 4, no. 1 (January 1935): 49–52.
31 Aspiring black attorneys had immense trouble getting into any American law schools, let alone the most exclusive. Northern, midwestern, and west coast law schools admitted only the most highly recommended, affluent, and academically promising black students. Southern law schools rejected them outright. Thus, most aspiring black law students remained stonewalled from most law schools until the 1960s. For more, see Meier and Rudwick, "Attorneys Black and White," 915–916, and Leonard, "Development of the Black Bar," 137–139.
32 Hill, *Big Bang,* 76–77.
33 Houston, "Need for Negro Lawyers."
34 Meier and Rudwick, "Attorneys Black and White," 916; Neil R. McMillen, "Perry W. Howard, Boss of Black and Tan Republicanism, 1924-1960," *Journal of Southern History* 48, no. 2 (May 1982): 205–224; Brown-Nagin, *Courage to Dissent;* and Sarvis, "Leaders in the Court and Community."

35 Leonard, "Development of the Black Bar," 139.
36 Mack, "Law and Mass Politics," 39–42; Mack, "Rethinking Civil Rights Lawyering," 266–268; and Meier and Elliott Rudwick, "Attorneys Black and White," 914–921.
37 William H. Hastie, "Toward an Equalitarian Legal Order, 1930–1950," *Annals of the American Academy of Political and Social Science* 407 (May 1973): 21.
38 G. Franklin Edwards, *The Negro Professional Class* (Glencoe, IL: Free Press, 1959), 137; and William H. Hastie, "Charles Hamilton Houston (1895–1950)," *Crisis Magazine*, 57, no.6 (June 1950): 364–365.
39 Mack, "Law and Mass Politics," 38–40; Mack, "Rethinking Civil Rights Lawyering," 278–279; Carter G. Woodson, *The Negro Professional Man and the Community* (Washington, DC: Association for the Study of Negro Life and History, 1934), 242–249; and St. Clair Drake and Horace R. Clayton, *Black Metropolis: A Study of Negro Life in a Northern City* (New York: Harcourt, Brace, 1945), 730.
40 Mack, "Rethinking Civil Rights Lawyering," 265–267; and Styles, *Negroes and the Law*.
41 McNeil, *Groundwork*.
42 Houston, "Need for Negro Lawyers," 49–52.
43 Roscoe Pound, "Theories of Law," *Yale Law Journal* 22, no.2 (December 1912): 114–150; Roscoe Pound, "A Survey of Social Interests," *Harvard Law Review* 57, no.1 (October 1943): 1–39; Felix Frankfurter, "Hours of Labor and Realism in Constitutional Law," *Harvard Law Review* 29, no.4 (February 1916): 353–373; and Sanford V. Levinson, "The Democratic Faith of Felix Frankfurter," *Stanford Law Review* 25, no.3 (February 1973): 430–448.
44 "Spottswood W. Robinson, III," *Washington Post*, October 17, 1998, A20.
45 Bond and Hill, "Interview with Oliver Hill," 11; and McNeil, *Groundwork*, 82.
46 Peter Wallerstein, *Blue Laws and Black Codes: Conflicts, Courts, and Change in Twentieth-Century Virginia* (Charlottesville: University of Virginia Press, 2004); Mollison, "Negro Lawyers in Mississippi," 38–71; and Meier and Rudwick, "Attorneys Black and White," 918.
47 Houston, "Need for Negro Lawyers," 52.
48 Kilpatrick, "(Extra)Ordinary Men," 299–398.
49 Jas. H. Hayes to Booker T. Washington, February 3, 1903, letter found in Louis R. Harlan and Raymond W. Smock, eds., *The Booker T. Washington Papers, 1903-4*, vol.7 (Urbana: University of Illinois Press, 1977); profile of Alfred William Harris (1853–1920) in *Dictionary of Virginia Biography*, http://mlkcommission.dls.virginia.gov/lincoln/pdfs/bios/harris_alfred_william.pdf; profile of James Apostle Field (1844–1903) in *Encyclopedia Virginia*, www.lva.virginia.gov/public/dvb/sources.asp?b=Fields_James_Apostle_1844-1903; profile of Andrew W. E. Bassette Jr. (1857-1942) in *Encyclopedia Virginia*, https://encyclopediavirginia.org/entries/bassette-andrew-w-e-1857-1942/; and Luther Porter Jackson, *Negro Office Holders in Virginia, 1865–1895*, (Norfolk, VA: Guide Quality Press, 1945), 1–45.
50 Ann Alexander Field, *Race Man: The Rise and Fall of the "Fighting Editor" John Mitchell, Jr.* (Charlottesville: University of Virginia Press, 2002), 128; and Joseph Gordon Hylton, "The African-American Lawyer, The First Generation: Virginia as a Case Study," *University of Pittsburgh Law Review* 56, no. 107 (Fall 1994): 107–164.

51 Mack, "Law and Mass Politics," 39; and Chiles, "Down Where the South Begins," 73–81.
52 "The Early Years: 1940–1950," Old Dominion Bar Association accessed April 22, 2024, https://olddominionbarassociation.com/history; and Leonard, "Development of the Black Bar," 140.
53 Houston, "Need for Negro Lawyers," 52.
54 "Table of Lawyers in Virginia by Race and Gender, 1880–1990," found in Wallerstein, *Blue Laws and Black Codes*, 65.
55 Hill, *Big Bang*, 76.
56 Bond and Hill, "Interview with Oliver Hill," 10.
57 Edds, *We Face the Dawn*, 63.
58 "In Memoriam Spottswood W. Robinson III 1916–1998," *Journal of Blacks in Higher Education* 22, no.1 (Winter 1998–1999): 39.
59 "New Chief Judge Robinson Has Passion for Work," *Washington Post*, May 27, 1981, A1.
60 John A. Kirk, "The NAACP Campaign for Teachers' Salary Equalization: African American Women Educators and the Early Civil Rights Struggle," *Journal of African American History* 94, no.4 (Fall 2009): 520–532.
61 W.E.B. Du Bois, "Louisiana Segregation Ordinance," *Crisis Magazine* 10, no. 4, (August 1915): 199–201; McCabe v. Atchison, T. & S.F. Ry. Co., 235 U.S. 151 (1914); Hopkins v. City of Richmond, 117 Va. 692 (1915); "Supreme Court of Appeals of Virginia: *Hopkins et al. v. City of Richmond*. (No. 1.), *Coleman v. Town of Ashland*" (No. 2.) September 9, 1915 [86 S. E. 139], *Virginia Law Register* 1, no. 7 (November 1915): 519–527; and Meier and Rudwick, "Attorneys Black and White," 921–922.
62 Meier and Rudwick, "Attorneys Black and White," 930–933.
63 Brochure and brief history of Richmond Branch from Richmond, Va., Annual State Conference Meeting, October 12–14, 1951, folder 4, box C:209 (NAACP Papers).
64 Armistead L. Boothe, "The Adequacy of the Virginia Constitution of 1902," *Virginia Law Review* 54, no.5 (June 1968): 981–993; and August Meier and Elliott Rudwick, "Negro Boycotts of Segregated Streetcars in Virginia, 1904–1907," *Virginia Magazine of History and Biography* 81, no. 4 (1973): 479–487.
65 Hopkins v. City of Richmond, 86 S.E. (1915), 139; Buchanan v. Warley, 245, US 60 38 S. Ct. 16 L. Ed (1917), 70–82; and Harmon v. Tyler US 668, 47 S. Ct. 471, 71 L. Ed (1927), 831.
66 "Credit Where Credit Is Due," *Norfolk Journal and Guide*, July 27, 1929, 14.
67 "Greatest Disparity in Pay of Races Found among Teachers," *Norfolk Journal and Guide*, January 27, 1934, 16; "Va Tutors Want Equal Pay Checks, Better Facilities," *Baltimore Afro-American*, December 8, 1934, 23; "Credit Where Credit Is Due"; City of Richmond v. Deans, 37 F.2d 712 (4th Cir. 1930); West v. Bliley, 33 F.2d 177 (E.D. Va. 1929), 42 F.2d 101 (4th Cir. 1930); "William Pickens To Speak Here," *Richmond Planet*, October 11, 1930, 1; "NAACP Organized In Response to Pickens' Speech," *Richmond Planet*, October 16, 1930, 1 and 4; "Branch News," *Crisis*, February 19, 1939, 56–57; Walter White to Dr. J. M. Tinsley, November 8, 1934; Dr. J. M. Tinsley to Walter White, November 10, 1934; and Membership Report, Branch Richmond, November 2, 1934,

folder 2, Richmond, VA, September–December 1934, box I: G211, NAACP Papers; and C. H. Thompson, "Equalization of White and Negro Teachers' Salaries in Virginia," *Journal of Negro Education* 7, no.2 (1938): 113–117.

68 Bruce Beezer, "Black Teachers' Salaries and the Federal Courts before *Brown v. Board of Education*: One Beginning for Equity," *Journal of Negro Education* 55, no. 2 (Spring 1986): 200–213; and Edgar A. Toppin, "Walter White and the Atlanta NAACP's Fight for Equal Schools," *History of Education Quarterly* 7, no.1 (Spring 1967): 3–21.

69 John J. Donohue III, James J. Heckman, and Petra E. Todd, "The Schooling of Southern Blacks: The Roles of Legal Activism and Private Philanthropy, 1910–1960," *Quarterly Journal of Economics* 117, no.1 (February 2002): 225–268.

70 McCabe v. Atchison, Topeka, & Santa Fe Railway Company, 235 U.S. 151, 161; Mark Tushnet, "The Politics of Equality in Constitutional Law: The Equal Protection Clause, Dr. Du Bois, and Charles Hamilton Houston," *Journal of American History* 74, no. 3 (December 1987): 884–903; Scott Baker, "Testing Equality: The National Teacher Examination and the NAACP's Legal Campaign to Equalize Teachers' Salaries in the South, 1936-63," *History of Education Quarterly* 35, no.1 (Spring 1995): 49–64; and Yick Wo v. Hopkins, 118 U.S. 356 (1886).

71 Luther P. Jackson, *A History of the Virginia State Teachers Association* (Norfolk, VA: Guide, 1937), 95–100.

72 Thompson, "Equalization of White and Negro Teachers' Salaries in Virginia," 113–117; "Greatest Disparity In Pay of Races Found among Teachers," *Norfolk Journal and Guide*, January 27, 1934, 16; and "State School System Under Investigation," *Norfolk Journal and Guide*, February 2, 1935, 11; Ada F. Coleman, "The Salary Equalization Movement," *Journal of Negro Education* 16, no.2 (Spring 1947): 235–241; Doxey A. Wilkerson, "The Negro School Movement in Virginia: From 'Equalization' to 'Integration,'" *Journal of Negro Education* 29, no.1 (Winter 1960): 17–29; and Jackson, *Virginia State Teachers Association*, 108–110.

73 "Chesterfield Teachers for Equal Salaries," *Norfolk Journal and Guide*, February 5, 1938, 11; "Virginia Principals Ponder Unequal School Cases," *Richmond Afro-American*, May 13, 1939, 17; "300 Petition against School Inequalities," *Norfolk Journal and Guide*, February 11, 1939, 1; "Sussex County Teachers Back Wage Drive," *Norfolk Journal and Guide*, February 26, 1938, 11; "900 Teachers in Tidewater Area Vote to Support Equal Pay Suit," *Norfolk Journal and Guide*, April 29, 1939, 4; Brian J. Daugherity and Alyce Miller, "A New Era in Building: African American Educational Activism in Goochland County, Virginia, 1911-32," *Virginia Magazine of History and Biography* 128, no. 1 (Fall 2020): 44–88.

74 Earl Lewis, *In Their Own Interests: Race, Class, and Power in Twentieth-Century Norfolk, Virginia* (Berkeley: University of California Press, 1991), 157.

75 "Teachers To Support Salary Move," *Norfolk Journal and Guide*, January 22, 1938, 2; "Salary Petition Denied, Lawyers Plan Early Court Action," *Norfolk Journal and Guide*, January 21, 1939, 10; "Move to Secure Better Schools On Wide Front," *Norfolk Journal and Guide*, February 11, 1939, 1 and 10; "Teachers Join Salary Fight," *Norfolk Journal and Guide*, February 12, 1938, 2; and "Equal Salaries for All Teachers Being Sought," *Norfolk Journal and Guide*, November 5, 1938, 20.

76 "Court Denies Salary Claim of Teacher," *Virginia Pilot*, June 1, 1939, 18; and "School Board Is Urged to Reappoint Fired Teacher," *Norfolk Journal and Guide*, July 1, 1939, 1.
77 Alston et al. v. School Board of City of Norfolk et al., 112 F. 2d 992 (4th Cir. 1940).
78 J. Douglas Smith, *Managing White Supremacy: Race, Politics, and Citizenship in Jim Crow Virginia* (Chapel Hill: University of North Carolina Press, 2003).
79 "Equal Pay Campaign Is Backed by Va. Teachers," *Norfolk Journal and Guide*, January 22, 1938, 22.
80 Oliver Hill to Dr. Leon Ransom and Thurgood Marshall, August 30, 1941; Dr. J. M. Tinsley to Thurgood Marshall, October 18, 1941; Summary of Bowler Petition and Events Leading Up to It, enclosed in a letter from Thurgood Marshall to "Peanuts" [Oliver W. Hill], December 19, 1941; Memorandum to The Legal Committee Richmond Branch NAACP, November 14, 1941, folder 7, box I: B208, NAACP Papers.
81 "Negroes Plea for Salary Rises Turned Down by School Board over Opposition Woman," *Richmond Times-Dispatch*, November 7, 1941; "Negro Teachers Will Sue," *Richmond News Leader*, November 26, 1941; Walter White to Douglas S. Freeman, December 3, 1941; Douglas S. Freeman to Mr. Walter White, December 6, 1941; Oliver W. Hill to Thurgood Marshall, December 26, 1941; J. H. Binford to Richmond Teachers' Association, December 29, 1941; Oliver Hill to Leon A. Ransom, December 30, 1941; "Copy of The December 27th Vote To Approve 5-Year Plan," enclosed in a letter from Charles E. Bentley to J. H. Binford, January 12, 1942; Oliver W. Hill to Thurgood Marshall and Leon Ransom, January 5, 1942; Thurgood Marshall to *Richmond Afro-American*, February 16, 1942; Thurgood Marshall to Dr. J. M. Tinsley, enclosed in a memo from Thurgood Marshall to Walter White and Roy Wilkins February 17, 1942; Antoinette E. Bowler to Walter White, February 20, 1942; Milton L. Randolph to Walter White, February 23, 1941; Dr. J. M. Tinsley to Walter White, May 11, 1942; John P. McGuire Jr. to Oliver W. Hill, March 30, 1942; and Final Judgment of *Bowler v. Richmond*, May 13, 1942, all in folder 7, box I: B208, NAACP Papers.
82 William A. Link, *A Hard Country and a Lonely Place: Schooling, Society, and Reform in Rural Virginia, 1870–1920* (Chapel Hill: University of North Carolina Press, 1986); James L. Leloudis II, "School Reforms in the New South: The Women's Association for the Betterment of Public Schools in North Carolina, 1902–1919," *Journal of American History* 69, no.4 (March 1983): 886; Carl V. Harris, "Stability and Change in Discrimination against Black Public Schools: Birmingham, Alabama, 1871–1931," *Journal of Southern History* 51, no.3 (August 1985): 375; Edwin R. Embree and Julia Waxman, *Investment in People: The Story of The Julius Rosenwald Fund* (New York: Harper, 1949); C. Vann Woodward, *Origins of the New South, 1877–1913* (Baton Rouge: Louisiana State University Press, 1951), 396–340; George Brown Tindall, *The Emergence of the New South, 1913–1945* (Baton Rouge: Louisiana State University Press, 1967), 268–272; *The Jeanes Story: A Chapter in the History of American Education, 1908–1968* (Jackson, MS: Jackson State University, 1979); Joan Malczewski, "Weak State, Stronger Schools: Northern Philanthropy and Organizational Change in the Jim Crow South," *Journal of Southern History* 75, no.4 (November 2009): 963–1000; James D. Anderson, *The Education of Blacks in the South, 1860–1935* (Chapel Hill: University of North Carolina Press, 1988); Eric Anderson and Alfred A. Moss Jr., *Dangerous Donations:*

Northern Philanthropy and Southern Education, 1902–1930 (Columbia: University of Missouri Press, 1999); Adam Fairclough, *Teaching Equality: Black Schools in the Age of Jim Crow* (Athens: University of Georgia Press, 2001); Robert J. Taggart, "Philanthropy and Black Public Education in Delaware, 1918–1930," *Pennsylvania Magazine of History and Biography* 103, no.4 (October 1979): 467–483; and Thomas W. Hanchett, "The Rosenwald Schools and Black Education in North Carolina," *North Carolina Historical Review* 65, no.4 (October 1988): 387–444.

83 Baker, "Testing Equality," 50; Leander L. Boykin, "The Status and Trends of Differentials Between White and Negro Teachers' Salaries in the Southern States, 1900–1946," *Journal of Negro Education* 18, no.1 (Winter 1949): 40–47 (the charts and tables in this article provided me with information on the pay disparity between white and black teachers between 1900 and 1930s); and *Twenty-Year Report of the Phelps-Stokes Fund, 1911–1931* (New York City: Phelps-Stokes Fund, 1932), 1–40.

84 Mills v. Anne Arundel County Board of Education, 30 F. Supp. 245 (D. Md. 1939); Davis v. Cook, 80 F. Supp. 443 (N.D. Ga. 1948); McDaniel v. Board of Public Instruction for Escambia County, Florida, 39 F. Supp. 638 (N.D. Fla. 1941); Thomas v. Hibbitts, 46 F. Supp. 368 (M.D. Tenn. 1942); Morris v. Williams, 59 F. Supp. 508 (E.D. Ark. 1944); Duvall, et al. v. J.F. Seignous, Case No. 1082 (1944); Abbington, et al. v. Louisville Board of Education, Civ. 243, W.D. Ky (1941); Turner v. Keefe, 50 F. Supp. 647 (S.D. Fla 1943); Lee v. Jefferson Parish School Board, ED. 721 La. (1943); Bates and Brown v. Board of Trustees of Jackson Separate School District and K. P. Walker, Superintendent of Jackson School (1950); and C. C. Bolton, "Mississippi's School Equalization Program, 1945–1954: A Last Gasp to Try to Maintain a Segregated Educational System," *Journal of Southern History* 66, no. 4 (2000): 781–814. Unfortunately, I was not able to find the name of each state's black teacher association; the names provided were the ones found in newspapers or lawsuits.

85 Charles Bolton, *The Hardest Deal of All: The Battle over School Integration in Mississippi, 1870–1980* (Jackson: University Press of Mississippi, 2005); and Edds, *We Face the Dawn*, 114.

86 "National Equal Salary Campaign Endorsed," *Pittsburgh Courier,* February 12, 1938, 7; Coleman, "Salary Equalization Movement," 235–241; "State School Head Opposed Bills For Equal Pay, Terms," *Baltimore Afro-American,* February 23, 1935, 14; "State Teachers To Fight Salary Scale Compromise," *Baltimore Afro-American,* November 16, 1935, 4; John R. Wennersten, "The Black School Teacher in Maryland, 1930's," *Negro History Bulletin,* 38, no.1 (April/May 1975): 370–373; "Unequal Pay Scale of Maryland Teachers To Be Attacked," *Norfolk Journal and Guide,* November 28, 1935, 3; "Unfair Teachers' Salaries To Be Fought," *New York Amsterdam News,* November 28, 1936, 19; "NAACP Will Attack Unequal Salary Scales of Maryland Schoolmarms," *Pittsburgh Courier,* November 28, 1936, 7; "Opening Gun Fired in War To Equalize Teachers' Pay," *Baltimore Afro-American,* December 12, 1936, 16; "NAACP Wins Teachers' Fight," *Atlanta Daily World,* August 2, 1937, 1; "Delaware Wants Teachers' Pay Equalized Too," *Baltimore Afro-American,* November 27, 1937, 13; "Alabama Conclude Session," *Atlanta Daily World,* March 29, 1938, 1; "NC Interracial Group Urges Salary Equalization," *Norfolk Journal and Guide,* May 14, 1938, 20; Charles W. McKinney Jr.,

"Multiple Fronts: The Struggle for Black Educational and Political Equality in Wilson, North Carolina, 1941-1953," *North Carolina Historical Review* 88, no.1 (January 2011): 1-39; "New Orleans School Teachers Equalization Case Under Fire," *Pittsburgh Courier,* June 4, 1938, 23; "The Digest," *Cleveland Call and Post,* January 26, 1939, 6; "Nashville Votes Equal Pay For Teachers," *Chicago Defender,* April 1, 1939, 4; Charles C. Bolton, "Mississippi's School Equalization Program, 1945-1954: A Last Gasp to Try to Maintain a Segregated Educational System," *Journal of Southern History* 66, no.4 (November 2000): 781-814; John Hale, "'The Fight Was Instilled in Us': High School Activism and the Civil Rights Movement in Charleston," *South Carolina Historical Magazine* 114, no.1 (January 2013): 9-10; "Fla. Teachers Press Fight On Salary Bias," *Chicago Defender,* November 19, 1938, 5; Irvin D. S. Winsboro and Abel A. Bartley, "Race, Education, and Regionalism: The Long and Troubling History of School Desegregation in the Sunshine State," *Florida Historical Quarterly* 92, no.4 (Spring 2014): 725-727; Barbara J. Shircliffe, "Rethinking *Turner v. Keefe*: The Parallel Mobilization of African-American and White Teachers in Tampa, Florida, 1936-1946," *History of Education Quarterly* 52, no.1 (February 2012): 99-136; Caroline Emmons, "Not a Single Battle but Rather a Real War: The Fight to Equalize Teachers' Salaries in Florida in the 1930s and 1940s," *Florida Historical Quarterly* 81, no.4 (Spring 2003): 418-435; "Ark. Teachers Seek Equal Pay," *Pittsburgh Courier,* December 3, 1938, 5; Ben F. Johnson III, "All Thoughtful Citizens: The Arkansas School Reform Movement, 1921-1930," *Arkansas Historical Quarterly* 46, no.2 (Summer 1987): 105-132.
87 Wilkerson, "Negro School Movement in Virginia," 17-29.
88 "Wesley Elam Dismissed as Head of Alexandria School," *Norfolk Journal and Guide,* April 2, 1938, 11.
89 Edds, *We Face the Dawn,* 111.
90 Baker, "Testing Equality," 50.
91 Kirk, "NAACP Campaign for Teachers' Salary Equalization," 520-532.
92 Edds, *We Face the Dawn,* 133-134.
93 "Irene Morgan v. Commonwealth of Virginia," Jim Crow Museum, December 2007, www.ferris.edu/HTMLS/news/jimcrow/question/2007/december.htm#:~:text=Unlike%20Rosa%20Parks%2C%20Irene%20Morgan,remove%20her%20from%20the%20bus; and "Freedom Riders: Before Rosa Parks, There Was Irene Morgan," PBSLearningMedia, clip for the American Experience, 0:52, https://virginia.pbslearningmedia.org/resource/arct14.socst.ush.fr06irenemorgan/before-rosa-parks-there-was-irene-morgan/
94 Herman H. Long, "Racial Desegregation in Railroad and Bus Transportation," *Journal of Negro Education* 23, no.3 (Summer, 1954): 214-221.
95 Gilbert Thomas Stephenson, *Race Distinctions in American Law* (New York: Appleton, 1910), chapter 9, www.gutenberg.org/files/65083/65083-h/65083-h.htm#Page_208; and Sarah M. Lemmon, "Transportation Segregation in the Federal Courts Since 1865," *Journal of Negro History* 38, no.2 (April 1953): 174-193.
96 Jack M. Beermann, *The Journey to Separate but Equal: Madame Decuir's Quest for Racial Justice in the Reconstruction Era* (Lawrence: University of Kansas Press, 2021); Hall v. Decuir, 95 U.S. 485 (1878); Green v. City of Bridgeton, 10 F. Cas. 1090 (S.D. Ga.

1879); *Civil Rights Cases*, 109 U.S. 3 (1883); Chiles v. Chesapeake & Ohio Ry. Co., 218 U.S. 71 (1910); Heard v. Georgia R. Co., 1 I.C.C. 428 (1888); and State ex rel. Abbott v. Hicks, 44 La. Ann. 770 (1892).

97 Barton J. Bernstein, "Case Law in *Plessy v. Ferguson*," *Journal of Negro History* 47, no. 3 (July 1962): 198.

98 Louisville, New Orleans & Texas Ry. Co. v. Mississippi, 133 U.S. 587 (1890); and August Meier and Elliott Rudwick, "The Boycott Movement against Jim Crow Streetcars in the South, 1900–1906," *Journal of American History* 55, no. 4 (March 1969): 756–757.

99 Charles E. Wynes, *Race Relations in Virginia, 1870–1902* (Totowa, NJ: Rowman and Littlefield, 1971), 68–80.

100 August Meier and Elliott Rudwick, "Negro Boycotts of Segregated Streetcars in Virginia, 1904–1907," *Virginia Magazine of History and Biography* 81, no. 4 (October 1973): 479–487; Wynes, "Evolution of Jim Crow Laws," 416–425; and Blair L. M. Kelley, *Right to Ride: Streetcar Boycotts and African American Citizenship in the Era of Plessy v. Ferguson* (Chapel Hill: University of North Carolina Press, 2010).

101 Barbara Y. Welke, "When All the Women Were White, and All the Blacks Were Men: Gender, Class, Race, and the Road to Plessy, 1855–1914," *Law and History Review* 13, no. 2 (Autumn 1995): 278.

102 *Hall v. DeCuir* (1868); and Railroad Company v. Brown, 84 U.S. 17 Wall. 445 445 (1873).

103 Brown v. Memphis & C. R. Co., 5 F. 499 (1880); United States v. Dodge, 25 F. Cas. 882, 1 Tex. Law J. 47 (1877); Chesapeake, Ohio & Southwestern Railroad v. Wells (1887); Logwood v. Memphis & C. R. Co., 23 F. 318 (1885); Chicago & Northwestern, R. Co., v. Williams, 36 N.W. 857 (Wis. 1888); and Houck v. Southern Pacific Ry. Co., Circuit Court, W.D. Texas, 38 F. 226 (1888).

104 Fields vs. The Baltimore City Passenger R.R. Co., 9 Fed. Cases, No. 4, 76; and Thompson v. The Baltimore City Passenger R.R. Co., 23 Fed. Cases, No. 13, 941, found in Robert W. Hughes, *Reports of Cases Decided in the Circuit Courts of the United States for the Fourth Circuit; Most of Them Since Chief Justice Waite Came Upon the Bench; and of Selected Cases in Admiralty and Bankruptcy, Decided in the District Courts of that Circuit. With an Appendix to the Second Volume, Containing the Rules in Admiralty and Bankruptcy of the District Court for the Eastern District of Virginia, and the Rules of the Circuit Court for that District, Etc.*, vol. 1 (Washinton, DC, Morrison, 1877), https://books.google.ad/books?id=0Pw7AAAAIAAJ.

105 Edds, *We Face the Dawn*, 143.

106 Edds, *We Face the Dawn*, 110–112, 145–147, 150–153; and Freeman v. County School Board, 82 F. Supp. 167 (E.D. Va. 1948).

107 "School Desegregation and Civil Rights Stories: Pulaski County, Virginia," National Archives, accessed April 22, 2024, www.archives.gov/education/lessons/desegregation/pulaski.html

108 Edds, *We Face the Dawn*, 199–201.

109 "Forum Speaker Says," *Norfolk Journal and Guide*, April 22, 1961, B1; and "Robinson Resigns NAACP Post," *Baltimore Afro-American*, July 1, 1961, 3.

110 "Oliver Hill Appointed Assistant to FHA Intergroup Relations Head," *Atlanta Daily World,* May 13, 1961, 1; and "Be More Active to End Bias, Hill Tells Race," *Atlanta Daily World,* December 21, 1961, 1.

111 "Spottswood W. Robinson, III," *Washington Post,* October 17, 1998, A20.

112 "Spottswood Robinson to Retire," *Washington Post,* August 12, 1989, A8.

113 "UVA Honors Legendary Oliver W. Hill," *Norfolk Journal and Guide,* September 20, 2007, 8.

114 "Oliver W. Hill Was Last of Famous *Brown* Lawyers," *Norfolk Journal and Guide,* August 9, 2007, 1; and "Brown v. Board of Ed Lawyer Oliver W. Hill—Dead at 100," *Chicago Defender,* August 10, 2007, 12.

115 "Students Urged to Go on By Wilder," *Philadelphia Tribune,* February 23, 1993, 3C.

116 "Civil Rights Lawyer Gets Honored," *Atlanta Daily World,* May 27, 1999, 2.

117 "State Building Re-Named for Legendary Black Virginian," *Norfolk Journal and Guide,* December 8, 2005, 1; and "State Monument to Honor Civil Rights Heroes," *Norfolk Journal and Guide,* May 24, 2008, 8.

118 "Spottswood W. Robinson, III," *Richmond Times-Dispatch,* September 19, 2019, https://richmond.com/spottswood-w-robinson-iii/article_50bb1c90-6bde-11e2-8fa5-0019bb30f31a.html; Spottswood Robinson III and Oliver Hill biographical sketches in PBS documentary "Beyond Brown: Pursuing the Promise," www.pbs.org/beyondbrown/history/spottswood.html and www.pbs.org/beyondbrown/history/oliverhill.html; Spottswood W. Robinson biographical sketch for the National Park Service, accessed April 23, 2024, www.nps.gov/people/spottswood-w-robinson-iii.htm; "A Civil Rights Champion," *Richmond Law Magazine,* July 9, 2018, https://lawmagazine.richmond.edu/article/-/15499/.html?utm_source=related-stories&utm_medium=referral&utm_campaign=lawmagazine-story; "An Unsung Civil Rights Icon: Bro. Oliver White Hill, Alpha '27," undated, https://omegapsiphi-xgg.wildapricot.org/oliverwhitehill; and "NAACP Honors Oliver W. Hill with Spingarn Medal," *Crisis Magazine* 112, no. 4 (July–August 2005): 57–58.

5

"Fighting the Good Fight"

Legal Influences and Experiences of Oscar W. Adams Jr. before and during the Second Reconstruction in Alabama, 1947 to 1967

BERTIS D. ENGLISH

Born February 7, 1925, and reared in Birmingham, Alabama, Oscar W. Adams Jr. was a brilliant student who earned a bachelor of laws degree from Howard University in Washington, DC, on June 6, 1947. Desirous of joining a small group of Black licensed attorneys in Alabama, Adams on July 22 traveled from Birmingham to the state's judicial building in Montgomery to sit for day one of the three-day bar examination. When he arrived, however, White bar personnel were reluctant to allow him entry. Adams persisted but, owing to segregation, had to complete his exam in a hot and damp basement instead of on the cool, dry, ground floor of the Supreme Court of Alabama's law library alongside White examinees. Despite that harrowing ordeal, he rejoiced when state bar officials mailed his license to him a few weeks later. According to the *Birmingham News*, one of the most prominent White-owned papers in the South, "Congratulations from friends and well-wishers" poured in when they learned about Adams's accomplishment.[1] From that moment until a cancer-related infection ended his life on February 15, 1997, Adams worked tirelessly to help remedy societal inequality wherever it existed.

Among numerous precedent-setting activities, Adams on July 8, 1966, became the first Black member of the Birmingham Bar Association. On April 4, 1967, after Alabama's Supreme Court justices licensed Harvey M. Burg, a White attorney from New York City, Adams and Burg cofounded the first ethnically integrated law firm in Alabama. Those two endeavors were meritorious, but one of the greatest precedents Adams set occurred on October 17, 1980, when a gubernatorial appointment enabled him to become the first Black person to occupy a seat on the state's Supreme Court. He retained the seat via a plebiscite held on November 2, 1982, making him the first Black person elected to a statewide constitutional office in Alabama's history. This chapter explores some of Adams's most significant personal and professional influences from his birth through the first two decades of his legal career amid the country's traditional civil rights movement, or second Reconstruction. For most of those years, the *Birmingham News* avowed, Adams was "linked with civil rights like bread with butter."[2]

Thanks in no small part to a lineage of learned, ethical, and accomplished parents, Adams developed lasting commitments to academic excellence, universal equality, and the law at an early age. His highly cerebral, unwaveringly moral, and socially active mother, Ella V. Adams (née Eaton), was a major inspiration. She was a beloved schoolteacher, loyal churchgoer, and talented musician whom people of all ethnicities respected immensely. Oscar W. Adams Sr. was proprietor of the *Birmingham Reporter*, Alabama's leading Black-owned newspaper. As a testament to the paper's standing, officers in the Colored Knights of Pythias Grand Lodge in Alabama, the Masons, the Order of Calanthe, and the Order of Eastern Star named the *Reporter* their official state organ.

Though a successful journalist, Oscar Adams Sr. contemplated becoming a lawyer. Oftentimes, while his family ate meals or gathered in its living room, he pretended to argue cases or to hold mock trials. Reminiscing about such activities following a long and successful legal career, Oscar Adams Jr. supposed his father "probably cleverly instilled" in him the desire to study the law.[3] That Adams Jr. frequented judicial proceedings during his early teen years was certain. "Every chance I got," he reflected in 1994, after retiring from the Supreme Court of Alabama, "I would go down to the Jefferson County Courthouse... and listen to the lawyers trying cases, and particularly their closing arguments to the jury. Some lawyers had deep, powerful voices and I would hear those voices ringing down the corridors of the courthouse. I visualized myself doing the same thing."[4]

Oscar Adams Jr.'s God-given abilities made his teenage vision seem practical to him. He was a prodigy whom public school administrators in Jefferson County advanced, or skipped, multiple classifications, or grades. Their acts helped facilitate his completing the A. H. Parker High School in Birmingham in May 1940. Adams was fifteen years old and already had a deep, melodious, baritone voice akin to the lawyers' voices he heard at the county courthouse. Besides those innate gifts, Adams was a voracious reader, critical thinker, and fine wordsmith who enjoyed analyzing, speaking, and writing. Such talents and interests proved invaluable when he began coursework at historically Black Talladega College, his mother's alma mater.[5] Adams Jr. entered Talladega in September 1940 and thenceforth amassed a superb academic record, though for him seeing a B grade on his transcript for the first time was disturbing. Younger brother Frank E. Adams was pragmatic about the grade. As Frank would recount decades later, the college "was way ahead of most black schools and probably most white schools."[6] Talladega's faculty and students held open "debates about *rights*, about freedom and the Constitution," Frank explained, "and it was like heaven on earth down there, as an incubator, for those who attended" the college.[7]

Oscar Adams Jr. engaged fully in debates and in other scholarly endeavors, but he also made time for extracurricular activities. The Adamses were devout members of the African Methodist Episcopal (AME) Zion Church, and the city of Talladega had several denominational churches Adams Jr. could attend while matriculating through the local college. In addition to ecclesiastical pursuits, he affiliated with multiple civic and social organizations. Omega Psi Phi Fraternity, Inc., was foremost. Adams Jr. was a second-generation Omega whose father cofounded the Alpha Phi graduate chapter in Birmingham. At Talladega College, Adams Jr. joined Gamma Psi, the first undergraduate chapter in Alabama. By his junior year, he was basileus, or chapter president.

Oscar Adams Jr. relished extracurricular activities, but earning a degree in philosophy on June 5, 1944, was the crowning event of his Talladega College tenure. He was nineteen years old and class valedictorian; moreover, eminent scholar William E. B. Du Bois delivered the keynote address. Du Bois spoke brilliantly about Judaic personalities Jacob and Esau, whom he used to interrogate unnamed European leaders' myriad treacheries as they scrambled for "division of power and profit" from the late nineteenth century onward.[8] According to Du Bois, the European leaders' "cheating, lying and killing" were unrivaled.[9] What, he queried, "was the initial right and wrong of the original Jacobs and Esaus and of their spiritual descendants the world over? We stand convinced today, at least those who remain sane, that lying and cheating and killing will build no world organization worth the building."[10] Then, speaking directly to Adams and his classmates, Du Bois proclaimed,

> In the days of the years of my pilgrimage, I have greeted many thousands of young men and women at the commencement of their careers as citizens of the select commonwealth of culture. In no case have I welcomed them to such a world of darkness and distractions as that into which I usher you. I take joy only in the thought that if work to be done is measure of man's opportunity you inherit a mighty fortune. You have only to remember that the birthright which is today in symbol draped over your shoulders is a heritage which has been preserved

all too often by the lying, stealing, and murdering of the Jacobs of the world, and if these are the only means by which this birthright can be preserved in the future, it is not worth the price. I do not believe this, and I lay it upon your hearts to prove that this not only need be true, but it is eternally and forever false.[11]

By the time Du Bois enthralled listeners with his acumen and oratory in June 1944, Oscar Adams Jr. had decided to challenge injustice through the legal system despite naysayers aplenty. Years earlier, when a teenaged Adams worked at the American Cast Iron and Pipe Company in Birmingham, Alabama, others in the "gang" to which supervisors assigned him devised the sobriquet "lawyer" to poke fun at his career aspiration.[12] Adams's desire seemed fanciful to them because there were only a few lawyers in the entire state who were not White. Several of Adams's friends also discouraged him from pursuing a legal career, but their reservations did not bother him as much as the discouragement of his maternal grandmother, Linette A. Eaton. Skeptical he would earn much money because "lawyering was a white man's business," she advised him to become a physician.[13]

Adams appreciated the advice, but he did not heed it. His mind was set on becoming a lawyer. Adams wanted to attend the University of Alabama School of Law in Tuscaloosa, but the state's legal color barrier prohibited him from enrolling. Administrators at Yale Law School in New Haven, Connecticut, admitted Adams, but they offered no scholarship to him. Therefore, he chose to attend the Howard University School of Law. In Washington, DC, Adams occasionally dined with US Supreme Court associate justice Hugo L. Black Sr., a native Alabamian whom Oscar Adams Sr. befriended despite Black's one-time affiliation with the Ku Klux Klan. Black warned Adams Jr. not to return to Alabama seeking to practice law when he completed Howard, though not because his legal preparation would be inadequate. Black knew the university was a fine institution whose law school faculty would equip Adams Jr. adequately to handle the nuances of Alabama law. Black doubted a single White judge in Alabama would desegregate a jury box. Owing to such bigotry, Adams Jr. would have an extremely difficult time winning a jury trial. Nevertheless, he returned to Birmingham and moved into his childhood home, but the familial environment was very different from erstwhile periods. The death of Adams Sr. was paramount. He died May 14, 1946, after suffering a heart attack.

As Oscar Adams Jr. adjusted to life at home without one of his greatest influences while trying to establish a law practice, some of Birmingham's most influential Black businesspersons invited him to join their operations. The entrepreneurism of one businessman, Arthur G. Gaston, resulted in Gaston becoming "a bona fide millionaire—one hundred times over."[14] Furthermore, he had deep ties to the Adamses. Among other things, Gaston was a childhood friend of Ella Eaton, on whom he had a deep crush. During their teenage years, her eventual husband, Oscar Adams Sr., provided Gaston with one of his first paying jobs, assisting with the *Birmingham Reporter.* In 1947, Gaston returned the favor by extending a job offer to Adams Jr. once he finished Howard University.

Oscar Adams Jr. appreciated the invitation to join Gaston's flourishing business operation, which ultimately included a business college, a burial insurance company, a construction company, a motel, a real estate company, a savings and loan bank, two cemeteries, and two radio stations. Adams, however, was determined to blaze his own professional trail instead of following someone else's route. A Birmingham office with a license to practice law hanging on the wall was Adams's favored destination, and bigoted Alabama State Bar officials tried hard to prevent him from reaching it. Despite their efforts, he passed the certifying examination from July 22 to 24, 1947, and the Supreme Court of Alabama admitted him to the state bar on September 30. He thereupon joined an older Talladega College alumnus, Birmingham neighbor, and legal pioneer named Arthur D. Shores to become the only Black lawyers practicing actively in Alabama. At the time, Shores was litigating a civil rights case whose plaintiffs sought to abolish ethnically discriminatory pay schemes for public schoolteachers in the state. A 1939 to 1940 case originating in Virginia and styled *Alston v. School Board of City of Norfolk* was a precedent, and Howard University law professors William H. Hastie Jr. and Leon A. Ransom helped litigate the case. The ruling the US Court of Appeals delivered in 1940 began a process that ultimately equalized pay for teachers in Norfolk.

Together with the clandestine prodding of Oscar Adams Sr. and the valiancy of Shores, who braved constant threats from violent White bigots in Birmingham—some of whom dynamited Shores's residence because he dared to challenge discrimination—the central roles that Howard-affiliated lawyers such as Hastie and Ransom performed in cases like *Alston* helped motivate Oscar Adams Jr. to study law at the university. Regrettably for Adams Jr., Ransom resigned from Howard in 1943 after not winning appointment as permanent dean of the law school. Ransom believed he earned the position because he served as acting dean for the academic year 1941 to 1942 when governmental responsibilities prevented Hastie from occupying the deanship full-time. Upon leaving Howard, Ransom joined the NAACP Legal Defense and Educational Fund, Inc., familiarly the LDF. Adams Jr. watched closely as

Ransom argued legal cases to secure equitable teacher pay and to abolish segregated busing, among other civil rights matters. Hastie, meanwhile, continued to be a pillar of civil rights scholarship and activism at Howard. Adams Jr. desired to emulate both men by litigating civil rights cases after hanging out his shingle in 1947; however, most prospective clients in Alabama preferred "the gentle giant," Shores.[15] In general, Adams Jr. focused on collections, probate, real estate, and tort matters.

Though busy professionally, Oscar Adams Jr. maintained a good work-life balance during the first years of his legal career. Spending time with his widowed mother, Ella Adams, and other family members was one of the most important personal duties he undertook. Adams Jr. also volunteered to assist with numerous community activities. Speaking to civic, educational, labor, religious, and social groups was an almost weekly occurrence. He was an officer at the Metropolitan AME Zion Church, worked tirelessly for the Young Men's Christian Association, and encouraged people to take part in the body politic, though the long and sharp claws of Jim and Jane Crow during the country's second Reconstruction caused him to tailor certain political messages when addressing public audiences, especially those in Alabama and its neighboring former Confederate states. Paying mandatory poll taxes, if possible, was a common theme of his speeches to Black, bi-ethnic, and broad-minded White citizens. He likewise encouraged them to learn about civics and history, particularly if they aspired to vote or to hold public office. In theory, familiarity with those two subjects would facilitate their passing the literacy tests bigoted White state lawmakers enacted primarily to disenfranchise non-White citizens. In practice, passing a literacy test usually depended on those who conducted it. Besides those endeavors, Adams Jr. tutored elderly military veterans in Birmingham on weekdays. Most were not high school graduates. Many worked in coal mines. Nearly all were illiterate or semiliterate.

The community service for which Oscar Adams Jr. volunteered in 1947 was commendable, but the lawyering services he provided mainly to Black and bi-ethnic citizens were invaluable from that year onward. One of the first potentially consequential cases Adams assisted in litigating while still a plebe civil rights attorney dealt with ethnically discriminatory franchise laws in the state. In 1948, a Black minister in Birmingham by the name of Eugene O. Braxter offered himself as lead plaintiff in a class-action lawsuit to challenge the franchise laws. Adams and Arthur Shores were co-lead attorneys. Full-time LDF lawyers Edward R. Dudley and Thurgood Marshall assisted Adams and Shores. Later, David H. Hood Jr., a recently minted lawyer at Shores's law firm, joined Braxter's legal team.

A 1946 amendment to the 1901 Alabama Constitution hindering the ability of Black and bi-ethnic citizens in Jefferson County to become duly registered voters was the target of Braxter's lawsuit. Edward C. Boswell, a White Democrat, lawyer, and state representative for Hartford in Geneva County, sponsored the 1945 legislative bill that resulted in the amendment. Boswell and his supporters desired to neutralize a 1944 ruling the US Supreme Court delivered in a case styled *Smith v. Allwright* deeming all-White political party primaries unconstitutional. The Boswell amendment required a prospective voter to articulate, express in writing, or otherwise communicate a solid understanding of any article in the US Constitution. The same citizen had to be employed for most of the year preceding the citizen's registration attempt, have good character, and "understand the duties and obligations of good citizenship under a republican form of government," as determined by at least one of three county registrars.[16]

Because the term *understanding* was subjective, lawyers Oscar Adams Jr., Edward Dudley, David Hood Jr., Thurgood Marshall, and Arthur Shores emphasized a fact in their 1948 legal argument that all knowledgeable citizens realized: The Boswell amendment was a "mere subterfuge" or literacy test enabling biased White registrars to arbitrarily disenfranchise non-White citizens; therefore, the amendment violated the Fourteenth and Fifteenth Amendments to the US Constitution.[17] The White-owned *Montgomery Advertiser* newspaper, a Democratic Party organ that had served as "the voice of Alabama's plantation elite since the Civil War,"[18] was candid about the main goal of the Boswell amendment: "If the Board of Registrars wants the Negro to vote, he understands the Constitution. If not, he does not comprehend."[19]

Adams, Dudley, Hood, Marshall, and Shores were confident they had a solid legal case. Their client, Braxter, met the four primary requirements to become a duly registered voter in Alabama: He was an employed, physically fit, literate property holder with high moral character. Furthermore, Braxter answered every question the Jefferson County registrar who tested him asked about the Constitution in a factually correct manner. Nonetheless, in February 1948, the complete three-member board of registrars in Jefferson denied his application. Creating more fodder for the legal fire Braxter and his fellow plaintiffs would light two months later, each county registrar qualified every White person who sought to vote without asking a single question about the Constitution.

Braxter filed a complaint in April 1948, demanding $5,000 in damages. Besides awarding that sum, lawyers Adams, Dudley, Hood, Marshall, and Shores requested a US district court grant a permanent injunction "restraining and enjoining the defendants and each of them from discriminating against the plaintiff and other qualified Negroes seeking to register solely on the basis of race or color."[20] Adams, Dudley, Hood, Marshall, and Shores also requested a declaratory judgment invalidating the Boswell amendment, which in their opinion amounted to a conspiracy disenfranchising almost 100,000 law-abiding, non-White, voting-age citizens from casting ballots.

Jefferson County's three registrars claimed a federal court lacked authority to hear Braxter's case. Moreover, Braxter could not file a legitimate class action because his interests were not "identical" with other Black or ethnically mixed citizens the Boswell amendment might have affected negatively.[21] The registrars' final major claims asserted that they had to determine whether to qualify or to disqualify every prospective voter on an individual basis and that no state law subjected any citizen to an "unreasonable test" to qualify to vote.[22]

In January 1949, a three-member panel constituted by the judge Leon C. McCord of the US Court of Appeals for the Fifth Circuit in New Orleans, Louisiana, and two district judges in Alabama, John McDuffie of Mobile and Clarence H. Mullins of Birmingham ruled the Boswell amendment was unconstitutional. Later in January, Adams, Dudley, Hood, Marshall, Shores, and other attorneys representing the Braxter class filed for dismissal and announced to the court their intention to join Harvard Law School graduate George N. Leighton in litigating another suit, called *Davis v. Schnell*. Lead plaintiff Hunter Davis and nine other Black aspiring voters in Mobile initiated the suit in February 1948 (the same month Jefferson County registrars denied Braxter's application and approximately two months before Braxter filed his complaint). Sponsored by the Mobile Negro Veterans Voters Association, Hunter and his eight co-plaintiffs sued John M. Schnell and two other county registrars pursuant to invalidating the Boswell amendment. Justices on the US District Court of the Southern District of Alabama ruled in favor of the plaintiffs, causing the defendants to appeal the ruling to the US Supreme Court. In March 1949, Hugo Black Sr. and his colleagues on the highest court in the land affirmed the ruling of the lower court: the Boswell amendment was unconstitutional because it violated the Fifteenth Amendment.

Adams enjoyed a respite from lawyering during the Christmas season in 1949. On Christmas Day, he married Willa I. Perkins, a Fairfield, Alabama, native who completed Fisk University in Nashville, Tennessee. A Black craftsman in Birmingham was responsible for Adams meeting Perkins. In 1947, while inspecting potential law offices in the Masonic Temple Building on Fourth Avenue in the center of the Black business district, Adams spoke with the craftsman about painting a sign for his present law office in the Pythian Temple Building on Eighteenth Street North. The craftsman not only agreed to perform the job, but he also recommended a woman for secretarial duties who "works cheap. And not only that, she's good looking. She has freckles and red hair," the craftsman averred.[23]

During a subsequent interview with Adams, Perkins's dictation skills impressed him, but he was apprehensive about employing her because his practice was fewer than two years old and he could not pay more than $15 per week. Perkins accepted that amount, which Adams increased as soon as he could afford to do so. Within 18 months, they were married. In time, the couple parented three children: Oscar W. Adams III, Gail I. Adams, and Frank T. Adams, named after his paternal uncle. Oscar III became a licensed attorney, Gail a sales representative, and Frank an oil engineer. Both parents supported them unconditionally, but their mother was more outgoing than their father, who described his wife as "vivacious, glamourous and provocative. She was a tempest in a teapot—a whirlwind."[24] Called "Sparky" by close adult relatives,[25] Willa "met no stranger [and seemed forever] ready to entertain."[26] Many people adored her bubbly personality, but she also was very smart and extremely organized. Willa's intellectual abilities along with her management skills contributed immensely to the success of Oscar Adams Jr.'s law firm.

Bigoted White state representative Edward Boswell was central to one broadly publicized legal case with which Willa Perkins assisted her beau and soon-to-be husband, Oscar Adams Jr., toward the end of 1949. In October, two months before Perkins and Adams wed, four Black law school graduates residing in Birmingham—Manley Banks, Clarence E. Moses, Henry C. Moss, and Henry L. Pearson—filed a petition with the Alabama State Bar challenging the diploma privilege that state law afforded University of Alabama School of Law graduates.[27] Banks, Moses, and Moss were Howard University alumni, while Pearson completed Lincoln University in Missouri. They petitioned Alabama State Bar officials to certify them to practice law without having to pass the state bar examination. Banks, Moses, Moss, and Pearson reasoned they should have a practicing allowance akin to a University of Alabama School of Law graduate because state law prohibited them from attending the university; hence, their becoming graduates was impossible.

Members of the Supreme Court of Alabama licensed prospective attorneys. State bar officials then certified the attorneys. Court members scheduled a hearing for Banks, Moses, Moss, and Pearson for December 1949. Of no surprise, considering their home state was one of the sturdiest perches for Jim and Jane Crow in the South, most Alabama State Bar officials objected to the hearing. One White male official, speaking anonymously, argued, "White boys who go out of the state to get their law training at Harvard and other fine schools of law, still have to take bar examinations. If we allowed the four

Negroes licenses without an examination, we would be discriminating against the white boys who go out of the state."[28]

Even if one ignored the bar official's reference to fine law schools such as Harvard almost certainly being a backhanded dig at Howard, Lincoln, and suchlike historically Black law schools, his argument was flawed. White law students from Alabama who undertook legal training elsewhere in the country did so voluntarily; state law in Alabama compelled non-White students to do so. All the same, the unanimous opinion issued by the state Supreme Court in June 1950 concluded that Banks, Moses, Moss, and Peterson pursued legal training outside Alabama by their own free will:

> We are fully conscious of the importance of the questions presented on this application and the arguments made in support of it. We are asked to ignore [state law] and grant petitioners a license without an examination and without a diploma from the Law School of the University of Alabama. This we believe has never been done by this Court in plain conflict with the statute. In all instances when any person has received legal education out of the State and out of the Law School of the University of Alabama an examination has been required under that statute. While the status of petitioners in that respect is not exactly the same as that of the others, they do occupy a status of voluntarily seeking legal education outside of the State, aided by the State [financially], knowing that in doing so the law does not justify a diploma license. We do not think we should set ourselves directly in conflict with the requirements of our statutes to favor petitioners who have not been denied any legal or constitutional right by the State or its authorities. The petition is denied as to each petitioner separately.[29]

The defeat Oscar Adams Jr. experienced in the diploma-privilege battle did not lessen his will to fight in the war against injustice. One of the next headline-making struggles in which he eventually participated involved an automobile theft and a capital murder three Black privates in the US Army—namely, Chastine Beverly of Balty, Virginia; James L. Riggins of Birmingham, Alabama; and Louis M. Suttles Jr. of Chattanooga, Tennessee—committed while absent without leave from Ft. Leonard Wood in Missouri. Beverly, Riggins, and Suttles beat and then robbed a White taxi driver named Harry A. Langley in September 1951. After pummeling him with their fists, metal rods, and rocks, they stole his money, commandeered his taxi, and left him bleeding profusely and barely conscious near a secluded country road. Within days, he was dead. In October, a court-martial composed of six male officers and three enlisted men reached a unanimous verdict regarding Beverly, Riggins, and

Suttles being guilty of premeditated murder and a lesser charge, automobile theft. The court-martial sentenced them to die by hanging. Military lawyers appealed the verdict and each sentence, but their appeals were unsuccessful. By the time Adams took on Riggins's case, as he was not the original lawyer, Riggins and his two codefendants, Beverly and Suttles, were awaiting execution in the US Disciplinary Barracks at Ft. Leavenworth in Kansas.

The appeals Adams and other lawyers filed on behalf of their clients did not dispute the guilt of a single client. Instead, the lawyers argued the military court proceedings were flawed and the death sentences were unjust. The lawyers postulated much of the circumstantial evidence against Riggins, Beverly, and Suttles was not strong enough to support the conviction of every soldier of premeditated murder. For instance, not one soldier intended to kill Langley; hence, premeditated murder was a bogus charge. Additionally, the law officer who presided over the initial trial did not give members of the court-martial any instruction regarding their being able to try a soldier as an aider or as an abettor to murder, as opposed to trying each defendant as a principal murderer. Adams and his fellow defense lawyers believed the law officer had a duty to instruct the court-martial on every degree of homicide because the evidence was circumstantial. The lawyers cited several civilian rulings to support their arguments, which, they declared, constituted a pressing and compelling reason for a new trial.

Ultimately, the arguments Adams and his fellow defense lawyers made on behalf of Riggins, Beverly, and Suttles failed to overturn the soldiers' death sentences. Consequently, each soldier faced a hangman's noose in March 1955. Riggins's execution, the final of the three, was most barbaric. The rope failed to snap his neck, so he twisted and turned for several minutes. At one point, Riggins lifted his strapped legs near his chest, as if sparring with death, before asphyxiation defeated him. His final punishment, which numerous observers deemed cruel and unusual, did not end governmental hangings in Kansas, but state lawmakers did revise hanging protocols.

Adams was not present to see Riggins's execution. Instead, he was in Birmingham, Alabama, trying to prevent the hangings, electrocutions, and related government-performed killings of other citizens whom law enforcement or judicial system personnel treated unfairly. Active civic engagement was another important function Adams stressed in his hometown, Birmingham. As president of the local Abraham Lincoln Republican Club, Adams oversaw numerous political debates. Most participants were Black Republicans, whom Adams often represented, or Black Democrats, of whom persons like Arthur Shores were representatives. One Black Republican with whom Adams associated denounced Shores and other Black or bi-ethnic Democrats as "yellow fence-sitters... voting under a white supremacy banner (the white rooster at the top of the ballot sheet)."[30] One of Shores's fellow Black Democrats countered by saying all Republicans, irrespective of skin color, belonged to a "Do-Nothing, Claim All-Credit" political party.[31]

In the wake of the Riggins execution, main subjects of debate among Adams, Shores, and their contemporaries in Birmingham included the second US Supreme Court ruling in *Brown v. Board of Education of Topeka* on May 31, 1955. The ruling fortified the first ruling on May 17, 1954, by ordering the desegregating of public schools deliberately and speedily. White adult male southerners' horrendous killing of 14-year-old Emmett L. Till on August 28, 1955, and yet another Supreme Court ruling on October 10 were two additional subjects of debate. The ruling ordered administrators at the University of Alabama in Tuscaloosa to desegregate the institution by admitting Black women Autherine J. Lucy and Pollie M. Hudson to graduate programs in library science and journalism, respectively. Shores and his close friend, Thurgood Marshall, both attorneys in *Brown I* and *II*, served as co-lead attorneys in the Lucy and Hudson case. On December 5, 1955, the Montgomery bus boycott resulting from the unjust arrest of Black NAACP member, professional seamstress, and civil rights activist Rosa M. Parks for refusing to yield a seat in which she sat legally to a White passenger rose to the top of debated subjects.

On June 1, 1956, as Parks and more than 50,000 other bus boycotters in Montgomery continued to demonstrate how effective a unified body of resilient foot soldiers could be at driving societal change via nonviolent direct action, Montgomery County Circuit Judge Walter B. Jones issued an order restraining the NAACP from operating formally in Alabama. Ironically, Jones served as a state bar examination tutor for Shores decades earlier. Since that time, Jones had decided to "speak for the White Race."[32] Among other statements, he was one of many White government officials who during the Montgomery bus boycott contended that the NAACP was a "clandestine arm of the Communist Party" whose leaders organized, financed, or supported the boycott in sundry other ways.[33] According to Jones, the NAACP leaders "employed or otherwise paid money" to Lucy and Hudson to enroll in the University of Alabama "to test the policy of that institution in denying entrance as a student to persons of the Negro race."[34] Jones, furthermore, avowed the NAACP operated illegally in Alabama because its leaders did not register the organization in the state. Shores was a well-known NAACP member. Adams did not attend every monthly NAACP meeting but, when Shores and other regular attendees called on him for legal or related services, he usually answered, one Adams relative confirmed.[35]

Oscar Adams Jr. played a more direct role in the 1956 founding of the Alabama Christian Movement for Human Rights, or ACMHR. Its president and Baptist minister, Fred L. Shuttlesworth, was a friend of Adams. Shuttlesworth joined the Birmingham chapter of the NAACP in 1955, so he was a neophyte when Jones enjoined its members from operating formally in Alabama in 1956. Shuttlesworth, Adams, and others established the ACMHR as a counterbalance to the injunction. In future years, Adams represented numerous ACMHR members in legal proceedings and in other matters about which scholars have written extensively. Scholars have given less attention to a 1956 legal case in which Adams served as lead defense attorney even though the case resulted in the US Supreme Court issuing a landmark ruling in 1961 regarding police detaining a suspected criminal and the legal representation of that suspect.

At some time between 11 p.m. on October 12, 1956, and 3 a.m. on October 13, White Birmingham police officers arrested a 25-year-old, mentally disabled, indigent, and illiterate Black citizen named Charles C. Hamilton. According to the officers, Hamilton entered a house in the Ensley community where a White, elderly, nearly blind, and physically ill Sicilian immigrant named Maria R. Giangrosso lived with the intention of robbing her. On November 9, a Jefferson County grand jury indicted Hamilton for breaking and entering, or burglarizing, an inhabited dwelling with intent to commit felony theft, which was a capital crime in Alabama. Owing to his indigence, he could not afford to pay for a lawyer, so the circuit judge Wallace C. Gibson Sr. assigned a public defender by the name of Clell I. Mayfield to represent Hamilton during his arraignment on January 4, 1957. In accordance with Gibson's assignment, Mayfield was present to witness Hamilton enter a plea of not guilty to burglary and theft during Hamilton's arraignment. As the accused lawbreaker awaited future proceedings, law enforcement personnel in Birmingham conducted an additional investigation and concluded he might have wanted to rape Giangrosso, so a grand jury returned a second indictment against Hamilton on February 12. That indictment contained the original count of burgling with intent to steal from Giangrosso as well as an additional count, burgling with intent to ravish her. The grand jury leveled those charges against Hamilton even though he did not have a burglary tool or a dangerous weapon during the October 1956 matter involving Giangrosso, whom Hamilton did not touch let alone inflict bodily damage on her.

A second arraignment, or rearraignment, took place on March 1, 1957. Hamilton still could not afford private counsel, and Mayfield did not show up for the arraignment despite being aware of it. Several observers presumed

Mayfield's original appointment did not carry over, but available public records did not indicate what caused his absence. Records, however, did indicate Hamilton entered a plea of not guilty and Gibson set April 23 as the trial date. Mayfield showed for trial, only to attempt to withdraw from the case because Hamilton acted unstably, at one point declaring Mayfield was not his lawyer. To Mayfield's dismay, Gibson did not permit him to resign because the Alabama State Bar Code of Ethics discouraged any officer of the court from seeking to retire from a case on account of a light cause, or minor reason. Furthermore, Gibson explained, Hamilton never stated he did not want Mayfield to represent him, nor did Hamilton contend Mayfield was disloyal or incompetent. Hamilton simply declared Mayfield was not his lawyer.

Jefferson County Deputy Solicitor Cecil M. Deason prosecuted the Hamilton case. Amid closing arguments on April 23, 1957, Deason admitted Hamilton did not ravish Giangrosso, as alleged in count two against Hamilton, but Deason implied the mere possibility of such Black-on-White criminality was enough to make an example of Hamilton. Deason thus asked the White men composing the jury if they were "going to wait until a man like this accomplishes his purpose before giving the extreme penalty."[36] Deason then challenged the jurors to prove they had "the guts to . . . send out the word from this courthouse this very day that anyone, anyone at all, who enters a house in the night-time with intent to ravish, will face death" by electrocution at Kilby Prison in Mt. Meigs, the birthplace of the Rev. Fred Shuttlesworth.[37]

Neither the jury nor the circuit judge, Wallace Gibson, disappointed Deason in April 1957. Within an hour of Deason's closing argument, the jury returned a guilty verdict against Hamilton for the March 1, or second, indictment of first-degree burglary. On April 24, Gibson sentenced Hamilton to death while discontinuing the January 4, or first, indictment. Because death was the sentence the jury recommended and Gibson ordered, a state statute entitled Hamilton to an automatic appeal to the Supreme Court of Alabama. Orzell Billingsley Jr., a Birmingham native who, not unlike Oscar Adams Jr., was graduated from the A. H. Parker High School in Birmingham, Talladega College, and the Howard University School of Law, was one lead counselor. Arthur Shores was the second. Adams and Peter Hall Sr. rounded out the defense team. Billingsley, Shores, Adams, and Hall acknowledged Mayfield's being present during arraignment on January 4 and representing Hamilton during trial on April 23, 1957, but averred no lawyer was present to represent Hamilton during arraignment on March 1. Billingsley, Shores, Adams, and Hall introduced into evidence an arraignment minute entry and certified copies of Gibson's bench memoranda, or notes, and his judgment of entry to support their averment. The same minute entry and bench memoranda indicated Mayfield did not begin representing Hamilton until March 4, several days after Hamilton pleaded not guilty on two separate occasions.

Inasmuch as Hamilton did not have legal representation during his second arraignment on March 1, Billingsley, Shores, Adams, and Hall argued Hamilton did not have a fair trial. They supported their argument by noting due process guarantees in both the US Constitution and the Alabama Constitution. As per both constitutions, a citizen accused of a capital offense had a right to legal counsel during each discussion the citizen had with any agent of the state from the opening of an initial plea hearing through the adjournment of a final court hearing. But being guided by a trial record indicating Hamilton had legal representation on January 4 and concluding that the absence of representation on March 1 did not affect Hamilton adversely or prejudice the case, members of the Supreme Court of Alabama did not reach the merits of Billingsley, Shores, Adams, and Hall's argument. Reaching said merits necessitated impeaching the trial's minute entries, which was illegal in the state for a case on appeal. Moreover, neither Billingsley nor Shores, as co-lead counselors for Hamilton, attempted to show there was an adverse effect or prejudice. Consequently, Alabama Chief Justice James E. Livingston issued an opinion on September 17, 1959, affirming Hamilton's conviction.

Not long after Livingston issued his opinion, he announced that officials at Kilby Prison would electrocute Hamilton on December 4, 1959. Proclaiming the Jefferson County jail was overcrowded, law enforcement personnel in Birmingham transferred Hamilton and two other inmates facing death penalties to Kilby where Hamilton planned to continue his stand against having to sit in the state's electric chair. A rehearing application his legal team filed with Livingston and others on the Supreme Court of Alabama provided Hamilton with an additional respite, but Livingston and his judicial associates eventually decided to overrule the application. Livingston announced their decision on January 21, 1960, and set April 15 as the new date Kilby officials would electrocute Hamilton. On January 28, however, a staffer in the office of Alabama governor and Democratic Party standard-bearer John M. Patterson publicized an opportunity for Hamilton to "plea for clemency before God" during a gubernatorial hearing on April 8.[38]

For some unpublicized reason, the hearing Patterson afforded Hamilton wound up taking place on April 15, 1960, mere hours before the scheduled electrocution. According to the White-owned *Birmingham Post-Herald*, among other newspapers, Hamilton without a hint of nervousness looked directly into the eyes of Patterson when trying to prove he was innocent of a vile act, rape: "I ask for mercy because I did not commit the crime[,] nor did I have any intention of committing the crime. I have a great respect for elderly people. I was too afraid to run because people would think I had stolen something or done something wrong."[39] Hamilton then beseeched Patterson to "spare his life and 'show the world that Alabama does believe in justice.'"[40] In the end, Patterson rejected Hamilton's emotional plea, condemning him to death via electrocution on April 20. When that date arrived, however, US Supreme Court Associate Justice Hugo Black Sr. stayed the execution pending the eventuation of a petition for a writ of certiorari. Black gave defense lawyers Oscar Adams Jr., Orzell Billingsley Jr., Peter Hall Sr., and Arthur Shores until May 20, 1961, to file the petition. Whether Adams, Billingsley, Hall, and Shores met that deadline remains unclear, but on May 27, they and full-time LDF lawyers Derrick A. Bell Jr., Jack Greenberg, Thurgood Marshall, and James M. Nabrit III petitioned Black and his colleagues on the high court to give the Hamilton case full review.

The petition Adams, Billingsley, Hall, Shores, Bell, Greenberg, and Nabrit submitted to the US Supreme Court emphasized federal and state laws, judicial decisions and precedents, and cognate items guaranteeing defendants who faced death penalties had competent legal representatives present at all stages of their detentions from arrest through sentencing. Adams, Billingsley, Hall, Shores, Bell, Greenberg, and Nabrit indicated Charles Hamilton had no legal representation, competent or otherwise, during his second arraignment on March 1, 1957. Likewise, the original trial on April 23, 1957, was unfair. Among other problematic acts, Wallace Gibson, the circuit judge who presided over the trial, invited Hamilton to conduct his own defense along with public defender Clell Mayfield. Hamilton was so deficient that Gibson had to reprimand him multiple times in open court. Nevertheless, justices on the Supreme Court of Alabama affirmed the conviction. Hamilton's legal team appealed the case to the US Supreme Court, whose justices heard it on October 17, 1961.

Constance B. Motley, the first woman to serve as an LDF staff lawyer, argued Hamilton's case before the country's highest court. Reared in New Haven, Connecticut, near Yale University, Motley attended Fisk University from 1941 to 1942 before transferring to New York University where she completed an economics degree in 1943. After clerking for Thurgood Marshall at the LDF in 1945, Motley earned a law degree from Columbia University in 1946 and proceeded to join him full-time at the LDF. Among other notable endeavors, Motley drafted the original 1952 complaint in *Brown I*, and she assisted Shores and Marshall in the Autherine Lucy and Pollie Hudson desegregation case against the University of Alabama from 1952 to 1956. Those activities helped prepare Motley for the 1961 Hamilton litigation, which made her a jurisprudential trailblazer and a neophyte simultaneously. Motley was the first Black lead attorney in the twentieth century to argue a case before the US Supreme Court, and the argument she made was her first before that court.

A 1932 Supreme Court ruling in *Powell v. Alabama*, a case Oscar Adams Sr. followed closely in the *Birmingham Reporter*, was a seminal piece in Motley's legal education as well as a saving grace for her eventual client, Hamilton. As per the ruling, any citizen facing a capital crime "requires the guiding hand of counsel at every step in the proceedings against him. Without it, though he be not guilty, he faces the danger of conviction because he does not know how to establish his innocence."[41] Those lines, among others in the *Powell* ruling, were crucial to the freeing of nine Black teenagers from Alabama whom judicial officials in the state incarcerated unfairly. Two White hitchhikers, one a teen and the other an adult, lied about the nine teens raping them onboard a freight train in Paint Rock, about 20 miles west of Scottsboro, in 1931. Before *Powell*, seven of the nine Black teens faced death by electrocution and one teen a lifetime of imprisonment. Justices on the Supreme Court of Alabama granted the ninth teen a new trial because he was a minor when the two hitchhikers lied about being raped.

Motley in consultation with Oscar Adams Jr., Derrick Bell Jr., Orzell Billingsley Jr., Jack Greenberg, Peter Hall Sr., James Nabrit III, and Arthur Shores based part of their defense strategy for Hamilton on the *Powell* ruling. Motley's argument before the US Supreme Court on October 17, 1961, emphasized Hamilton's intellectual disability, which required him to have effective legal representation from his arraignment onward. Motley also emphasized an Alabama statute requiring a defendant to introduce, present, or raise certain issues (e.g., regarding the ethnic composition of a grand jury) during arraignment lest the defendant waived the ability to raise those issues in a future proceeding. Moreover, the evidence against Hamilton was flimsy, as ravishing a person without touching the person was impossible. Even so, Hamilton's public defender, Clell Mayfield, did not offer to point out that impossibility during trial. Mayfield's glaring omission, Motley concluded, was only one problem that made his counsel ineffective and hence violative of due process.

Associate Justice William O. Douglas authored the November 13, 1961, opinion for the Supreme Court. "Whatever may be the function and importance of arraignment in other jurisdictions," Douglas wrote, "in Alabama it is a critical stage in a criminal proceeding. What happens there may affect the whole trial. Available defenses may be as irretrievably lost, if not then and there asserted, as they are when an accused represented by counsel waives a right for strategic purposes."[42] Douglas then borrowed the line from *Powell* regarding any defendant facing capital punishment needing the guiding hand of a counselor lest the defendant risked conviction and execution simply for not knowing how to establish innocence. For that reason, among others, Douglas and his judicial associates on the Supreme Court unanimously set aside the death penalty Hamilton faced because no lawyer represented Hamilton at his second arraignment on March 1, 1957.

Oscar Adams Jr. helped litigate another precedent-setting Supreme Court case during the early 1960s. Mary L. Hamilton was plaintiff. Of no relation to Charles Hamilton, she was a light-skinned, freckled-faced, unabashedly militant State University of Iowa graduate, one-time schoolmarm, and Freedom Rider who became the first woman to serve as field secretary for the Congress of Racial Equality. After participating in a June 25, 1963, demonstration in Gadsden, Alabama, local police officers arrested her for violating a court injunction against certain protests. During a habeas corpus hearing on the same date, Etowah County Circuit Solicitor William W. Rayburn referred to her by Mary instead of by Miss Hamilton, a titular courtesy he almost certainly would have granted a White woman in a judicial proceeding. Hamilton did not take his insult lightly. She proclaimed, "My name is Miss Hamilton. Please address me correctly."[43]

Ignoring Hamilton's legitimate request, Rayburn continued to ask questions, but she declined to answer him because he did not address her respectfully. His antics made newspaper headlines across the country, especially in the North. The Dayton, Ohio, *Daily News* and the *New York Times* reported: "Whisperings, gasps and shufflings of feet rustled through the courtroom" after Hamilton's valiant stance against a "key part of the South's 'racial caste system' [i.e., someone White addressing a non-White person by a first name]."[44] "Down came the gavel. Contempt of court. Fifty dollar fine. Five days in jail," the *Daily News* went on, describing the ostensible reaction of Etowah County Circuit Judge Augustus B. Cunningham Sr.[45] In reality, a furious Cunningham erroneously ordered Hamilton to serve fifty days in jail and to pay a fine amounting to $5. Cunningham did not correct the error until Adams informed him the extent of his jurisdiction permitted only a five-day jail sentence and a $50 fine.

Cunningham had regained control of his temper by the close of business on June 25, 1963. Having rethought what transpired among Rayburn and Hamilton, Cunningham summoned Adams to his chambers and encouraged him to "bring that girl down here, get her to apologize, and let's just forget about this thing."[46] Adams doubted Hamilton would agree to those terms, but Cunningham asked him to approach her anyhow. Adams complied and, as he expected, she rejected the offer. In his opinion, Hamilton was prepared to remain incarcerated "till hell freezes over."[47] All the same, Cunningham directed jail personnel to escort Hamilton from her cell to his chambers where he expressed being "sorry they called you Mary. I don't mind them calling you Miss Hamilton. In fact, I think they ought to call you Miss Hamilton," as did Cunningham himself when explaining to her a primary reason for his not correcting Rayburn: "He's influential with a lot of powerful people. If I had done that, come election time I wouldn't get a single vote."[48] When Hamilton remained steadfast in refusing to apologize for not accepting Rayburn's disrespect, Cunningham agreed to release her on bond so she could "take this thing all the way to the U.S. Supreme Court."[49]

Members of the Supreme Court of Alabama ruled on Hamilton's case before their contemporaries on the US Supreme Court agreed to hear it. Associate Justice Pelham J. Merrill authored the September 26, 1963, opinion for the state court. Because it was "every man's duty to give testimony before a duly constituted tribunal unless he invokes some valid legal exemption in withholding it," Merrill wrote, Hamilton was obligated to answer Rayburn's question regarding who arrested her on June 25 because she did not invoke an exemption to legitimize a refusal to answer the question.[50] Furthermore, the "record conclusively shows that petitioner's name is Mary Hamilton, not Miss Mary Hamilton," Merrill declared.[51] "Many witnesses are addressed by various titles," he expounded, "but one's own name is an acceptable appellation at law. This practice is almost universal in the written opinions of courts. In the cross-examination of witnesses, a wide latitude is allowed resting in the sound discretion of the trial court and unless the discretion is grossly abused, the ruling of the court will not be overturned. [Inasmuch as we] hold that the trial court did not abuse its discretion and the record supports the summary punishment inflicted," Merrill concluded, he and his colleagues on the Supreme Court of Alabama denied the petition for a writ of certiorari Adams, Jack Greenberg, and James Nabrit III submitted to the court.[52]

Adams, Greenberg, and Nabrit represented Hamilton when the US Supreme Court released an unsigned decision on March 30, 1964. The decision overturned the September 26, 1963, opinion of the state court and set a precedent for the proper way to address a person in a judicial proceeding. The legal victory delighted Hamilton, but she was skeptical that many White judges in the South would comply. Hamilton knew that addressing someone respectfully whom they deemed inherently unworthy of respect was "a bitter pill for them to swallow."[53] But if a judge did not comply, she resolved on second thought, he "could never get any convictions against a Negro" because an appellate court would declare a mistrial whenever the judge was noncompliant.[54]

By the time the US Supreme Court issued its precedent-setting ruling in the Hamilton case in March 1964, Adams had helped successfully represent a Black minister in Birmingham, Alabama, named Calvin W. Woods Sr. after Woods's unlawful arrest in November 1958 and his wrongful conviction in December for a bogus misdemeanor charge the Black-owned *Pittsburgh Courier* newspaper described as "boycott preaching."[55] Birmingham court officials convicted Woods, who pastored the East End Baptist Church and who cofounded the ACMHR, of encouraging his parishioners not to ride segregated buses. Not unlike countless other freedom fighters, Woods believed peaceable passengers who "paid their money . . . were entitled to sit wherever they pleased."[56] His ministerial ACMHR associate, Fred Shuttlesworth, called Woods's arrest "an unwarranted and illegal invasion of the inviolability of the Christian pulpit."[57] In December 1959, a second Black-owned newspaper, the Huntsville, Alabama, *Mirror*, announced that "a ray of hope" shown when Adams and Orzell Billingsley Jr. persuaded an appellate court to reverse the conviction of Woods, whose original penalties included a $500 fine and six months hard labor while he served jail time.[58] The court agreed with Adams and Billingsley regarding there being no legitimate reason to arrest, try, or convict Woods because state lawmakers repealed the city ordinance he purportedly violated years before his arrest.

Another late 1950s civil rights case Adams helped litigate involved Black husband and wife Carl L. and Alexinia Y. Baldwin. White police officers arrested the Baldwins in December 1956 for sitting in an area of the Birmingham Terminal Station reserved for White people and interstate travelers. In February 1961, after more than four years of litigation, the USCourt of Appeals for the Fifth Circuit ordered city officials to "obliterate the supposed distinction between interstate and intrastate passenger status as well as the use of race or color as the basis for occupancy of either one or both of the waiting rooms of the Terminal."[59] Elaborating, the appellate court stated, "Negroes are entitled to be free of . . . discrimination at the hands of state, city, and police officials," as per the Fourteenth Amendment to the US Constitution and a federal civil rights law effected in September 1957—not long, incidentally, after Adams and other founders of the Charles H. Houston Legal Study Club in Birmingham elected Adams as their inaugural president.[60]

Of no surprise, considering Adams's central involvement in the Baldwins' legal case and his devotion to the broader civil rights movement, he supported the Freedom Rides of May to December 1961. According to the *Alabama Tribune*, a Black-owned newspaper in Montgomery, Adams believed the riders' "use of 'unconventional weapons'" represented the types of "new tools, sharper methods, and lofty ideas" needed to meet "novel resistance . . . and fresh barriers" to universal equality.[61] Recognizing Adams for the various roles he had performed to combat bigotry and thereby advance the movement by the early 1960s, Arthur Shores—the "dean of the Alabama black bar"—said Adams established himself firmly within a cohort whose members Shores heralded as the first generation of civil rights lawyers in the state.[62]

Adams's efforts with the LDF were particularly noteworthy. As its Birmingham counsel during the 1950s and 1960s, Adams litigated more civil rights cases than any other lawyer in Alabama. His work desegregated or helped lay the foundations to desegregate airports, libraries, medical centers, parks, schools, and other taxpayer-sponsored places. One case Adams litigated resulted in the desegregation of the Birmingham Police Department. And, despite risking grave harm to not only himself but also his loved ones, he protested the recurrent bombings that Klansmen and other violent White Alabamians carried out in the Smithfield community where the Adams and Shores families resided. After Klansmen bombed the Shores residence on August 20, 1963, and again on September 4, or twice in a two-week span, they executed a third bombing on September 15. It occurred roughly a mile northeast of Smithfield and ended the lives of four young, innocent, female members of the Sixteenth Street Baptist Church. That bombing remains one of the most notorious single acts of White domestic terrorism in US history.

About 17 months after the Sixteenth Street Baptist Church bombing, a White state trooper in Alabama fatally shot a 26-year-old Black deacon, family man, and hardworking laborer named Jimmie L. Jackson. The shooting took place on February 18, 1965, during an originally peaceful civil rights demonstration in Marion, the county seat of Perry County, about 75 miles southwest of Birmingham. Adams represented Jackson, who while fighting for his life in a Selma hospital called Good Samaritan on February 25 described seeing another White trooper strike his mother a week earlier. Jackson said he "couldn't stand it, 'cause Mother wasn't doing anything." [Jackson] remembered having a bottle, but that if he used it at all, and he wasn't sure, it must have been after he himself was clubbed" by multiple troopers.[63] Not long after the clubbing, Jackson felt a bullet penetrate his abdomen. Unable to recover, he died in Good Samaritan on February 26.

Civil rights icons Coretta S. and Martin L. King Jr. were close friends of Jackson, whose death helped motivate the Kings and hundreds of other nonviolent foot soldiers to march from Selma to Montgomery to protest injustice. As one source noted, "the first attempt to reach Montgomery on March 7 resulted in 'blood [flowing] in the street . . . like water' at the foot of the Edmund Pettus Bridge in Selma. A second attempt on March 9 was not bloody, but it was not successful, either. Success did not come until March 25. After five days and four nights of trekking fifty-four miles altogether, an estimated twenty-five thousand individuals arrived in the state capital."[64] Stepping onto the flatbed of a trailer serving as a makeshift riser, Rev. King positioned himself behind a rostrum and proclaimed in his typically eloquent and idealistic manner, "The end we seek is a society at peace with itself, a society that can live with its conscience. And that will be a day not of the white man, not of the black man. That will be the day of man as man."[65] Attempting to facilitate the societal peace about which King spoke, Adams helped craft one of the loftiest mechanisms to unperch Jim and Jane Crow in modern US history: the Voting Rights Act of 1965. The following year, Adams became the first Black member of the Birmingham Bar Association. A year later, Harvey Burg and Adams established the first ethnically mixed law firm in Alabama.

Adams celebrated his twentieth anniversary as a licensed attorney on September 30, 1967. From that date until his retirement from the Supreme Court of Alabama on October 31, 1993, he amassed a sterling record as both a litigator and a jurist. His close friend and law partner, U. W. Clemon, spoke glowingly about him during a June 10, 2006, interview conducted at the Birmingham Civil Rights Institute, on whose original task force Adams served. Clemon, a Fairfield native who finished Columbia Law School en route to becoming the first Black federal judge in Alabama, declared:

> Aside from [being] the first Black to be elected to statewide office in the history of the state, I think that Oscar's legacy will be one of subtle commitment to Civil Rights at a time when it was not an easy thing to do. Because in the days when Oscar filed the [principal] cases, even if you won, you didn't get attorney's fees and so much of that had to be a labor of love. Often the NAACP legal defense fund, if it could be convinced... to sponsor a case, would pay you $50 a day for working in the office and $100 a day for each trial. Other lawyers in those days[,] in the 60s, were making $50 per hour and most of the work was done outside of court. So you didn't make money by handling civil rights cases, but Oscar handled them and didn't complain about it. He did very well because in the process, he made friendships and Civil Rights clients brought other kinds of cases into the office, which did pay money and it worked out nicely.[66]

Deemed a legal "gladiator but also a man of charm and good humor, courage and... insight" by a White-owned Anniston, Alabama, newspaper known as the *Star*, Adams represented more than 20,000 clients.[67] That list included the Alabama Christian Movement for Human Rights, the NAACP, and the

Southern Christian Leadership Conference, among other organizations, as well as civil rights foot soldiers and commanders such as Coretta and Martin King Jr., Rosa Parks, and Fred Shuttlesworth. While Adams did not gauge his worth by the sums he obtained for his clients, one monumental equal-employment case against the United States Steel Corporation in which Adams served as lead attorney resulted in a monetary award exceeding $30 million for the class he represented. Throughout those proceedings, which were microcosms of others, Adams prepared diligently, spoke eloquently, and cared equally as much about the law as about the people for whom he lawyered. His LDF associate, Jack Greenberg, described him as "courageous, forthright, humble, sensitive and strong."[68] Without Adams, Greenberg asserted, "nothing would have happened" to advance civil rights in Alabama.[69] "I packed my . . . bags and went home" to New York, Greenberg continued, while Adams "stayed down there and lived with the problem and dealt with it and he overcame."[70] Concluding, Greenberg said Adams "showed that someone who is prepared and energetic and optimistic and courageous can make a big difference."[71]

Adams expressed corresponding beliefs about preparation, energy, optimism, and courageousness. Youth constituted his favorite audience. He liked to say, "You can go as far as your talents will take you, if you study and be ready or get ready," adding pragmatically: "It doesn't necessarily mean the opportunity will come, but don't be lacking preparedness in the event that the opportunity does come."[72] Adams, a talented cook, imparted such kernels of wisdom generously, particularly when communicating with those he loved most: his family members. Reminiscing fondly about him in March 2006, his widow, Anne-Marie B. Adams, confirmed that he "was a very devoted family man—to his wife, and his children and I guess one of the significant things is that when we married, he was devoted to my two sons" from a previous marriage, Kynath J. Bradford and his younger sibling, Kevin J. Bradford.[73] Adams Jr. treated his and Anne-Marie's adopted grandchildren, Kynath J. Adams and Kyndra J. Adams, with similar degrees of love and care, exposing "them to the finer things in life as if they were his own blood kin," Anne-Marie noted happily.[74] According to her, the final words he spoke to Kynath and Kyndra before succumbing to cancer on February 15, 1997, were "Granddaddy wants you to always remember that I love you."[75]

Oscar Adams Jr.'s survivors interred him in a Birmingham cemetery called Elmwood. It was a fitting resting place for him considering that he assisted in litigating the federal case that desegregated Elmwood in 1969. Although underrepresented in civil rights scholarship, that legal victory and others discussed in this chapter help prove Adams was a conscientious lawyer and jurist worthy of emulation and further study. As his fellow Black lawyer, Julian M. Davis Jr., attested during an interview at the Birmingham Civil Rights Institute in 2006, Adams loved his family, cherished academic education, and respected the law. Davis characterized his friend and professional associate, Adams, as "a sincere man. He was concerned about his practice [and] did an excellent [job] in the cases that he had."[76] Unwaveringly committed to family and God, Adams was one of the Metropolitan AME Zion Church's most outstanding members in Davis's judgment. Quoting Paul the Apostle, Davis concluded his characterization of Adams with a line from which this chapter draws its title. Adams, Davis posited, "fought the good fight, he finished the course, he ran the race."[77]

Notes

1 Mattie B. Rowe, "What Negroes Are Doing," *Birmingham News*, September 7, 1947, 14A.
2 Frances Spotswood, "The End of an Era for Black Law Firm," *Birmingham News*, October 19, 1980, 1F (quotation), 4F.
3 Oscar W. Adams Jr., "Remarks by Retired Justice Oscar W. Adams, Jr.: Opening of Court Ceremony 1994-95, Term October 3, 1994," *Alabama Lawyer* 56, no. 1 (January 1995): 33.
4 Adams, "Remarks," 33.
5 Ella V. Eaton finished Talladega College on June 3, 1914.
6 Frank Adams and Burgin Mathews, *Doc: The Story of a Birmingham Jazz Man* (Tuscaloosa: University of Alabama Press, 2012), 225.
7 Adams and Mathews, *Doc*, 225.
8 W. E. B. Du Bois, "Jacob and Esau," in *W. E. B. Du Bois Speaks: Speeches and Addresses, 1920-1963*, ed. Philip S. Foner (New York: Pathfinder, 1970), 137-149 (quotation on p. 146).
9 Du Bois, "Jacob and Esau," 147.
10 Du Bois, 147.
11 Du Bois, 148-149; James W. Kelsaw to W. E. B. Du Bois, April 3, 1951, in W. E. B. Du Bois Papers, MS 312, Special Collections and University Archives, University of Massachusetts Amherst Libraries (cited hereinafter as Du Bois Papers and UMAL, respectively). See also Oscar W. Adams Sr. to W. E. B. Du Bois, June 6, 1944, in Du Bois Papers, UMAL.
12 Adams, "Remarks," 33; Stan Bailey, "Justice for All: The First Black to Sit on Alabama's Supreme Court Says He Never Wanted to Be More than a Good Lawyer," *Birmingham News*, October 31, 1993, 1A, 12A.
13 Adams, "Remarks," 33.
14 Carol Jenkins and Elizabeth Gardner Hines, *Black Titan: A. G. Gaston and the Making of a Black American Millionaire* (New York: One World/Ballantine Books, 2004), 3.

15 Helen Shores Lee and Barbara S. Shores, *The Gentle Giant of Dynamite Hill: The Untold Story of Arthur Shores and His Family's Fight for Civil Rights* (Grand Rapids, MI: Zondervan, 2012).
16 "An Act to Propose an Amendment to Section 181 of the Constitution of Alabama and to Order Thereon an Election for the Qualified Electors of the State of Alabama at the General Election Next Succeeding the 1945 Regular Session of the Legislature," June 13-27, 1945, in *General Laws (and Joint Resolutions) of the Legislature of Alabama Passed at the Session of 1945* . . . (Birmingham, AL: Birmingham Printing Company, 1945), 551-552 (quotation on p. 551); Joseph M. Brittain, "The Return of the Negro to Alabama Politics, 1930-1954," *Negro History Bulletin* 22, no. 8 (May 1959): 197.
17 Edwin Strickland, "Boswell Amendment Facing Federal Court Validity Test," *Birmingham News*, May 30, 1948, 4A.
18 Samuel L. Webb, "Hugo Black, Bibb Graves, and the Ku Klux Klan: A Revisionist View of the 1926 Alabama Democratic Primary," *Alabama Review* 57, no. 4 (October 2004): 244.
19 "The Boswell Amendment," *Montgomery Advertiser*, August 25, 1947, 4.
20 "First Suit Is Filed against Boswell Rule by Birmingham Negro," *Birmingham News*, April 27, 1948, 1.
21 Strickland, "Boswell Amendment."
22 Associated Press, "Jefferson Board of Registrars Asks Suit Action," *Talladega Daily Home and Our Mountain Home*, December 9, 1948, 2.
23 Kelly Dowe, "Judge Adams Wins Statewide Race," *Down Home* 3, no. 2 (Winter 1983): 29.
24 Dowe, 32.
25 Adams and Mathews, *Doc,* 203.
26 Wayne Coleman, interview with Gail Harden, August 19, 2006, transcript, 3-4, Birmingham Civil Rights Institute Oral History Project (cited hereinafter as BCRIOHP).
27 In 1897, the all-White Alabama legislature passed an act providing everyone who finished the ethnically segregated University of Alabama School of Law in Tuscaloosa with a diploma privilege authorizing justices on the Supreme Court of Alabama to admit the graduate to the state bar without completing a certifying examination. The attendant law took effect in 1898.
28 "Ala. Suit Opposes Four Negro Lawyers on Bar Exemptions," *Pittsburgh Courier*, December 17, 1949, 11.
29 Ex Parte Banks et al., 6 Div. 972, 254 Ala. 117 (June 30, 1950).
30 "Demo and GOP Speakers Urge All to Vote Nov. 6 for Either Candidate" (Tuscaloosa, AL), *Alabama Citizen*, November 3, 1956, 1, 8 (quotation).
31 "Demo and GOP Speakers," 8.
32 Walter B. Jones, "I Speak for the White Race," *Alabama Lawyer* 18, no. 2 (April 1957): 201-203.
33 J. Mills Thornton III, *Dividing Lines: Municipal Politics and the Struggle for Civil Rights in Montgomery, Birmingham, and Selma* (Tuscaloosa: University of Alabama Press, 2002), 108.
34 "Jones Grants Writ on Patterson Plea" (Montgomery), *Alabama Journal*, June 1, 1956, 1A (quotation), 2A.

35 See Horace Huntley, interview with Anne-Marie Adams, March 7, 2006, transcript, 10, BCRIOHP (cited hereinafter as Huntley–Anne-Marie Adams interview, even though the transcriber did not hyphenate Anne-Marie).
36 Jane Aldridge, "Young Negro Captured in White House," *Birmingham Post-Herald*, Aril 24, 1957, 1 (quotation), 2.
37 Aldridge, "Young Negro Captured in White House," 1.
38 "Two Clemency Hearings Get Governor's Nod," *Alabama Journal* (Montgomery), January 28, 1960, 2A.
39 United Press International, "Negro Asks Mercy in Death Sentence," *Birmingham Post-Herald*, April 19, 1960, 17.
40 "Negro Slated for Chair Has Hearing," *Montgomery Advertiser*, April 19, 1960, 2A.
41 Ozie Powell, Willie Roberson, Andy Wright, and Olen Montgomery v. Alabama, Haywood Paterson v. Same, Charley Weems and Clarence Norris v. Same, Nos. 98, 99, 100, 287 U.S. 45 (November 7, 1932).
42 Hamilton v. Alabama, No. 32, 368 U.S. 52 (November 13, 1961).
43 Frye Gaillard, *Alabama Civil Rights Trail: An Illustrated Guide to the Cradle of Freedom* (Tuscaloosa: University of Alabama Press, 2010), 242.
44 "Tom Who?" *Dayton (OH) Daily News*, February 17, 1964, 18 (first quotation); "Negro's Dignity Basis of Appeal," *New York Times*, January 31, 1964, 15 (second quotation).
45 "Tom Who?"
46 Dowe, "Judge Adams Wins Statewide Race," 29.
47 Dowe, 29.
48 Dowe, 29.
49 Dowe, 29.
50 Ex Parte Mary Hamilton, No. 7 Div. 621, 275 Ala. 574 (September 26, 1963), quoting Ullmann v. United States, No. 58, 350 U.S. 422 (March 26, 1956).
51 Ex Parte Mary Hamilton.
52 Ex Parte Mary Hamilton.
53 Larry Still, "Court Decision on Miss Mary Will Change South's Social Customs," *Jet* 26, no. 2 (April 23, 1964): 51.
54 Still, "Court Decision," 51.
55 Trezzvant W. Anderson, "Ala. Group Plans Park Bias Fight after Legal Bout," *Pittsburgh Courier*, May 2, 1959, sec. 2, p. 4.
56 Andrew M. Manis, *A Fire You Can't Put Out: The Civil Rights Life of Birmingham's Reverend Fred Shuttlesworth* (Tuscaloosa: University of Alabama Press, 1999), 192.
57 Scott News Syndicate, "B'Ham Ministers Speak for Freedom in Bus Protest," *Alabama Tribune* (Montgomery), December 19, 1958, 1, 8 (quotation).
58 "Judge Cates Voids Woods Bus Boycott Case Charges," *Huntsville Mirror*, December 19, 1959, 1.
59 Carl L. Baldwin and Alexinia Baldwin, Appellants, v. J. W. Morgan et al., Appellees, No. 18280, 287 F. 2d 750 (February 17, 1961).
60 *Baldwin and Baldwin v. Morgan et al.*
61 Emory O. Jackson, "The Tip-Off," *Alabama Tribune* (Montgomery), June 2, 1961, 8.

62 U. W. Clemon and Bryan Fair, "Making Bricks without Straw: The NAACP Legal Defense Fund and the Development of Civil Rights Law in Alabama 1940–1980," *Alabama Law Review* 52, no. 4 (Summer 2001): 1128.

63 Jack Mendelsohn, *The Martyrs: Sixteen Who Gave Their Lives for Racial Justice* (New York: Harper and Row, 1966), 146.

64 Bertis D. English, *Civil Wars, Civil Beings, and Civil Rights in Alabama's Black Belt: A History of Perry County* (Tuscaloosa: University of Alabama Press, 2020), 240, quoting Deric A. Gilliard, *Living in the Shadows of a Legend: Unsung Heroes and 'Sheroes' Who Marched with Dr. Martin Luther King, Jr.* (Decatur, GA: Gilliard Communications, 2003), 149.

65 Martin L. King Jr., "Address at the Conclusion of the Selma to Montgomery March," in *A Call to Conscience: The Landmark Speeches of Dr. Martin Luther King, Jr.*, ed. Clayborne Carson and Kris Shepard (New York: Warner Books, 2001), 119–132 (quotation on p. 130).

66 Horace Huntley, interview with U. W. Clemon, June 10, 2006, transcript, 4, BCRIOHP.

67 "Legal Precedent: Adams and Justice," *Anniston Star*, August 2, 1993, 4A.

68 Jack Greenberg, interview with Wayne Coleman, November 17, 2006, transcript, 5, BCRIOHP (cited hereinafter as Greenberg-Coleman interview).

69 Greenberg-Coleman interview, 6, BCRIOHP.

70 Greenberg-Coleman interview, 6, BCRIOHP.

71 Greenberg-Coleman interview, 6, BCRIOHP.

72 Huntley–Anne-Marie Adams interview, 12, BCRIOHP.

73 Huntley–Anne-Marie Adams interview, 6, BCRIOHP.

74 Huntley–Anne-Marie Adams interview, 6, BCRIOHP. Kynath J. Adams and Kyndra J. Adams are Kynath J. Bradford's biological children.

75 Huntley–Anne-Marie Adams interview, 6, BCRIOHP.

76 Horace Huntley, interview with J. Mason Davis Jr., October 5, 2006, transcript, 4, BCRIOHP (cited hereinafter as Huntley-Davis interview).

77 Huntley-Davis interview, 4, BCRIOHP.

III

Sports Pioneers

6

Robert Lee Elder and the African American Golf Legacy

MARVIN P. DAWKINS AND JOMILLS HENRY BRADDOCK II

Robert Lee Elder was recognized as one of the trailblazing African American golfers whose achievements contributed to the Black presence in a sport where only a few players of African descent have ever participated in mainstream competition.[1] Among them, only Tiger Woods, who turned professional in 1996, has played regularly on the Professional Golfers Association Tour for at least the past two decades. Lee Elder, who joined the PGA Tour in the 1960s, became the first Black golfer to play in the prestigious Masters Championship Tournament in Augusta, Georgia in 1975.[2] Yet African Americans have participated in golf since its earliest appearance in the United States in the late 1800s.[3] While the tributes paid to Elder upon his passing on November 28, 2021, have been wide and well deserved, critical assessments of questions surrounding the reasons for the absence of a significant presence of Black golfers in this white-dominated sport are lacking.[4] This chapter addresses this issue by focusing on the impact of systemic racism in sports in America, especially in golf. We argue that Lee Elder's achievements, which we shall review, can be better understood in the broader social context of systemic racism and its manifestation in golf. In response to racial barriers, Blacks resisted and developed parallel structures to compete in their own venues behind the veil of segregation while seeking changes to remove institutional barriers, some of which remain in the sport. Thus, Robert Lee Elder is part of a long and ongoing history and struggle among Black golfers, which we refer to as the African American golf legacy.

Racism and Sports in America: A Framework

Sports in America were originally organized to reflect mainstream realities of racial inequality. Thus, whites have maintained control and exploitation of

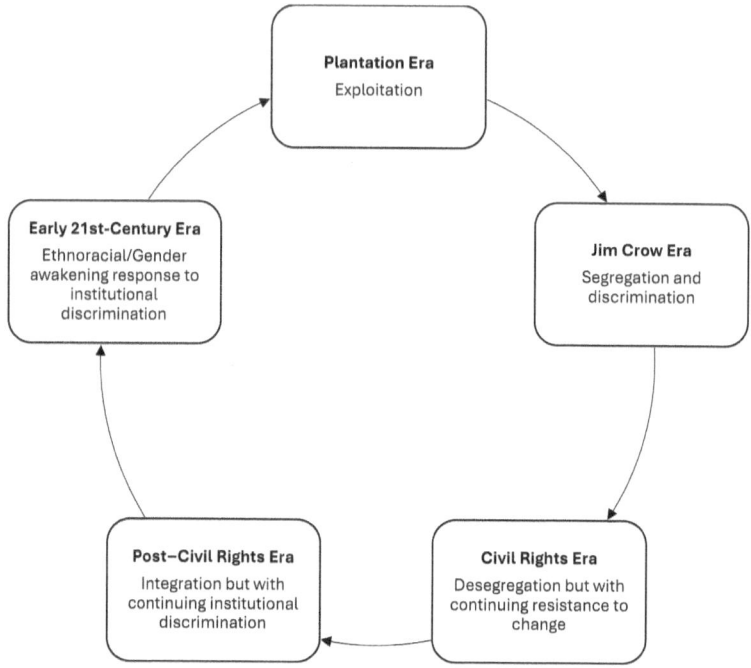

Figure 6.1. Systemic racism and black participation in sports—a framework.

Blacks and other minorities in sports for centuries. Institutionalized racism in sports has been a part of the larger pattern of systemic racism in America, which Feagin has identified as Euro-American oppression of African Americans since the seventeenth century resulting in the reproduction of white power and privilege.[5] Systemic racism in American sports has progressed across five historical stages: the plantation era, the Jim Crow era, the civil rights era, the post–civil rights era, and the early-twenty-first-century-to-the-present era.[6] These stages are depicted in figure 6.1 and described below. The plantation era was characterized by Black exclusion or exploitation and where formal participation in sports was confined to white elites.

During the eighteenth and nineteenth centuries, slaves were exploited for betting purposes (e.g., boxing and horse racing). During the late nineteenth and early twentieth centuries, the initiation of professional sports was established on a "whites-only" basis and Blacks engaged in sports activities as within-group play and recreation.[7] The Jim Crow era was characterized by segregation and discrimination with African Americans stereotyped as inferior and formally excluded from participation in most sports. Blacks responded by developing their own organizational activities (i.e., "parallel structures") and producing their own sport "stars" and role models.[8] During the civil rights era, limited desegregation began after World War II in such major professional sports as baseball and basketball and reinitiated in football. Unlike most major professional sports during the Jim Crow era, the National Football League (NFL) allowed a limited number of African Americans to play. For example, Fritz Pollard, who had been the first African American to play in the Rose Bowl in 1916, played professional football for some seven years leading the Akron Pros to an NFL championship in 1920. He took over as head coach of the team, becoming the first African American head coach in the NFL and went on to coach two other NFL teams before the color line was drawn in 1934, in the middle of the Great Depression.[9] Desegregation was slower in some sports, such as tennis, while white organizations maintained private exemption from compliance with desegregation laws in golf. White owners reacted to desegregation in some sports by continuing to display racial prejudice (e.g., Marge Schott, owner of major league baseball's Cincinnati Reds was widely chastised for using racial slurs in referring to Black star players on the team, resulting in being banned from the position of team president and CEO for two years) along with isolated and small-group discrimination. Black athletes who displayed temperate behavior gained greater acceptance than others who were more critical and radical. Consequently, challenges to discriminatory treatment resulted in negative impacts on their careers.[10] During the post–civil rights era, the white power structure adapted to integration by resisting full Black inclusion through indirect means. For example, Black access to managerial and coaching positions was limited relative to whites. Although not usually expressed openly, a statement by Al Campanis, general manager of the Los Angeles Dodgers major league baseball team (being interviewed by Ted Koppel on an episode of the ABC news show *Nightline* in 1987), may have summarized the sentiment of upper management regarding hiring Black persons as managers and coaches in baseball and other sports. Campanis stated, "They [Black people] may not have some of the necessities."[11] Black athletes and coaches were also subjected to higher performance demands than their white counterparts. In a groundbreaking study on discrimination in managerial hiring in the NFL, Jomills Braddock found that even when potentially prospective Black candidates for coaching and manager positions in the NFL surpassed white counterparts, they were passed over.[12] In this era, efforts to promote gender equity (e.g., Title IX) were initiated. However, Black and white girls and women have not benefited equally.[13] Finally, organizational actions on behalf of players increased efforts to address the lack of full Black inclusion. One example is the "Rooney

Rule" in professional football, which was created, originally, to increase the low number of minorities in head coaching positions in the NFL. The policy required every NFL team with a head coaching vacancy to interview at least one diverse candidate before hiring a new head coach. Such policies as the Rooney Rule (named for late owner of the Pittsburgh Steelers professional football team and head of the NFL diversity committee) enacted at the close of the post–civil rights era (2001) met with only modest success.[14] During the early-twenty-first-century-to-the-present era, a reawakening of Blacks in the context of racial injustices (especially police-involved killings of Blacks) increased Black activism and social protest movements (e.g., Black Lives Matter), including participation by prominent Black athletes reminiscent of the "committed Black athletes" of the civil rights era (e.g., The "Call to Action" challenge issued by leading Black professional basketball players LeBron James, Chris Paul, Dwayne Wade, and Carmelo Anthony at the 2016 Espy Awards ceremony; pro football player Colin Kaepernick's action in "taking a knee" at the playing of the US national anthem at the beginning of games in protest of racial injustices).[15] Such protests against racial and other forms of social injustices were not restricted to examples cited above, but reverberated across many sports and countries throughout the world where athletes joined a reawakening and used their notoriety and platforms to protest injustices in the larger society.

Racism in Golf: The African American Golf Legacy

The systemic racism framework in sports can be applied to golf in America and its long history of institutional barriers to inclusion of African Americans and other minorities, as reflected in the PGA's infamous "Caucasians-only" constitutional clause.[16] The legacy of African Americans in golf traces the actions taken by whites to erect barriers to Black participation in golf from its earliest appearance in America, as well as the actions by African Americans in response to exclusion, in terms of erecting their own institutional golf activities and challenging barriers (both unsuccessfully and successfully) across historical periods as depicted in the systemic racism framework described above (see table 6.1 for some key actions in the African American golf legacy).

The earliest African American presence in golf occurred during the same period that the game was introduced to white elites in the United States in the late nineteenth century. Blacks began in their youth as caddies for wealthy white golf patrons at exclusive country club settings. In this role, Blacks also developed as players. However, unlike their white counterparts (some of whom advanced as youthful golfers to become successful later as professional

Table 6.1. The African American Golf Legacy: Some Key Actions by Year (1896–2019)

Year	Action
1896	John Shippen becomes first African American to play in the United States Golf Association (USGA) championship tournament (over objections of white entrants)
1926	African Americans establish the United Golfers Association (UGA) as a "parallel structure" for Black golfers and hold the first UGA championship tournament
1932	Robert Ball wins motion filed for Philadelphia court injunction to gain entry to the national public links tournament
1934	Professional Golfers' Association (PGA) inserts "Caucasians-only" clause into its constitution
1937	Pennsylvania Open becomes first interracial golf tournament sponsored by a private organization (Eastern Golf Association-affiliate of UGA)
1938	Robert Ball becomes first Black golfer–appointed teaching pro at an interracial (public) golf course (Palos Park, near Chicago)
1939	Public golf course (Langston) is built for African Americans in the nation's capital (Washington, DC)
1941	Joe Louis, world heavyweight boxing champion, launches richest Black golf tournament in the nation (Joe Louis Open)
1942	Black golfers invited to first Tam O'Shanter All American and World Golf Championship Tournament (a major interracial golf venue)
1948	Black golfers (Ted Rhodes, Bill Spiller, and Madison Gunter) threatened a suit against the PGA for excluding them from entering a PGA tournament (Richmond Open)
1952	Joe Louis becomes first African American golfer to play in a PGA-sponsored tournament (San Diego Open) as fellow Black golfer (Bill Spiller) denied entry to the same tournament
1955	In *Holmes v. Atlanta,* the US Supreme Court ended segregation at municipal (public) golf courses
1959	Charlie Sifford is granted "approved tournament player" status by the PGA
1961	PGA removes "Caucasians-only" clause from its constitution
1964	Pete Brown becomes first Black golfer to win a PGA tournament (Waco Turner Open)
1964	Charlie Sifford becomes first Black golfer to gain PGA membership
1975	Lee Elder becomes first Black golfer to play in the Masters Golf Championship Tournament (Augusta, GA)
1997	Tiger Woods becomes first Black golfer to win the Masters and go on to win four more Masters championships
2006	Charlie Sifford becomes first Black golfer to be inducted into the World Golf Hall of Fame
2009	Black golfers John Shippen, Bill Spiller, and Ted Rhodes are posthumously granted PGA membership (Joe Louis is awarded honorary membership posthumously)
2019	Lee Elder becomes first Black golfer to receive the Bob Jones Award, the USGA's highest honor

golfers), Black youth who began as caddies with aspirations for advancement were restricted from achieving this goal by racial barriers erected in the context of Jim Crow practices reflective of the larger society.

The first Black golfer recognized for mounting a challenge to the Jim Crow norms of racial exclusion was a young, teenage caddie named John Shippen, who, along with his Native American (Shinnecock Indian) friend, Oscar Bunn, sought and gained entry to a major, national golf tournament.[17] As Marvin Dawkins and A. C. Tellison Jr. describe, "Shippen was introduced to golf in the 1890s and became involved in tournaments held by the United States Golf Association (USGA) [in] the mid-1890s. Shippen competed in the second USGA championship tournament in 1896 over the objections of some of the white entrants who didn't want to play with him [or Oscar Bunn]. . . . Amazingly, at a time when the top golfers were transplants from England, who would dominate major American golf tournaments for many years to come, this young African American caddie finished tied for fifth place."[18] Later, when the PGA was formed in 1916, Shippen was not invited to join. Clearly, Shippen's appearances in the USGA championship tournaments represented an aberration during the racial climate of Jim Crowism and was not to be repeated by the PGA. Thus, the African American golf legacy can trace its origin to this period of the Jim Crow era.[19] As a result, John Shippen and other Blacks who began as caddies became recognized as golf "pros" only in Black communities. They also served as catalysts for the spread of golf, joining with elite African Americans who, in response to segregation, established organizational golf activities behind the veil of racial segregation. For example, Shippen quietly established himself as a prime mover of golf for over 30 years throughout the Northeast, especially in the Washington, DC–Baltimore area during the 1920s and later while serving as club professional at one of the earliest Black-operated resorts, the Shady Rest Golf and Country Club in Westfield (Scotch Plains), New Jersey. Like Shippen, other African American golfers drew upon experiences gained initially through exposure to golf by caddying to become successful players. However, Black golfers, most of whom began as caddies, did not get opportunities to compete with whites, some of whom advanced through the caddying ranks or followed other routes to advancement in the sport. The cultural norms of Jim Crowism led to the codification of racial restriction when the PGA amended its constitution in 1934 to insert a clause that confined membership in its organization to "Caucasians only."

A major organization created by African Americans to serve as a "parallel structure" and respond to white exclusion of Black golfers from mainstream, white-controlled golf participation was the United Golfers Association

(UGA).[20] The UGA was founded in 1926 and established regional affiliates. The UGA also created its own national golf championship tournament called the National Negro Open, which ran annually from 1926 to 1976 (except during World War II, from 1942 to 1945), produced many and star performers who were better known throughout Black communities in America. Recent scholarship on the UGA has assembled and disseminated evidence more widely to support greater recognition of UGA-era golfers and to view the African American golf legacy as an alternative, critical lens to interrogate previous historical information on the activities and contributions of Blacks to golf; the aim of such scholarship is to explain the lack of a significant historical presence of African Americans competing in golf in America. In adopting the term "trailblazing" in golf, it is not sufficient to simply compile a list of achievements of Black golf pioneers. Drawing upon a critical race approach, the African American golf legacy considers the social context of achievements that often constitute acts of resistance and persistence in overcoming barriers to advancement of Blacks in golf. For example, one of the earliest barrier-breakers was Robert "Pat" Ball, a four-time winner of the UGA Negro National Open Championship from Chicago. Ball was an Atlanta, Georgia, transplant, who, during his teenage years, caddied for the legendary golf pioneer, Bobby Jones, before migrating to Chicago seeking greater opportunities for golf competition. When applying the critical lens of the African American golf legacy, Ball's most notable contribution in advancing Black golf is identified as the role he played in resisting discrimination. For instance, as an action of resistance, Ball filed an injunction in a Philadelphia court against organizers of the 1932 National Public Links Golf Championship Tournament, which sought to deny his entry to that year's championship tournament despite his qualifying by winning the Chicago Public Links Tournament. Also, in 1938 when Ball became the first Black golfer to be named "teaching pro" at an interracial municipal golf course in the Chicagoland area (Palos Park), he had engaged in contestation and resistance to achieve significant goals for himself and successfully achieved progress and advancement for Black golf in America.[21] Solomon Hughes followed a similar path in his resistance to being excluded from the St. Paul (Minnesota) Open, a PGA-sponsored tournament in 1948.[22] As another example, at the opening of the historically Black Langston golf course in Washington, DC, in 1939, which was the culmination of a long battle by prominent and rank-and-file African American golfers of that city, progress came as a result of persistence by African Americans who faced resistance by the white power structure.[23] Through the critical lens of the African American golf legacy (as an exposé of systemic racism in golf in America), we are reminded that the opening of Langston in 1939 was viewed as pacification, disguised as progress. Black Washingtonians continued to be denied entry to the other five public golf courses in the District of Columbia. To their credit, the leaders of the fight for Black golf access that led to the creation of the segregated Langston golf course, dissatisfied with the quality and maintenance of the course (along with the fact the Langston was built with only nine holes after being promised 18 holes), after only two years elected in 1941 to mount a protest (which was successful) to gain access to all public golf courses in Washington, DC.[24] As a third example, ex–world heavyweight boxing champion Joe Louis is noted for the achievement of becoming the first African American golfer to participate in a PGA-sponsored tournament when he accepted the invitation to play at the 1952 San Diego Open. However, Louis's acceptance was made on the condition that fellow Black golfers Eural Clark and Bill Spiller were also invited to play. Clark and Spiller were then required to meet additional qualifying criteria, which only Spiller met. Nevertheless, Spiller was denied entry to the tournament, even though he met the additional qualifications set up by the PGA, when the organization decided to invoke its "Caucasians-only" rule to support the denial of Spiller while waving this rule and upholding the invitation to participate in the tournament for Joe Louis as an amateur guest. Although Joe Louis played in the tournament, he became a more radicalized supporter and advocate for inclusion of Black golfers in mainstream golf activities.[25]

Although the most significant organization developed by African Americans to promote golf in the Black community in response to white exclusion, the UGA exhibited a level of resource support and organizational sophistication that was well below that of the white-controlled PGA. Additionally, the UGA may have been less distant from the masses of rank-and-file (as opposed to elitist) members of the Black golfing community than either the USGA or PGA. The UGA had a network of local and regional affiliates in addition to sponsoring the national championship tournament. Much like Negro league baseball, the heydays of Black golf were reached in the 1940s. Although actions of challenge and protest persisted, long-standing racial barriers only began to change during the civil rights and post–civil rights eras in major sports. However, the pace of change in golf was slower than in other sports. The UGA played an important role in the African American golf legacy in terms of facilitating the advancement of Black golfers by serving as a "springboard" to the PGA for such UGA Negro National Open champions as Charlie Sifford, Pete Brown, Lee Elder, and others. As the protests and demands of the civil rights era began to mount, however, the UGA faded with the dismantling of segregation in some areas of mainstream golf activity.

The actions of African American golfers, themselves, in some areas, were part of the African American golf legacy, including the actions of well-known amateur champion Alfred "Tup" Holmes and the Holmes family leading to the 1955 decision of the US Supreme Court in *Holmes v. Atlanta,* which ended the racial barrier to Black access to municipal (public) golf courses.[26] Also, trailblazing Black baseball star Jackie Robinson, "the golfer," brought significant social pressure that led to the PGA's decision to remove the "Caucasians-only" clause from its constitution in 1961.[27] Robinson was an avid golfer and supported Black golfers in their effort to break through the racial barrier just as he had done in baseball. Lane Demas notes that, "as a youngster he sneaked onto Pasadena's private courses to steal golf balls and sell them back to players . . . [and began playing golf seriously only after arriving at the University of California, Los Angeles] By the end of his college tenure, he had won the Pacific Coast Intercollegiate Golf Championship."[28] When Robinson retired from major league baseball in 1957, he wrote a syndicated column in the *New York Post,* where he launched a fierce writing campaign criticizing the PGA for maintaining its infamous racial exclusionary rule.[29] Despite these efforts, only a handful of Black golfers ascended to the top levels of professional golf and competed on the PGA Tour, leading to the lament by Sifford who recalled this moment in his 1992 autobiography, *Just Let Me Play: The Story of Charlie Sifford, the First Black PGA Golfer.* He referred to the many aging star Black golf performers of an earlier generation at the time of the breakthrough, saying that "most of the black guys who had come up with me had long since given up the idea of playing for a living. They might come out for a Negro tournament here or there, but they'd lost their dedication to the game. The struggle was just too hard and was obviously a losing battle. They went back to their homes and their jobs at the fertilizer plant or the grocery store or the post office, and golf was just an old memory to them."[30] Nevertheless, among the few Black golfers who would play on the PGA Tour following Sifford's breakthrough, the outstanding performance of Lee Elder in becoming the first Black golfer to earn a berth in the famed Masters Golf Championship in Augusta, Georgia, in 1975 and Tiger Woods's record-setting win in the 1997 Masters, as the first golfer of African descent to win the Masters, stand out as perhaps the most significant achievements of the African American golf legacy of the post–civil rights era up to the close of the twentieth century. Lee Elder played in the Masters six times with his top finish a tie for seventeenth place in 1979.[31] Tiger Woods has played in the Masters 24 times since his first appearance in 1995 as an amateur. Since turning pro in 1997, Woods has failed to appear in the Masters only in 2014, 2016, 2017, and 2021. He has won the Masters five times (in 1997, 2001, 2002, 2005, and 2019), including a record-setting victory of finishing 12-under par in his first appearance as a professional in 1997. The five victories at the Masters place him second only to Jack Nicklaus, who has six.[32]

In the early-twenty-first-century-to-the-present era, the African American golf legacy has drawn attention to the need for greater recognition of Black golf pioneers and trailblazers as the larger society moved toward a period of "reckoning" in the face of greater awareness of racial injustices and the lack of diversity, equity, and inclusion in all sectors of society, including sports. Thus, in 2006, Charlie Sifford became the first African American inducted into the World Golf Hall of Fame,[33] followed by the awarding of PGA membership, posthumously, in 2009 to Black golf trailblazer John Shippen and pioneers Bill Spiller and Ted Rhodes along with an honorary membership being granted to Joe Louis.[34] Finally, the USGA in 2019 bestowed its highest honor, the Bob Jones Award, to Lee Elder, as the first Black golf recipient.[35] However, while Tiger Woods has been competing on the PGA Tour in the professional division for more than 25 years, no other golfer of African descent has appeared on the PGA Tour on a regular basis over this period, which continues to raise the question of how to address the cumulative effect of long-term barriers to Black participation in golf.

Lee Elder: Breaking Barriers and Continuing the Legacy

In referring to Lee Elder and his golf accomplishments, such terms as "trailblazer," "barrier-breaker" and "Black golf pioneer," among others, were used following his death in 2021. In addition, Elder has also been applauded for possessing strong endurance and restraint, which enabled him to overcome racism and other adversities that he and other Black golfers of his generation faced as obstacles to their advancement in the sport. Given the history of golf in America, characterized by white domination and control, from the perspective of the African American golf legacy, Lee Elder also faced indirect barriers reflecting institutionalized racism in golf, which prevented Black golfers from competing on an equal basis as their white counterparts. As Adrienne Milner and Jomills Braddock's examination of sex discrimination in sports (*Women in Sports: Breaking Barriers, Facing Obstacles*) notes, trailblazing involves breaking barriers in the context of facing obstacles that require making changes, such as enacting policies (e.g., Title IX) to improve access and equity.[36] Therefore, Lee Elder's career in golf should be viewed in the context of racism in golf and the larger society that served as obstacles that he and other Black golfers faced during their careers. Table 6.2 lists selected highlights of Elder's golf career.

Table 6.2. Lee Elder: Selected Golf Career Highlights

Year	Action
1959	Turned golf professional
1963	United Golfers Association (UGA) Negro National Open Champion (Langston Golf Course, Washington, DC)
1964	UGA Negro National Open Champion (Douglass Park Golf Course, Indianapolis, IN)
1966	UGA Negro National Open Champion (Palos Park Golf Course, Chicago)
1967	UGA Negro National Open Champion (Miami Springs Golf Course, Miami)
1967	Joined the regular PGA Tour
1968	American Golf Classic (tied Jack Nicklaus, lost in sudden-death playoff; Akron, OH)
1974	Monsanto Open Champion (earned invitation to 1975 Masters; Pensacola, FL)
1975	Became the first Black golfer to play in the Masters (Augusta, GA)
1976	Houston Open Champion (Houston)
1978	Greater Milwaukee Open Champion (Milwaukee)
1978	American Express Westchester Classic Champion (Rye, New York)
1979	Became the first Black golfer named to the US Ryder Cup team
1984	Joined the Senior PGA Tour (won eight tournaments in a four-year span)
1996	Forced to withdraw from 5 of 8 Senior Tour events entered due to health problems
2019	Became first Black golfer to receive Bob Jones Award, the United States Golf Association's highest honor
2021	Became honorary starter at Augusta National in April

Robert Lee Elder was born in Dallas, Texas on July 14, 1934, to Charles (a coal truck driver) and Sadie Elder as one of ten siblings. He was introduced to golf at a young age while caddying at a local, all-white golf course, Tenison Park Golf Course, to assist the family by bringing in additional income from caddying. Caddying was the usual route to learning the game of golf for Black youth during the Jim Crow era. Caddies were often taught by white professional golfers who would take them under their wings and teach them to play, while serving as the Head Teaching pros at exclusive (whites-only) golf and country clubs.[37] According to Pete McDaniel, "Elder and several other caddies were favored by Tenison Head pro, Erwin Hardwick, who looked the other way when they slipped on to the course late in the afternoon and played the six holes that were obscured from view of the clubhouse."[38] When Elder was nine, his father was killed in combat during World War II and his mother died three months afterward. Elder moved from place to place among his siblings and other relatives. At the age of 12, Lee left Dallas to live with a relative in Los Angeles, where he continued to caddie and work at a golf shop and locker room at a San Bernardino country club. Given his love of golf, Elder was not interested in school and dropped out of Manual Arts High School in Los Angeles after attending for two years so that he could spend more time improving his golf game. Elder met Moses Brooks, a fellow caddie and small-time golf hustler. The two became close friends and began to make money by baiting unsuspecting players to place bets on golf matches with them in a scam where they convinced their marks that as caddies neither of them knew how to play golf. According to John H. Kennedy, Brooks and Elder returned to Dallas, continuing to hone their skills and continuing to hustle. It was there that Elder met Alvin Thomas, an accomplished con man and golf hustler, better known as "Titanic Thompson."[39] Thompson was a big-time gambler and creative golf hustler. According to Moses Brooks, "Titanic Thompson would come to town and stay most of the summer. . . . Lee and I would caddie for him, and he'd set up matches for us with different city players. He was the best I ever saw at baiting a player. He'd do stuff like dress us up in chauffeur clothes and bet that he could take his chauffeur as a partner and beat a club's best players."[40] As another example, Elder would pose as Thompson's caddie and at some point Thompson would tell his golf competitor that he will bet that even his caddie could out-play him. The stakes would be increased, and when Elder won the match with the mark Thompson would split the winnings with Elder.[41]

Lee Elder began traveling with Thompson and participating in golf hustles to scam players out of their money, Elder used his winnings to help his impoverished family out, purchase golf gear, and pay entrance fees to tournaments. Perhaps, Elder's biggest "break" toward entering the inner circle of accomplished Black golfers began in 1951 while playing at a UGA tournament (the UGA National Championship Amateur Division) in Cleveland, Ohio, where he finished as runner-up in a close match against world heavyweight boxing champion Joe Louis, who had retired from boxing in 1949. Impressed by the young Elder, who was only 16, Louis introduced him to Ted Rhodes, his personal golf tutor at the time. Louis was known for supporting top Black golfers and employing them to be his personal instructors. Rhodes was, unquestionably, the best Black golfer in America during this period. Rhodes had won back-to-back UGA National Championships in 1949 and 1950 and held four consecutive championships titles at the Joe Louis Open (in 1946, 1947, 1948 and 1949), among many other golf accomplishments.[42] Joe Louis, like other celebrities, including pro athletes in boxing, baseball, and other sports as well as the entertainment world, included golf tutors like Rhodes as members of their traveling entourage. Louis also paid for Rhodes's tournament entry fees among other expenses, along with allowing time for him to practice. Rhodes took Elder under his wing and immediately became Elder's teacher and mentor. The day after Rhodes died in 1969, Elder stated that "Ted Rhodes was like a father to me. He took me under his wing when I was 16 years old and completely rebuilt my golf game and my life."[43] In his travels with Rhodes, Elder was greatly influenced by Rhodes's laid-back attitude and easygoing demeanor, which would later become invaluable personality assets that were necessary on some occasions when confronted by racist taunts while playing golf. Elder would continue to hone his skills during the 1950s. At the age of 18, he won the 1952 UGA statewide golf tournament held annually to name the best Black golfer in Texas.

Elder officially turned professional in 1959 and was also drafted into the US Army that same year. He was able to further polish his golfing skills during the two years he spent in the military. Elder was stationed at Ft. Lewis, in Washington. The commanding officer, Colonel John Gleaster, an avid golfer, assigned Elder to a special services unit, putting him on "golf duty," where Elder, essentially, played golf for 16 months. Elder won his post championship at Ft. Lewis twice and performed well against white PGA golfers also serving in the military, finishing "second to Phil Rogers in the All-Service tournament in 1960 and second to Orville Moody [future US Open champion] in the Sixth Army Championship."[44] When he was discharged from the army in 1961, Elder began to compete as a professional on the UGA circuit.

Although earnings from the UGA tour were not great, Elder had received a substantial stake from Los Angeles night club owner, Moses Stevens, to cover his expenses.[45] Elder dominated the Black golf tours winning four UGA National Open championship titles between 1963 and 1967 and 18 of the 22 UGA tournaments he entered over this period (see table 6.2). By 1967, Elder had stockpiled "enough savings to try the PGA Tour's qualifying school in November of 1967 . . . documenting savings of $6,500-a requirement for prospective PGA Tour members in those days. . . . Elder left his home in Washington, DC for West Palm Beach, Fla [and] easily qualified."[46] Like the other Black golfers who had joined the PGA Tour before him, including Charlie Sifford, Pete Brown, and others, at some sites he would face such racist practices as not being allowed to enter the clubhouse or use the dining facilities.

After joining the PGA Tour in December 1967, it took little time for Elder to draw attention to his golf talents as he faced off against the number one golfer on the PGA Tour, Jack Nicklaus, in his rookie season (1968) at the American Golf Classic in Akron, Ohio, when the tournament ended with Nicklaus and Elder tied for the lead. Although Elder lost in a sudden-death playoff to finish as runner-up, the five holes of dueling with the top golfer in the world before falling to defeat drew attention to Elder as a rising star on the tour.[47] Even more eventful, however, was his victory on the PGA Tour six years later at the Monsanto (now Pensacola) Open in 1974, which earned an invitation to play in the Masters at Augusta (Georgia) National, becoming the first Black Golfer to play in this prestigious event.[48] It is important to note that Elder's victory at the Monsanto Open, his first on the PGA Tour, and invitation to play in the Masters was shrouded in the issue of race that continued to exist in golf. As an "invitational," event, before 1972, winning a PGA tournament did not automatically qualify one to receive an invitation from the all-white Augusta National Golf Club to the Masters tournament. Thus, Charlie Sifford, the first Black golf to play on the PGA Tour and be granted membership into the PGA of America, was repeated snubbed by the club and was never invited to the Masters, despite, seemingly, meeting "criteria" that merited an invitation. Even before his victory at the Monsanto Open in 1974, Elder, too, seemed to have met criteria that merited an invitation to the Masters.[49] Eighteen members of the US Congress had "formally asked Augusta national to invite 'the most prominent black golfer' [Lee Elder] and urged the tournament to take 'affirmative action.'"[50] Augusta National refused to act on the request from members of Congress, and Elder, too, rejected their attempt to help in the matter, insisting "he not want to be a test case in one of the first popular controversies over affirmative action [and] would refuse an invitation unless it was achieved on merit."[51]

Another major tournament in Elder's career that should be highlighted was a thrilling event that saw famed Mexican American golfer, Lee Trevino, duel with Elder in a sudden-death shootout. According to Rob Hernandez, "Lee Elder etched his name in Wisconsin golf history at the 1978 Greater Milwaukee Open when he battled Lee Trevino in an epic, sudden-death playoff at Tuckaway Country Club in Franklin, winning with a par on the eighth extra hole. It remains the second-longest sudden-death playoff in PGA Tour history."[52] *Wisconsin State Journal* sports editor Glenn Miller estimated that 35,000 to 40,000 fans attended the tournament on its final day, the largest crowd in the history of the Greater Milwaukee Open. The victory for Elder also represented a reverse of the outcome of an earlier sudden-death playoff between the two, where Trevino defeated Elder at the 1972 Greater Hartford Open.[53] The 1978 victory at the Greater Milwaukee Open was significant in that it qualified Elder for the 1979 Masters at Augusta National, the last of his six appearances. Elder was also named to the US Ryder Cup team in 1979, the first African American to be accorded this honor. Elder, who had joined the regular PGA Tour at age 33, joined the senior PGA Tour in 1984, winning eight tournaments in a four-year period before his health began to decline in the early 1990s. He officially retired from playing professional golf in 2005.

As a Black golf trailblazer and icon, Lee Elder continued to amass awards up to the final years of his life. In 2019 he became the first African American to receive the Bob Jones Award, and in 2021 he was the honorary starter at the Masters. These honors do not overshadow the fact that Elder's career was part of a long history where Black golfers had confronted racism in the sport. From the perspective of the African American golf legacy, Elder's career can be traced across the Jim Crow, civil rights, and post–civil rights eras. This perspective, therefore, connects him to the social context of the past and links him to barriers that impact the progress to inclusion for Blacks and other minorities. The racial barriers faced by Elder and other Black golfers of his generation ranged from overt, perpetuated by individuals and small isolated groups, such as racial slurs and threats on his life, to covert and institutionalized, such as the slow pace of Black inclusion and lingering effects after removal of the Caucasians-only clause. The lack of a significant presence of Black golfers playing at the highest levels of the sport and represented in the golf-related industry may also reflect the maintenance of restrictive policies by prestigious, private golf clubs and private corporations and other sponsors of golf activities in local communities.

Often neglected as part of the response to racism and removal of barriers that served as obstacles to Black golf advancement is the role that many Black golf pioneers played in preparing young, aspiring Black golfers to become future contributors to the African American golf legacy. Lee Elder devoted much of his time engaged in such efforts. For example, after turning pro in 1959, he moved to Washington, DC, in 1961, where he established strong ties with the historic Langston golf course. In 1974, "Lee Elder Day" was declared by the District of Columbia government, and by the late 1970s Lee and his wife, Rose Harper Elder, launched a variety of programs to attract both black and white youth to golf and to support educational growth and social development.[54] After his time in Washington, DC, at Langston, Elder continued his affinity for supporting young people, especially Black and other minority youth, in their social development, including golf-related aspirations.

In a recent analysis comparing the pioneering and trailblazing efforts and endeavors of four Black golfers—Ted Rhodes, Charlie Sifford, Lee Elder and Tiger Woods—Lucas Skelton describes Elder as the "Resilient and Determined Trailblazer," in comparison to his predecessors Rhodes the "Calm and Courageous Trailblazer" and Sifford the "Outspoken and Militant Trailblazer." According to Skelton, in facing such racial discrimination as threatening phone calls or being barred from clubhouses and forced to change shoes and eat meals in golf course parking lots or the caddie quarters, Elder would face these obstacles not just with calmness or militancy but with the added resiliency and determination he acquired from the advice and mentoring of his predecessors and fellow Black golf trailblazers. No wonder that Tiger Woods, who Skelton describes as the "Restrained and Steadfast Trailblazer," paid homage to Rhodes, Sifford, and Elder as Black golf pioneers at the traditional ceremony of donning the green blazer in the post-Masters interview immediately after winning his first of five Masters championships in 1997.[55] He recognized his role as a barrier-breaker and trailblazer in continuing the African American golf legacy. Woods had been introduced to Charlie Sifford, Lee Elder, and other Black golf pioneers by his father from the beginning of playing golf in childhood. Although Ted Rhodes died in 1969, before Tiger's birth, Woods was aware of the perseverance of African American golf champions who came before him and confronted racism. However, there was a special connection between Woods and Elder. In the beginning of the final round of the 1997 Masters, Lee Elder also felt the connection. As Vartan Kupelian, author of *Stalking the Tiger: A Writer's Diary,* describes Elder's expressing his emotions when Tiger Woods neared the final round on what would become a record-setting performance:

> Elder . . . was home in Florida during Masters week and watched on television as Woods neared the historic moment. "I told my wife if he were anywhere near the lead, I was going to be there. . . . This has more potential than Jackie Robinson breaking the color barrier in baseball." . . . [the next day] He took a 7 a.m. flight to Atlanta but couldn't connect to Augusta. He rented a car for the 2½-hour drive . . . When Elder finally arrived at Augusta, where he played seven times in the Masters, the drive down Magnolia Lane gave him goosebumps. "It was wonderful." . . . He visited briefly with Woods on the putting green before the final round.[56]

After achieving this barrier-breaking victory at the 1997 Masters, Woods expressed what that brief meeting with Elder before the final round meant to him:

> That meant a lot to me because he was the first, he was the one I looked up to. Because of what he did I was able to play on the PGA Tour. When Lee came down that really inspired me and reinforced what I had to do. I wasn't the pioneer. Charlie Sifford, Lee Elder and Ted Rhodes, those are the guys who paved the way. All night I was thinking about them,

what they've done for me and all the game of golf. Coming up 18, I said a little prayer of thanks to those guys. Those guys are the ones who did it.[57]

Conclusion

While the long history of racism in American sports has been well documented, the relatively slow pace of progress and change in the participation of African Americans in golf continues to be a challenge. In this essay, we developed a framework drawing upon systemic racism in sports and applying it to golf. This model is referred to as the African American golf legacy. We used the model as a context for assessing the career of Lee Elder, who was among a cadre of Black golf pioneers serving as trailblazers and agents of change. In this context, Lee Elder's stellar golf career and life achievements can be viewed as a continuation by Black golfers to confront obstacles faced during the history of the African American golf legacy. Lee Elder's contributions in overcoming complex barriers that Black golfers have faced solidifies his place in this legacy.

While Lee Elder will be forever remembered as the first African American golfer to play in the Masters at Augusta National, his most important contribution to the sport may perhaps be remembrance of the positive personal character and spirited optimism he displayed and maintained during his life. Elder was held in the highest regard by organizations and individuals in golf and across other realms. Among many honors that he received from organizations, the one that stands out was the USGA Bob Jones Award in 2019. This award "recognizes an individual who demonstrates the spirit, personal character and respect for the game exhibited by Jones, winner of nine USGA championships."[58] As the first Black golfer to receive this award, Lee Elder joined such notable golfers as Jack Nicklaus, Arnold Palmer, Ben Hogan, Francis Ouimet, Byron Nelson, Mickey Wright, Nancy Lopez, and others.

Among the many tributes paid to Elder by individuals in golf, one that stands out was made by African America female golf trailblazer Renee Powell, who in 1967 became only the second African American to join the Ladies Professional Golfers Association (LPGA) Tour.[59] The following excerpts from Renee Powell's tribute to Lee Elder demonstrate the powerful impact he had on individuals in the sport of golf:

> When I was young, I viewed him as an uncle. He wasn't the only one.
> There were plenty of Black men who loved golf and kept their eye out for a teenager trying to make her way in the game. Charlie Sifford, Pete

Brown, George Johnson.... At an event in Miami, I met Lee for the first time. He threw his head back and smiled, greeting me like I was a long, lost relative. As an 18-year-old on the road trying to navigate my way through tournament golf, there was comfort in the friendship of an older man. We played a practice round together that week and he could not have been more complimentary.... Everything about Lee was polished, then and to the end.... He and I both won the UGA National Championship in 1966. The next year, 1967, we both qualified for our respective tours. Lee played the PGA Tour and PGA Tour Champions from 1968 until his retirement in 2005.... I was so honored to be asked to join in the celebration this past April [2021] when Augusta National and the Masters honored Lee on the first tee prior to Jack Nicklaus and Gary Player hitting the ceremonial first tee shots.... That day in Augusta the last time I saw him face to face, he was moved by the fact that Augusta National Golf Club, the place where people like Charlie Sifford weren't allowed to play, had helped create a women's golf program at Paine College, an Historically Black College in Augusta, and endowed a golf scholarship in the name of Lee Elder. That meant more to him than any tournament win. He knew that the golfers who went to school on the Lee Elder Scholarship would keep the game moving. Always forward. Just like Lee.[60]

Notes

1. For a list of African Americans competing on the PGA and LPGA Tours between 1960 and 2016, see Lane Demas, *Game of Privilege: An African American History of Golf* (Chapel Hill: University of North Carolina Press, 2017), 216. See also Pete McDaniel, *Uneven Lies: The Heroic Story of African Americans in Golf* (Greenwich, CT: American Golfer, 2000), 167; and Marvin P. Dawkins and A. C. Tellison Jr., "Golf," in *African Americans and Popular Culture*, vol. 2, *Sports,* ed. Todd Boyd (Westport, CT: Praeger, 2008), 61.
2. Demas, *Game of Privilege,* 232–236.
3. See Calvin H. Sinnette, *Forbidden Fairways: African Americans and the Game of Golf* (Chelsea, MI: Sleeping Bear Press, 1998); Marvin P. Dawkins and Graham C. Kinloch, *African American Golfers during the Jim Crow Era* (Westport, CT: Praeger, 2000); Pete McDaniel, *Uneven Lies: The Heroic Story of African Americans in Golf* (Greenwich, CT: American Golfer, 2000); John H. Kennedy, *A Course of Their Own: A History of African American Golfers* (Lincoln: University of Nebraska Press, 2005), and Demas, *Game of Privilege.*

4 See, e.g., Renee Powell, "Missing My Friend: A Tribute to Lee Elder," LPGA, Ladies Professional Golf Association, November 30, 2021, www.lpga.com/news/2021/missing-my-friend-a-tribute-to-lee-elder; Andrew Reid, "'Lost a Hero': World Mourns Death of Golf Pioneer Lee Elder," November 29, 2021, Retrieved from https://au.sports.yahoo.com/golf-lee-elder-death-world-pays-tribute-first-black-masters-player-pioneer-201050324.html?soc_sre=social-sh&soc_trk=ma; Amey Kulkarni, "A Tribute to Lee Elder," November 29, 2021, retrieved from www.essentiallysports.com/golf-news-a-tribute-to-lee-elder/

5 Joe R. Feagin, *Systemic Racism: A Theory of Oppression* (New York: Routledge, 2006).

6 For an examination of the first four of these eras in golf, see Dawkins and Kinloch, *African American Golfers*.

7 See David K. Wiggins, "Good Times on the Old Plantation: Recreations of the Black Slave in Antebellum South, 1810–1860," *Journal of Sport History* 4 (1977): 260–284; David K. Wiggins, "The Play of Slave Children in the Plantation Communities of the Old South, 1820–1860," *Journal of Sport History* 7 (1980): 21–39; David K. Wiggins, "Sport and Popular Past-Times: Shadow of the Slave Quarter," *Canadian Journal of History of Sport and Physical Education* 11 (1980): 61–88; David K. Wiggins, "From Plantation to Playing Field: Historical Writings on the Black Athlete in American Sport," *Research Quarterly for Exercise and Sport* 57 (1986): 101–116; Al-Tony Gilmore, "Black Athletes in an Historical Context: The Issue of Race," *Negro History Bulletin* 58 (1995): 7–14.

8 See Arthur Ashe, *A Hard Road to Glory: A History of the African American Athlete, 1919–1945* (New York: Warner Books, 1988); David K. Wiggins, "Great Speed but Little Stamina: The Historical Debate over Black Athletic Superiority," *Journal of Sport History* 16 (1989): 158–185; Dawkins and Kinloch, *African American Golfers;* Marvin P. Dawkins, "Race Relations and the Sport of Golf: The African American Golf Legacy," *Western Journal of Black Studies* 27 (2003): 231–235.

9 David K. Wiggins and Patrick B. Miller, *The Unlevel Playing Field: A Documentary History of the African American Experience in Sport* (Urbana: University of Illinois Press, 2003), 226–227. See also T. Smith, "Outside the Pale: The Exclusion of Blacks from the National Football League, 1934–1946," *Journal of Sport History* 15 (1988): 255–281.

10 See Ezra Edelman, dir., *The Curious Case of Curt Flood* (New York: HBO Sports, 2011), a documentary about major league (St. Louis Cardinals) baseball player Curt Flood's legal challenge to MLB's restrictive "reserve clause," which for decades had unconstitutionally prevented MLB players from benefiting from free agency; and see "The Supreme Court Overturns Muhammad Ali's Conviction," a documentary clip about the 1971 unanimous ruling by the US Supreme Court to overturn Ali's conviction for refusing his call to military service due to his religious beliefs, September 21, 2021, 7:38, PBS, pbs.org/video/supreme-court-overturns-muhammad-alis-conviction-b8jypt/. See also Harry Edwards, *The Revolt of the Black Athlete* (New York: Free Press, 1969); Arthur Ashe, *A Hard Road to Glory: A History of the African American Athlete* (New York: Warner Books, 1988b); Donald Spivey, "End Jim Crow in Sports: The Protest at New York University, 1940–1941," *Journal of Sport History* 15 (1988): 282–303; Kenneth Shropshire, "Private Race Consciousness," *Detroit College of Law at Michigan State University Law Review* 3 (1996): 628–652.

11 "Al Campanis," Wikipedia, last modified April 25, 2024, https://en.wikipedia.org>wiki>Al_Campanis
12 Jomills Braddock Henry Braddock II, *Institutional Discrimination: A Study of Managerial Recruitment in Professional Football* (Washington, DC: National Football League Players Association, 1980).
13 Moneque Walker Pickett, Marvin P. Dawkins, and Jomills Henry Braddock II, "Race and Gender Equity in Sports: Have White and African Americans Benefited Equally from Title IX?" *American Behavioral Scientist* 20 (2012): 17–32.
14 See William C. Rhoden, *Forty Million Dollar Slaves: The Rise, Fall and Redemption of Black Athletes* (New York: Three Rivers Press, 2006); Jomills Henry Braddock II, Eryka Smith, and Marvin P. Dawkins, "Pathways to Power in the National Football League," *American Behavioral Scientist* 20 (2012): 1–16; Moneque Walker Pickett, Marvin P. Dawkins, and Jomills Henry Braddock II, "Challenges to Title IX: A Critical Race Perspective," *Negro Educational Review* 70 (2019): 78–99.
15 See Karen Toulon, "Colin Kaepernick, the QB Who Became a Civil Rights Trailblazer." *Bloomberg Businessweek,* December 3, 2020, www.bloomberg.com/news/articles/2020-12-03/colin-kaepernick-civil-rights-trailblazer-supporter-of-blm-bloomberg-50-2020; "Lebron James on Social Activism: 'We All Have to Do Better,'" ESPN, July 13, 2016, www.espn.com/espys/2016/story/_/id/17060953/espys-carmelo-anthony-chris-paul-dwyane-wade-lebron-james-call-athletes-promote-change
16 This clause (Section I, Article III) was inserted into the PGA constitution in 1934 and restricted membership to "professional golfers of the Caucasian race;" see Demas, *Game of Privilege,* 116.
17 See Sinnette, *Forbidden Fairways,* 15–25; Dawkins and Kinloch, *African American Golfers,* 13–17; McDaniel, *Uneven Lies,* 26–27; and Demas, *Game of Privilege,* 34–39.
18 Dawkins and Tellison Jr., "Golf," 54.
19 See Marvin P. Dawkins, "Race Relations and the Sport of Golf: The African American Golf Legacy," *Western Journal of Black Studies* 28 (2004): 327–333.
20 Dawkins and Kinloch, *African American Golfers,* 35–64.
21 Dawkins and Kinloch, 50–51.
22 Thomas B. Jones, "Caucasians Only: Solomon Hughes, the PGA, and the 1948 St. Paul Open Golf Tournament," *Minnesota History* (Winter 2003–2004): 382–393.
23 Marvin P. Dawkins and Jomills Henry Braddock II, "Teeing Off against Jim Crow," in *DC Sports: The Nation's Capital at Play,* ed. Chris Elzey and David K. Wiggins (Fayetteville: University of Arkansas Press, 2015), 57–72.
24 Dawkins and Braddock II, "Teeing Off against Jim Crow."
25 Marvin P. Dawkins and Walter C. Farrell, "Joe Louis and the Struggle of African American Golfers for Visibility and Access," *Challenge: A Journal of Research on African American Men* 14 (2008): 72–90.
26 Demas, *Game of Privilege,* 149–159.
27 Garrett Morrison (producer and host), "Fried Egg Stories: Jackie Robinson the Golfer" (featuring Rosemary Maravetz, USGA Curator, and authors Lane Demas and Marvin Dawkins), September 2020, 36:00, in *The Fried Egg Golf Podcast,* https://podcasts.apple.com/nz/podcast/fried-egg-stories-jackie-robinson-the-golfer/id1131723994?i=1000490527001

28 Demas, *Game of Privilege*, 129.
29 Morrison, "Fried Egg Stories."
30 Taken from Dawkins and Tellison Jr., "Golf," 59; original quote in Charlie Sifford and James Gullo, *Just Let Me Play: The Story of Charlie Sifford, The First Black PGA Golfer* (Latham, NY: British American Publishing, 1992).
31 Richard Goldstein, "Lee Elder, Who Broke a Golf Color Barrier, Dies at 87" *New York Times*, November 29, 2021, www.nytimes.com/2021/11/29/sports/golf/lee-elder-dead.html
32 Jacob Camenker, "Tiger Woods' Worst Masters Finishes: How Golfer Has Fared at Augusta since 1995 Debut," *Sporting News*, April 10, 2022; see also "Tiger Woods," Wikipedia, last modified April 25, 2024, https://en.wikipedia.org>wiki>Tiger_Woods
33 "Sifford Set to Break Another Barrier, World Golf Hall of Fame Will Welcome First Black Member," MSNBC.com, November 13, 2004, https://web.archive.org/web/20041114151220/http://www.msnbc.msn.com/id/6463067/
34 "PGA Bestows Membership on African-American Pioneers," PGA.com, February 4, 2011,www.pga.com/archive/pga-america-bestows-membership-african-american-pioneers
35 "USGA Bob Jones Award," USGA, accessed April 25, 2024, www.usga.org/content/usga/home-page/about/usga-bob-jones-award.html
36 Adrienne N. Milner and Jomills Henry Braddock II, eds., *Women in Sports: Breaking Barriers, Facing Obstacles* (Santa Barbara, CA: Praeger, 2017).
37 Dawkins and Kinloch, *African American Golfers*, 13–20.
38 McDaniel, *Uneven Lies*, 113.
39 Kennedy, *A Course of Their Own*, 153–162.
40 McDaniel, *Uneven Lies*, 113.
41 Kennedy, *A Course of Their Own*, 156.
42 Dawkins and Farrell, "Joe Louis," 79–82.
43 Demas, *Game of Privilege*, 109.
44 Kennedy, *A Course of Their Own*, 162; see also "Elder, Lee 1934–," ENCYCLOPEDIA.com, https://encyclopedia.com/education/news-wires-white-papers-and-books/elder-lee-1934
45 McDaniel, *Uneven Lies*, 114.
46 McDaniel, 114.
47 Demas, *Game of Privilege*, 223; Sinnette, *Forbidden Fairways*, 172.
48 Demas, *Game of Privilege*, 231–236.
49 Demas, 231.
50 Demas, 231.
51 Demas, 232.
52 Rob Hernandez, "Masters Pioneer Lee Elder, Who Outlasted Lee Trevino in Eight-Hole Playoff to Win 1978 Greater Milwaukee Open, Dies at Age 87," November 29, 2021, Wisconsin.Golf, https://www.wisconsin.golf/men/mens_professional/masters-pioneer-lee-elder-who-outlasted-lee-trevino-in-eight-hole-playoff-to-win-the/article_04b8b2d6-5152-11ec-a609-f31ba0028178.html.
53 Hernandez, "Masters Pioneer Lee Elder."

54 Dawkins and Braddock II, "Teeing Off against Jim Crow," 71–72.
55 Lucas Skelton, "Trailblazing: A Historical Overview of the Advocacy Work of Four Legendary Black Golf Professionals," *Journal of Black Studies* 53 (2022): 441–463.
56 Vartan Kupelian, *Stalking the Tiger: A Writer's Diary* (Chelsea, MI: Sleeping Bear Press, 1997), 60.
57 Vartan Kupelian, *Stalking the Tiger,* 61.
58 "USGA Bob Jones Award."
59 Demas, *Game of Privilege,* 215–220.
60 Powell, "Missing My Friend."

7

Clarence Gaines

An Athlete and Coach Who Made a "Big House" of the Central Intercollegiate Athletic Association

ARTHUR SMITH

Clarence "Big House" Gaines was larger than life—and not just because he had been an intimidating lineman for Morgan State College who became a famous basketball coach as well as the first African American to mentor a national championship squad. A fascinating anecdote from his personal archives seems to show how his baptism in the Ohio River as a child was such an event that it stopped barges and other river traffic.[1] For even as a child, Gaines was larger than normal, and he drew attention throughout his life for his size and formidable stature. But Gaines's physical size and presence, though perhaps a critical element in his personal success as a coach and recruiter, are not what make him a formidable historical presence.[2] Gaines's life is central to the story of the Central Intercollegiate Athletic Association (formerly, the Colored Intercollegiate Athletic Association, CIAA) and how it developed in the 1940s, 1950s, and 1960s as an institution that affected African American men as a positive force. Best known for his Hall of Fame exploits as a basketball coach, perhaps more interesting is the path he took first as an athlete and then as a coach; this path never left the sanctuary that the CIAA established for him and indeed he thrived there. His career is an excellent example of the way individuals strengthen and develop the institutions in which they work. From his arrival on campus at Morgan State in the fall of 1941 to his retirement from coaching in 1993, Gaines had a 53-year association with the CIAA.

Born in 1923 in rural Paducah, Kentucky, Gaines was the great-grandson of slaves. In his autobiography, Gaines attributes his own remarkable size of six feet five inches and 265 pounds to his great-grandfather Ambrose, a blacksmith remembered in family history as being the biggest slave on the Kentucky plantations when the Civil War ended.[3] Gaines credits his interest in sports and education to his parents. While his father was a sports fan, it was his mother's insistence on education and that he pursue—and finish—a college degree that Gaines cited later in life as an inspiration for him to continue a career in higher education.[4]

The journey Gaines took from small-town Kentucky to play football for one of the CIAA's founding colleges, Morgan State, is instructive. White colleges relied on organized recruiting, utilizing mass mailings and paid trips to campus for top prospects (even in the late 1930s and 1940s). The route for talented African American athletes to find a home in the CIAA, however, more often depended on a network of alumni, friends, and community leaders. Coming from Kentucky, Gaines was virtually unknown to Morgan State head football and track coach Eddie Hurt. Morgan State, like other CIAA schools and most of the HBCUs that supported athletics, did not have the budget to bring a talented, young high school football player like Gaines to campus. In turn, a prospect like Gaines had few chances to find out about the opportunities available to him at schools like Morgan State in faraway Baltimore. Instead, coach and athlete relied on a network that spread across the South. Thinking back, Gaines wrote,

> Black colleges, even the largest of them, had no recruiting budgets and no talent scouts paid to watch for news coverage or to visit the high-school games to evaluate promising athletes . . . black colleges relied on people in communities to send them good prospects. My own acceptance at the colleges had all been on the strength of my network of contacts in Paducah calling their network of contacts at those schools and assuring them that I could not only make it academically but also perform on the football field.[5]

Gaines would later rely on this very same network to establish his own basketball dynasty at Winston-Salem Teachers College (WSTC).[6]

Gaines chose to attend Morgan State instead of its fiercest rival, Howard University, in nearby Washington, DC. As Gaines and others have noted, Howard was the "crown jewel" of African American higher education. The Morgan State and Howard rivalry was among the oldest in the CIAA. As with other rivalries, such as St. Augustine's and North Carolina College, this heated competition was fueled by geographical[7] proximity but also by the fact that CIAA schools were often recruiting from the same pool of top athletes. The common recruiting trail only heightened the level of familiarity and motivation that fueled the energy in these contests. Gaines's budding relationship with coach Hurt was the deciding factor in his decision to attend Morgan over Howard, though Gaines graduated third in his high school class and was academically qualified to attend either.[8] Gaines had a solid but otherwise unremarkable academic career. Although Gaines did not choose Howard, he would have found the academic and social experience at either school similar. The experiences that he valued at Morgan State—the bond forged with teammates, or the strong community support from Baltimore African Americans—were very similar to what was found on the Washington, DC, campus.[9]

It was while at Morgan State as a football star that Gaines not only garnered his nickname Big House but also developed a real feel for the importance of the team and coach in a young man's development.[10] Coach Hurt taught him, among many other things, "that a coach can inspire young men" and that this inspiration came in a number of different forms.[11] But perhaps most inspirational was that a young person could be rewarded through athletic competition, and not just through notoriety gained in the Baltimore *Afro-American* sports pages or from being an object of attention on campus, but also from the camaraderie of teammates, the approval of a well-respected coach, and the lessons of hard work.

Gaines developed a great deal at Morgan State and, by his own admission, much of this was physical as well as mental and emotional. Coach Hurt demonstrated to him the value of hard work and that, to succeed, he needed to do more than rely on his own prodigious physical talent. Gaines entered college a solid 265 pounds but graduated with a sculpted 238-pound frame, and he credits that physical transformation to Hurt's demands and motivations. But the conditioning that Hurt expected from stars like Gaines became personal habits that were to suit them well later in life (in Gaines's case, as a coach). Gaines was dominant at left tackle and was a part of CIAA championship teams in his favorite sport, football, but also in the sport at which he ultimately would become most famous, basketball.[12]

Sam Lacy of the Baltimore *Afro-American* focused a number of his columns during Gaines's undergraduate years on the prowess of the Morgan State football team. Indeed, his repeated theme was the size of the Morgan State offensive and defensive line, of which Gaines was the anchor and leader. Lacy noted in one typical column, "I am not alone in noticing but it needs to be pointed out that surely the success of the Morgan State football team lies with the offensive line outweighing opponents by an average of 20 pounds!"[13]

Gaines was well known among sports fans in African American communities, not just in Baltimore where Lacy and other sportswriters added to stories about his legendary size and abilities with flowery prose. The CIAA had developed into a close-knit institution, and educators from each school met twice a year. The yearly *Bulletin* summed up achievements in each sport and provided commentary on issues affecting black higher education through the prism of athletics. At these annual meetings, much like other academic or professional conferences, networking and job-placement efforts were standard fare. Although Gaines did not attend the CIAA meetings in those days (he did when he became established as a head coach), word of mouth led coach Howard Wilson of the Winston-Salem Teachers College (also the athletic director of the nearly all-female school) to offer Gaines a job assisting him as the coach of all of Winston-Salem's sports once Gaines graduated. He hired Gaines in the summer of 1945, with no formal interview, after coach Hurt recommended him to Wilson at the annual meetings.

Coaching and the CIAA

Like many coaches, Gaines did not move to Winston-Salem intending to coach for long. Instead, he saw the position as a means to an end before going on to dental school.[14] He was also certainly qualified to attend dental school, but chose coaching because it offered an immediate paycheck.[15] As at many other CIAA schools, the budget for athletics was very small at Winston-Salem, and Gaines did not make a great deal in annual salary even though he was the assistant athletic director and assistant coach to Wilson for football, soccer, track, and basketball.[16] Coincidentally, Gaines's arrival at WSTC was the first year the Rams entered CIAA competition. When Wilson soon took a position at Bluefield State College, Gaines was appointed as athletic director and head coach of all sports in the summer of 1946.

The years Gaines spent in Winston-Salem mirrored a period of remarkable transition for African Americans. WSTC was the educational epicenter of the city's black community, but as in Durham, North Carolina, and other southern cities with a significant African American population, a number of black high schools offered an opportunity for connection between athletes, coaches, and educators. Although they did not compete against each other, African American high schools and Winston-Salem Teachers College formed an almost symbiotic relationship. Gaines opened his gym to local high schools when they were in need of facilities, and he was a well-known figure at local high school events.[17]

The tobacco industry was the defining work experience for most African Americans in Winston-Salem, and the opportunities presented by employment and unionization provided the impetus for voter registration and job improvement measures.[18] This working-class background also inspired an affection and passion for education. Historian Robert Korstad describes the efforts of the African American community, both working class and professionals, to transform Winston-Salem Teachers College into "a symbol of hope for the future" of the community.[19] Although Gaines recruited from around the South, he often benefited from local networks that introduced him to the hardworking sons of tobacco workers as well as young men raised in the growing middle class of Winston-Salem.[20]

The African American community in Winston-Salem asserted its identity and rights in a period of statewide disfranchisement, lynchings, and job discrimination. Blacks also sought civic harmony with the local white community. In 1905, sociologist Robert E. Park called Winston-Salem a "city of racial peace" where blacks' deference to whites and frequent financial aid from white philanthropists created a model in race accommodation.[21] Yet, as historian Bertha Hampton Miller described in her 1981 PhD dissertation, the African American community in Winston-Salem did not simply accept the status quo but maintained autonomy and expanded its economic and educational potential.[22] Miller traces the growth of African American high school and college efforts, noting that a mixture of Booker T. Washington accommodation–style tactics as well as the principles of W.E.B. Du Bois's "Talented Tenth" philosophy guided the early years of WSTC. Winston-Salem blacks founded and supported enduring institutions, including WSTC, elementary and high schools, and one of the earliest (1918) and strongest chapters of the National Association for the Advancement of Colored People (NAACP) in the state.[23]

Working-class African Americans became supporters of the educational aspirations of the NAACP and its push toward economic and political civil rights. In Winston-Salem, African American tobacco factory workers for companies like R. J. Reynolds Tobacco Company joined forces with their white coworkers to stand up against the economic and political inequalities that they faced. This interracial cooperation is a major theme in Korstad's *Civil Rights Unionism: Tobacco Workers and the Struggle for Democracy in the Mid-Twentieth Century South,* but also cogent is its description of conflict within the black community in Winston-Salem. The marriage between working-class and professional blacks, as Korstad describes, was not always simple or smooth.[24]

The tension between middle- and upper-class blacks "demolished the notion of an automatically unified and undifferentiated black community."[25] Korstad describes an evolving black populace in Winston-Salem: a majority made up a growing working class that was increasing as new workers steadily migrated into the area; a middle class composed of teachers and business owners; and a small black elite who were administrators and professionals. Even as black elites (the self-styled "better class") felt a sense of entitlement, because of advantages of income and education, to speak for the entire black community, black workers often chafed at this "false leadership." Black industrial workers were concerned that upper and middle-class blacks were more inclined to preserve the status quo, and hence their more comfortable position in Jim Crow Winson-Salem.[26] On the other hand, this group of more established blacks who had associated themselves with Du Bois's concept of a "Talented Tenth" were more likely to seek respect from white power brokers and were distrustful of the growing number of working-class blacks who threatened to upset the delicate balance of accommodation with white society that the "better class" had established.[27]

Black workers joined Local 22-CIO, a leftist, biracial union of tobacco workers, participated in a "wildcat strike" against R. J. Reynolds (the first on record is in 1943), registered to vote, and helped elect a black city councilman (the first since Reconstruction) in 1948 while helping to build a distinctive cultural voice through their churches and community groups like the Local 22 singers. To the black elite, which had worked hard to negotiate educational institutions like WSTC and other beneficiaries of white philanthropy, these protests were a direct challenge to their vision of the black community's future in Winston-Salem.[28] Korstad also describes how black workers, despite a dearth of facilities and free time, formed baseball teams and used old or abandoned lots as the site of pickup games across a variety of sports. Blacks relied on the local YMCAs and the city for many of these leagues and fields of play because recreational facilities allocated for blacks was meager at best: whereas 27 baseball diamonds were accessible for white neighborhoods, there were only eight such parks for blacks.[29] Local 22 even sponsored a team, described by Korstad as a "hard-hitting" squad that won the all-black city championship in 1946. Over 100 blacks signed up to play in the league; despite hardships associated with hard industrial work and low pay, the desire to play and support sporting events was a part of black life in Winston-Salem. Although the vast majority of the workers who made up the city leagues did not have access to a college education, they became a significant part of the fan base for CIAA sports and intercollegiate athletics generally.

Despite real differences between the mass of black workers who were employed by R. J. Reynolds and the smaller group of established black professionals who felt that the workers' challenge posited a grave danger to the structure of race relations in Winston-Salem, educational institutions like WSTC were a unifying force in the black community. Aspiration for advancement through education was a theme shared by blacks of various economic and social backgrounds and cheering the exploits of WSTC sports teams was a shared passion. Although the Atkins family that helped found WSTC were unlikely to attend Local 22 baseball games, CIAA basketball contests were venues where blacks of different economic and social status mingled.[30]

When Gaines arrived in Winston-Salem, therefore, he became part of a community that was attempting to negotiate a place in the harsh structures of the Jim Crow South while also entering a black social and economic sphere that supported African American educational and athletic endeavors. This process of racial advancement was complicated by class and educational differences within the black community, but the role his basketball teams would play in providing a sense of identity to this somewhat fragmented community is important. Gaines's career did not happen in a vacuum but was instead very much a partnership with the larger African American community of Winston-Salem, which held its college and its athletic teams in the highest regard.

His career as a head coach in football and basketball was remarkable. Despite a predominantly female enrollment at a school with no football tradition, in Gaines's last year as coach, the team went 8–1 and he had an overall record of 20–124.[31] Gaines was a hard-nosed competitor, and he saw that to be successful year in and year out in the CIAA Winston-Salem would need to focus on sports other than football, at least as long as the student body was less than 25 percent male. Football simply required too many players. It would be more efficient and realistic to recruit 12 basketball players to his new school than to recruit 40 men for football.[32] Gaines, therefore, turned over the head football coaching duties in 1950 and retained the titles of athletic director and head basketball coach, titles he would continue to hold until 1993. His career record as a basketball coach was 828–445. The 828 wins were at the time of his retirement, fourth all-time in collegiate basketball history and, in 1982, he became only the second African American elected to the Naismith Basketball Hall of Fame as a coach.[33] When he coached Winston-Salem to the NCAA Division II (Small Schools, as it was called then) championship in 1967, it was the first national title in NCAA-sponsored competition for an HBCU.

Gaines's experiences as a student-athlete introduced him to the CIAA and provided him with a road map toward a career in coaching. Nevertheless, it was during the decades at WSTC that he was most able to influence and inspire others. Coaching allowed Gaines the means to work with young men and aid in their personal and educational development; how this worked in the context of the CIAA was unique. Along the way, Gaines's efforts helped validate the high level of play occurring in the CIAA and brought him national renown as well. But the emergence of Gaines as a national sporting figure should not be highlighted without understanding the impact he was having on a day-to-day basis with his players and within the CIAA.

One key to success in collegiate coaching in any era is to have talented players. As Gaines is quick to point out throughout his autobiography, it was his success at finding talented players and ultimately convincing them to attend his college that enabled him to have successful teams. Gaines realized early on that his own athletic talents and motivational abilities were not enough to succeed as a basketball coach. Although he was constantly in search of new strategies and techniques, it was his ability to connect with young African American men across the South, and later the Northeast, that laid the foundation for his basketball dynasty.[34] Despite Gaines's success, the problems associated with recruiting African American athletes to southern HBCUs was a central concern to CIAA coaches and demonstrates not only the challenges they faced but also the unique ways in which they turned obstacles into advantages. It was often despite the many challenges that Gaines faced at a small CIAA school that made him an effective recruiter of talented African American basketball players.

Traveling in the 1950s and 1960s South was not an easy task for African Americans. Gaines and other coaches who hit the road searching for top players in faraway towns made do with substandard lodging, the indignities of eating outside white restaurants, suspicion and hostility from whites, and a great many other discomforts in the Jim Crow South. In addition, CIAA schools were not overflowing with cash, so travel budgets for coaches were based on very small allowances. To save costs, CIAA coaches traveled together in search of talent, a practice unheard of among their peers in white conferences. Gaines, in a move that reveals his underlying passion to get better as a coach over any other concern, befriended rival John McLendon, the even more successful head basketball coach at North Carolina College. Gaines writes:

> John thought we were riding together just to save gas money, but the truth is I wanted to get him alone to talk about basketball plays, strategy on the court, and how to motivate players. As amazing as it might seem to people wondering about competition for hot players, neither John nor myself ever sandbagged the other while on the recruiting trail.[35]

The need to save on costs forced Gaines and McLendon into collaborative ventures that not only helped them recruit better players but also established a venue for the sharing of ideas and the building of relationships usually not found in other collegiate sports or associations. As Murray Sperber explains in *Onward to Victory*, the intercollegiate landscape in white America ca. 1950 had strayed dramatically from its turn-of-the-century roots. What was initially hoped to be a forum for the promotion of sportsmanship and fair play had already devolved into big business, marred by gambling controversy, academic cheating, and recruiting scandals.[36] Although the rivalries and stakes within the CIAA were high, it is fair to say that a higher degree of sharing and promotion of sportsmanship endured within black schools. HBCUs chose cooperation when attempting to overcome the obstacles that segregation placed in front of their athletic goals.

Gaines attached himself to John McLendon, an innovator who developed a fast-breaking style of play that revolutionized CIAA basketball and ultimately ushered in the modern era of basketball all around the country. In his autobiography, Gaines makes no secret of using recruiting trips to gain more knowledge from McLendon, who gave him advice freely.[37] Gaines and McLendon traveled throughout the South in the summer months checking on various friends and contacts to learn more about top high school talent. Gaines claimed that neither attempted to poach the other's contacts unless given permission. In fact, in looking through the rosters of his teams from 1946 to 1952, when he and McLendon traveled the South together, none of Gaines's players came from the Midwest, which was McLendon's recruiting base. Similarly, McLendon had no players from Kentucky in that time period, which was Gaines's only realistic place for attracting out-of-state talent. That was where he had grown up and, at this stage of his young coaching career, where he had the most contacts.[38]

There is no question that Gaines used these contacts to help WSTC attract top players from the Midwest after McLendon left North Carolina College and the CIAA for Hampton Institute in the summer of 1952. In the 1950s, the demographics of Gaines's teams changed dramatically as the fruits of his recruiting efforts began to pay off. No longer was he relying on homegrown North Carolina talent, nor on the occasional player pried from his connections back home. Instead, his roster included players from Virginia, Tennessee, and (in an indication that his time at Morgan still played a role in his career) four players from Baltimore in the 1950s alone.[39]

In the mid-1950s and early 1960s, Gaines made inroads in the Midwest and the Northeast despite the challenges of persuading young African American stars to move to the Jim Crow South. While discrimination and the realities of segregation were still facts of life in the North, the indignities of life for African Americans in the South were significantly harsher. For three years during his teens, Gaines had lived in Newark, New Jersey, with an uncle. Gaines thus knew that the better athletic facilities and larger populations meant a greater pool of more polished and accomplished players than what many smaller, rural African American communities could provide. But he had to rely on his powers of persuasion as well as cultivate his reputation as a coach to help and mentor young African Americans, in order to persuade these athletes to join him in the South.

To students of contemporary basketball and hip-hop culture, the Rucker playground basketball tournament in New York City is legendary and to this day produces remarkable players as well as its own mythology.[40] Gaines was among the first collegiate coaches to attend these games. His persona and physical presence gave him a special reputation in New York.[41] Gaines successfully recruited a number of top players from New York in the 1950s and 1960s. While pursuing a master's degree in physical education at Columbia University in the early 1950s, he had ample opportunity to make himself a well-known figure at Rucker. He never promised his recruits an easy time in the South but did point out to them that blatant racism existed in the North just as it did in the South and that competing at a small teachers' college in a welcoming African American community had many benefits.[42]

Two of his earliest New York City stars were Jack DeFares and Wilfred John, both of whom would have been prime recruits for white New York City colleges. While tournaments like the Rucker extravaganza gave Gaines visibility and a platform upon which to extol the virtues of playing at his college in the CIAA (where Rucker veterans would find a familiar brand of fast break basketball), it was a betting scandal at the City College of New York (CCNY) that began a trend that would send a number of young black players from traditional Northeast NCAA powers to smaller schools in the CIAA. The top programs at CCNY, Long Island University, and Manhattan College reeled after betting scandals involving their players and the New York City mafia became public. Also, with Kentucky coach Adolph Rupp alleging that black players were more susceptible to the allure of gambling, young black men began looking at the CIAA as a viable, more welcoming, and less contentious option for college than the power programs of NCAA Division I white schools.[43] Amid scandal in the North, Gaines and other CIAA coaches gained top players and the reputation of caring for African American players in a way that white coaches were unwilling or unable to do.

With both DeFares and John, Gaines did not even need to persuade their parents; both young men knew their opportunities to play intercollegiate basketball were best at an HBCU.[44] John recalls that Gaines's everyday presence made an indelible impression on him and made the "culture shock" of moving to Jim Crow Winston-Salem more palatable.[45] But the academic environments available at HBCUs like WSTC were also important recruiting tools.

Students at WSTC enjoyed a diverse curriculum that was designed to provide them with a liberal arts education that would also prepare them for the realities of the professional world. WSTC was a teaching preparatory program, so courses in English, mathematics, and science were required each year beginning in 1950. The papers of longtime (1938–1974) WSTC registrar Francis L. Ross Coble also make it clear that success in the classroom was required for continued enrollment: 120 credit hours were required to graduate, and a student was expected to complete half of those hours with a grade of "C" or better by the beginning of the third year.[46] This was not unusual. Other CIAA schools had similar degree requirements. At Shaw University, for example, a student was expected to reach 60 credit hours (of 126 for graduation) at the end of the second year.[47] For prospective teachers at WSTC, courses in elementary education, elementary art, physical education, music, and home economics were listed in the 1951 catalogue as additional course requirements on top of courses in English, history, math, and science that were expected of students in their first two years.[48]

At Shaw, students were only permitted to engage in multiple extracurricular activities if they maintained a certain grade point average. Students with less than a "B" average, for example, were limited to only one activity and could pursue up to three if their academic record was better.[49] Coble's records indicate a somewhat less restrictive set of guidelines, though 70 percent of the students in 1950 were women and the athletic extracurricular activities were considerably less prominent for women, which may explain why the guidelines were less restrictive.

The registrar's office at WSTC also offers a fascinating guide to class attendance, which is mirrored in the records of Shaw University. HBCUs were serious about student attendance, and strict guidelines were in place at both institutions to ensure that students didn't miss class. These guidelines provided instructors with clear rules on what constituted a "tardy" notation in a student record and how this should affect grading.[50] Not surprisingly, Shaw received an "A" from the North Carolina State Board of Education for its positive record of encouraging academic participation and achievement.[51] An array of extracurricular activities was offered, but it is clear that the mission of the colleges resided in the classroom. As long as students did maintain a focus on their academic work, the life of a student at an HBCU in the first half of the twentieth century meant opportunities to be involved in student publications, theater, and musical groups as well as sports. By 1939, Shaw had 35 extracurricular groups, and WSTC had at least 28 in 1950.[52]

Athletics became a prominent part of the extracurricular offerings. And at both Shaw and WSTC, women's basketball was part of the winter sports scene, as was men's, from the early twentieth century through the middle part of the century. Both schools did away with women's intercollegiate athletic teams in the early 1950s, mostly due to a sense—fairly common at the time—that since fewer women seemed interested in being on teams, limited money in athletic department budgets should be spent elsewhere. And since the CIAA as an organization did not sponsor a women's championship, both schools invested their dollars in men's teams that did compete for championships. As Gaines noted in 1958 in a letter to fellow coaches at WTSC, "I see no interest at our rival schools to put forth the effort to put a girls team on the floor."[53] Evidence suggests, however, that this sensibility in the 1950s was inaccurate. Both Shaw and WSTC did have a history of women's participation: Shaw had women's basketball and croquet teams as early as 1908. In fact, the team played games with WSTC in 1926, the earliest game on record between the schools.[54]

Gaines never coached women, and during the vast majority of his years coaching there were no formal women's sports organized on a codified institutional level. Also, in his autobiography, Gaines makes no mention of the advent of women's intercollegiate athletics in 1975. It would be a stretch to call Gaines a champion of women's equal opportunity, but his records indicate that he made no effort to hinder innovation. While athletic director, he encouraged women's intramurals and taught physical education courses for women.[55] He was typical of his era rather than an innovator in women's athletics. In the years when the CIAA operated within the worst of Jim Crow, women did not compete in CIAA competition at Winston-Salem Teachers College, mostly due to custom (that was not an opportunity for women around the country either) but also due to financial constraints. Women were not far absent from Gaines's world, however, as his wife was a constant presence at the over 1,200 basketball games that he coached; his mother was a fixture and inspiration throughout his life.[56] And what's more, though not known as being a taskmaster (since he had very few team rules), Gaines would phone his players' mothers and sisters back home to help instill a lesson when he was upset at a player.[57] Mothers and sisters were the critical members of his players' families, and he cultivated relationships with them to mentor his players most efficiently.

Gaines and others may have misunderstood or underestimated the interest of college-aged women in the 1950s, and while he may have been correct, technically speaking, that other teams in the CIAA did not have teams for WSTC women to compete against, the reality was that women did want to play and had a tradition of competing at schools like Shaw, WSTC, and Bennett College.[58] Unfortunately, that tradition did not mean a level of organized intercollegiate play sponsored by a conference like the CIAA until 1975.

Emergence of CIAA Men's Basketball

Although women's intercollegiate athletic competition was never officially endorsed by the CIAA before the 1970s, men's basketball was emerging as an important institution when Gaines took over the reins of the WSTC program. A combination of factors, including innovative young coaches attracting top African American athletic talent to the rich academic opportunities of HBCUs, helped provide an environment ready to celebrate athletic excellence. But Gaines played an important role in expanding the position of the CIAA in the consciousness of southern black communities. Just as Gaines and McLendon were expanding the horizons of CIAA coaches by looking for top talent outside the South, Gaines helped create a uniquely southern institution: the annual CIAA basketball tournament. The tournament was born in 1946, Gaines's first year as the head basketball coach at Winston-Salem Teachers College. Along with McLendon, he was instrumental in promoting the event.[59] McLendon's teams were the dominant force in the CIAA in the early years of the tournament, but Gaines's defensive-oriented approach (which was gradually mimicking elements of McLendon's rollicking fast break attack on offense) meant for spirited and exciting games. The tournament became the signal event in southern African American communities every February. Gaines witnessed its evolution from an annual athletic event into the cultural and educational extravaganza that it is today. From modest beginnings that attracted 3,000 fans to the four-day tournament hosted by Howard University, the annual CIAA tournament now attracts 80,000 fans each year for the weeklong extravaganza.

Gaines speaks passionately of how the tournament not only "made" him the coaching legend he is today but also preserved space where athletes, teams, and spectators reunited each year to reminisce about years past and shared experiences in college. "Whatever reputation I have," he states, "was built on those courts during those games" in the CIAA tournament.[60] Moreover, teams and athletes "going back fifty years use it to keep track of each other, help each other out."[61] Just as the semiannual meetings of athletic directors, presidents, and coaches served to strengthen the mission and growth of the association, the basketball tournament became the place for the vast majority of the association's population—its players, coaches, and fans—to meet in athletic competition and socially renew their ties and share a sense of community.

The tournament did not merely involve the playing of games; it was also a venue for black businessmen and educators to make their mark. To this day, the tournament provides opportunities for black publishing companies, clothing companies, fashion consultants, religious groups, insurance salesmen, and many others to hawk their wares to the African American community. High school coach Russell Blunt recalls the event as far more than simply a sporting one: it was a place, much like church, where all elements of the community could come together.[62]

The CIAA basketball tournament proved to be a real boon for the member schools as it dramatically increased revenue.[63] While a large-scale event like this within the African American community could and did bring together an impressive amount of dollars and entrepreneurial spirit, it did not solve the financial woes of CIAA schools like Winston-Salem Teachers College. Gaines still had a limited budget for travel and facilities. Gaines's recruiting and scholarship budget were never even remotely close to white collegiate powerhouse programs in his own state, such as those of the universities of North Carolina, Duke, or Wake Forest, all members of the Atlantic Coast Conference (ACC), which was founded in 1953. Gaines did work hard to get special permission from WSTC to fund the educational expenses of top players recruited out of state. But it took constant vigilance on his part with each new board of directors to continue this financial support of his athletes. When his already relatively meager recruiting budget was slashed in half in the later 1980s, he saw a steady decline in his teams.[64]

Not only were budgets for recruiting and scholarships tight, but team travel during the season was also difficult and unreliable. Far more so than their peers at white colleges, African American athletes in the CIAA were faced with substandard housing while on the road. Although many of the CIAA schools were in proximity to one another, overnight team travel was still a necessity in many cases if players had any hope of attending class. A constant indignity included having to stand at the back of public buses. Unlike teams in the ACC in the 1950s and 1960s, CIAA squads traveled to competitions by public bus or carpooling with private automobiles, and they often camped out in warm weather or slept in the gymnasiums of the schools against which they competed. By contrast, other NCAA schools across the country relied on hotels for big sports like basketball and football. Yet frequently CIAA players stayed in the dormitories of their opponents. Competing within the realities of Jim Crow and budgetary constraints, athletes from CIAA schools formed real friendships and lasting respect because of relationships formed while traveling to compete.[65] Gaines and McLendon were not alone in forming a friendship across team boundaries. For instance, Wilfred John (who was a New York City product and among Gaines's first real stars from the Northeast) recalls the special friendships he formed not only with teammates but also with opponents during his years playing for Gaines.[66] Gaines kept many of the letters that his former athletes sent him, and it is a card from Jack DeFares, one of his earliest "finds" in New York City, that probably sums up Big House's effect on his young men: "Thanks, Coach, for making me the man I am today."[67]

Another measure of how Gaines's teams were able to turn the indignities of Jim Crow into a positive was in fostering a special brand of play that soon became a model for basketball generally and the envy of collegiate basketball around the country. Gaines employed a defensive-minded approach that, when blended with McLendon's revolutionary use of the fast break, quickly wore down white opponents. Throughout the 1950s and 1960s, Gaines's teams frequently scrimmaged ACC power Wake Forest, a neighboring institution. Wake Forest stars like Billy Packer found the Rams of Winston-Salem State to be better conditioned and far more organized than anticipated.[68] Gaines combined McLendon's fast break with his punishing, football-style defense, and developed a number of fitness and coordination drills, including jump roping and running. These were new to basketball purists but made the Rams, and other CIAA schools, formidable opponents.[69]

Soon absorbed by the Harlem Globetrotters and then the National Basketball Association, the pin-point accuracy, flexibility, and crowd-pleasing style of McLendon's fast break offense caught on more rapidly in the professional ranks. But while the Harlem Globetrotters became an entertainment phenomenon that combined the aesthetic values of McLendon and Gaines's passing and physical-fitness innovations, with elements reminiscent of carnival shows, CIAA basketball—and its style of play—remained serious business for its competitors.[70] Although NCAA basketball coaches at the "powerhouse" Division I schools were slower to change playing tactics and recruiting pools, they were soon forced to reconsider their practices as small schools like WSTC and North Carolina College demonstrated prowess in their pickup games with affluent Wake Forest and Duke.[71]

Furthermore, young ambitious coaches like Dean Smith at North Carolina and Bob Knight at Indiana saw the uses of the passing and cutting elements inherent in the new CIAA style of play. Although their teams did not play one another in formal competition, white coaches attended CIAA games and learned from observing and scouting.[72] The fast break was honed in countless games throughout the 1940s, 1950s, and 1960s, becoming a source of pride within the CIAA. In some ways its dramatic success both contributed to and coincided with the CIAA's decline as a home to marquee black athletes.

The success of Gaines's 1967 Winston-Salem team, led by future Hall of Famer Earl Monroe of New York City, only presaged the decline of CIAA basketball as a home to top talent. For the first time, the CIAA's signature style of fast break basketball built on quick decision-making and use of passing fundamentals, as well as outstanding conditioning, surprised the general basketball public. What once may have been dismissed as ragtag basketball was now a winning formula that many coaches around the country began attempting to copy.[73] By the time Texas Western University started five African American players to defeat Adolph Rupp's all-white Kentucky squad in the 1966 NCAA Division I Championship, it was apparent that African American players—exhibiting a style of play fostered at HBCUs—could win at the highest levels of collegiate basketball.[74]

As white coaches scrambled to copy this style and recruit more and more black players, Gaines and others found their traditional recruiting pools in the Midwest, South, and New York City increasingly shrinking. Bigger white programs with greater financial resources began wooing the very best black players away. With the Jim Crow laws of the South disappearing only at a glacial rate, more and more young African American players found it hard to listen to the call of coaches like Gaines when more attractive conditions beckoned elsewhere.[75] The level of play did not drop off significantly in the CIAA; after all, CIAA teams still maintain competitive Division II programs. But with the very top African American athletes able to take advantage of the resources of major white state universities, like North Carolina and Kentucky, and private institutions such as Duke and Vanderbilt, the ability of smaller, less well-funded HBCUs to remain in contention with the upper echelon of intercollegiate basketball diminished markedly. This did not mean that success could not and did not happen for CIAA teams. In fact, the success of Virginia Union in the 1980s with future NBA star Charles Oakley leading the nation in rebounding demonstrated that the CIAA occasionally still produced teams that could play with the very top teams that had formerly been for whites only.[76]

The fast break itself produced a problem of sorts. As is often the case with innovation, a trademark and source of pride soon became a tradition not to be tampered with. Although the CIAA brand of basketball had changed the way the game was played, Gaines and others grew older and less willing to make any changes to a winning formula. When younger coaches entered the CIAA less adept at teaching that style, the CIAA brand of basketball became less competitive than what was being played in other major basketball conferences like the ACC and Big 10.[77] But as Gaines argued, in the end, the decreasing ability of CIAA coaches to attract top talent ultimately led to the decline in the level of play more than any stylistic problems. The biggest drain on the CIAA, and Gaines's teams in particular, was the loss of star players.

Scholars have looked thoughtfully at the impact of desegregation on black athletic teams and their communities.[78] Players make up teams, but it is the fans and family members drawn to games who ultimately dictate how much a sports team can affect the broader community. Given the carefully nurtured and symbiotic relationship between black high schools and HBCUs, a path existed for young African American athletes to follow that kept them within the gaze and focus of their community. Many of these stars found homes in larger white institutions as Jim Crow died; many fans, friends, and family members followed them. That is not to say that they abandoned the CIAA, but networks became fragmented in a way that was detrimental to the CIAA. Unlike the Negro leagues, CIAA athletic teams did not cease to exist, nor did they become unimportant. In fact, the continuing success of the CIAA basketball tournament and the continued relevancy of HBCUs allowed the CIAA to survive where professional associations like the Negro leagues failed. But the CIAA, and other conferences like the SEAC and SWAC, no longer monopolized African American athletic talent, and the repercussions were felt beyond a decline in performance and a drain of top performers; this shift also predicted a siphoning of interest from within the black community.

Gaines had held throughout his career that it was the talent of the players upon which any coach built his reputation. And it was in working with these players and in imparting life's lessons that Gaines was at his best. First and foremost a teacher, he was also a disciplinarian and a father figure and mentor for his players. His considerable physical presence was memorable as far north as the basketball playgrounds of New York, but it was his concern for his players' education and life that made his vast network of friends, teachers, and associates want to send the young men of their particular communities to play for him.[79]

What perhaps most endeared him to his players, and an aspect of his coaching style that provided the best life lessons, was that he had very few rules.[80] Insisting that it was more important that his players learn how to make their own decisions, he merely laid out the schedule and left it to them to choose whether or not a late night spent socializing was worth it when a 6 a.m. training run and a full day of classes were on the next day's agenda. Earl Monroe, whom Gaines has described as his best player, remains loyal to the memory of his coach today for instilling those adult lessons of mature decision-making in him at a young age.[81]

Coach Gaines distilled his own hopes for how he wanted to influence young people into these words:

> A coach's job is to teach his boys the fundamentals of the game and then to teach them how to be men. Any coach's job is to teach boys to live up to their potential, to do their best, to never be satisfied with what they are but to strive to be as good as they can be.[82]

Gaines took great pride that many of his former athletes followed him into a career in coaching and education, thus continuing the cycle that defined his own life: student-athlete, and then coach in the CIAA in the same community of HBCUs that helped shape him. But he was also proud that his athletes were not one-dimensional, that they were students first who went on to become doctors, businessmen, politicians and, in the case of Earl Monroe, an NBA star.

Yet as with many coaches—both black and white—whose tenure spans decades and generations, Gaines's time at Winston-Salem State ended in a slightly ignominious fashion. A new administration gradually hamstrung his budget and administrative responsibilities in the late 1980s and early 1990s. Classy to the end, Gaines did not publicly criticize the administration, which encouraged him to retire before he was ready and, by all accounts, well before any of his coaching skills had begun to diminish. Gaines's legacy is not his final few years but the life and coaching career that so imposingly spanned five decades.

Introduced to the CIAA through its unique network of alumni and well-wishers as a prospective student, Gaines became a two-sport star at Morgan State College and an athlete of no small renown within the CIAA community. Given the opportunity to coach at a young age through the CIAA's network of coaches, Gaines became a legendary basketball coach who helped develop the CIAA brand of basketball into a national model and whose recruiting efforts demonstrated that it was possible to attract top talent from all over the country to the HBCUs of the CIAA. Indeed, his competitive zeal to be the best within the CIAA helped bolster the quality of the association's athletes and style of play. His career saw the famous CIAA basketball tournament grow from a small athletic event into an annual extravaganza that continues to be the social and economic event among CIAA member schools each February. His tenure as a coach reflected many of the inequities of budget, travel, and discrimination that CIAA schools, coaches, and athletes fought to overcome. His own successes help highlight how many coaches in the CIAA turned these disadvantages into shared values, athletic strategies, and close personal relationships that strengthened their careers and community.[83]

Notes

1. Clarence Gaines, with Clint Johnson, *They Call Me Big House* (Winston-Salem, NC: John F. Bair, 2004), 27; "Resolutions," Clarence Edward "Big House" Gaines Sr. Collection, C. G. O' Kelly Library, Winston-Salem State University, Winston-Salem State, NC, series 58, box 21, folder 1.
2. Gaines's fame in the broader context of American society came at a time when large African American men were often considered dangerous and threatening to white society, particularly in the South. There is a considerable body of literature on the subject of black manhood and white society during Jim Crow. Gaines's ability to survive in a position of notoriety for so many decades is indeed an important theme in his career. See Earnestine Jenkins and Darlene Clark Hine, eds., *A Question of Manhood: A Reader in U.S. Black Men's History and Masculinity* (Bloomington: Indiana University Press, 2001), for a good collection of essays on the subject.
3. Gaines, *They Call Me Big House*, 18.
4. "Resolutions," series 8, box 21, folder 1.
5. Gaines, *They Call Me Big House*, 44.
6. Gaines.
7. Gaines.
8. Gaines.
9. Rayford W. Logan, *Howard University: The First Hundred Years, 1867–1967* (New York: New York University Press, 1968), chapter 4. Logan describes in great detail the student life at Howard in the years Gaines was at Morgan State. Logan's study makes it clear that Howard and other HBCUs were centers of African American culture and community.
10. Upon seeing Gaines for the first time, older teammates declared that he was "as big as a house" and the nickname stuck.
11. Gaines, *They Call Me Big House*, 50; "Outgoing Letters," Clarence Edward "Big House" Gaines Sr. Collection, series 1, box 1, folder 8. Letters to Coach Hurt as well as anecdotes in his autobiography shed light on Gaines's affection for his college coach.
12. A far less successful player in basketball than football, he was a far more successful coach, in terms measured by longevity and won-loss records, in basketball. As Gaines says in *They Call Me Big House*: "When sports historians look at my contributions at Morgan State, they rightly concentrate on my four All-CIAA seasons as a football tackle. Though I became a very fair basketball coach, I never excelled at playing the game" (56).
13. Baltimore *Afro-American*, 22 October 1943, 12.
14. Gaines, *They Call Me Big House*, chapter 4, for a description of Gaines's decision to choose coaching for two years over immediately heading to dental school.
15. Gaines, *They Call Me Big House*, 51.
16. His annual starting salary as an assistant coach was $1,800. The next year as head coach that salary increased to $2,400.
17. Gaines, *They Call Me Big House*, 153.
18. Robert Rogers Korstad, *Civil Rights Unionism: Tobacco Workers and the Struggle for Democracy in the Mid-Twentieth-Century South* (Chapel Hill: University of North Carolina Press, 2003), 61–92.

19 Korstad, *Civil Rights Unionism*, 77.
20 Gaines, *They Call Me Big House*, 176.
21 Robert E. Park, "A City of Racial Peace," *World Today* 9 (August 1905): 897–899.
22 Bertha Hampton Miller, "Blacks in Winston-Salem, North Carolina, 1895–1920: Community Development in an Era of Benevolent Paternalism" (PhD diss., Duke University, 1981), 1–3.
23 Hampton Miller, "Blacks in Winston-Salem," 148–195; Raymond Gavins "The NAACP in North Carolina during the Age of Segregation," in *New Directions in Civil Rights Studies,* ed. Armstead L. Robinson and Patricia Sullivan (Charlottesville: University of Virginia Press, 1991), 105–125.
24 Korstad, *Civil Rights Unionism,* 183–184.
25 Korstad, 183.
26 Korstad, 9, 184–185.
27 Korstad, 76–77.
28 Korstad, 78, 79.
29 Korstad, 235–236.
30 *Bulletin of the CIAA* (1949): 38. Attendance figures from 1939 indicate that 6,281 paying customers attended WSTC's 14 home contests. Assuming an average of nearly 500 spectators, it is fair to say that this crowd was likely a diverse group of African Americans and unlikely to have come solely from one particular social stratus. Students would have made up a portion of this crowd, as well as professionals who worked at WSTC, but it would have been impossible for this crowd to only be WSTC staff and students. These types of crowds certainly indicate a broader base of support within the black community.
31 *Bulletin of the CIAA* (1950): 41.
32 "Incoming Letters," Clarence Edward "Big House" Gaines Sr. Collection, series 1, box 1, folder 1 and folder 2; Gaines, *They Call Me Big House,* chapter 5.
33 The first was John McLendon.
34 Gaines describes in *They Call Me Big House,* chapters 5–6, his willingness to attend coaching clinics as the only black coach in attendance. He notes that he was accepted in nearly all cases because of his passion for the game and for learning. Gaines also learned from other coaches in the CIAA such as John McLendon. He deemed McLendon to be far more knowledgeable regarding basketball.
35 Gaines, *They Call Me Big House,* 90.
36 Murray Sperber, *Onward to Victory: The Crises That Shaped College Sport* (New York: Henry Holt, 2000), 157.
37 "Incoming Letters," series 1, box 1, folders 1–16 document the strong coaching and personal friendship of McLendon and Gaines; Gaines, *They Call Me Big House,* 89–90.
38 *Bulletin of the CIAA* (1945–1952) provides roster information.
39 *Bulletin of the CIAA* (1945–1952).
40 Nelson George, *Elevating the Game: Black Men and Basketball* (Harper Collins: New York, 1992), 72.
41 Gaines was in attendance, according to the New York *Amsterdam News* (July 24, 1955): 15. Gaines himself describes how his network of friends and Winston-Salem alumni

gave him acceptance into the Rucker tournaments in *They Call Me Big House*, 109–110.
42 Gaines does admit to a little bit of salesmanship in *They Call Me Big House*, 124: "Another thing that I never made a point of warning these New York recruits about was what life was really like in the segregated South. If I had, they may have skipped college entirely."
43 George, *Elevating the Game*, 87.
44 Gaines, *They Call Me Big House*, 121–124. "Incoming Letters," series 1, box 1, folders 1–16.
45 Gaines, *They Call Me Big House*, 125.
46 Francis L. Ross Coble Papers, C. G. O'Kelly Library, Winston-Salem State University, Winston-Salem, NC, box 1, folder 4.
47 Wilmoth A. Carter, *Shaw's Universe: A Monument to Educational Innovation* (Raleigh: Shaw University, 1973), 149.
48 "1951 Catalogue," Francis L. Ross Coble Papers, box 1, folder 6. These expectations were similar at other HBCUs in North Carolina. E.g., see Hugh Victor Brown, *A History of the Education of Negroes in North Carolina* (Raleigh: Irving Swain Press, 1961), 16–44, and Brown, *E-Qual-ity Education in North Carolina among Negroes* (Raleigh: Irving-Swain Press, 1964), 123–133. For further detail on the academic history of another CIAA school, see Cecil D. Halliburton, *A History of St. Augustine's College: 1867–1937* (Raleigh: St. Augustine's College, 1937).
49 "1951 Catalogue," 152.
50 "1948 Teaching Manual," Francis L. Ross Coble Papers, box 1, folder 5; Carter, *Shaw's Universe*, 149–150.
51 Carter, *Shaw's Universe*, 148.
52 Carter, *Shaw's Universe*, 202; Francis L. Ross Coble Papers, box 1, folder 6.
53 "Memoranda (Outgoing)," Clarence Edward "Big House" Gaines Sr. Collection, series 6, box 20, folder 1.
54 Carter, *Shaw's Universe*, 202–203.
55 "Memoranda (Outgoing)," series 6, box 20, folders 1.
56 "Memoranda (Outgoing)," 9–10; "Incoming Letters," series 1, box 1, folder 1.
57 "Memoranda (Outgoing)," 179.
58 Rita Liberti, "'We Were Ladies, We Just Played Basketball Like Boys': A Study of Women's Basketball at Historically Black Colleges and Universities in North Carolina, 1925–1945" (PhD diss., University of Iowa, 1998), 1, 8–9, 36–37.
59 "Central Intercollegiate Athletic Association," Clarence Edward "Big House" Gaines Sr. Collection, series 5, boxes 8–12.
60 Gaines, *They Call Me Big House*, 77.
61 Gaines, 80.
62 Russell Blunt, interview by Arthur Smith, tape recording, Durham, NC, March 6, 1997, BTV; "The Magic of The CIAA Basketball Tournament," *Ebony* 57 (February 2003): 128.
63 By the 1950s, the tournament accounted for over 30 percent and nearly 50 percent in some years of the CIAA's total revenue; see *Bulletin of the CIAA* (1959): 34–36.

64. For more on his efforts to keep his recruiting budget at a competitive level, see "Outgoing Letters," Clarence Edward "Big House" Gaines Sr. Collection, series 1, box 2, folder 8. For his description of the decline in his teams in the late 1980s, see Gaines, *They Call Me Big House*, 247–276.
65. Gaines, *They Call Me Big House*, chapters 12 and 13.
66. "Incoming Letters," series 1, box 1, folders 10–16 contain letters from former players.
67. "Incoming Letters," series 1, box 1, folders 1–16. John Dell, "Goodbye, Big House," Winston-Salem *Journal* (April 23, 2005): 1.
68. "Coaching Techniques," Clarence Edward "Big House" Gaines Sr. Collection, series 7, box 21, folder 24; Gaines, *They Call Me Big House*, 176.
69. For more on how the Harlem Globetrotters combined athletic prowess with minstrelsy, see David Wiggins and Patrick B. Miller, eds., *The Unlevel Playing Field: A Documentary History of the African American Experience in Sport* (Champaign: University of Illinois, 2003), 229–233, and Ben Green, *Spinning the Globe: The Rise, Fall, and Return To Greatness of the Harlem Globetrotters* (New York: Harper Collins, 2005).
70. Scott Ellsworth "Jim Crow Losses: The Secret Game," *New York Times Magazine* 99 (March 31, 1996): 28.
71. Dr. Leroy T. Walker, interview by Arthur Smith, tape recording, Durham, NC, December 9, 2005.
72. Peter Bjarkman, *The Biographical History of Basketball* (New York: McGraw-Hill, 1999), 400.
73. Gaines, *They Call Me Big House*, 217–220.
74. Gaines, *They Call Me Big House*, 225.
75. Dr. Leroy T. Walker, interview by Arthur Smith. Walker highlighted the example of Charles Oakley as an example of a player who was undiscovered by the traditional powerhouse programs of NCAA Division I but who flourished in the CIAA and proved to be a national-caliber star.
76. Bjarkman, *Biographical History of Basketball*, 404.
77. Neil Lanctot, *Negro League Baseball: The Rise and Ruin of a Black Institution* (Philadelphia: University of Pennsylvania Press, 2004) does so most directly in terms of how the loss of star players and Negro League Teams impacted the economy and daily life of black communities.
78. "Incoming Letters," series 1, box 1, folder 5.
79. "Incoming Letters," series 1, box 1, folder 14.
80. Gaines, *They Call Me Big House*, 184.
81. Gaines, 190.
82. Gaines, 190.
83. Gaines, 190.

IV

Musical Geniuses

8

Count Basie

Red Bank's Soulful Original

Matthew Buttermann

As the evolution of large ensemble jazz, or the "jazz orchestra," has progressed from the days of the dance halls, individual players have exhibited unique styles that shaped the sound of jazz for every generation. Musicians continually look to the players before them for guidance and inspiration as they form their musical identity both through their instruments and with the ensembles they lead. As much as the sound of big band has evolved in tandem with individual development, few, if any, big bands have had the prolonged influence as the Count Basie Orchestra. We know the about immense influence Duke Ellington has had on American music, as much as we know about the popularity of Benny Goodman and many innovations of the Stan Kenton Orchestra. But how can we look to those characteristics to shape our current understanding of their music? As listeners, players, and students, we can ask, What does it mean to play like the Fletcher Henderson Orchestra, the Duke Ellington Orchestra, or even the Mel Lewis/Thad Jones Orchestra? The immense impact of each of these artists and ensembles, as well as numerous others, is profoundly important to understanding jazz music and how it is performed today. Yet the "Basie" style elicits clear performance guidelines that inform players from the most advanced to those just beginning to experience the richness of large ensemble playing. The Count Basie band of the late 1930s and early 40s was the embodiment of swing so that "whatever their other attributes, to one degree or another most of the big bands that followed aspired to Basie's quality of swing."[1] To play like "Basie" means to be bluesy while sophisticated, soulful while innovative, and simple to a degree hard to attain but pioneered by Count Basie and the many iterations of his orchestra.

Simplicity does not mean unsophisticated. In the case of Count Basie, simplicity was the catalyst for the creativity and supportive risk-taking his musicians needed to shape their sound in the jazz world. Composition, arrangement, and orchestration led the way in the large ensemble development. Bandleaders employed sophisticated and complex techniques for their ensembles and ultimately to create their ensemble identity. Duke Ellington wrote compositions and arrangements with his orchestra players' capabilities in mind—Ellington's keen awareness of the sounds he could evoke from his players showed us Bubber Miley and "East St. Louis Toodle-Oo" with a new and iconic sound for the trumpet soloist that has been emulated by trumpeters ever since. Stan Kenton's link to "cool jazz" and the concept influenced by Claude Thornhill moved away from dance music and presented rich harmonies in intricate arrangements. There might not have been a Maria Schneider Orchestra had it not been for the innovations of Stan Kenton. The same could be said about Charlie Parker and the countless others who came after him if it were not for Lester Young and the unique platform Count Basie gave him to develop his iconic brand of improvising.

A native of Red Bank, New Jersey, William James Basie Jr. was born on August 21, 1904, to his father, Harvey Lee Basie, and mother, Lillian Childs Basie.[2] Both parents were born and raised in Chase City, Virginia, and came to Red Bank after they were married.[3] Young Basie had a tight-knit relationship with family members who all worked various jobs around Red Bank. In the early twentieth century, automobiles were only just coming into communities and Basie's father worked as a coachman and caretaker for Judge White, who owned a large estate along the Shrewsbury River just north of Red Bank.[4] When Judge White exchanged horse and carriage for an automobile, Harvey transitioned to caretaker work for the estate as well as the estates of several other prominent families in the area. The Whites were kind to the Basie family and often their daughter, Margarette, would drive William to his piano lessons. That was the first time he ever rode in a car. The salary paid to Harvey for looking after the White estate was good and enough for the Basie family to afford their own house.[5]

William's mother, Lilly Ann, worked as a laundress and would sell her baked cakes for 40 cents each to neighbors. While William appreciated the work his parents did it pained him even as a child to see his mother work so hard. "I never did like the idea of my mother having to work at anything like washing and ironing and cooking and all that jive. I used to tell her that all the time, and one day I drew the picture of an automobile and showed it to her and said, 'One of these days I'm going to get you a car just like that, and I'm going to stop you from working.'"[6] He never forgot that as he got older at every stage of his career, he would always send something back to his mother.

There was always a piano in the house, and William's mother made him take lessons, which she paid 25 cents per lesson to Miss Vandevere. However, the strict formality of piano lessons did not resonate with the young William. He managed to play through basic exercise assignments and could read a few pieces, but he was keener to pick songs up by ear, particularly ragtime tunes that were popular in the day. Because he was so good at picking up tunes quickly, he managed to get a gig playing for silent pictures at the Palace Theatre in Red Bank one day when the regular pianist couldn't make it. William had spent time working in the theater learning how to rewind the reels, switch projectors, and operate the spotlight. He had spent enough time watching the other pianist at the movies that he knew the songs and how to follow the film, so when the owner needed someone to fill in at the last-minute William jumped at the chance. Although the manager was skeptical at first due to his age, he was impressed with that matinee performance and invited William to play again for the evening show.[7]

But it really was not the piano young Basie was most interested in, he wanted to be a drummer. "I didn't start out to be a piano player. The first thing I really wanted to be was a drummer . . . I was attracted to the trap drums very early."[8] His mother would take William to dances around Red Bank, and the local drummer, who played several of these dances, taught William a few things and let him sit in during some intermissions.[9] He was enamored by the drums, so his father bought him a small set and soon enough William picked up small jobs around Red Bank playing with a piano player.[10] However, it wasn't long before William shifted his attention away from drums and focused on the piano, and that motivation came from hearing Sonny Greer for the first time. "It was Sonny Greer, who later on went on to become one of the greatest and most famous drummers in the world with the Duke Ellington Orchestra, who got the notion of being a drummer out of my head once and for all."[11]

Basie would later become known as an ever-swinging bandleader and pianist whose seemingly simple approach to the music was steeped in short and fully effective motifs. The later Basie rhythm section would be dubbed the "All-American Rhythm Section" due to the strong cohesion among the four rhythm section members and the never-wavering sense of swing and solid timekeeping. The influence of Greer and Basie's early ambition to be a drummer laid a foundation that would define the Basie sound as his career unfolded. But it wasn't a competitive relationship between Greer and Basie, and they began working together as a piano and drummer duo for dances around Red Bank. It was from the early opportunities to play for dancers and an intuitive understanding of how music functions (while supporting the lively entertaining quality of dancing) that locked Basie into a state of constant groove and swing. It is also during these formative years that Basie first demonstrated his entrepreneurial spirit. He was so taken by the dancing scene and opportunities to work around town as a musician that he got the idea to make his own gig rather than find ways to be hired by dance halls and managers. When he was still a teenager, he decided to put on his own dance and acquired the help of his parents to make some food and sell the tickets for an evening at the K&P Hall.[12] Although he didn't make any money after paying the musicians, it was another way Basie set himself apart from his peers—you could get hired by musicians or managers, or you could take a new initiative as a musician and put it on yourself. Basie was remembered as a pianist and bandleader, and some of those band-leadership qualities were established before he left Red Bank for New York City and then on to the Midwest.

Basie is most associated with the "Kansas City" sound, but his early days in Red Bank and time in New York City instilled in him a musical aesthetic that grounded his playing before developing as the musician best known from his Kansas City days. In 1924, when William was just nineteen years old, he made the move to New York City where a growing and vibrant music scene was what he needed most. After settling in Harlem, New York, near the Alhambra Theatre at Seventh Avenue and 127th Street, Basie took to exploring the neighborhood and soon ran into Sonny Greer, who was between sets with the Washingtonians, led by Duke Ellington, at the Capital Palace near the center of Harlem at 140th Street and Lenox Avenue. It was the first time he met Ellington and the same day he made the acquaintance of Willie "the Lion" Smith as the house piano player in the same building.[13] He played around New York with Elmer Snowden at the Nest Club, a dance hall with June Clark, and with a band at Leroy's in Harlem.[14] A cornet player from back home in Red Bank who also relocated to New York City, Freddie Douglas, got Basie his first steady gig in New York at Leroy's.[15] The club was owned by Leroy Wilkins, the brother of Barron Wilkins, who was the first New York club owner to give the Washingtonians a break at his Exclusive Club, known just as Barron's.[16] Otto Hardwick, a member of Ellington's Washingtonians, hired Basie as his pianist at Barron's while the Washingtonians were on a hiatus.[17]

In these formative New York days, Basie was heavily influenced by the popular entertainer and stride-pianist Fats Waller. Although they first met at Leroy's, which was the spot where James P. Johnson and Willie "the Lion" Smith were having piano sessions, Basie became friends with Waller at Harlem's Lincoln Theatre at 135th Street and Lenox Avenue, where Waller was playing organ for the movies. He would sit and watch Waller play the Wurlitzer pipe organ and ask him questions about playing that instrument. Waller gave Basie the only lessons he ever received for the organ.[18] In 1923, Basie followed Waller as the pianist with Liza and Her Shuffling Sextet, a job that Ellington made his second trip to New York in hopes of acquiring.[19] It was the first tour for Basie.[20] Basie maintained a strong stride tradition even during his time in Kansas City and the subsequent leading of his orchestra as his piano playing developed new styles after the popularity of stride pianists like Fats Waller, Willie Smith, and James P. Johnson. Basie innovatively "extended the Harlem Stride extension of the ragtime piano in the very process of stripping it down for use as an element of Kansas City riff-style orchestration."[21] The same evening he first met Ellington and Smith Basie persuaded a bandleader working in a nearby club to let him sit in, and that was his first set in New York. It went well and the leader, Lou Henry, told him about an audition for a traveling show the following day. It turned out to be for a burlesque show—*Hippity Hop*—heading out on the Columbia circuit. Basie and his friend Elmer Williams got the gig and negotiated a salary of $40 a week—later doubled to $80 a week on the second tour. The show traveled around the country and included his first, albeit short, visit to Kansas City and a performance at the Apollo Theatre on 125th Street in Harlem before it became the iconic theater known the world over.[22]

It was through his work at Leroy's that Basie became aware of an opening for a pianist for a new vaudeville act known as Gonzelle White and Her Jazz Band. Gonzelle White's trumpet player Harry Smith got Basie the audition to replace the pianist who cut out earlier. The band worked around the New York area for a while mostly on weekends in Brooklyn, Long Island, and New Jersey. The proximity to New York City allowed Basie to stay close to the Harlem scene as the Gonzelle White show was not a lot of work. But as the show grew in popularity, White's husband, saxophonist and manager Ed Langford, decided to set up the ensemble's own road company and arrange a trip to Havana, Cuba. The newly expanded show had a comedy team, a chorus line, and a new singer. However, the deal to Cuba fell through and Langford decided to take the newly formed show on the TOBA (Theatre Owners and Bookers Association) circuit.[23] That was an entirely new experience than Basie had had with the vaudeville and theater circuits operated by Columbia, Keith, Orpheum, and Poli that were white or mixed. "On the TOBA audiences were strictly colored, but sometimes there was a special section for a few white people. Some TOBA theaters were owned by white people, but most were operated by colored people."[24] When Langford became ill during performances in Indianapolis, Basie filled in for the skit with Gonzelle. The show adjusted after Langford's death in Chicago to continue with the TOBA circuit commitments, which took them to Kansas City and Tulsa, Oklahoma. Basie explained, "So about the time we reach Kansas City, the unit was in pretty bad shape and then came the inevitable folding. When we folded, I was broke and didn't have any way to get out of town."[25]

Basie worked in vaudeville for about four years and heard the Blue Devils, a popular territory band led by Walter Page, for the first time in 1926 when he traveled through Tulsa, Oklahoma, performing at the Dreamland Theatre with Gonzelle White. The experience of first hearing, and sitting in with, Walter Page and the Blue Devils changed his ambitions for and perceptions of music. About a year after hearing the Blue Devils, Basie was back in Kansas City with the Whitman Sisters. The show broke up in Kansas City and left Basie stranded there looking for odd jobs, where he found work playing organ for silent movies at the Eblon Theatre.[26] He was quickly trying to insert himself into the Kansas City music scene outside the Eblon, "without really being aware of the big change I was making, I was becoming more and more tied up with music itself and less and less concerned with show business and entertainment in general . . . after playing with those Blue Devils, being a musician was where it was really at for me."[27]

Kansas City was ripe for new opportunities and shows in need of musicians, during what has been called the Pendergast era, from around 1927 through 1938, when Tom Pendergast was the leader of the Democratic Party in Kansas City. Tom Pendergast first came to Kansas City to work for his brother James at a saloon in the First Ward, which was solidly a Democratic constituency. The Pendergast family used their businesses to gain favor within the community and exert significant influence on elections by delivering the First Ward vote. Tom Pendergast's first public appointment came as deputy county marshal and later Kansas City's superintended of the streets. When James Pendergast died in 1910, Tom took over the family business, now including wholesale liquor distribution, and was predictably elected to the city council of Kansas City. When the US Congress passed of the Volstead Act in 1919 outlawing the sale of liquor, Tom Pendergast diverted his legitimate business to the Ready Mix Concrete Company that "supplied every cubic foot of concrete and asphalt used in the construction of streets, highways, and public buildings" while relinquishing control of liquor distribution to an old friend from the First Ward, Johnny Lazia.[28] Pendergast now had control over nearly every layer of Kansas City government from council chambers and judgeships down to police departments and inspectors.[29] "Pendergast encouraged gambling and all forms of night life. . . . Whatever one may think of Pendergast's dubious behavioral role as a leading light in KC, it is true to say that all the significant musical developments, including the formative work of Basie, Jay McShann, Charlie Parker, etc., took place when Pendergast ran the city his way, with dozens of excellent bands playing at the many places of entertainment."[30]

The popularity and styles of territory bands were on the rise and allowed Basie to hear bands like George E. Lee's and Andy Kirk and his Twelve Clouds of Joy, featuring Mary Lou Williams on piano.[31] Of course, the most important territory band in those days was led by Bennie Moten. It was common for bands to compete in a battle of the bands, but despite rumors to the contrary Bennie Moten band never held a battle with Walter Page and the Blue Devils. It was in 1928 that Basie joined the Blue Devils.

Walter Page took over running the Blue Devils when the previous bandleader, trombonist Ermir Coleman, retired. Page persuaded some businessmen to back him in expanding the ensemble to a big band. Some of the new members could not read music, so Page, who studied music at Kansas University, began to teach the members how to read and coalesce them into a solid group.[32] He began to add talented young musicians to the group as they toured the territories: Jimmy Rushing was picked up from Oklahoma City; Buster Smith, on alto and clarinet, from Dallas; Oran Page in Texas; and tenor saxophonist Lester Young, picked up on a tour through Minnesota.[33] While Page was the de facto leader of the group, it was organized more as a collective with all members making contributions. By the time Basie joined in 1928, the Blue Devils was considered the best band in the territory and Page was eager to challenge Bennie Moten, who claimed most of the jobs in Kansas City. While Basie insists an official battle never occurred, Moten was thoroughly impressed with the Blue Devils and offered to hire the entire band with Page as music director. When Page refused, Moten proceeded to recruit one player at a time with better pay and opportunities in Kansas City.[34] Basie officially joined Bennie Moten in 1929, and by 1933 Moten had successfully absorbed the Blue Devils into his band, including Lester Young.

For Basie, the Moten band was *the* destination. He heard recordings after settling in Kansas City that fixated him on joining the group, even though Bennie himself was already the piano player in the band. Basie explained, "I have always been a conniver and began saying to myself, I got to see how I can connive my way into that band. I like that band. I got to play with that band . . . I don't know why the fact that Bennie Moten himself was such a good piano player didn't faze me. All I know is that I just had to play with them, and I was going to do everything I could to get myself in there. I kept watching for my first chance."[35] The chance came when Basie learned about Eddie Durham and his role as an arranger for Moten. He asked Durham if he could notate what he played on the piano and took those arrangements to the next rehearsal. Moten liked them and asked Basie to travel with them to Wichita to hear the band more and work on arrangements with Durham. That was it—he was in. It was soon after he found a way to sit in at the piano for Bennie while he attended to some business matters, which turned into more regular subbing in with the band. Moten and everyone agreed to chip in some money and make Basie's first salary $15 a week as the second piano player at the same time Moten secured a deal with the Victor Record Company.[36]

Moten was ambitious and looked forward to the day when the band would move outside the territories and into bigger markets. He started to book the band in Chicago and New York, and places along the way, to get their sound out into the world more. Moten bought stock arrangements from Benny Carter and Horace Henderson in 1931 before heading east to perform in the Savoy Ballroom in New York, the first such occasion performing opposite the house band led by Chick Webb—Benny Carter was their chief arranger at the time.[37] Emer Williams, Basie's longtime friend from Red Bank, was the tenor saxophonist.[38] Moten's drive to modernize the band and grow the audience base created repercussions back in Kansas City when they returned. The audiences of Kansas City rebuffed the smoother sounds that ran contrary to the Kansas City ethos. They were humiliated at the annual Musicians' Ball at Paseo Hall in Kansas City, when alongside bands like Andy Kirk and Clarence Love. It was the former Moten band member, trombonist Thamon Hayes, whose new band the Kansas City Rockers sent Moten down the ranks of the territory bands.[39]

Moten managed to follow George E. Lee's band at the new club Cherry Blossom for the summer, formerly known as the Eblon Theatre where Basie played organ for the silent films. Moten was trying to cook up another opportunity and take the band out of the Cherry Blossom, but the members were keen to stay. In the spirit of maintaining a commonwealth band, Moten stepped out of the room for the band to vote and they collectively decided to stay at the Cherry Blossom and voted to remove Bennie Moten as leader. Basie couldn't believe Moten would be the one voted out and was even more surprised when he was voted the new leader. Basie was eager to step into the shoes of bandleader and prove he could make it in the role. But he was honest with Moten by telling him the truth of the matter was that his removal as leader was not his doing and he would happily step aside when Moten was ready to return. In the meantime, the band was now called Count Basie and His Cherry Blossom Orchestra. It was the first time he was publicly billed as Count Basie, but not the first time going by that name. Basie gave himself the name "Count" when the Cherry Blossom was still the Eblon Theatre.[40] As the band began to dissolve, Bennie Moten went to Club Harlem with George

E. Lee on a version of their original arrangement taking some of the Moten band members with him while the others continued with Basie at the Cherry Blossom.[41] The lack of momentum for Basie and the new role became evident when they traveled to Little Rock, Arkansas—his name was simply not enough of a draw. Moten was happy to take the previously departed members back into his group and by 1934 was on a better footing in the Kansas City scene and ready to move out of the territories again with a new booking at the Rainbow Gardens in Denver. However, Moten became too ill to travel and stayed behind to have a tonsillectomy—tragically, Moten died during the operation. The band was devastated and unable to attend the funeral since they were booked at the Rainbow Gardens for a solid week. They wanted the Rainbow Gardens performances to reflect well on Moten's name and finished the week engagement, but overall, morale was at the bottom and the group disbanded in the summer of 1935 after returning to Kansas City.[42]

Basie did not immediately take over leadership of the band after Moten's death. Instead, he started looking around town for a little joint he could book a small ensemble rather than pursue any notion of reforming a big band. But soon after leaving Moten, Basie got a chance to go into the Reno Club "way downtown at Twelfth and Cherry."[43] Someone was already playing there and asked him to fill in while he was away for a few days. That was an unfamiliar part of town and, as far as Basie was concerned, not a part of town where anything was happening. But he needed a job and went there to check it out and see what the group was like. He was filling in for the piano player, and a tenor saxophonist by the name of Slim Freeman was calling the tunes. "I was curious about what it would be like to work in that part of town for a change. And the pay was eighteen dollars a week."[44] Basie became friends with the manager, Sol Steibold, and after only a week Sol asked if he wanted the piano chair permanently. Not long after that, he then suggested Basie be the new bandleader. Sol gave Basie the green light to add members to the band, and Basie quickly got to work adding former Moten bandmates to his new lineup at the Reno Club. After the Moten band broke up, the members scattered to different cities, so Basie had to go to Oklahoma City for Jack Washington and Big 'Un and then onto Dallas for Buster Smith and Joe Keys. Lips Page and Jimmy Rushing came to the club as singles, not as part of the band, but regularly performed with the band. Page was the master of ceremonies and would play in the trumpet section from time to time while Rushing was part of the floor show. Eventually he was able to get Jo Jones back from St. Louis, and that's "when the band really started swinging."[45]

While his new group at the Reno Club was taking shape, Basie was becoming more familiar with that part of town and learned he could practice the organ at Jenkin's music store. An executive from the WHB radio station heard him practicing and asked if he would like to have a small organ program on the radio in the afternoons, which became his first broadcasts as a single. It was about 15 minutes every day during the week in the middle of the afternoon. Frequency and regularity of the organ program forced Basie to compose new tunes or just make it up as he went along.[46]

The hours in the Reno Club were long, often twelve hours with Basie receiving $21 a week as the leader and the band members paid $18. The club was nothing special at the time, and all indicators pointed to the Reno Club catering to all kinds of less-than-upstanding clientele. But the Reno Club happened to have broadcasting capabilities over a local Kansas City station, W9XBY. It was still experimental, as each Sunday night the band went on the air and Jimmy Rushing sat in.[47] It was about a year before the weekly broadcasting took hold, but when it did it irrevocably changed the way forward for Basie. For starters, Lester Young heard the broadcasts and came down to replace Slim Freeman as the tenor saxophonist. Roy Eldridge said he and Fletcher Henderson used to listen to the broadcasts from Chicago, which prompted Henderson to send Basie some arrangements.[48]

Around the time that Basie was making his way at the Reno Club in Kansas City, Benny Goodman was rising to star power around the country. He was already dubbed "King of Swing" and performing at the Congress Hotel in Chicago. Alongside Goodman was young promoter John Hammond, who wrote for the British journal *Melody Maker* and had a contract to produce records for the British market. He was a longtime friend of Goodman, who married John's sister Alice in 1941. It was during a break in the engagement at the Congress Hotel that Hammond tuned his car radio into W9XBY and heard Basie's evening broadcast for the first time. He was so taken by what he heard on the radio that he went to Kansas City to hear the band for himself firsthand and relay those transformative experiences in *DownBeat* magazine.[49]

Hammond urged Dick Altschuler of the American Record Company to sign the band to his Brunswick label. Although Altschuler agreed, Decca, a competing record label, got to Basie first via Dave Kapp. Basie signed a contract for 24 sides a year for three years, for a fee of $750 a year with no royalties to Basie for the 61 tracks he would make for Decca between January 1937 and February 1939. Many of Basie's best-known songs were recorded during this time, including "One O'Clock Jump," "Jumpin' at the Woodside," and "Topsy."[50]

Hammond soon brought Benny Goodman to hear Basie. Goodman was equally enthused by the music and referred his own agent, Willard Alexander, to find bookings for Basie outside Kansas City.[51] Alexander was with Music

Corporation of America and signed Basie to an MCA contract with a new booking at the Grand Terrace Hotel in Chicago.[52]

By all accounts, the Grand Terrace Hotel engagement was a disaster. The Basie band was taken out of their element from playing head arrangements of blues and riff-tunes to a proper show for the Grand Terrace audience. "There was nothing in the show that gave us a real chance to displace ourselves properly."[53] Fletcher Henderson bailed them out by lending Basie his whole book of pop tunes.[54] The band played at the Grand Terrace for nearly a month in late 1936, during a period the owner claimed the Terrace did its smallest business in years and tried to cancel the Basie show before the contract expired. But MCA kept it on since they had a larger interest in the radio wire at the club as part of Hammond's plans to expand the Basie audience. Before the Chicago residency concluded, Hammond recorded the band on what later came out on the Vocalion label and included seminal recordings of Lester Young on "Lady Be Good" and "Shoeshine Boy."[55] Since the Count Basie name was tied up with the Decca contract, the recordings would be released under the name Jones-Smith, Inc.[56]

The band made a ragged trip along the way to New York with disappointing stops in Connecticut before arriving in New York for a gig at the Roseland Ballroom just before a New Year's Day that turned things around for them with a slightly more positive reception, a reception that continued at the famed Apollo Theatre in Harlem. The new momentum sent them to the William Penn Hotel in Pittsburgh for an overwhelmingly positive review in an otherwise stale environment. The band was in solid form with a newfound attraction in the tenor battles between Lester Young and Herschel Evans. MCA felt a female singer would add to the ensembles sound and popularity and brought in Billie Holiday in 1937 after Basie heard her sing at Clark Monroe's in Harlem.[57] She did not make records with Basie and only lasted less than a year. Hammond now turned his attention to recommending that Basie bring in Freddie Green—Basie's left hand—to replace Claude Williams and a new female vocalist in Helen Humes.[58]

The Count Basie Orchestra was no longer a territory band. After broadcasting, recording, and performing successes around the country, the Basie name was established in the world of big band jazz with the likes of Benny Goodman, Duke Ellington, Cab Calloway, and Chick Webb. In January 1938 Basie took part in a cutting contest at the Savoy Ballroom against Chick Webb, the same day as Benny Goodman's Carnegie Hall concert that Basie participated in the same afternoon. The collective understanding of the scene was that Basie did it: he had beaten the hometown favorite Chick Webb, though Basie himself would never admit such a thing happened that way.[59] Basie suspected they came out on top due to the fact the sound system failed nearly every time Ella Fitzgerald came out to sing with Chick Webb and miraculously worked properly when Billie Holiday sang with Basie's band.[60]

Willard Alexander had Basie booked for a six-month engagement starting mid-1938 until January 1939, at the Famous Door on Fifty-Second Street, run by Jerry Brooks and Al Felshin. The Famous Door was a small venue, and Jerry and Al were not keen to have a large group in the space that was better suited for small combos with singers. Hammond and Alexander saw promise in the residency and loaned the club money to install air conditioners to convince the owners and attract customers during the summer months. The stage was tighter than the one at the Reno Club in Kansas City.[61] The prolonged engagement allowed the band to develop their sound more accurately by leaning into certain soloists in the group, particularly the growing popularity of the tenor saxophonists. Basie was paid $1,300 per week at the Famous Door, but the most significant element was the CBS radio network installed to broadcast the group on a regular basis across the country. The residency was followed by another six-month engagement in Chicago.[62] The stability allowed the band to develop and featured musicians in a growing book of repertoire, and producers found it beneficial to have stellar musicians available for other recording projects with Billie Holiday and Teddy Wilson, among others. By January 1939 Basie was fulfilling his Decca contract with the "All-American Rhythm Section" featuring Jo Jones on drums, Walter Page on bass, guitarist Freddie Green, and Basie on piano.[63] Decca was eager to continue their relationship with Basie and offered him an additional $1,000 to sign a new contract, but Basie refused and signed with Columbia instead—a contract that would remain intact until 1946. The new contract put Count Basie in direct competition with Duke Ellington, who at the time, was the only "Negro band on the Columbia label." Therefore, Basie's records had to be released on the Okeh label, a subsidiary of Columbia.[64] When Basie did officially move to Columbia, Ellington left and went to Victor.[65] Unfortunately, just at the end of the Decca recordings, Basie's tenor saxophonist Herschel Evans collapsed and died from a cardiac condition in January 1939, eventually replaced by Buddy Tate.[66] There was speculation that the tenor battles between Lester Young and Herschel Evans in some way reflected actual feelings of animosity among the players, but nothing was further from the truth. Evans and Young were close friends on and off the bandstand. "Nobody missed him [Herschel] more than Lester. For a while, Lester really didn't want to go on. It was a problem every night just trying to get him to go on the bandstand, and Jack Washington would have to spend most of the gig just trying to keep him up there. It was rough, and naturally the rest of us understood how he felt."[67]

The first part of 1940 saw Basie's relationship with MCA turn sour, largely due to Willard Alexander's move to another agency and Basie being booked on engagements through MCA without radio airtime that Alexander deemed crucial early on.[68] It sparked a series of setbacks, Basie threatened to dissolve the band to release himself from the MCA contract and took short gigs with Benny Goodman while the rest of his musicians found small jobs around New York City. Eventually, MCA and Basie's manager, Milt Ebbins, agreed to have MCA take less in commissions considering MCA's poor handling of booking Basie that year. Another setback came when Lester Young failed to show up for a recording session in December 1940, forcing Basie to give Young's intended solos on four tunes to Buddy Tate. It marked Young's temporary departure from the band to be replaced by Don Byas in 1941.[69] Basie would soon buy his release from MCA for $10,000 and join the William Morris agency—the same agency Willard Alexander joined the year prior. Now that Alexander was back in charge of bookings for Basie, things improved with engagements at ballrooms and theaters.[70] Despite a recording ban and musicians being drafted into the US Army for the war, Basie made some important personnel changes, most importantly the return of Lester Young at the end of 1943. The band was touring around the country and made it to California, where a number of new opportunities in the film industry emerged and where Basie can be seen in *Hit Parade of 1942, Reveille with Beverley,* and *Stage Door Canteen.* The most significant engagement in 1943 came at the Lincoln Hotel in New York. "It was the breaking down of multiple barriers. It was Count's first booking into a New York hotel and the first time the Lincoln had ever played host to a coloured band. No doubt Willard Alexander was the power behind the move and the Lincoln booking was an immediate success."[71]

By the time World War II ended in 1945, the music across the United States was changing and Basie was aware of where these musical trends were headed. His orchestra was also adjusting in personnel—Jo Jones was back from the army—while holding on to key elements that sent him apart. One such element was maintaining a strong tenor saxophone soloist, which he found in Illinois Jacquet. The management and recording contracts of Count Basie also evolved. Basie was still being booked through the William Morris agency, but Willard Alexander was no longer with the agency. Basie soon signed a new recording contract with RCA Victor—a move that John Hammond signaled as the end of the Basie band on records.[72] Meanwhile, the music of Charlie Parker and Dizzy Gillespie was taking hold and younger musicians wanted to follow. The Basie rhythm section was "highly influential and led directly into bop's subsequent revision of the rhythm section's function . . . it changed the relationships between solos and ensemble."[73] Furthermore, "bop's harmonic intricacies changed jazz, but the music's fundamental characteristic remained, for coursing through it in the mid-forties was the rhythmic pulse that distinguishes jazz from other music and gave the swing era its name."[74] Basie explained, "The youngsters in my band support the modern part of the music. And I definitely approve of the way jazz is going. As far as bebop is concerned, it's real great if it's played right, and I think it's really taking effect."[75] Some of those youngsters in his group included trumpeter Clark Terry and tenor saxophonist Paul Gonsalves. The business side of big bands, especially of the Count Basie Orchestra, was taking issue again from the management of General Artists Corporation. GAC handled his booking throughout the RCA Victor contract, and Basie was able to release himself of the agreement in January 1950 and return to Willard Alexander. That same month Basie completed a weeklong engagement at the Blue Note in Chicago but broke up the band four weeks later to regroup as a small group considering the ongoing business pressures of sustaining a big band.[76] He formed a sextet with Clary Terry (trumpet), Buddy DeFranco (clarinet), Gus Johnson (drums), Jimmy Lewis (bass), and Bob Graf (tenor). "Freddie Green, who was not originally re-engaged after the breakup of the bi ban in January, joined the sextet one night much to Basie's surprise and please."[77]

The way forward for Basie at this point was to take the bookings he could with the small group and rejoice in the few opportunities he was given to reboot his big band. One such occasion was putting together a 16-piece band for a weeklong engagement at the Apollo Theatre in Harlem. The big band was on again and off again most of that year with engagements at Chicago's Capitol Lounge, the Savoy Ballroom in New York, and the Oasis Theatre in Los Angeles. Big bands were fading fast or disappearing entirely. "It would have seemed incredible in 1936 that twenty-odd years later there should be only two big jazz bands in regular existence. Had that possibility been entertained, it would have seemed reasonable enough that one should be Duke Ellington's. But the other should be Count Basie's—that, too, would have seemed incredible!"[78] Despite these realizations, 1952 saw of mix of success, one of which was the signing of a recording contract with Norman Granz for three years and two sessions lined up in January.[79] Basie started to delegate some of his band-leadership responsibilities to a new alto saxophonist, Marshall Royal, who also shaped up the saxophone sections into one of the best there has ever been. "The blend of the five men, their time keeping and their ability to play quietly has been a hallmark of the Basie band since the early fifties and the major credit must go to Royal."[80] The formation of the "new" Basie band relied more on arrangements than head charts in his previous edition, giving the "section leaders the task of achieving technical perfection and a proper regard for dynamics."[81]

The Basie reputation was recentering back in New York City after disappointing returns from national tours. In 1953 Frank Wess joined the band, who introduced the flute as a new color, followed by Frank Foster, who would provide iconic compositions like "Shiny Stockings" for the band. The impetus for the ensemble was not about paving the way forward, as some might have thought of Basie twenty years earlier, rather refining his sound and preserving those rich elements that were evaporating from modernizations of jazz. Over the next "three decades for no barrier-breaking soloist was to emerge from the Basie ranks, rather it was a band which became the curator of jazz big band tradition."[82] But new things were on the horizon, and in 1953 Norman Granz put together an album called *Count Basie Dance Session* that was so well received that *Count Basie Dance Session No. 2* was soon in the works. These proved important on multiple levels: first, it demonstrated that Basie still considered himself the leader of a band for dancers; and, second, the fact that LPs were given titles was an innovation itself. Follow-up examples like *The Atomic Mr. Basie,* of Neal Hefti music, and *On My Way and Shoutin' Again* have become a significant piece of jazz history.[83]

The band was doing better than ever and embarked on their first tour of Europe in 1954, but they still needed something extra to take them to the next level. That extra bump came from vocalist Joe Williams with hits "Every Day" and "The Comeback." When Basie recorded these hits with Joe Williams—arrangements supplied by tenor saxophonist Frank Foster and alto saxophonist Ernie Wilkins—in 1955, they also recorded their instrumental hit, *April in Paris*. With more bookings coming in for concert halls rather than dances, Basie was looking for showmanship on the bandstand to support the newfound momentum and brought back drummer Sonny Payne to replace Gus Johnson in 1955.[84]

In the fall of 1957 Basie signed a new recording contract with a relatively new label, Roulette, and release the critically acclaimed *Atomic Mr. Basie*. The contract lasted five years, and Basie went on to record twenty albums for the label.[85] For the most part, the band comradery remained high with Basie always friendly, approachable, and just one of the band. There were some rough moments that tested Basie's resolve as the leader, but nonetheless, the band recorded some of the most prominent music for the Roulette label. Neal Hefti wrote music for two albums, as did Quincy Jones and Frank Foster. Benny Carter contributed the *Kansas City Suite* and *The Legend*.[86]

The Basie band was at its best during the Roulette days and just before recording *The Atomic Mr. Basie,* the band completed thirteen weeks at the

Waldorf-Astoria Hotel in New York City and later that year a Royal Command performance in London. They performed at the inauguration of President John F. Kennedy in 1961.[87] The profile growth of Basie led directly to recordings with Billy Eckstine, Sarah Vaughan, and Tony Bennett, as well as classic and popular work with Frank Sinatra. These combinations expanded the profile of the Basie Orchestra at the expense of deflecting attention from the band itself. Between 1962 and 1966, Basie moved between Verve and Reprise labels with a new emphasis on the idea of concept albums devoted to the work of individual arrangers, including Neal Hefti and Quincy Jones. Albums like *Basie's Beatles Bag, Basie Meets Bond,* and *More Hits of the 50's and 60's* seem especially out of the Basie aesthetic.[88] The vocalist pairings, while fruitful and at times musically enriching, opened an area of recording collaborations on a non-exclusive basis that resulted in quickly forgettable albums, like *Two Much* and *Basie's in the Bag.*

However, the period of some mediocre recordings was capped off with two albums in the late 60s as some of Basie's best work. Trombonist and arranger Sammy Nestico entered the Basie world and made an immediate impact with *Basie Straight Ahead.* "Sammy obviously grasped the band's strengths immediately and camp up with sores which the men seemed to enjoy playing. Moreover, he had the ability to make the band sound the way that audiences identified with Basie."[89] At the end of 1973 Basie started to record again for Norman Granz and the Pablo label. "Granz had little time for adding unsuitable vocalists or placing the band in a role which made them subservient to a 'concept' programme."[90] Granz created recording dates as jam sessions with Basie alongside Ray Brown and Louie Bellson, and later a pairing with pianist Oscar Peterson. Basie was featured in several small groups for studio sessions and concerts at various jazz festivals put on by Granz.

In September 1976 Basie suffered a heart attack but came back to the group in January 1977. Nat Pierce filled in on piano and Clark Terry took over as leader while Basie recovered. He was back in the studio recording more of Nestico's works for the *Prime Time* album. Pierce was always on hand to step in as needed and recorded, often uncredited, for several tracks. He was happy to do it: "I feel very privileged to be Basie's number one substitute pianist."[91] As Basie's health slowly declined, he still made memorable performances and recordings with the help of Norman Granz. In 1981, Granz put Basie in a new Kansas City Six to "make music as blues-filled and as timeless as anything he had ever done before."[92]

Basie was the last of the great pianist bandleaders when he passed away on April 26, 1984. He left a profound legacy that remains deeply influential to players and jazz audiences today. To say "like Basie" conjures sounds and images immediately identifiable as a style all his own. The Basie sound was straight ahead, seemingly understated, and always swinging like no other band could achieve. The underlying philosophy, "Keep it simple," might sound easy enough, but "so many others have tried and failed; they have found that *simple is difficult.*"[93] The band created a beautiful platform for musicians to expand and showcase their individual talent. Such a platform has sparked endless creativity from soloists and inspired generations of players from that original Basie ethos, whether they were aware of it or not. It is impossible to know how jazz would have developed were it not for Count Basie, but we do know the world of jazz and American music was forever changed because Basie navigated a challenging and continuously changing landscape of music while forever preserving his identity as a powerful, empathetic, and diligent creator of beautifully engaging music. Basie was a compassionate leader and truly loved working with the musicians in his band. The longevity of Basie band members, namely Freddie Green, who remained in the band for nearly fifty years until his death in 1987, speaks to the inviting uniqueness that was the Basie aura and "happy family atmosphere" he engendered through all the years.[94] When Basie was not on the road, he settled in St. Albans in Long Island with his with his wife, Catherine, whom he met when she was a dancer with the Whitman Sisters years earlier, and his daughter, Diane. The true impact of Basie's legacy is immeasurable and still present. Audiences around the world will forever revere the incomparable Basie sound, while history will remember a kid from Red Bank who discovered his pathway through life as a soulful, transformative, and true American original.

Notes

1 Bill Kirchner, ed., *The Oxford Companion to Jazz* (New York: Oxford University Press, 2005), 405.
2 "William J. 'Count' Basie (1904-1984)," Count Basie Center for the Arts, accessed May 12, 2022, https://thebasie.org/countbasiebio/.
3 Count Basie and Albert Murray, *Good Morning Blues: The Autobiography of Count Basie* (New York: Random House, 1985), 24.
4 Basie and Murray, *Good Morning Blues,* 25.
5 Basie and Murray, 26.
6 Basie and Murray, 26.
7 Basie and Murray, 27.
8 Basie and Murray, 26–33.
9 Basie and Murray, 33.
10 Basie and Murray.

11 Basie and Murray.
12 Basie and Murray, 34–35.
13 Basie and Murray, 52.
14 Rex Stewart, *Jazz Masters of the Thirties* (New York: Da Capo Press, 1972), 196.
15 Basie and Murray, *Good Morning Blues*, 67.
16 Basie and Murray.
17 Basie and Murray, 83.
18 Basie and Murray, 69.
19 Stewart, *Jazz Masters of the Thirties*, 197.
20 Hadlock Richard, *Jazz Masters of the Twenties* (New York: Da Capo Press, 1988), 150.
21 Albert Murray, *Stomping the Blues* (New York: Da Capo Press, 1976), 126.
22 Murray, *Stomping the Blues*, 62.
23 Marshall Stearns, *The Story of Jazz, with an Expanded Bibliography and a Syllabus of Fifteen Lectures on the History of Jazz* (New York: New American Library, 1958), 106.
24 Basie and Murray, *Good Morning Blues*, 92
25 Alun Morgan, *Count Basie* (New York: Spellmount, 1984), 10.
26 Stewart, *Jazz Masters of the Thirties*, 197.
27 Basie and Murray, *Good Morning Blues*, 108.
28 Ross Russell, *Jazz Style in Kansas City and the Southwest* (Los Angeles: University of California Press, 1971), 25.
29 Russell, *Jazz Style in Kansas City*, 26.
30 Morgan, *Count Basie*, 12.
31 Basie and Murray, *Good Morning Blues*, 111.
32 Stewart, *Jazz Masters of the Thirties*, 197.
33 Stewart, 198.
34 Stewart, 198.
35 Basie and Murray, *Good Morning Blues*, 113.
36 Basie and Murray 117.
37 Stewart, *Jazz Masters of the Thirties*, 200.
38 Basie and Murray, *Good Morning Blues*, 129.
39 Morgan, *Count Basie*, 13.
40 Basie and Murray, *Good Morning Blues*, 146.
41 Basie and Murray, 147.
42 Basie and Murray, 154.
43 Basie and Murray, 157.
44 Basie and Murray, 157.
45 Basie and Murray, 160.
46 Basie and Murray, 160.
47 Morgan, *Count Basie*, 15.
48 Basie and Murray, *Good Morning Blues*, 161.
49 John Hammond and Irving Townsend, *John Hammond on Record: An Autobiography* (New York: Penguin, 1977).
50 Morgan, *Count Basie*, 17.
51 Stewart, *Jazz Masters of the Thirties*, 202.
52 Morgan, *Count Basie*, 17.

53 Morgan, 20.
54 Stewart, *Jazz Masters of the Thirties*, 202.
55 Morgan, *Count Basie*, 21.
56 Morgan, 21.
57 Basie and Murray, *Good Morning Blues*, 188.
58 Morgan, *Count Basie*, 23.
59 Morgan, 24.
60 Basie and Murray, *Good Morning Blues*, 209.
61 Basie and Murray, 217.
62 Morgan, *Count Basie*, 25.
63 Morgan, 28.
64 Morgan, 29.
65 Morgan, 29.
66 Morgan, 30.
67 Basie and Murray, *Good Morning Blues*, 233.
68 Morgan, *Count Basie*, 32.
69 Morgan, 33.
70 Morgan, 33.
71 Morgan, 39.
72 Morgan, 41.
73 Kirchner, *Oxford Companion to Jazz*, 284.
74 Kirchner, 405.
75 Morgan, *Count Basie*, 44.
76 Morgan, 44.
77 Morgan, 46.
78 Stanley Dance, *The World of Count Basie* (New York: Scribner, 1980), 4.
79 Morgan, *Count Basie*, 47.
80 Morgan, 50.
81 Morgan, 50.
82 Morgan, 51.
83 Morgan, 52.
84 Morgan, 53.
85 Morgan, 56.
86 Morgan, 57.
87 Basie and Murray, *Good Morning Blues*, 338.
88 Morgan, *Count Basie*, 58.
89 Morgan, 61.
90 Morgan, 64.
91 Dance, *World of Count Basie*.
92 Morgan, *Count Basie*, 67.
93 Morgan, 69.
94 Morgan, 69.

9

Max Roach

Deeds, Not Words

KEVIN C. McDONALD

Within the jazz canon and its pantheon of horn-playing heroes, including Charlie Parker, John Coltrane, Miles Davis, and Louis Armstrong, the contributions of American jazz drummer, percussionist, composer, and bandleader Max Roach (1924–2007) have been woefully muted. Roach has been pigeonholed as either a "bop" pioneer within a linear doctrine of jazz evolution or as a revolutionary civil rights activist.[1] Even in the third edition of Ted Gioia's *The History of Jazz*, for example, Roach figures most prominently in the section "The Mainstreaming of Bebop" and within a discussion of "hard bop."[2] While brief mentions are made of Roach's explorations in free jazz, percussion ensemble, and hip-hop,[3] Gioia's narrative overlooks both drummers in general and Roach in particular. That Roach was a percussionist, composer, bandleader, pianist, multi-instrumentalist, and business pioneer has been ignored within the canonic narrative. In a 1982 interview with Scott Fish for *Modern Drummer*, Roach made clear his disdain for this canonic bias:

> I notice in the history books, when they talk about new trends and things that happened, they say, "This is the period of Dizzy Gillespie and Charlie Parker; This is the period of Miles Davis; This is the period of Louis Armstrong." They never say anything about the drummers! Now this is the period of fusion. They say this is the period of rock. But, you know, for every one of those things, the reason that there is a change is rhythmic things. It has nothing to do with the horns![4]

The disproportionate name recognition of Louis Armstrong, Sidney Bechet, and Bix Beiderbecke as compared with "Baby" Dodds, Zutty Singleton, Sid Catlett, Kaiser Marshall, Chauncey Morehouse, Tony Sbarbaro, and

Paul Barbarin underscores the canonic dominance of horn players throughout the earliest iterations of jazz.[5] After the heyday of big bands and amid the emergence of what has become known as the "bop" style, the disproportionate name recognition of Dizzy Gillespie, Charlie Parker, and Miles Davis as compared with O'Neill Spencer, Shadow Wilson, Roy Haynes, and Stan Levey attests to the canonic marginalization of drummers continuing through the 1930s, 1940s, and into the early 1950s.

The root of this canonic bias is two-pronged. First, beginning with the earliest iterations of jazz as functional dance accompaniment, drummers have traditionally taken both a literal and figurative "back seat" on the bandstand as compared with their horn-playing, "front-line" counterparts.[6] In *Thinking in Jazz*, Paul Berliner has argued that, the standard "front-line" instruments—clarinet, trombone, and, most especially, cornet or trumpet—dominated early jazz, while the other performing forces, including percussion, primarily provided musical accompaniment.[7] Moreover, "convention commonly dictates that drummers and bass players receive proportionately fewer solos than other musicians."[8]

In a 1979 interview with Harold Howland for *Modern Drummer*, Roach staunchly opposed these hierarchical conventions: "Drummers are required to support constantly. We're expected to be the rhythmic foundation. . . . You're almost like a slave. . . . I think the instrument goes beyond that."[9] In the 1982 *Modern Drummer* interview, Roach specifically lamented hierarchical performance dynamics during his years collaborating with Charlie Parker: "Then, the only thing was the so-called 'front-line.' The horns were the front-line and the drummer was like the nigger [sic] of the band. He was the guy who was always waiting, and then when he did play an extended solo, everybody would go off the stage and leave him up there, . . . I resented all that."[10]

Second, music historians traditionally look to documentation and music notation as the primary source material on which to construct historical narratives. Not only has the orality of the jazz tradition made scarce this source type, but the problem has been compounded for the histories of drummers who, when given musical parts at all, are often handed "lead sheets" or a copy of a horn part rather than musical notation intended specifically for the drumset. Moreover, scholars who have attempted to circumvent jazz's source material problem with human-subject interviews have invariably descended the rabbit hole of a storytelling literature ripe for the formation of mythology.[11]

Not all drummers, however, passively kowtowed to the hierarchical status quo. In an interview with Burt Korall for *Drummin' Men: The Heartbeat of Jazz—The Bebop Years*, Roach cast drummer Chick Webb as an inspiration:

"He [Webb] made a major impression and brought attention to the instrument, which for so long was used only for timekeeping. . . . I've always felt the drummer shouldn't be a subservient figure."[12] Roach channeled this musical impetus himself. In a 1979 interview with Stanley Crouch for *Village Voice*, Roach recounted, "I played in a way that meant that the drums weren't in the background anymore, they were front-line, with everybody else."[13] In so doing, Roach transformed perceptions of the drum chair from those of vaudevillian novelty and subservience to those of multidisciplinary, promethean artistic independence. Archival sources, published interviews, and comparative musical analysis together demonstrate that Roach's performance practices and musical ethos—including his drum tuning, comping concepts, improvisational voice, engagement with music education and pedagogical philosophy, band leadership, ever-diversifying ensemble instrumentations, prolific composing, and vanguardist business ventures—challenged jazz's functionality as dance accompaniment and revolutionized the drummer's conventionally subservient role.

The son of Alphonso and Cressie Roach, Maxwell Lemuel Roach was born on January 10, 1924, in the township of Newland in Pasquotank County, North Carolina, south of the Great Dismal Swamp and northwest of Elizabeth City.[14] After the Roach family moved to Brooklyn, New York's Bedford-Stuyvesant neighborhood in 1928, they moved from apartment to apartment, ultimately settling in a fourth-floor walk-up on Gates Avenue, where they inherited a piano left behind by former tenants.[15] The Roach family maintained an active musical life at nearby Concord Baptist Church of Christ: Roach's mother sang in the chorus and his aunt played piano.[16] Beginning at the age of eight, Roach began playing drums and studying piano at Concord Baptist.[17] Shortly after having graduated from Brooklyn's Boys High School in 1942, Roach's "big break" came on a three-night engagement with the Duke Ellington Orchestra at Manhattan's Paramount Theater when regular drummer Sonny Greer had fallen ill.[18]

Drum Tuning

The sounds Roach drew out of the drumset were unique as compared with those of his predecessors. Specifically, Roach's *tuning* of the drums was not only unique, but it also reflected a distinct departure from conventional drumset functionality. Jazz before the midcentury, including styles known as "early jazz" and "swing," was primarily functional entertainment that accompanied dancing. Period drum equipment reflected this functionality, and the sonic requirements for various twentieth-century professional environments varied widely. For example, a larger bass drum tuned for low-end resonance and propulsive "kick" was needed to keep patrons on their feet through storied early morning breakfast dances at large ballrooms like the Savoy and Roseland.[19]

During and after World War II, however, the Gretsch drum company pioneered smaller drum sizes to facilitate "gig-hopping" from Fifty-Second Street clubs Royal Roost, Three Deuces, and Onyx, to uptown haunts like Minton's.[20] Even so, the functionality of the drum chair persisted amid traditional ensemble power dynamics. While the recording studio afforded opportunity, for example, the studio could also signify frustrations with burgeoning technologies and the magnification of traditional power dynamics within ensembles, especially for drummers. When saxophonist Coleman Hawkins called Roach for the drummer's first recording date in 1943, it was this dynamic labyrinth of functionality into which Roach stepped:

> Yeah, but you know in those days the recording industry always messed up the drummer in the back. This was really . . . what do you call it . . . cultural discrimination. The first record date I had. Dizzy had gotten me to do this date with Coleman Hawkins. When I got to the studio they put a lot of blankets over the drums [for muffling] and everything else. I said, "Dizzy, listen! If you don't want a drummer on the date, *I'm going home*." . . . [A]t that time, the drums were always felt and not heard.[21]

Determined to be both felt *and* heard, Roach tuned the drums differently: "I don't tune for a particular pitch like thirds and fifths. But, I do tune for a 'live' sound. . . . Each drum has its own character. . . . the snare always sounded crisp and the tom-toms always rang. That flat sound wasn't there. It was always a ringing sound. . . . the main thing was that you want it to project. . . . So everything was tuned up."[22] Scholars agree that Roach's drum tuning departed from convention. Kenny Washington, for one, has argued that Roach was "the first drummer in modern jazz to tune the drums up high."[23] Jack DeJohnette, for another, has argued, "He [Roach] tuned high, and that cut through the ensemble."[24] Roach's drum tuning, therefore, reflects an assertive self-determination aimed at establishing the drummer's musical voice as equal, rather than subservient, to those of other ensemble instrumentalists.

Solo Order and Comping Concepts

During the late 1940s and early 1950s, Roach performed and recorded extensively with saxophonist Charlie Parker. While this music, primarily framed by scholars, journalists, and critics as "bop," has been lauded as a liberating departure from performance practices of the so-called big band era, it still exemplifies distinctly hierarchical performance practice conventions. In *Thinking in Jazz,* Paul Berliner has argued that rhythm section players, especially drummers and bassists, perform disproportionately fewer solos than do horn players, pianists, and guitarists.[25] Significantly, the solos of drummers and bassists tend to appear last within the order of solos.

Among many possible examples, Parker's 1952 recording of "Laird Baird" (Clef 89144), which includes Roach on drums, illustrates the conventional order of jazz solos. After an eight-measure solo introduction by pianist Hank Jones, Parker, accompanied by a rhythm section comprising Jones, bassist Teddy Kotick, and Roach, performs the tune's "inhead." Parker solos first, followed by Jones, Kotick, and Roach, respectively. The piece ends after Parker's performance of the "outhead."

Roach's musical responses to these hierarchically stratified performance practices not only magnify the remarkability of the recordings on which they can be found, but they also reflect his pursuit of greater equality within the jazz ensemble. Recorded on December 2, 1955, Sonny Rollins's *Work Time* (Prestige PRLP-7020), which also features Roach, pianist Ray Bryant, and bassist George Morrow, demonstrates intriguing departures from performance practices governing conventional solo order. On the group's interpretation of the Billy Strayhorn tune "Raincheck," for example, Rollins solos first. Significantly, the second solo is performed not by piano, as might be expected, but rather by Roach.

In *Thinking in Jazz,* Paul Berliner has argued that the collective function of the jazz rhythm section is to "comp," "a term that carries the dual connotations of *accompanying* and *complementing.*"[26] Yet, examples from Roach's discography demonstrate intriguing departures from this hierarchically functional dogma. On "Nickels and Dimes" from J. J. Johnson's 1957 release *First Place* (Columbia CL 1030), for example, Roach "lays out" and does not accompany the first sixteen measures of bassist Paul Chambers's solo. Roach makes a similar performance decision during sections of Charles Mingus's bass solo on "Machajo," a John Dennis composition from the pianist's 1956 release *New Piano Expressions* (Debut DEB-121). While "laying out" was popularized by such performances as that of Tony Williams on "There Is No Greater Love" from Miles Davis's 1964 recording *Four & More* (Columbia CL 2453/9253), the practice was notably employed by Roach almost a full decade prior.

Although drum solos are most frequently performed unaccompanied, there are many recorded examples of Roach performing drum solos that are accompanied by other instrumentalists.[27] These examples underscore the idea that Roach envisioned the drummer as an instrumentalist equal to others in the ensemble: if other instrumentalists' solo with accompaniment, so, too, can the drummer. In the 1982 *Modern Drummer* interview, Roach stated, "I'd tell the front line, 'You know, I'm breaking my back accompanying you folks, and then when I play a solo, an extended solo, which is usually once a week, everybody just lays out! Why can't you accompany me as well?'"

Indeed, on trumpeter Booker Little's composition "Gandolfo's Bounce," from Roach's 1959 record *Award-Winning Drummer* (Time T/70003), Roach's drum solo is accompanied by both bass and horns. Examples of Roach solos with piano accompaniment include "Mr. X" from *Max Roach +4* (EmArcy MG-36098), Charlie Parker's "Now's the Time" (Clef MGC-157), "The Scene is Clean" from *At Basin Street* (EmArcy MG-36070), "If I Love Again" from Thad Jones's *The Magnificent Thad Jones* (Blue Note BLP 1527), and both "Paradox" and "Raincheck" from Sonny Rollins's *Work Time* (Prestige PRLP-7020). Examples of Roach's solos with bass accompaniment include "Henry Street Blues" from *In the Light* (Soul Note SN 1053), "Juliano" from *Quiet as It's Kept* (Mercury MG-20491), "Mama" from *Percussion Bitter Sweet* (Impulse! A-8), "Sadiga" from *Award-Winning Drummer* (Time T/70003), "Jodie's Cha-Cha" from *Deeds, Not Words* (Riverside RLP 12-280), and both "Connie's Bounce" and "Lepa" from *The Many Sides of Max* (Mercury MG-20911).[28]

Improvisational Voice

In *Freedom Sounds,* Ingrid Monson has argued that the cultivation of one's unique concept, one's individual voice, or one's own improvisational identity has always been a manifestation of self-determination among the highest aesthetic ideals of the jazz art form.[29] Indeed, Roach's improvisational voice is instantly recognizable throughout his prolific discography. Kenny Washington has argued that "Max's rhythms were more varied than those of the drummers that came before him."[30] John Riley has offered insightful Roach analysis and has codified important Roach "licks."[31] However, just as Scott DeVeaux has taken issue with narrow, style-focused readings that inevitably impose upon jazz a linear doctrine of progress,[32] extant stylistic readings of Roach have primarily linked his contributions to the so-called bebop period, effectively muting Roach's broader and more far-reaching significance. Musical analysis can add specificity to, and broaden the scope of, the impact of Roach's improvisational voice.

Roach's unique improvisational voice challenged the dogmatic functionality and conventional subservience of the drum chair in three specific ways. First, Roach diverged from the right-hand-lead stickings inextricably linked to functional martial drumming. Second, Roach challenged the functionality of jazz as dance accompaniment by employing unprecedented limb independence in the vocabulary for both feet. Third, Roach's motivic development and large-scale formal structures elevated the perception of drum solos, transforming them from excursions in primitivist, vaudevillian novelty to masterclasses in musical composition.

Roach diverged from the right-hand-lead stickings inextricably linked to martial snare drum études. Elsewhere, I have contrasted the prolific penchant for right-hand lead favored by Gene Krupa, Buddy Rich, and "Philly" Joe Jones with intriguing alternatives from Roach's discography.[33] On "The Scene Is Clean" from *At Basin Street* (EmArcy MG-36070), "Drum Conversation" from Miles Davis's *At Last* (Contemporary C-7645), and "Sandu" from *Study in Brown* (EmArcy MG-36037), for example, Roach relies on both right *and* left hands to "steer" from drum to drum around the kit.[34] On "Swingin'" from *Study in Brown,* Roach arguably leads with the left hand.[35]

Roach challenged the functionality of jazz as dance accompaniment by employing unprecedented limb independence in the vocabulary for both feet. To the present day, jazz drummers often "feather" the bass drum in conjunction with the notes played by the upright bass—electric bass, tuba, bass saxophone, and Hammond organ have also shouldered this role, albeit less frequently. Historically, such rhythm section shifts between playing "in two" and "in four" were done to encourage dancers, the proverbial "butts in seats" that pay the bills, as it were. These rhythm section shifts exist today primarily to change between energy levels in a performance, and they are executed today with less regard for dancers. While there are plenty of examples of Roach "feathering," including on his solo on "Sandu" from *Study in Brown* (EmArcy MG-36037), Roach also departed from this trend.[36]

Roach's departures from feathering have attracted scholarly attention. John Riley, drummer for the renowned Vanguard Jazz Orchestra, has argued that Roach was "the first to play over ostinatos, and the first to integrate the bass drum in a linear fashion."[37] Recordings of Roach soloing with his hands atop ostinatos in his feet include "The Drum Also Waltzes" from *Drums Unlimited* (Atlantic LP 1467), "Blues Waltz" from *Jazz in 3/4 Time* (EmArcy MG-36108), and "Triptych" from *We Insist! Freedom Now Suite* (Candid CJM 8002).

Concerning Roach's solo on "Parisian Thoroughfare" from *Clifford Brown and Max Roach* (EmArcy MG-26043), Riley has argued that "Max incorporates his bass drum into his melodic lines as if it were a third hand."[38] Similarly, Dave Goodman has noted that, in Roach's playing, "the bass drum becomes a part of the melodic contour."[39] Illustrative examples include vocabulary from Roach's solos on "Juliano" from *Quiet as It's Kept* (Mercury MG-20491),

"Mama" from *Percussion Bitter Sweet* (Impulse! A-8), "Sadiga" from *Award-Winning Drummer* (Time T/70003), "Mr. X" from *Max Roach +4* (EmArcy MG-36098), and both "Connie's Bounce" and "Lepa" from *The Many Sides of Max* (Mercury MG-20911).[40]

Kenny Washington has argued, "Max took the idea of four-limb coordination to an entirely new level."[41] Yet much discussion about four-voice coordination has focused on Roy Haynes and Tony Williams. In a 2007 interview for *JAZZIZ*, for example, Lewis Nash has argued, "Roy wasn't just comping with his left hand. . . . He comped pretty much with all four limbs and wasn't afraid to do things that highlight the basic pulse, rather than stating it. Nobody else was doing this to the degree he did."[42] Yet, vocabulary from Roach's solos on "Mr. X" from *Max Roach +4* (EmArcy MG-36098) and "Drum Conversation" from Miles Davis's *At Last!* (Contemporary C-7645) demonstrate true four-voice coordination chronologically earlier than examples from the catalogues of either Roy Haynes or Tony Williams.[43] Roach contributed greatly to mid-century developments in limb independence, he did so to a greater extent than the canon indicates, and he explored alternative performance practices to the feathering associated with functional dance accompaniment.

Motivic development and large-scale formal structures in Roach's improvisations not only differentiate his unique musical voice from those of other drummers, but the improvisations also elevated the perception of drum solos from exoticist excursions in vaudevillian novelty to masterclasses in musical composition. Comparing Roach's motivic development on "Stompin' at the Savoy" from *Clifford Brown and Max Roach* (EmArcy MG-26043) to that of Art Blakey on "Wail March" from *Sonny Rollins, vol. 2* (Blue Note BLP 1558) yields intriguing insights[44]: whereas Blakey presents three motives, Roach presents five; whereas Blakey's motives largely return in the same form in which they were originally presented, Roach consistently recasts, reframes, and revoices motives in diverse ways; last, the final eight measures of Roach's solo on "Stompin' at the Savoy" recapitulate material not only from the beginning of the second chorus but also from the very beginning of the two-chorus solo. Other examples of Roach's motivic concept include his solos on "Blues on Down" from the Benny Golson Sextet's *The Modern Touch* (Riverside RLP 12-256), "Paradox" from Sonny Rollins's *Work Time* (Prestige PRLP-7020), and "Sandu" from *Study in Brown* (EmArcy MG-36037).

Marked by recapitulating thematic content, large-scale structural features in Roach's pieces for solo drumset demonstrate striking connections to "classical" forms. "Drum Conversation" from Miles Davis's *At Last!* (Contemporary C-7645) exhibits a "sonata-like" form: the piece exhibits ternary structure, ABA'; the two themes of A recapitulate in A' and briefly do so at the end of A; last, A' contains a closing coda. Similarly, "The Drum Also Waltzes" and "For Big Sid" from *Drums Unlimited* (Atlantic LP-1467) exhibit rondo-like structures, ABACADAEA and ABACADAEAFA, respectively.[45]

Group Leadership and Ensemble Instrumentation

Most notably from the drum chair, to which "sideman" status had been conventionally ascribed, Roach led ensembles prodigiously. In an interview for Burt Korall's for *Drummin' Men: The Heartbeat of Jazz—The Bebop Years,* Roach recalled having been inspired by Chick Webb, the drummer whose orchestra featured Ella Fitzgerald at its regular engagements at Harlem's celebrated Savoy Ballroom: "There's another reason I was so impressed with Chick [Webb]. He was a leader—a bandleader, certainly not a second-class citizen."[46] Recorded May 15, 1949, in Paris during a European tour with Charlie Parker, *(A Session with) Max Roach* (Vogue LD 014) was Roach's self-titled debut. Other notable early releases led by Roach include the 1953 albums *The Max Roach Septet* (Debut DEP-451) and *The Max Roach Quartet Featuring Hank Mobley* (Debut DLP-13).

During the mid-1950s, Roach co-led the celebrated Clifford Brown and Max Roach Quintet for acclaimed releases including *Clifford Brown and Max Roach* (EmArcy MG-26043), *Study in Brown* (EmArcy MG-36037), *Brown and Roach Incorporated* (EmArcy MG-36008), and *At Basin Street* (EmArcy MG-36070). Tragically, both Clifford Brown and the group's pianist Richie Powell were killed in an automobile accident in June 1956.[47] In September 1956, Roach held his first sessions as a leader since the deaths of Brown and Powell. Roach assembled an ensemble that comprised trumpeter Kenny Dorham, saxophonist Sonny Rollins, pianist Ray Bryant, and bassist George Morrow, and the sessions resulted in the 1956 release *Max Roach +4* (EmArcy MG 36098). During the second half of the 1950s, Roach also led the release of *Jazz in 3/4 Time* (EmArcy MG-36108), *Deeds, Not Words* (Riverside RLP 12-280), *Quiet as It's Kept* (Mercury MG-20491), and *The Many Sides of Max* (Mercury MG-20911).

The instrumentations of the ensembles with which Roach performed challenged the drummer's functionally subservient role in conventional big bands and combos by reframing that role within ever-diversifying performing forces.[48] On December 10, 1947, one of the first such examples was a session with Coleman Hawkins's orchestra, vocalist Leslie Scott, and a strings section.[49] Roach again recorded with strings on both Charlie Parker's *Live at the Rockland Palace September 26, 1952* (Charlie Parker CP 502) and *Clifford Brown with Strings* (EmArcy MG-36005), the 1955 collaboration with

Neal Hefti's orchestra. On both January 21, 1949, and March 9, 1950, moreover, Roach recorded as part of Miles Davis's renowned *Birth of the Cool* sessions (Capitol T-792), which featured an expanded chamber jazz ensemble that included both tuba and French horn. Additionally, Roach filled the drum chair for Kenny Dorham's 1957 release *Jazz Contrasts* (Riverside RLP 12-239), which features harpist Betty Glamann. On Roach's 1958 recordings *Deeds, Not Words* (Riverside RLP 12-280), *Award-Winning Drummer* (Time T/70003), and *Max Roach +4 at Newport* (EmArcy MG-36140), tubist Ray Draper appears as part of the ensemble's complement of front-line horns, rather than as a substitute for upright bass as might otherwise be expected. Odeon Pope, moreover, plays both oboe and alto flute on Roach's 1981 release *Chattahoochee Red* (Columbia FC 37376). Last, 1985's *Easy Winners* (Soul Note SN 1109) and 1986's *Bright Moments* (Soul Note SN 1159) both feature Roach's ensemble augmented by the Uptown String Quartet, which notably includes Roach's daughter Maxine on viola.

Roach's first release with section percussion dates to 1958 on *Max Roach with the Boston Percussion Ensemble* (EmArcy/Mercury MG-36144). Not only does the record feature French horn player Al Portch and soprano Corrine Curry, but it also features Boston Percussion Ensemble members Irving Farberman, Everett "Vic" Firth, Lloyd McCausland, Arthur Press, Charles Smith, Harold Thompson, and Walter Tokarczyk. In 1970, Roach cofounded his own percussion ensemble, M'Boom, whose releases include 1973's *Re: percussion* (Strata-East SES-19732), 1979's *M'Boom* (Columbia IC-36247), and 1984's *Collage* (Soul Note SN 1059).

Roach appeared with symphony orchestra numerous times throughout his career. In 1958, Roach performed Peter Phillips's *Concerto for Max* at the Monterey Jazz Festival, and he performed Henry Threadgill's *Mix for Orchestra* with the Boston Philharmonic in 1993.[50] Roach performed Fred Tillis's *Festival Journey*, a three-movement work orchestrated for Roach and orchestra with the Atlanta Symphony Orchestra in 1992.[51] The work was recorded in 1993 with the New Orchestra of Boston. Including a 1995 recording of "Ghost Dance" with the So What Brass Quintet, *Max Roach with the New Orchestra of Boston and the So What Brass Quintet* (Blue Note CDP 7243 8 34813 2 3) was released in 1996.

In addition to outwardly expanded ensemble instrumentations, Roach experimented within intimate, duo settings, instrumentations in which Roach frames the drumset as a conversational voice liberated from conventional functionality. Roach and saxophonist Archie Shepp collaborated for 1976's *Force* (Uniteledis UNI 28.976) and again for 1979's *The Long March* (hat Hut 2R13). Similarly, Roach collaborated with pianist Abdullah Ibrahim for 1977's

Streams of Consciousness (Baystate RVJ-6016) and with pianist Cecil Taylor for *Historic Concerts* (Soul Note SN 1100/1), recorded at Columbia University's McMillin Theatre on December 15, 1979. Duo collaborations with saxophonist Anthony Braxton include 1978's *Birth and Rebirth* (Black Saint BSR 0024) and 1979's *One in Two/Two in One* (hat Hut 2R06).

Critics expressed mixed opinions concerning Roach's duo recordings. In a review of *One in Two/Two in One* for *All About Jazz,* Chris May, on the one hand, has argued, "This is music which demands the full attention of the listener to reveal all of its considerable beauty—but it's not 'difficult' music. It's consistently melodic, and often, but not always, played with a fixed meter. It's subtle, it's layered and it's got depth. It's a blast."[52] On the other hand, Burt Korall's review of *Historic Concerts,* Roach's duo recording with the polarizing pianist Cecil Taylor was not as warm: "The generally precise, thoughtful, inventive Roach is hammered by the combative Taylor. There are rewarding moments when Roach breaks away and intelligently cools the atmosphere. But overall, I couldn't wait for the CD to come to an end."[53]

Roach also released mixed-media works. On "The Dream/It's Time," from Roach's 1981 *Chattahoochee Red* (Columbia FC 37376), Roach performs drumset alongside excerpted audio samples from Dr. Martin Luther King Jr.'s "I Have a Dream" speech. In the 1982 *Modern Drummer* interview, Roach discussed the work: "That was a duet with voice. I think it grows out of some of the things I'm interested in besides playing with bands and with other instruments. I'm also interested in doing 'mixed' or multimedia things: using a drummer in contexts other than just drums."[54] In 1983, moreover, Roach performed with hip-hop pioneer Fab 5 Freddy and a break dancer.[55] Roach collaborated with Amiri Baraka for a spoken-word duo with drumset at Paris's La Villette Jazz Festival in 1996.[56] In *Digging: The Afro-American Soul of American Classical Music,* Baraka recounted the engagement: "But then the last night, Max and I did a word-music performance. My reading to his playing, improvising together, myself raised in expanded understanding creating at the top of anything I've ever done, raised by the 'oom boom ba boom' of the all the way back to the beginning of what we still presume to be humanity."[57]

Music Education, Pedagogy, and Composition

In *Drummin' Men: The Heartbeat of Jazz—The Swing Years,* Burt Korall has argued that, before the "star" drummers of the swing era, including Gene Krupa and Buddy Rich, drummers were not considered complete musicians: "'How many in your band, Charlie?' 'Twelve musicians and a drummer.' That's how it was."[58] Stereotypes marginalizing drummers as incomplete musicians persist to the present day.[59] By contrast, Roach's extensive engagement with music education and his pedagogical philosophy directly challenged the narrative construct marginalizing drummers as incomplete musicians. First, dating back to his childhood and the bop gigs on which he performed as a pianist, Roach always practiced multi-instrumentalism. Second, Roach pursued formal education at Manhattan School of Music. Third, Roach's own pedagogical philosophy stressed music theory and, significantly, composition for all instrumentalists, drummers and other instrumentalists alike.

Roach's multi-instrumentalism dates to his formative years and earliest musical experiences. In Geoffrey Haydon's documentary film *Sit Down and Listen: The Story of Max Roach*, Roach makes remarks upon visiting Mount Carmel Baptist Church, the congregation in North Carolina of which Roach's family was a part during Roach's early childhood:

> The church . . . has been a fountainhead, and actually the school, the music school if you will, of some of the greatest artists that America has produced; since Mahalia Jackson and on up through to Aretha Franklin, and well as Michael Jackson and people like that. All these roots come from our religious background . . . this is where I come from. If there is anything musical about me, its roots started in this kind of environment and the church, the Mount Carmel Baptist Church.[60]

After the Roach family moved to Brooklyn in 1928, Roach's musical focus at Brooklyn's Concord Baptist Church was as much on piano as it was drumset.[61] Notably, Roach played piano, not drums, on some of his earliest Fifty-Second Street jazz engagements of the 1940s.[62] In the 1982 *Modern Drummer* interview with Scott Fish, Roach recounted these club dates: "No, No. When I first came on 52nd St., I was playing piano. I played drums as well, but I'd get calls sometimes to play piano."[63]

Amplified by Miles Davis's 1989 autobiography, the most renowned stories of jazz musicians pursuing college-level music education include those of Davis and pianist Thelonious Monk. Davis, for example, matriculated at the Juilliard School in 1944, but dropped out during the fall of 1945.[64] Monk's stint enrolling in theory classes at Juilliard reflects similar brevity.[65] By contrast, Roach's history at Manhattan School of Music is not only lesser known, but also Roach's time at Manhattan School seems to have initiated a lifelong relationship with formal higher education. Roach was admitted to Manhattan School of Music for the fall of 1950; from 1950 to 1952, he completed 59 credits toward an undergraduate degree, having enrolled in an impressively diverse blend of courses covering music history, diction, theory, piano, percussion, and language.[66] While Roach did not enroll after 1952 and did not complete an undergraduate degree, Manhattan School of Music awarded Roach a Doctorate of Musical Arts, honoris causa, in 1990.[67]

In 1956, Roach formally began his pedagogical career by teaching summer sessions on improvisation at the Lenox School in Massachusetts.[68] From 1972 to 1994, Roach held a faculty position at the University of Massachusetts at Amherst.[69] In the 1982 *Modern Drummer* interview, Roach articulated his pedagogical philosophy, one focusing on multi-instrumentalism, theory, and composition as channels for musical self-determination for *all* instrumentalists, drummers included:

> I'm a firm believer that every drummer should also perform on a melodic instrument—mallet instrument preferably, and, of course, keyboard harmony on piano. I teach theory at the school [University of Massachusetts at Amherst]. That was my major in school; not percussion. So, when I get a student who plays a melodic instrument, I insist that they learn how to keep time on drums. . . . The drummers should do the same kind of thing. They should have the melodic and harmonic properties available to themselves and learn these properties. It all helps, even though their major is percussion. So, that when you sit down you're not just sitting in there as a percussionist and that's all you're aware of. . . . I think that musicians who play instruments of determinate pitch can play an instrument of indeterminate pitch and vice versa. That completes the musician. It makes the musician a complete person, musically speaking. . . . I believe strongly in drummers dealing with the compositional aspect of music. . . . Heretofore, all the composers have been pianists and people who played instruments of determinate pitch.[70]

Indeed, Roach composed prodigiously. In *The Birth of Bebop*, Scott DeVeaux argued that composition has been a means through which jazz artists have self-determined by exercising both financial and legal autonomy within an industry that has rewarded composers more than performers.[71] Through his prolific composition, Roach not only exercised financial and legal autonomy over mechanical copyrights, but he also dispelled myths that drummers' compositional potential was any less than that of other instrumentalists.[72] Concerning the intersection of self-realization and composing, Roach argued, "I really didn't start dealing with myself musically until I started having my own groups, writing my own music, and designing things that I could deal with."[73]

In the most conventional of iterations, Roach composed "tunes" for small jazz ensembles. Roach's tunes "Sfax," "Cou-Manchi-Cou," "Just Moody," and "Maximum" appear on his earliest releases as a bandleader, including *(A Session with) Max Roach* (Vogue LD 014), *Max Roach Septet* (Debut DEP-451), and *The Max Roach Quartet featuring Hank Mobley* (Debut DLP-13). Roach's combo compositions pervade his discography: "Dr. Free-Zee" and "Mr. X" were released on *Max Roach +4* (EmArcy MG-36098), "Blues Waltz" and "Little Folks" are amid the track listings of *Jazz in 3/4 Time* (EmArcy MG-36108), "Audio Blues" and "Four-X" appear on *MAX* (Argo LP-623), and both "A Little Sweet" and "Tympanalli" were released on *The Many Sides of Max* (Mercury MG-20911). Additionally, Roach challenged the limits of "jazz tunes" by composing suites. One such example is Roach's 1960 release *Parisian Sketches* (Mercury MG-60760), which includes the title work *Parisian Sketches*, a suite comprising "The Tower," "The Champs," "The Caves," "The Left Bank," and "The Arch."

Roach even composed for chorus. On 1962's *It's Time* (Impulse! A-16), Roach's conventional sextet is augmented by Abbey Lincoln and a 16-voice chorus conducted by Coleridge-Taylor Perkinson. All selections, including "It's Time," "Another Valley," "Sunday Afternoon," "Living Room," "The Profit," and "Lonesome Lover," were composed by Roach. Moreover, Roach included the 22-voice J. C. White Singers on the 1971 release *Lift Every Voice and Sing* (Atlantic SD-1587). While the record primarily features arrangements of traditional hymns and spirituals, "Garden of Prayer" was co-composed by Patricia Curtis and Roach.

Lesser-known examples of Roach's compositional prowess include his works for film and theater. Backed by his quartet and vocalist Abbey Lincoln, for example, Roach both composed and performed the music for the 1964 film *(The) Black Sun*.[74] In 1984, moreover, Roach began composing the music for *Shepardsets*, an off-Broadway collaboration with Sam Shepard for which Roach won an Obie award in 1985.[75] In 1987, Roach composed the music for the San Diego Repertory Theater's production of *A Midsummer Night's Dream*.[76] Similarly, Roach composed the music for Amiri Baraka's *The Life and Life of Bumpy Johnson*, which premiered at the San Diego Repertory Theater in 1991.[77] At Lincoln Center in 1994, Roach premiered *Ju-Ju*, a mixed-media work featuring M'Boom, Kit Fitzgerald, and the Donald Byrd Dance Group.[78] Roach's prolific history of composing not only assertively exercised financial and legal autonomy over his oeuvre but also departed from the idea that composers before Roach were primarily horn players, pianists, and other individuals whose primary instrument was of determinate pitch.

If Roach composed as a means of liberating the drummer from subservience and marginalization, the musical mechanics of time and meter—odd meters, mixed meters, and "free jazz" techniques—were key factors in accomplishing that work. As Burt Korall has argued in *Drummin' Men: The Heartbeat of Jazz—The Swing Years*, much jazz modernism of the 1940s and 1950s was centered around the idea that the new music was neither appropriate for nor intended for dancing.[79] One method to deter dancers was to perform at tempos too brisk for conventional dance styles. As Kenny Washington has noted, "No one could play faster than Max Roach. Listen to 'Just One of Those Things' from *Max Roach +4*. That's as fast as I've heard anyone play."[80] John Riley has argued that Roach was responsible for finding new ways to both accompany and improvise at breakneck tempos, pointing to "B. Quick" and "B. Swift" from Sonny Rollins's *Tour De Force* (Prestige PR 7126) as examples.[81]

Likewise, explorations in meter suggest an assertive self-determination that departed from functional compatibility with popular swing dances. The most canonically renowned example of jazz in odd meters is Dave Brubeck's *Time Out* (Columbia CS 8192), recorded and released in 1959. Yet not only does Roach's oeuvre exhibit varied explorations in meter before 1959, but Roach's contributions to the odd-meter jazz strain have largely been overlooked within the canon, too. Kenny Washington has pointed out Roach's omission from the literature: "Max sketched out the blueprint for playing in 3/4 time. And not only 3/4, but 5/4, 7/4 and he did it a few years before Dave Brubeck hit with 'Take Five.'"[82] Indeed, Roach filled the drum chair for Thelonious Monk's 1952 version of "Carolina Moon" (Blue Note 1603) in 6/4. Moreover, mixed-meter explorations on the 1954 recording of "I Get a Kick out of You" (EmArcy MG-36008), the 1956 version of "Love Is a Many Splendored Thing" from *At Basin Street* (EmArcy MG-36070), and Roach's entire 1957 record *Jazz in 3/4 Time* (EmArcy MG-36108) all predate Brubeck's 1959 release of *Time Out*.

Similarly, the genesis of "free jazz" has canonically been associated with two releases by saxophonist Ornette Coleman: 1959's *The Shape of Jazz to Come* (Atlantic 1317) and 1961's *Free Jazz* (Atlantic SD 1364). Yet Roach began employing free jazz procedures as early as 1954, five years before Coleman. Roach's composition "Mildama" from *Brown and Roach Incorporated* (EmArcy MG-36008) and the tune's alternate takes released on *Brownie: The Complete EmArcy Recordings of Clifford Brown* (EmArcy 838 306-2) demonstrate free jazz techniques. Using timpani mallets and with the snares turned "off," Roach plays a free, nonmetric drum solo that spans about one minute, before introducing the brisk tempo that serves as the improvisational canvas for both himself and Brown on the rest of the piece.

Pioneering Corporate Savvy

Throughout the twentieth century, the music industry disproportionately disadvantaged jazz musicians, especially noncomposing jazz performers, through a tight, interconnected web of licensing and distribution.[83] As Ingrid Monson has argued in *Freedom Sounds*, moreover, midcentury union practices disproportionately disadvantaged Black musicians as compared with their white counterparts.[84] Roach's business ventures, therefore, seem to have been overlooked as a vanguardist model for financial self-determination, agency, and Black entrepreneurship in the twentieth century.

To circumvent the "big box" studios and major record labels, Roach incorporated his own businesses. With the explicit purpose of opening a record label owned by musicians themselves, Roach, Charles Mingus, and Celia Mingus Zaentz, Mingus's spouse for a time, founded Debut Records in 1952.[85] As Brian Priestley has argued in *Mingus: A Critical Biography*, Debut Records initially thrived with such releases as *Jazz at Massey Hall*, vols. 1–3 (Debut DLP-2, DLP-3, and DLP-4): "The Massey Hall issues not only put Debut on the map as a company specializing in quality East Coast jazz, ready to rival Blue Note and Prestige, but brought about distribution and leasing deals with European companies, including the independent Danish Debut label."[86] Featuring trumpeter Dizzy Gillespie, saxophonist Charlie Parker, bassist Charles Mingus, pianist Bud Powell, and Roach, the *Jazz at Massey Hall* recordings are not only considered seminal within jazz history, but also the recordings were used as justification to induct Roach into the Grammy Awards Hall of Fame in 1995.[87]

Debut's ambitious releases came to an end in 1957; however, "in Mingus's words, the A.F.M. [American Federation of Musicians] 'stopped our license ... and ... said we didn't pay our debts.' It is not known who filed the complaint against Debut, whether fellow A.F.M. members or perhaps pressing plants or studios, but, either at this stage or earlier, there had been dissension between Mingus and Max Roach about the running of the company."[88] Including the mention of "old unpaid bills," June 9, 1960, correspondence from the Danish Debut Records president Ole Vestegaard Jensen to Roach confirms Debut's financial woes.

In the 1960s, Roach formed Milma Publishing Company for the purpose of registering, retaining, and collecting the financial rewards of copyrights, especially within the international market.[89] While records are unclear as to exactly when Roach began publishing under the Milma umbrella, a certificate dated July 26, 1966, qualifies the operational continuation of the business entity.[90] On June 24, 1964, the Royalties Department manager of a British conglomerate including Electric & Musical Industries, Gramophone, Columbia, Parlophone, and EMI wrote to Milma Publishing regarding "an amount of Copyright Royalties accruing" and requesting confirmation of address and bank information to execute a bank transfer.[91] In a telegram dated January 13, 1969, the Nordisk Copyright Bureau in Copenhagen, Denmark, reached out to Milma Publishing regarding "The Drum Also Waltzes" and "For Big Sid," among other recordings, seeking Milma's territorial copyright representative with whom to account mechanical royalties.[92] Last, a 1972 agreement between Milma Publishing and London's Mechanical Copyright Protection Society, Ltd., articulates the society's role as sole agent for the purpose of collecting and obtaining payment of all fees, royalties, or other sums of money to which the owner of Milma Publishing may be paid within territories of the United Kingdom.[93]

In the early 1970s, Roach formed "Max Roach Industries, Inc." While the archived proposal draft is undated, the document indicates a projected opening date in 1971: "Attached is a proposal to establish a Record Pressing Company, a Recording Studio and Record Distributorship which will be a private, employee and community owned and operated venture prepared through the coordinated efforts of Max Roach, noted percussionist, the Harlem Commonwealth Council Local Development Corporation and the New York Urban League."[94] The document includes cosignatories President Max Roach, Deputy Director Lloyd Terry, and Vice President Douglas S. Gray. Notably, the document specifically refers to the entity as one of private, employee, and community ownership and operation.

While Roach pursued traditionally capitalist avenues of reaping the economic rewards of artistic endeavors, he also pursued anticapitalist economic models. In the 1979 *Modern Drummer* interview, Roach expressed his preference for such economic models: "I noticed the audiences in Europe. . . . so many things are supported by the government. . . . But that's a different situation; those are Euro-Socialist countries. Here we're high on profit. Cultural development suffers as a result, which is a tragedy."[95] For example, Roach and bassist Charles Mingus co-organized the 1960 Newport Rebel Festival, an alternative to what they considered the Newport Jazz Festival's conservative programming and underpayment of artists.[96] Embattled in divorce proceedings with Louis Lorillard, a prominent Newport Jazz Festival figure, Elaine Lorillard facilitated the Rebel Festival's use of Cliff Walk Manor; the festival's artists kept all proceeds from entrance fees, since Cliff Walk Manor owner, Nick Cannarozzi, anticipated profits from hotel lodging and bar receipts.[97]

Launched from the success of the 1960 Newport Rebels Festival, the Newport Rebels, including Roach, organized the Jazz Artists Guild (JAG), whose mission was "to book concerts and sponsor projects over which musicians would have both economic and artistic control."[98] As Monson has argued in *Freedom Sounds*, "Although short lived, the JAG demonstrated that it was possible for jazz musicians to form collectives to advocate on their behalf both artistically and economically."[99] It is important to note that Roach's business ventures were not all proverbial cash cows. The "collective" business models in particular, including Debut Records and the Jazz Artists Guild, seem to have run into rocky fiscal terrain. Through his vanguardist business ventures, however, Roach continually endeavored for financial autonomy by circumventing the big box studios and major record labels.

Max Roach and the Modern Civil Rights Movement

Stemming from Roach's involvement with Sonny Rollins's 1958 *Freedom Suite* and Roach's own 1960 recording *We Insist! Freedom Now Suite* (Candid CJM 8002), much discourse has focused on articulating connections between Roach's musical life and the civil rights movement.[100] In *Freedom Sounds*, however, Ingrid Monson has argued that some of the political messaging from Roach's oeuvre—and the scholarly analysis that has amplified that messaging—has received disproportionately more attention than the music.[101] Yet, in the most explicit form of activism, Roach marched the picket line himself. On May 19, 1961, the Miles Davis Quintet and the Gil Evans Orchestra played Carnegie Hall as part of a benefit concert in support of the African Research Foundation (ARF).[102] During "Someday My Prince Will Come," the opener for the concert's second half, Roach and other protesters emerged from the crowd with signs that read "Africa for Africans," "Freedom Now," and "Medicine without Murrow Please." Roach was under the impression that the ARF had connections with CIA front groups, and was, therefore, playing into the hands of colonialism.[103]

Several musical works from Max Roach's oeuvre suggest connections to the civil rights movement through subject matter, lyrics, and libretto, and supplementary material including liner notes and cover art. Roach's 1960 recording *We Insist! Freedom Now Suite* (Candid CJM 8002) is the most renowned of these works. Cowritten by Roach and Oscar Brown, the suite includes movements "Driva' Man" and "Freedom Day." In the album's liner notes, Nat Hentoff included a stirring quotation by A. Philip Randolph:

> *A revolution is unfurling—America's unfinished revolution. It is unfurling in lunch counters, buses, libraries and schools—wherever the dignity and potential of men are denied. Youth and idealism are unfurling. Mass-*

es of Negros are marching onto the stage of history and demanding their freedom now![104]

Randolph's words underscore connections between *We Insist!* and the civil rights movement by invoking the cultural revolution generally and by subtly referencing specific civil rights events, including Rosa Park's 1955 bus boycott in Montgomery, Alabama, and the North Carolina A&T students' sit-ins at Woolworth's in Greensboro, North Carolina, during February and March 1960.[105] Making visually explicit the link between political events of 1960 and Roach's suite, the iconic image of the Woolworth's lunch counter sit-in was used in album promotional materials and as the cover art for *We Insist!*[106] Unpacking the music of the suite, Alisa White has argued, "The *Freedom Now Suite* emphasizes the similarities between the American and African 'revolutions' not only through topical juxtaposition but also by placing elements of traditional African American and African music into a modern jazz context."[107] While perhaps the most renowned, *We Insist!* is not the only of Roach's works to suggest topical connections to the civil rights movement. "Mendacity," from Roach's 1961 *Percussion Bitter Sweet* (Impulse! A-8), for example, includes lyrics that address voting rights and lynching: "Now voting rights in this fair land we know are not denied, But if I tried in certain states, from treetops I'd be tied."

Roach's performances at numerous fundraising events benefiting civil rights organizations have fortified connections between his musical career and the civil rights movement. Roach appeared at the Nation of Islam's African-Asian unity bazaars of the early 1960s.[108] On January 15, 1961, the Congress of Racial Equality sponsored a benefit performance of *We Insist!* at the Village Gate in New York City, and Roach performed excerpts from *We Insist!* for the 1961 NAACP Annual Convention in Philadelphia.[109] Although Roach was not directly involved with the August 28, 1963, March on Washington, he performed on a bill with Abbey Lincoln, Duke Ellington, Billy Taylor, Nat "King" Cole, Frank Sinatra, and Sammy Davis at one of the march's two major New York benefit concerts on August 25, 1963.[110] Alongside Abbey Lincoln, Blue Mitchell, Roy Haynes, and Lonnie Smith, moreover, Roach performed at a December 1964 benefit concert for *Freedomways*, a publication covering politics, art, and culture whose first editor was Shirley Graham Du Bois, wife of W.E.B. Du Bois.[111]

Yet, as I have argued elsewhere, musical analysis can dig deeper in substantiating links between Roach's musical life and the civil rights movement.[112] In *Freedom Sounds*, Ingrid Monson has argued that, while Jim Crow legislation did not *cause* jazz, it "functioned as a structural condition over which the emergence of the genre took place, and its effects were not limited to the South."[113] Federal legislation of the 1960s, however, pointed to change: the Equal Pay Act of 1963 prohibited wage discrimination on the basis of sex; the Civil Rights Act of 1964 barred discrimination on the basis of race, color, religion, sex, and sexual orientation; and the Voting Rights Act of 1965 dismantled the legal basis for racial discrimination. Significantly, while racial equality was a primary driver of the civil rights movement, it was not the only driver. In addition to legal protections from racial discrimination, the Equal Pay Act and Civil Rights Act make specific provisions for other qualifiers. Consequently, the civil rights movement can be viewed as not only a push for racial equality but also a push for equality more generally.[114]

In such light, Roach confronted marginalization on two fronts: as a Black American, he faced racial discrimination within society generally and within music industry economics specifically.[115] As a drummer, he faced marginalization within hierarchical jazz performance practices and within historical construction of the jazz canon. Therefore, I have argued that expressions of self-determination from Roach's musical life and career, many of which have been discussed herein, can be viewed as a nexus between his pursuit of racial equality and his quest to challenge the marginalization of the drum chair within the conventionally hierarchical performance practices of jazz.[116]

As such, expressions of self-determination from Roach's musical life bridge a connection with a broader civil rights impetus: Roach's drum tuning reflected an impetus to establish the drummer's musical voice as equal to those of other ensemble instrumentalists. He challenged the drummer's conventional role as a "comping" accompanist. Characterized by unconventional stickings, unprecedented limb independence, and large-scale formal structures, Roach's improvisational voice reframed drum solos from excursions in vaudevillian primitivism to masterclasses in musical composition. From the drum chair, to which "sideman" status had been ascribed, Roach led ensembles prodigiously. He challenged the drummer's functional role big bands and combos by reframing that role within ever-diversifying performing forces. Roach's pursuit of music education and his pedagogical philosophy challenged the narrative construct that marginalized drummers as incomplete musicians. Through prolific composition, Roach not only exercised financial and legal autonomy over his oeuvre, but he also dispelled myths that drummers' compositional potential was any less than that of other instrumentalists. Within the arts community and society more broadly, Roach's business savvy and pioneering economic self-determination piloted a vanguardist model for agency and Black entrepreneurship in the twentieth century.

Coda

Roach won the *DownBeat* critic's poll for drums in 1955 and each year from 1958 to 1961.[117] In 1984, Roach was named a National Endowment for the Arts Jazz Master and was inducted into the International Percussive Arts Society Hall of Fame.[118] In 1985, Roach won an Obie award for having composed the scores to *Shepardsets*, a collection of three Sam Shepard plays.[119] In 1988, Roach was the first jazz musician to receive a MacArthur Foundation Fellowship.[120] In 1989, he was granted the title of Commander in the French Order of Arts and Letters, France's highest cultural honor.[121] Roach was twice awarded the French Grand Prix du Disque.[122] In 1992, Roach was inducted into the American Academy of Arts and Letters as an Honorary Member.[123] Roach was inducted in to the Grammy Awards Hall of Fame in 1995.[124] In 1998, Roach received the Avedis Zildjian Cymbal Company's Lifetime Achievement Award.[125] Roach died in Manhattan on August 16, 2007, and was buried at Woodlawn Cemetery in the Bronx.[126]

Within twentieth-century intellectual discourse, especially that concerning jazz, scholars, journalists, and critics have debated whether art transcends or reflects its cultural context. In *Aesthetic Theory*, philosopher Theodor Adorno argued for art's transcendent nature: "Their [artworks'] transcendence is their eloquence, their script, but it is a script without meaning, or, more precisely, a script with broken or veiled meaning.... Art fails its concept when it does not achieve this transcendence; it loses its quality of being art."[127] In *Freedom Sounds*, Ingrid Monson has argued that, because the idea of transcendent art has historically provided musicians entrée into the world of "high culture," some jazz musicians of the 1960s cloaked themselves in eccentricity and basked in the idea of iconoclast genius.[128] Monson has pointed to Sun Ra and John Coltrane as classic examples of artists whose works have been read through the lens that "true art" is demeaned when it is deputized for political and social purposes.[129]

In the 1979 *Modern Drummer* interview, by contract, Roach decidedly endorsed the cultural contextualization of art: "There are those who think that art is for the sake of art, but actually it never is. Art is a powerful weapon that society, or the powers that be, use to control or direct the way people think."[130] In Arthur Taylor's 1977 *Notes and Tones: Musician-to-Musician Interviews*, moreover, Roach argued, "Two theories exist. One is that art is for the sake of art, which is true. The other theory, which is also true, is that the artist is like a secretary.... He keeps a record of his time, so to speak.... My music tries to say how I really feel, and I hope it mirrors in some way how black people feel in the United States."[131]

Through some lenses, Roach's career can certainly be viewed as decidedly transcendent. Some of Roach's colleagues, including trumpeter Clifford Brown, pianist Richie Powell, and saxophonist Charlie Parker, met untimely and tragic deaths. Others, like Coleman Hawkins, lived to see their musical relevance slowly fade from the fore. By contrast, Roach's musical life spanned seven decades and actively engaged with the myriad musical, economic, political, cultural, and aesthetic issues of the twentieth century. Roach's story, therefore, is that of survival, of perseverance, of continuous renewal, and of transcendence above the controversial compartmentalization of jazz history's "styles" and "periods" that serve merely as convenient signposts on the superhighway of the pedagogical jazz canon. American jazz drummer, percussionist, composer, and bandleader Max Roach should be viewed as a trailblazer, a pioneer, and a vanguardist that boldly confronted entrenched dogmas—those of jazz, of the music industry, and of society more broadly.

Notes

1 This "revolutionary" versus "evolutionary" terminology is recycled from Scott DeVeaux, *The Birth of Bebop* (Berkeley: University of California Press, 1997), 4. Judy Lochhead, "Naming: Music and the Postmodern," *New Formations*, no. 66 (Spring 2008): 161. In the article, Lochhead describes a similar duality between "journalistic" and "technical" scholarship. "Revolutionary" readings of Roach tend to rely on methodologies including human-subject interviews and secondary sources, a literature ripe for the formation of mythology and one that places tremendous emphasis on canonic construction by relying on scholarship, journalism, and critical reception. While "revolutionary" readings steep Roach's work in context, they generally shy away from musical analysis itself. "Revolutionary" readings include the following sources: Sean Leah Bowden, "Max Roach and M'Boom: Diasporic Soundings in American Percussion Music" (DMA diss., University of California at San Diego, 2018); LeRoi Jones [Amiri Baraka], *Blues People: Negro Music in White America* (New York: William and Morrow, 1963); Amiri Baraka [LeRoi Jones], *Digging: The Afro-American Soul of American Classical Music* (Berkeley: University of California Press, 2009), 1 and 106–109; Guthrie Ramsey, *Race Music: Black Cultures from Bebop to Hip-Hop* (Berkeley: University of California Press, 2003). Focusing too narrowly on linear canonic construction, "evolutionary" readings, by contrast, have portrayed Roach as a bebop pioneer, manifestly ignoring Roach's work as a composer and muting Roach's contributions to odd meters and free jazz. That Roach was a percussionist, composer, bandleader, pianist, and multi-instrumentalist is seemingly read out of the narrative. "Evolutionary" readings of Roach include the following sources: John Riley, "Tone Poems and Drum Conversations: A Max Roach Style & Analysis," *Modern Drummer* 31, no. 12 (December 2007): 98–103; John Riley, *The Art of Bop Drumming* (New York: Manhattan Music, 1994); Burt Korall, *Drummin' Men: The Heartbeat of Jazz—The Bebop Years* (New York: Ox-

ford University Press, 2002); Ted Gioia, *The History of Jazz*, 3rd ed. (New York: Oxford University Press, 2021); Thomas Owens, *Bebop: The Music and Its Players* (New York: Oxford university Press, 1995); Jonathan McCaslin, "Melodic Jazz Drumming" (DMA diss., University of Toronto, 2015); Dave Goodman, "Tony Williams' Drumset Ideology to 1969" (PhD diss., University of Sydney, 2011); Anthony Brown, "The Development of Modern Jazz Drumset Performance 1940 to 1950" (PhD diss., University of California at Berkley, 1997); Rande Paul Sanderbeck, "Homage to Max: A New Work for Solo Drumset Based on the Style of Max Roach" (DMA project, University of Kentucky, 1997).
2 Gioia, *History of Jazz*, 257 and 371–373.
3 Gioia, 373.
4 Scott Fish, "Max Roach," *Modern Drummer* 6, no. 4 (June 1982): 50.
5 While pianists Scott Joplin, "Jelly Roll" Morton and, later, James P. Johnson, Willie "The Lion" Smith, Fats Waller, and Art Tatum, represent notable exceptions to the dominance of horn-playing bandleaders, pianists rather than drummers or bassists have most often served as leaders within stand-alone piano trios. Even within the rhythm section itself, therefore, drummers have traditionally taken a "back seat."
6 Matt Brennen, *Kick It: A Social History of the Drum Kit* (New York: Oxford University Press, 2020), 7–8. Brennan's work surveys the historical stereotyping and marginalization of drummers, despite the centrality of both the drumset and its practitioners. Paul Berliner, *Thinking in Jazz* (Chicago: University of Chicago Press, 1994), 291. Berliner has argued that the standard "front-line" instruments (clarinet, trombone, and most especially cornet or trumpet) dominated early jazz in New Orleans, St. Louis, Chicago, and New York; the other performing forces (piano, banjo, guitar, tuba, bass saxophone, upright bass, and percussion) primarily provided musical accompaniment.
7 Berliner, *Thinking in Jazz*, 291.
8 Berliner, 299.
9 Harold Howland, "Max Roach: Back on the Bandstand," *Modern Drummer* 3, no. 1 (January/February 1979): 22.
10 Fish, "Max Roach," *Modern Drummer* 6, no. 4 (June 1982): 48. I have not redacted Roach's strong language because his language reflects the marginalization he so staunchly opposed.
11 Kevin McDonald, "Hearing the American Civil Rights Movement in the Music of Max Roach" (PhD diss., Catholic University of America, 2021), 45–57. My research relies upon a methodological synthesis: archival research surveying primary source material, secondary sources, audio-visual transcription, and comparative analysis together form a methodological bridge connecting the orality of jazz with the musical analysis required to substantiate musicological claims.
12 Korall, *Drummin' Men: The Heartbeat of Jazz—The Bebop Years*, 97.
13 Riley, "Tone Poems and Drum Conversations," *Modern Drummer* 31, no. 12 (December 2007): 98. Unfortunately, neither ProQuest's Music Periodicals Database nor RIPM archive Crouch's 1979 *Village Voice* article.
14 1995 National Medal of Arts nomination form, March 14, 1995, box 154, folder 35, Max Roach Papers, Music Division, Library of Congress, Washington, DC. Peter Keepnews, "Max Roach, Master of Modern Jazz, Dies at 83," *New York Times*, August

17, 2007; Keepnews cites "New Land, N.C." as Roach's birthplace. Thomas Barrick and Christopher Hartten, "Max Roach Papers: Guides to Special Collections in the Music Division of the Library of Congress," 2016, revised May 2019, Music Division, Library of Congress, Washington, DC, 5: "Newland, North Carolina" is listed as Roach's birthplace. Conversely, Roach simply listed Elizabeth City, NC—the largest nearby city—as place of birth on the 1995 National Medal of Arts nomination form.

15 Korall, *Drummin' Men: The Heartbeat of Jazz—The Bebop Years,* 90.
16 Barrick and Hartten, "Max Roach Papers," Music Division, Library of Congress, 5.
17 Keepnews, "Max Roach."
18 Keepnews. Roach also mentions this engagement with Ellington in Geoffrey Haydon, dir., *Sit Down and Listen: The Story of Max Roach* (London: Third Eye/Channel Four Television Company, 1984).
19 Brennan, *Kick It,* 176–177: "Roy Haynes remembers getting a 20-inch Ludwig bass drum while on tour with Lester Young in Chicago in 1947. Similarly, Dave Tough came to Gretsch in 1948 requesting a more portable 20-inch bass drum—much smaller than the standard 24 and 26-inch bass drums advertised in the company's catalogue that year—and Gretsch obliged." Moreover, sonic requirements for popular dance musics remain strikingly similar even to the present day: punchy low-end achieved through powerful subwoofers.
20 Chet Falzerano, "Gretsch Progressive Jazz Kits: Origin of Cool," *Drum!* January 17, 2013, https://drummagazine.com/gretsch-progressive-jazz-kits-origin-of-cool/
21 Fish, "Max Roach," *Modern Drummer* 6, no. 4 (June 1982): 52.
22 Fish, "Max Roach," 12.
23 Kenny Washington, "Guest Editorial: On Max Roach," *Modern Drummer* 31, no. 12 (December 2007): 10.
24 Jack DeJohnette, "Max Remembered," *Modern Drummer* 31, no. 12 (December 2007): 79.
25 Berliner, *Thinking in Jazz,* 299.
26 Berliner, 315.
27 McDonald, "Hearing the American Civil Rights Movement," 159–168. This discussion unpacks Roach's explorations challenging the drummer's conventional role as a "comping" accompanist.
28 Transcriptions of many of these solos can be found in the appendix to my dissertation, McDonald, "Hearing the American Civil Rights Movement," 196–241.
29 Ingrid Monson, *Freedom Sounds: Civil Rights Call Out to Jazz and Africa* (New York: Oxford University Press, 2007), 286–287.
30 Washington, "Guest Editorial," 10.
31 Riley, "Tone Poems and Drum Conversations," 102–103.
32 DeVeaux, *Birth of Bebop,* 3.
33 McDonald, "Hearing the American Civil Rights Movement," 116–128.
34 In correspondence from 2021, John Riley has suggested that Roach's unconventional drumset stickings could be related to Roach's extensive study of timpani.
35 McDonald, "Hearing the American Civil Rights Movement," 126–127.
36 For an exhaustive discussion, see McDonald, 128–136.
37 Riley, "Tone Poems and Drum Conversations," 98.

38 Riley, 100–101.
39 Goodman, "Tony Williams' Drumset Ideology to 1969," 279.
40 Transcriptions of these solos are included in the appendix to my dissertation: McDonald, "Hearing the American Civil Rights Movement," 196–241.
41 Washington, "Guest Editorial," 10.
42 Ted Panken, "I Am Not a Metronome: The Complicated Elegance of Roy Haynes," *JAZZIZ* 24, no. 3 (March 2007): 34.
43 For annotated examples, see McDonald, "Hearing the American Civil Rights Movement," 135–136. For complete transcriptions, see McDonald, 196–241.
44 For a lengthier discussion, see McDonald, 140–147.
45 See also McDonald, 148–159.
46 Korall, *Drummin' Men: The Heartbeat of Jazz—The Bebop Years*, 97.
47 Keepnews, "Max Roach."
48 To the present day, many of these varied instrumentations challenge perceive boundaries between jazz, "chamber jazz," "third stream," and broader syntheses with classical music.
49 The recordings were initially released as the singles RCA Victor 20-2919 and RCA Victor 20-2745 before their inclusion on the compilation *The Complete Coleman Hawkins*, vol. 2 (RCA PM 42046).
50 Barrick and Hartten, "Max Roach Papers," 6–7.
51 Barrick and Hartten, "Max Roach Papers," 7.
52 Chris May, "Max Roach & Anthony Braxton: One in Two, Two in One," *All About Jazz*, December 7, 2007, www.allaboutjazz.com/max-roach-and-anthony-braxton-one-in-two-two-in-one-by-chris-may.php
53 Korall, *Drummin' Men: The Heartbeat of Jazz—The Bebop Years*, 108.
54 Fish, "Max Roach," 9.
55 Adam Budofsky, "Max Roach through the years," *Modern Drummer* 31, no. 12 (December 2007): 70. See also Barrick and Hartten, "Max Roach Papers," 6.
56 "La Villette Jazz Festival: Max Roach duo avec Amiri Baraka," July 6, 1996, Philharmonie à la Demande, https://pad.philharmoniedeparis.fr/doc/CIMU/0082225/la-villette-jazz-festival-max-roach-duo-avec-amiri-baraka
57 Amiri Baraka, *Digging: The Afro-American Soul of American Classical Music* (Berkeley: University of California Press, 2009), 213.
58 Burt Korall, *Drummin' Men: The Heartbeat of Jazz—The Swing Years* (New York: Oxford University Press, 1990), 50.
59 Brennen, *Kick It*, 7–8. Brennan's work surveys the historical stereotyping and marginalization of drummers, especially during the twentieth century, despite the centrality of both the drumset and its practitioners.
60 Haydon, *Sit Down and Listen*; Brian Edward Jones, "'Members, Don't Git Weary': Max Roach, 'Treme,' and the Sound of Resistance" (MA thesis, College of William and Mary, 2015), 12.
61 Keepnews, "Max Roach."
62 Korall, *Drummin' Men: The Heartbeat of Jazz—The Bebop Years*, 91.
63 Fish, "Max Roach," 50.

64 Miles Davis, *Miles: The Autobiography* (New York: Simon and Schuster, 1989), 45–47, 56, 58, and 70.
65 Saheed Adejumobi, "Thelonious Monk (1917–1982)," BlackPast, June 16, 2007, https://www.blackpast.org/african-american-history/monk-thelonious-1917-1982/
66 Transcript of Record, Maxwell Roach, February 1951, Office of the Registrar, Manhattan School of Music, 130 Claremont Avenue, New York City. This information was confirmed in the author's correspondence of October 6, 2020, with John K. Blanchard, Manhattan School of Music's institutional historian and director of archives. Blanchard has framed Roach's major as classical percussion and has given no indication of a change of major. Yet Roach's transcript of record does not itself specifically designate a major.
67 Correspondence from Peggy L. Tueller (vice president for Administration, Manhattan School of Music) to Roach, March 2, 1990, box 152, folder 8, Max Roach Papers. Correspondence from Peter Simon (president, Manhattan School of Music) to Roach, February 19, 1990, box 152, folder 8, Max Roach Papers. President Simon's letter offers the degree; Vice President Tueller's letter confirms Roach's acceptance of the degree.
68 Barrick and Hartten, "Max Roach Papers," 5.
69 University of Massachusetts Amherst Office of Equity and Inclusion, "Max Roach," www.umass.edu/diversity/blackpresence/maxroach. Iain Anderson, *This Is Our Music: Free Jazz, the Sixties, and American Culture* (Philadelphia: University of Pennsylvania Press, 2007), 8: Anderson has argued that academic appointments afforded a springboard from which artists could launch more avant-garde musical experiments of the 1960s and 1970s. Roach seems to have been no exception to this rule, and his duo records of the 1970s exemplify such niche releases: 1976's *Force* (Uniteledis UNI 28.976), 1977's *Streams of Consciousness* (Baystate RVJ-6016), 1978's *Birth and Rebirth* (Black Saint BSR 0024), and the 1979 recordings *Historic Concerts* (Soul Note SN 1100/1), *The Long March* (hat Hut 2R13), and *One in Two/Two in One* (hat Hut 2R06).
70 Fish, "Max Roach," 10–11, 48.
71 DeVeaux, *Birth of Bebop*, 9–10.
72 Whereas Mel Lewis, Buddy Rich, and Art Blakey also led ensembles from the drum chair, Roach distinguished himself from this group by composing prolifically.
73 Fish, "Max Roach," 48.
74 Koreyoshi Kurahara, dir., *(The) Black Sun* [Kuroi taiyô] (Tokyo: Nikkatsu Films, 1964).
75 1995 National Medal of Arts nomination form. Jon Pareles, "Music to Match the Beat in Early Shepard," *New York Times*, November 18, 1984.
76 Thomas K. Arnold, "Max Roach Scoring the Bard: Jazzman's Dream," *Los Angeles Times*, August 17, 1987. Aljean Harmetz, "San Diego Is Now a Boom Town for New Theater," *New York Times*, August 24, 1987. See also box 15, folders 8–9, Max Roach Papers.
77 Nancy Churnin, "Playwright Hopes to Bring Harlem Hero Bumpy Johnson into the Light," *Los Angeles Times*, February 2, 1991. Don Shirley, "Stage Review: 'Bumpy Johnson' a Strange Tribute—Portrait of Harlem Gangster as a Kind of Black Robin Hood Remains More an Angle than a Play," *Los Angeles Times*, February 1, 1991.
78 Budofsky, "Max Roach through the Years," 72. See also Barrick and Hartten, "Max Roach Papers," 7.

79 Korall, *Drummin' Men: The Heartbeat of Jazz—The Swing Years,* 335.
80 Washington, "Guest Editorial," 10.
81 Riley, "Tone Poems and Drum Conversations," *Modern Drummer* 31, no. 12 (December 2007): 98.
82 Washington, "Guest Editorial," 10.
83 Monson, *Freedom Sounds,* 29–30. DeVeaux, *Birth of Bebop,* 9–11. A. B. Spellman, *Four Jazz Lives* (Ann Arbor: University of Michigan Press, 2004), xx.
84 Monson, *Freedom Sounds,* 39–41 and 48.
85 Korall, *Drummin' Men: The Heartbeat of Jazz—The Bebop Years,* 103. Brian Priestley, *Mingus: A Critical Biography* (New York: Quartet Books, 1983), 45–46. Harvey Pekar, "A View of Debut," *Metro,* October 30–November 5, 1997, www.metroactive.com/papers/metro/10.30.97/jazz-9744.html
86 Priestley, *Mingus,* 54.
87 Grammy Hall of Fame, box 147, folder 39, Max Roach Papers.
88 Priestley, *Mingus,* 80. Correspondence from Ole Vestegaard Jensen (president, Danish Debut) to Roach, June 9, 1960, box 146, folder 8, Max Roach Papers.
89 Correspondence from Bruce Wright to Roach, February 1, 1962, box 154, folder 7, Max Roach Papers.
90 Business Certificate, July 26, 1966, box 154, folder 7, Max Roach Papers.
91 Correspondence from Royalties Department manager to Milma Music Publishing, June 24, 1964, box 154, folder 7, Max Roach Papers.
92 Correspondence from Nordisk Copyright Bureau to Milma Publishing Co., January 13, 1969, box 154, folder 7, Max Roach Papers.
93 Contractual agreement between Milma Publishing Co. (EMI) and the Mechanical-Copyright Protection Society Limited, March 28, 1972, box 154, folder 7, Max Roach Papers.
94 Proposal to Establish Max Roach Industries, box 152, folder 28, Max Roach Papers.
95 Howland, "Max Roach," 21.
96 Monson, *Freedom Sounds,* 184: after George Wein offered Mingus $700 for the 1960 Newport Jazz Festival, Mingus declared that he would not perform for less than $5,000.
97 Monson, *Freedom Sounds,* 184.
98 Jazz Artists Guild, box 149, folder 25, Max Roach Papers. Monson, *Freedom Sounds,* 184. Monson cites an interview conducted with Nat Hentoff and two other sources: Gene Lees, "Newport: The Real Trouble," *DownBeat* 27, no. 17 (August 1960): 20–23, 44; Michael Cuscuna, liner notes, *The Complete Candid Recordings of Charles Mingus, 1960* (Mosaic III).
99 Monson, *Freedom Sounds,* 184.
100 Examples of sources that articulate connections between Roach and the civil rights movement include the following: Bowden, "Max Roach and M'Boom"; Benjamin Anderson, "Blue Notes and Brown Skin: Five African-American Jazzmen and the Music they Produced in Regard to the American Civil Rights Movement" (MA thesis, College of William and Mary, 2005); Jack Marchbanks, "Pride and Protest in Letters and Song: Jazz Artists and Writers during the Civil Rights Movement, 1955–1965" (PhD diss., Ohio University, 2018); Jones, "'Members Don't Git Weary'"; and Lucas A. Henry,

"Freedom Now! Four Hard Bop and Avant-garde Jazz Musicians' Musical Commentary on the Civil Rights Movement, 1958–1964" (MA thesis, East Tennessee State University, 2004).
101 Ingrid Monson, "Revisited! The Freedom Now Suite," *Jazz Times* 31 (September 2001): 54.
102 The 19 May 1961 concert was recorded and later released as *Miles Davis at Carnegie Hall* (Columbia CL 1812 and CS 8612).
103 Monson, *Freedom Sounds*, 188–189.
104 Nat Hentoff, liner notes to Max Roach, *We Insist! Freedom Now Suite*, 1960 (Candid CJM8002 and CCD9002). See also Ingrid Monson, *Freedom Sounds*, 172 and 362.
105 Monson, "Revisited!" 54–59.
106 Monson, *Freedom Sounds*, 152.
107 Alisa White, "'We Insist! Freedom Now': Max Roach's Transatlantic Civil Rights Imperative," *Jazz Education Journal* 40, nos. 2–3 (October 2007): 52.
108 Monson, *Freedom Sounds*, 227.
109 Barrick and Hartten, "Max Roach Papers," 6.
110 Monson, *Freedom Sounds*, 209.
111 Monson, *Freedom Sounds*, 230.
112 For a lengthier discussion, see McDonald, "Hearing the American Civil Rights Movement," 1–9.
113 Monson, *Freedom Sounds*, 6.
114 McDonald, "Hearing the American Civil Rights Movement," 3–12.
115 Monson, *Freedom Sounds*, 29–65. While Monson's book in its entirety is a masterclass on the subject, her second chapter ("Jim Crow, Economics, and the Politics of Musicianship") specifically engages with union segregation and copyright law, both of which are issues that relate to my arguments about Roach.
116 McDonald, "Hearing the American Civil Rights Movement," 3–9. For a description of musical self-determination, see Ralph Ellison, "The Golden Age/Time Past—Manners and Morals at Minton's, 1941: The Setting for a Revolution," *Esquire*, January 1, 1959, 110. To my mind, self-determination centers on the idea of controlling one's destiny—the extent to which outside factors affect the agency of the individual in life pursuits. Yet any comprehensive definition of self-determination must include an array of ideas and different channels for expression, including financial, artistic, political, and cultural self-determination.
117 Monson, *Freedom Sounds*, 68.
118 1995 National Medal of Arts nomination form.
119 Keepnews, "Max Roach."
120 Keepnews, "Max Roach."
121 1995 National Medal of Arts nomination form.
122 Herb Wong, *Jazz on My Mind* (Jefferson, NC: McFarland, 2016), 47.
123 1995 National Medal of Arts nomination form.
124 1995 National Medal of Arts nomination form.
125 Zildjian 1967–1998, box 163, folder 31, Max Roach Papers. See also Barrick and Hartten, "Max Roach Papers," 7.

126 Ginia Bellafante, "Pearly Gates, Velvet Rope," *New York Times,* November 1, 2015.
127 Theodor Adorno, *Aesthetic Theory,* trans. Robert Hullot-Kentor (Minneapolis: University of Minnesota Press, 1997), 78. Adorno's *Aesthetic Theory* was originally published posthumously in 1970.
128 Monson, *Freedom Sounds,* 205.
129 Monson, *Freedom Sounds,* 262 and 265.
130 Howland, "Max Roach," 23.
131 Arthur Taylor, *Notes and Tones: Musician-to-Musician Interviews* (New York: Coward, McCann and Geoghegan, 1977), 112.

10

Roland Hayes

The Quiet Social Activist?

Christopher A. Brooks

When we envision African American activists of the 1910s and '20s, Roland Hayes (1887–1977) is not one of the names that readily comes to mind. In fact, Hayes was known during his time as a celebrated tenor who sang on the world's greatest concert stages but was a reasonably engaged albeit quiet activist. In modern times however, some of his actions might be construed as timid if not anti-Black even during his era. This chapter explores that complicated legacy from this once-great artist.

At his height, he was referred to as the "Black Caruso," one of the greatest concert performers of the twentieth century. During his 60-year career, the gifted American singer packed concert halls all over Europe, in South America, and throughout the United States. At the zenith of his popularity, along with other renowned world-class musicians like Fritz Kreisler, Ignaz Paderewski, Tito Schipa, John McCormack, Nellie Melba, Feodor Chaliapin, and Pablo Casals, he was one of the few artists who could sell out famous venues like New York's Carnegie Hall, Washington's Constitution Hall, Boston's Symphony Hall, Covent Garden and Wigmore Hall in London, and the Hollywood Bowl, among other major auditoriums throughout this country and Europe. In 1923, he was the first African American musician to solo with a major symphony orchestra in the country, which led to him singing with many world-renowned orchestras under the batons of celebrated conductors, including Eugene Ormandy, Leopold Stokowski, Otto Klemperer, Bruno Walter, Pierre Monteux, Serge Koussevitzky, Sir Henry Wood, Walter Damrosch, Willem Mengelberg, and Gabriel Pierné.[1] Following the tradition of other celebrated musicians, he sang for crowned heads of Europe, prime ministers, presidents, and other heads of state.

His trailblazing career carved the paths for Paul Robeson, Marian Anderson, Todd Duncan, Dorothy Maynor,[2] among other African American classical vocalists. He was also one of the first concert artists to routinely program African American spirituals (then known as "Negro" spirituals) on his recitals, and thereby began a tradition that continues among African American concert vocalists today.

As a celebrated African American between the 1920s and the 1970s, his life was peppered with relationships that placed him among the most influential thinkers and artists of the twentieth century. Hayes counted among his personal friends and acquaintances George Washington Carver, Mary McLeod Bethune, Walter White, Eleanor Roosevelt, Pearl S. Buck, General Dwight D. Eisenhower, Alaine Locke, and Langston Hughes. He also crossed paths professionally with Booker T. Washington, Dr. W.E.B. Du Bois, A. Philip Randolph, and Thurgood Marshall. With great stealth, he also engaged with Emperor Haile Selassie of Ethiopia, and Marcus Garvey, the founder of the Universal Negro Improvement Association and African Communities League. Less well known, however, was the tenor's involvement in African American social causes in this country and in Europe where he was in residence during the 1920s, 30s, and 40s. Those issues he engaged in were not always successful, and he was not well known for being outspoken.

Having been born in northwest Georgia in 1887, Hayes was the sixth of seven children of William and Fannie Hayes. His mother had been enslaved on the very plantation where Hayes and his older siblings were born. After the accidental death of his father due to a mining incident in 1898 when Hayes was 11, his mother, determined to get her three sons educated, moved with them to Chattanooga, Tennessee, where she had support of her relatives there. Fannie Hayes's oldest surviving son, John, was on his own by then.[3] This period in Hayes's life was a mixture of discovery and wonder that came about because of several important life-changing "epiphanies," as he called them. Among them was a near-death experience where he was accidently pulled onto a conveyor belt where he worked and was nearly mangled as a teenager.[4] He likened that experience to the apostle Paul's Christian conversion on the road to Damascus. Another took place after he began studying with a local voice teacher, Arthur Calhoun, who took him to a local newspaper editor who played a recording of the celebrated Italian opera singer, Enrico Caruso. Hayes was transformed by his singing and that of the equally celebrated Polish American soprano, Marcella Sembrich. He was determined that he, too, would become a great singer.[5]

After matriculating at Fisk College (later University), Hayes pursued a musical career with the goal of becoming a world-class singer in the tradition of

Caruso and his contemporaries. Under the watchful eye of his teacher, Jennie Robinson, the young tenor was exposed to vocal repertory and remedial subjects such as reading and writing as he had entered Fisk with a fifth-grade education. In May 1908, Hayes performed at the Negro Music Festival in Louisville, Kentucky. There he met the singer and accompanist, Daisy Tapley,[6] who boosted his confidence and helped to refine his repertoire and vocal technique. She accompanied his recital at the festival and became a supporter early in his career.[7]

In 1910 at the end of his fourth year at Fisk, however, Hayes was summarily dismissed from the school after it was determined that he had founded a singing group, performed, and accepted payment as a Fisk-sanctioned organization.[8] After returning to Louisville for a year to make a living as a singing waiter, the young tenor was invited back to Fisk to rejoin the renowned Jubilee Singers. The group had been invited to Boston to perform at the World Exposition being staged in that city, which became Hayes's home base for the balance of his life. Throughout the 1910s the tenor performed around the country mostly through self-managed engagements. After establishing himself in Boston and bringing his mother Fannie to live with him, Daisy Tapley introduced him to the well-known baritone, Harry Burleigh. In 1914, through Burleigh's connections, Hayes met and sang at an engagement for the celebrated Tuskegee Institute president, Booker T. Washington, while the senior educator was on a speaking and fundraising tour. The year before, Hayes met Dr. W.E.B. Du Bois, Washington's chief nemesis in his capacity as editor of the NAACP magazine, *The Crisis,* where Hayes advertised his availability for engagements. The Washington/Du Bois philosophical debate regarding the appropriate direction for African Americans in the country at the time manifested itself in Roland Hayes's life experience. Because of his humble southern beginnings and background, and having experienced many menial jobs to support his family, Hayes was clearly a "Washingtonian" believing in the dignity of work.[9]

In April 1920, Hayes and his accompanist Lawrence Brown embarked on the SS *Mauretania* destined for Africa along with an extended stay in London. Although Hayes never made it to the African continent, his time in Europe would be a revelation for him in many ways as an artist and burgeoning activist.[10] Once they landed, the two musicians needed to find accommodations. After spending a day walking around different neighborhoods, they were directed to Duse Mohammed Ali, the Black nationalist, born in Egypt and raised in Sudan.[11] London at the time had become the epicenter of Black organizations protesting British colonial administrative abuses on the African continent and within the Black diaspora.[12] At the center of that activity was

Duse Mohammed Ali and a hand full of other activists. Ali offered the newly arrived Americans accommodations in his St. John's Wood boarding house where they met many continental African elitists and other brahmins from the diaspora.

Duse Mohammed Ali had been born in 1866 in Egypt and was from a large upper middle-class family. He was sent to study in Britain as a teenager, but when his father and brothers died in the British occupation of the country in the 1880s, the family could no longer afford his education.[13] Supporting himself as an actor and playwright, Ali traveled to the United States where he eventually became involved with the American Muslim movement. His animus toward the British manifested itself in his edited London-based weekly, *African and Orient Review,* where he decried British colonial policies in Africa and spoke out for "Africans" in the diaspora, specifically in the United Sates, the Caribbean, and Latin America.[14] It was Duse Mohammed Ali's one-time protégé, Marcus Garvey, who made his presence felt throughout the Black world in ways that the teacher could only dream of.[15] Duse Mohammed Ali's activities, however made him the target of the British intelligence apparatus, which routinely kept him under surveillance. Because of his artistic background, he was ideally suited to coach Hayes on the arts movement in London, but he also exposed him to a myriad of Black political activity in and around the city.

As it turned out, Ali's St. John's Wood rooming house was the perfect environment for Hayes to soak up events taking place on the African continent where he would meet many among the African and diasporan aristocracy. Within months of his arrival, he met the Yorùbá chief Amodu Tijani Oluwa and the other celebrated Nigerian nationalist of the era, Herbert Macaulay.[16] The two were also guests in Ali's rooming house and were on a mission in London to sue the British government for land that had been forcefully appropriated by colonists in southwestern Nigeria.[17] The success of their case set a legal precedent used by other British colonies for the restoration of illegally seized lands.[18]

With Duse Ali's encouragement, Hayes took full advantage of meeting Macaulay, Oluwa, and many other guests to strengthen his knowledge of the events on the African continent. He asked about their musical customs, learned songs, and generally soaked up whatever information they could provide him with. In addition, Hayes met several well positioned Afro-Britons who were also politically connected. Among this august group, Hayes met Dr. John Alcindor, a Trinidadian-born physician who trained and settled in London, John Archer, a British politician, and the first president of the African Progress Union (APU), and his longtime friend and well-connected

Afro-Briton of Ghanaian background, Robert Broadhurst. John Alcindor succeeded John Archer as president of the APU (after the former resigned from the position). Founded in 1918 by "an Association of Africans from various parts of Africa, the West Indies, British Guiana, Honduras and America, representing advanced African ideas in liberal education," the organization argued for human rights issues for continental and diasporan Africans throughout the greater London area and around the world.[19] While the organization was made up mostly of men, by 1921, after Hayes had established his presence in London, there were at least eight women who served either on the committee or held roles such as secretary for the organization.[20]

Hayes continued cultivating relationships among these well-placed Africans, Afro-Britons, and Afro-Caribbeans who quickly became some of his most ardent supporters. Barely six months into Hayes's stay in London, on October 28, an impressive assemblage of the African Progress Union along with other important members of the greater London Black community, expressed their admiration, encouragement, and support for the African American tenor.

> Roland Hayes
> The Negro Tenor
>
> We, the undersigned, having closely observed your interesting rise to a pre-eminent and enviable position in the realm of music, and being members of the various races that go to make up the families who comprise the inhabitants of Africa as well as those who have descended from the same parent stock as yourself, beg to tender you our high felicitations and regard on this your visit to the seat of the British Empire.
>
> We realize that your success is our success and that by proving that you are capable of the higher musical culture you are rendering incalculable benefits to your race. As blood of our blood, flesh of our flesh, and bone of our bone, we wish you continued success in all your undertakings praying that an All-Wise Creator will graciously grant you health and strength to complete the task you have so nobly undertaken which must indubitably redound to His Glory and to the amelioration and recognition of the undoubted mental capacities and endowments of your brothers of the Negro Race.
>
> We, therefore, beg that you will accept this slight token of our undying admiration and esteem.
>
> [Signatories]
London 28 October 1920.[21]

Among the signatories were Alcindor, Duse Mohammed Ali, and Robert Broadhurst, who served as the honorary secretary of the APU.[22] In its 1921–1922 annual report, the APU thanked Hayes for giving a fundraising concert on behalf of the organization.[23]

By early 1921, Hayes's name appeared in the *London Times,* the weekly *West Africa,* and other local publications. The culmination of the tenor's first year in London took place after his successful April 21 Wigmore Hall debut. Hayes reported being ill before the start of the recital and had to be assisted by Duse Mohammed Ali, who even helped dressed him for the performance. However, the singer managed to pull off a sensational performance resulting in strong reviews in many of the area's publications.[24] The success of his Wigmore Hall concert led to him being presented in a "command" performance at Buckingham Palace for King George and Queen Mary.[25] The news of his appearance before the royals catapulted the tenor to international stardom. Still maintaining his commitment to the Pan-African organizations, Hayes attended the August 1921 London session of the Second Pan-African Congress. There were several important resolutions to emerge from the London congress denouncing colonial activities on the African continent, including enslavement of the Black population in Abyssinia (modern-day Ethiopia), indigenous riots in Nairobi, land restoration in Nigeria and Uganda, and establishing an APU branch in Cameroon.[26]

One of the most enduring documents to emerge from the meetings was Du Bois's *London Manifesto.* In it, Du Bois made an impassioned argument acknowledging the strength of the British legal system as a model that many developed democracies could follow, but he was also critical of its practices. Specifically, Du Bois wrote:

> The absolute equality of races, physical, political and social, is the founding stone of World Peace and human advancement. No one denies great differences of gift, capacity, and attainment among individuals of all races, but the voice of Science, Religion and practical Politics is one in denying the God-appointed existence of super races or races naturally and inevitably and eternally inferior.[27]

Du Bois ended the document with several specific demands.

The Suppressed Races through their thinking leaders are demanding:
  1. The recognition of civilized men as civilized despite their race and color.
   2. Local self-government for backward groups, deliberately rising as

experience and knowledge grow to complete self-government under the limitations of a self-governed world.

3. Education in self-knowledge, in scientific truth and in industrial technique, undivorced from the art of beauty.

4. Freedom in their own religion and customs and with the right to be non-conformist and different.

5. Co-operation with the rest of the world in government, industry, and art on the basis of Justice, Freedom, and Peace.

6. The ancient common ownership of the Land and its natural fruits and defense against the unrestrained greed of invested capital.

The world must face two eventualities; either the complete assimilation of Africa with two or three of the great world states, with political, civil and social power and privileges absolutely equal for its black and white citizens, or the rise of a great black African State.[28]

Du Bois's manifesto resonated around the world, especially among the nascent nationalist movements on the African continent. Hayes and his accompanist Lawrence Brown were present when the manifesto was read at the congress. Although the tenor did not set foot on the continent during his lifetime, because of his exposure to the African nationalists of the early 1920s, he kept abreast of various independence movements in Africa and continued to cultivate and develop deep relationships among continental and diasporan Africans. During the balance of his first few years in London, he gave benefit recitals for the APU as well as the National Congress of British West Africa, and his name was routinely mentioned in Anglophone African serials during this period.

In the spring of 1922, Hayes and Lawrence Brown made a return trip to Paris after previously vowing never to return to the city after a racial incident the year before.[29] The second trip was very different and professionally profitable for the tenor. Hayes met many people with whom he would form long-lasting relationships, including another Pan-Africanist firebrand, Prince Tovalou Houénou of Dahomey (modern-day Benin Republic). Born the same year as Hayes, in Porto-Novo, Dahomey, the Parisian-educated lawyer became a fierce critic of French colonial rule in Africa.[30] As the nephew of the deposed and exiled Dahomean ruler, King Behanzin—or "Tova," as he was known to Hayes—came from a royal background as did his cousin, Prince Oanilo. Hayes credited Tova and Oanilo with validating his claim to African royalty, based on the name of the tenor's maternal great-grandfather, Abá 'Ougi.[31]

Hayes had an up-and-down relationship with Tovalou as he turned out to be more radical than the singer was prepared for. Before arriving in the United States in 1924, Tovalou founded an organization, La Ligue Universelle pour la Défense de la Race Noir (The universal league for the defense of the Black race), which was his principal platform for railing against the abuses of the French colonial system in Africa.[32] When he arrived in the United States, he quickly sought an association with Garvey and attended the Universal Negro Improvement Association meeting in New York. He also toured several cities with the Jamaican leader. All of this was too rich for Hayes's blood. He calculated that Tova's association with Garvey—who was generally seen as a "Black radical" by most white Americans (many of whom were the tenor's core supporters)—could damage his image and hence his livelihood. In a letter, Tova hinted at a passed meeting Hayes had with Garvey. The subject of the meeting is not known.[33]

Hayes's carefully cultivated public image was that of a humble performer wanting to share his art. He had seen how the fickle white American public had turned on the renowned boxer, Jack Johnson, who brazenly flaunted his relationships with several white women.[34] After the birth of his daughter, Maya, in 1926 with Countess Bertha, Hayes made at least two efforts to "adopt" his child and raise her in the United States as a foreign-born adoptee. The countess, however, would not agree to the arrangement.[35] By the early 1930s, Hayes had taken up romantically with Alzada Mann, whom he would eventually marry. They had a daughter, Afrika. With his "official American family intact," Hayes's reputation as a respectable family man was enhanced for press purposes.

Throughout the 1920s, 30s, and 40s, African Americans were increasingly waging war against Jim Crow segregation in housing, restaurant accommodations, and integrated seating at performing arts events. This was the area in which Hayes entered the arena of Black social activism. The publicly reserved Hayes was generally not inclined to "rock" the segregation boat. Even with his recent celebrity, he still did not have the leverage (especially not in the South) to challenge these ironclad segregation rules of the 1920s, even if he were so disposed. The accepted norms where that African American concertgoers typically sat in the balcony of theaters and churches when there were such seating arrangements.

By 1926, however, Hayes had sung with many of the country's major orchestras, performed with some of the world's preeminent conductors, sung for the British royalty in Europe, and been awarded the NAACP's coveted Spingarn Medal (for his service to "the race"). Without question these achievements made him a model for Black America regardless of whether he thought so or not. Nonetheless, his artistic influence and integrity was put to the test in Maryland's most populated and racially diverse city. On January 5, Hayes had been booked to sing in the nation's capital at the Washington Auditorium, to be followed two days later by a concert in Baltimore at that city's Lyric Theater by Mrs. Kate Wilson-Green, a highly respected concert promoter.[36] She had presented the likes of Jascha Heifetz and Sergei Rachmaninoff, among other A-list artists in the DC area, so she was more than capable of producing someone of Hayes's caliber. Mrs. Wilson-Green had booked the now celebrated tenor in the respective venues at least six months before the scheduled concerts.

Leading the onslaught against Jim Crow segregation rules was the NAACP, among other civil rights groups. It had been agreed that Hayes's Washington Auditorium concert would be integrated, but the Lyric Theater engagement on January 7 would not be. The racial slight was enough to attract the attention of the *Baltimore Afro-American*. As a well-established artist, Hayes's prior appearances in the city had drawn large and appreciative audiences and included critical reviews from the best-known and most widely circulated African American newspaper.[37] Like other news outlets which primarily catered to African American communities around the country, the *Afro-American* was also in the forefront of challenging Jim Crow segregation wherever and whenever it could.[38] As with his previous concerts in the city, the paper began announcing the tenor's recital as far back as the previous November, when Hayes's 1925–1926 national tour had gotten under way.

Hayes's January 5 Washington recital was reviewed in the *Washington Daily American* the following day with the headline,

> Roland Hayes Given Ovation at Washington Auditorium: Colored People Scattered throughout Orchestra as Result of the Strenuous Protests against Attempted Segregation.[39]

The January 6, 1926, editions of the *Washington Tribune* and *Washington Daily American* reported more enthusiastic reactions to the tenor's recital:

> Roland Hayes . . . delighted his hearers by his artistry, his dramatic expression and fine restraint in tone effects. . . . Throughout the evening the audience was most enthusiastic, and the applause at times amounted to an ovation.[40]

> Roland Hayes Given Ovation at Washington Auditorium—Famous Tenor Stirs vast audience almost to point of frenzy with Wonderful Rendition of Negro Spirituals.[41]

The reporter from the *Washington Daily American*, however, was less generous in discussing Hayes's participation in Jim Crow segregation. When the *Tribune*'s reporter attempted to seek Roland's opinion about his integrated Washington recital on the evening of the concert, the reporter said the tenor "feigned fatigue and referred him to his secretary—without results."[42] The singer obviously knew of the land mines that lay in wait were he to have answered any questions related to his integrated audience at his Washington concert, especially with the Baltimore engagement coming two days later. Anything said in Washington would easily be relayed in Baltimore just 45 miles north.

As expected, news of the integrated recital in the nation's capital reached Baltimore. Ominously, the city's Black ministers and anti–Jim Crow demonstrators found Roland's "double" standard outrageous. News of his refusal to speak with reporters also did not play well in the city's African American press. The Washington *Afro-American* (a branch of the Baltimore-based paper) ran a story confirming the incident. When Roland and his small entourage arrived in the city, once again, he, his secretary, and William Lawrence stayed at a private residence, the home of Baltimore physician Dr. Edward Wheatley and his wife, Laura.[43]

Hayes arrived by train at Baltimore's Penn Station and encountered a vociferous protest. There were calls for him to cancel his concert if it remained segregated, and he was even called demeaning names in signs which read "Roland 'Uncle Tom' Hayes," and "Jim Crow Roland."[44] From their pulpits the Sunday before, several prominent Baltimorean African American ministers had denounced Hayes's apparent willingness to sing before a Jim Crow segregated audience in the city.[45] The Reverend Dr. Ernest Lyons had said that no "self-respecting colored person" would pay to be Jim Crowed.[46] Some ministers cited the example of the less well-known Hampton Institute conductor, Nathaniel Dett, who had refused to perform at a segregated auditorium in Washington, DC, as setting an appropriate example. Added to that, Dett was an Afro-Canadian who was willing to take a moral stand against segregation, but not the American-born Roland Hayes!

Hayes's stay at the Wheatleys' was anything but peaceful. The deluge of calls from reporters and anti–Jim Crow protesters led the family to temporarily disconnect their telephone. After some orchestrated delays, Hayes agreed to meet with several Baltimore ministers, an *Afro* representative, and other prominent equal rights advocates at the Wheatleys' home the afternoon of his Thursday evening recital. Out of this meeting, it was agreed that he would wire his managers in Boston and ask them to cancel that evening's concert.

Hayes dressed and readied himself to perform, and arrived at the Lyric Theater that evening, where yet another obstreperous group of protesting African Americans waited. He endured a barrage of insults that made the protest at Penn Station the day before appear mild. Some, who had withstood the cold January weather for hours anticipating the tenor's arrival, turned mean-spirited and spat at him while he entered the back entrance of the Lyric. As always, Hayes was publicly dignified, even in the face of such treatment. Kate Wilson-Green, the promoter, was at the theater waiting for the tenor to arrive. When Hayes refused to go through with the recital, describing what he had just endured entering the building, her desperate pleas quickly turned into tears, as she begged the singer to go onstage. Hayes was guaranteed at least $1,000 whether he performed or not, but she and the theater stood to lose much more, had he canceled at the eleventh hour. The standoff took more than half an hour to resolve. Calmly, Hayes walked on onstage followed by an anxious William Lawrence, and made an announcement with a quavering voice and shaking hands, "I may not be able to finish my program. And if I do not finish it, you will know why."[47] Hayes began his concert with the unscheduled arrangement of the "Crucifixion," for which he was well known. When he completed the work, the polite applause made clear that the audience was receptive, with a few exceptions. He also sang Schubert's "Du Bis die Ruh" (You Are the Calm), which worked for him in 1924 when he confronted a hostile Berlin audience and won them over by the sheer beauty of his singing.[48] But Baltimore in January 1926 was no Berlin. Hayes had transformed that irate German audience's hisses and boos into adulation when he had handily demonstrated his artistry. But the tenor's primary detractors that wintry Thursday night at Baltimore's Lyric Theater were his own people!

Although the Lyric concert was a success, various Baltimore readers and opinion makers wrote to the *Afro-American* and would not let the issue go away. Beginning with the January 9 edition of the weekly, the editorials and commentaries poured in. "Flay Roland Hayes for Jim Crow" was the headline of the early edition of the paper. Predictably, there were calls for him to return his Spingarn Medal, saying he had failed to stand up for "the race" on this crucial issue. An editorial in the January 9 *Afro* said that African American restaurants should refuse to serve the singer, and if he wanted to eat let him go to "Mrs. Wilson Green's kitchen for a meal."[49] An editorial one week later titled "'Rolling' Hayes" said that, despite his education at Fisk University in Tennessee, as well as in New England, Hayes was ultimately from rural Georgia. Thus, it said, proving that old adage that it was easier to "take the man out of the country than it was to take the country out of the man."[50] The same editorial also decried Kate Wilson-Green, who had "ignorantly" declared that one part of the theater was as good as the other.[51] Some of Hayes's white supporters who had attended his concert praised his bravery for singing under such difficult conditions and denounced his critics as unsophisticated troublemakers. Such callous remarks from whites (however well-meaning) only fueled this very volatile issue.

Eventually, average *Afro* readers weighed into the fray. With the simple heading, "'Afro' Readers Blame Roland Hayes for Lyric Jim Crow," more than twenty individual views were expressed. Starting with Laura Wheatley, who had hosted the tenor and his small entourage when they were in the city:

> Mr. Hayes was my house guest while in the city. The circumstance at the theater was most unfortunate. Mr. Hayes seemed really not to know that there was going to be any separation in the audience until he got to the theater. Had he known before, I believe he would not have sung. However, as matters stand his singing here has softened many of our enemies, has gained new friends for us and bound many of our old friends closer to us.
>
>   Mrs. Laura D. Wheatley, 1230 Druid Hill Avenue.[52]

> I think that Roland Hayes should not have sung before a segregated audience.
>   Mrs. Mary Brown, 226 W. Chase Str.

> It is unfortunate for the colored [sic] people of the city that Roland Hayes performed before a separate audience.
>   Mrs. Lula Richardson, 216 Dolphin Street.

> Personally, I feel Mr. Hayes committed no imposition upon his race in performing for a segregated audience inasmuch as he was engaged by the whites.
>   Rev. J. J. Barnes, 553 W. Biddle Street.

> Mr. Hayes was right in performing before a separate audience as his concerts are for monetary gain.
>   David H. Parham, musician, 229 W. Hamburg Street.

> Mr. Hayes should not have violated the integrity of his race for gold.
>   William H. Brown, musician 278 St. Mary Street.

Mr. Hayes committed a serious infringement against the integrity of his race in singing before a segregated audience.
Milton Green, 1406 Myrtle Avenue.

An article in the following issue of the *Afro* stated that Hayes heroically gave Kate Wilson-Green a piece of his mind, while he delayed the concert. But in the minds of many African American Baltimoreans, they believed that Hayes in the end had taken his 30 pieces of silver and *sang!* The debate over Hayes's performance at the Lyric Theater in Baltimore that January 1926 continued in the *Afro* off and on for another three years. The Baltimore incident aside, Hayes was at his performing height throughout the 1920s. However, the effect of the Depression would affect him as it did many of his friends, colleagues, and family. A few years later, Roland Hayes went yet another round with Jim Crow and segregated seating in the concert hall. The setting of this brawl was Washington, DC, in 1931, and once again it was Kate Wilson-Green who was the promoter at the center of the drama. Five years after presenting Hayes at the Lyric Theater in Baltimore, Wilson-Green had scheduled the tenor to sing a recital at Constitution Hall, which had been built by the Daughters of the American Revolution (DAR). She had presented him in the city at least two times since Baltimore without incident. Hayes's January 1931 appearance at Constitution Hall had been announced in the *Washington Post* nine months earlier and at least twice afterward before the concert.[53]

The custom of the period was for African Americans to be segregated when they were allowed to attend an event in the theater, but tickets could be sold in blocks through a surrogate organization or society. Constitution Hall's general manager, Fred Hand, had apparently allowed limited use of the facility by African American groups or individuals before the Hayes incident.[54] The evening of the Saturday concert, Hayes walked on stage followed by Percival Parham, his latest accompanist[55] and immediately noticed a block of African Americans sitting together in the orchestra left. He recognized it as a classic hallmark of a Jim Crow–style segregated group sell, which he had seen on countless occasions. Although there were a few African Americans scattered in other parts of the theater, Hayes announced to the audience that he would not sing to a segregated gathering. After a pregnant pause of a minute or so, he turned, motioned to Parham and the pair walked off stage.

The singer insisted that he would not return until the audience was desegregated.[56] Hayes remained backstage for more than 30 minutes, while no one in the audience, Black or white, budged from their seats. Unbeknownst to him at the time that he was backstage, Fred Hand, the hall's manager, had walked down the aisle and stood with folded arms where African Americans were segregated, as if to intimidate them from leaving their seats.[57] Bewildered by Hayes's pronouncement, they stayed where they were. Kate Wilson-Green's role in this scenario is a mystery, but after the Baltimore incident, it is certain that she would have been mindful of the tenor's sensitivities around Jim Crow segregation. Hayes eventually returned to the stage and sang the recital, ignoring his earlier demand. Fred Hand, in the meantime, was so "infuriated" with the tenor's petulant demonstration that he vowed no other African American artist would perform at Constitution Hall while he was manager.[58]

The *Washington Post*'s next-day review, "Negro Spirituals Win Hayes Praise," focused on the "scope of the [tenor's] genius," and described how artistically he delivered the works of the great art music composers. As the headline implied, of course, his interpretation of spirituals was the most noteworthy.[59] The review said nothing of the singer's staged demonstration before the concert.[60] Although Hayes had made yet another gallant attempt to stand up to segregation at his Constitution Hall concert, after the bout was over and the dust had settled, the score was Jim Crow–2 wins, Roland Hayes–0.

A year after Hayes's demonstration, Fred Hand, and the board of the DAR formally adopted a "White Artists–Only" policy for the use of Constitution Hall. Apparently, there had earlier been a quietly kept agreement between a few board members of the DAR and a major donor to exclude all but white artists once the Constitution Hall was completed. After Hayes's brief protest, Fred Hand simply invoked that policy openly.[61] It took the highly publicized 1939 Marian Anderson incident, denying her use of the venue, and the subsequent international controversy (including First Lady Eleanor Roosevelt resigning her membership in the DAR) to focus attention on Constitution Hall's discriminatory practice.[62]

By late 1931, Hayes was increasingly becoming involved with Alzada. She had moved into his home in Brookline, Boston, and managed it during his travels. Although they quietly wedded in the spring of 1932 in California, he kept his relationship with another woman, Countess Bertha (as well as their daughter in France) a secret.[63] Still the countess's influence on the tenor had been significant. Following her lead, Hayes began consulting astrologers and numerologists, a practice he continued for the remainder of his life.[64] His relationship with Alzada was very different from that with Countess Bertha. His letters lacked the passion and flowery language he used with the European aristocrat like "my revealer of wonders," or "my comfort," or "I need you so." Instead, his letters referred to Alzada as "Tootsie, Wootsie—How is my child today? So glad to get your letter, dear. I just love you, my little darling!" He concluded his letter with, "Much love, my little 'Brown doll' from Rolly."⁶⁵

The impact of the Depression throughout the 1930s was devastating in most sectors of the American economy, and Hayes's career was no exception. Still, the wily tenor, always career-conscious, was determined to remain before the public and artistically relevant. By the mid-1930s, he was forced to accept $750 per performance when just a few years earlier he would have received $2,500.⁶⁶ Seeking to imitate the success of Paul Robeson in the movie industry, Hayes made overtures to various Hollywood managers and producers to have a movie of his life produced. When those efforts were not successful, Hayes attempted to capitalize on the situation. On January 20, 1934, an article appeared in the *Boston Chronicle* with the headline, "Noted Tenor Cancels Race Libel Film" with the subheading "Refuses to Accept Hollywood's Version of His Life's Story."⁶⁷ On the same date, an article appeared in the *Pittsburgh Courier* with similar information. It's heading and subheading read "Roland Hayes, Despite Success, Turns Back on Fame to Join Hands with His Own People; White Management No Longer Directs Singer's Concerts; Will Try to Build New Contacts after Movie Failure."⁶⁸ Although the *Chronicle* and *Courier* articles both mention that the tenor did not approve of some of the content of a movie project, rather than betray his race for money, he simply walked away from the project. No other specifics were mentioned. This was most certainly a publicity effort to spin his failed negotiations. Hayes was the only source for both stories. It is more likely that this was his attempt to resuscitate his floundering career during the national Depression.

BEATEN IN GEORGIA
SAYS Roland HAYES
Negro Singer Asserts He and
Wife Were Put in Cell After
a Store Dispute
POLICE MAKE A DENIAL
Charges of Being Slugged and
Dragged Into Patrol Car Are
Not True, Says Chief⁶⁹

This was the headline (and bylines) of the July 17, 1942, *New York Times* reporting on events that took place in Rome, Georgia, just six days earlier. The news account came from the African American owned *Atlanta Daily Word* on July 15.⁷⁰ On Saturday, July 11, the Hayes family went shopping for tennis shoes for their nine-year-old daughter Afrika in nearby Rome. While Hayes went to try on hats, Alzada and Afrika went to Higgins Shoe in the downtown area. Alzada and Afrika briefly sat under a fan on the sweltering day, which happened to be in a segregated white area. When she was ordered to move by a store clerk, Alzada protested, "This is not the time to talk about racial prejudice and segregation. [Adolph] Hitler ought to have you,"[71] before leaving the store to shop elsewhere. After she found her husband, he insisted it had to be a misunderstanding and returned to the store to speak to the owner, Fred Higgins. He asked a salesperson in the store to assist Alzada, but she politely declined indicating that she had gone to another store.[72]

Alzada left Afrika with her father, but in minutes heard her daughter's unmistakable scream coming from the direction of Higgins's store. By the time she made it to her daughter standing alone, a crowd had formed, and she instinctively knew her husband was at the center of it. When Alzada made it through, she witnessed her husband being beaten by several local police in the back of a police car. She began protesting right away, but that only encouraged the police to become more aggressive. Eventually, she was ordered into the car along with Afrika and they were all taken to the local jail.[73] Hayes and Alzada were booked and placed in jail cells. When she was asked her name, Alzada defiantly said, "*Mrs. Hayes!*" The policemen drew back his fist as if he was going to punch her and said, "God dammit! Don't ch'u say no 'Mrs.' to me."[74] The couple were placed in a cell together with their daughter crying on the outside staring at them.[75] The celebrated tenor and his wife were incarcerated for at least an hour before he was allowed to post the $50 bail. After the event was reported by the *Atlanta Daily Word*, the story took on a life of its own. By then, Hayes had amalgamated a Who's Who of prominent African Americans who championed his cause. The reaction to the *Times* story was swift and sustained. One day after the July 17 article appeared, Hayes began receiving letters and telegrams of condolence and support. Hayes's New York manager, Ray Halmans, who, having read the story in the *Herald-Tribune*, wrote to him saying that her heart "ached" that he would be subjected to such "indignities and vile treatment."[76] Other communications from around the country came pouring into Hayes at Angelmo Farm. "Sister Mary" (McLeod Bethune as she was known to Hayes) wrote:

> Not until last night did the distressing news of the outrage upon you and your family reach me. I have failed to sleep. My wails and prayers have been loud to a God who must hear and understand why should such treatment come to you and yours. All America is distressed—white and black. All that can be done will be done. Our souls are stirred. WE are suffering with you. If I am needed in person, let me know.
> Mary McLeod Bethune[77]

Hayes received official communications from several organizations like the Department of Race Relations of the Federal Council of the Churches of Christ in America; the United Christian Youth Movement; the Boston Symphony Orchestra; the president and alumni association of Fisk University (encouraging all Fiskites to rally to the side of their famous alum); the Haines Normal and Industrial Institute in Augusta, Georgia; African American (and white) Freemason lodges from around the country; the Workers Defense League; and various boards of education throughout the United States. Lawyers from around the country offered their services pro bono to sue the guilty parties.[78] The National Association for Improving Negro Country Life, based at Georgia State College, invited him to sit on the board of directors. He received letters of solidarity and support from the composer William Grant Still, who was in Los Angeles; he heard from his good friend from his early days in Boston, Charles Harris (not to be confused with the Rome, Georgia, chief of police by the same name), who was still teaching at South Carolina State in Orangeburg.

Hayes also heard from many unknown well-wishers, Black and white. Such letters came from concerned individuals like Mrs. Valeno Costello and her family in Biloxi, Mississippi, who said, in part,

> I want to say this to you. This thing happened to you, true enough, but, just be thankful to our God that they did not take away your life completely. I imagine, that really was what they were trying to do.
>
> They are jealous of you because you have climbed your ladder to success in your singing. Now they want to destroy you because your skin is dark.
>
> It seems to us, that God is taking his own time in giving our race a brake [sic]. . . . What has been done to you will never be forgotten, but, try to be strong and courageous.[79]

An even larger number of well-meaning European Americans wrote Hayes from different parts of the country. When the incident was reported in *Time* magazine,[80] it brought another round of letters like those from H. L. Smith of Madison, Wisconsin, who wrote:

> You will probably receive many crackpot letters after the article in TIME magazine, but there must hundreds who are thoroughly indignant at the way you and Mrs. Hayes were treated. It may make some of us wonder what we are fighting for, when such a large section of the country doesn't even know the meaning of the word Democracy.

One thing is clear, and that is that every time an intelligent, useful member of your race reacts with dignity and largeness of spirit, you put us one step nearer to the ultimate brotherhood of man, for which we are really fighting. In the encounter you came out second best, but because you acted with restraint, you arouse the sympathy of thousands who believe in fair play and democracy.[81]

To many of these well-wishers, Hayes sent a generic response. That is, that he was grateful for their concern and support; that the assault was an outrageous and shameful act; that while his head was bloodied, it was not bowed; that the unfortunate policemen of Rome, Georgia, brutalized and manhandled him and threw him and his wife in a dingy cell and exposed his young child to such unnecessary indecencies. But that ultimately, he had confidence in *all* people who worked for justice and decency throughout the land.[82] That was Hayes's official and public position. Behind the scenes, however, the tenor was totally degraded and outraged. He wanted certain and swift redress for the dastardly behavior for all of those who had carried off this humiliation against him and his family. Whether it was the influence of "Sister Mary," or his close friend and fellow Georgian, Walter White ("Mr. NAACP" as he had come to be known), or a combination of many others, the Roland Hayes case resonated at the highest levels of the state and federal government. It eventually spread beyond the shores of the country.

In the meantime, the Hayes assault in Rome, Georgia, had become an international cause célèbre. Hayes received a letter from a Senor M. A. Contreras of Havana, Cuba, who described himself as "100% white," expressing outrage at the attack that he had suffered and solidarity with him in the tenor's conciliatory statement that "the humiliation [was] on the other side." An even stronger and more personal expression of support came from the United Kingdom. Robert Broadhurst, the singer's beloved "Tarah" (the "African" name that Hayes had called Broadhurst, and he was called "Cunjah") bemoaned the fact that he and Hayes had been out of contact with each other for such a long time, but wanted to assure his friend that he and many others of African ancestry throughout greater London were in total solidarity with him and his family.[83] After Broadhurst's communication came a more formal letter of support signed by many of the important continental Africans and Afro-Britons, similar to the one the tenor had been given 22 years earlier. This letter, however, was far from congratulatory. It had as its basis, an indictment against the United States and its regressive social policies regarding its African American citizenry:

5 September 1942

Mr. Roland Hayes
58 Allerton Street
Brookline, Boston,
Mass., U.S.A.

Dear Mr. Hayes:
We the undersigned, British Colonials of African descent in London, have heard with profound indignation of the cowardly assault made upon you and your family in Rome, Georgia. Permit us to avail ourselves of this opportunity to express to you and Mrs. Hayes our heartfelt sympathy. At a time like this when our two nations are supposed to be fighting to uphold democratic institutions and the Rights of Man, the disgraceful behavior of public officials in Rome and the cynical attitude of Governor Talmadge can only serve to undermine the faith of Coloured peoples everywhere in the cause of the United Nations.[84]

As was the case with the October 1920 document, the most eminent scholars, physicians, lawyers, diplomats, students, and businesspersons of African ancestry in London at the time, signed it.

Some months after Hayes experienced the most humiliating and overtly racial incident of his life, his friend Langston Hughes published an essay titled "My America."[85] In it, Hughes with "clear and unprejudiced eyes," set out to assess social conditions in the 1940s United States, as it was defending democracy in Europe and in other parts of the world. In this somewhat toned-down reality check on the record of the country, Langston Hughes pointed out that while foreigners of European extraction could come to this country and become naturalized citizens; could subsequently be guaranteed the right to travel throughout the land as they desired; buy food anywhere they chose; stay in a hotel anywhere where they were inclined to rest their heads; buy tickets to concerts of their liking; attend theater productions anywhere in the land as they so fancied; travel on any railroad; and vote in Texas, and Mississippi as it was their constitutional right to do so; *he,* as a native-born citizen of African ancestry, could not. Hughes then focused on the celebrated singer's Rome, Georgia, incident specifically:

America is a land where the best of all democracies has been achieved for some people but in Georgia, Roland Hayes, the world-famous singer is beaten for being colored and nobody is jailed—nor can Mr. Hayes vote in the State where he was born. Yet America is a country where Roland Hayes *can* come from a log cabin to wealth and fame in spite of the segment that still wishes to maltreat him physically and spiritually, famous though he is.[86]

There were few who knew how to capitalize on the Rome, Georgia, assault better than Roland Hayes. It placed him back on the front pages of many papers throughout the country, and in 1942 he was 55 years old when many singers are beginning to anticipate retirement. Added to that, Hayes's autobiographical account, *Angel Mo' and Her Son Roland Hayes,* was released that year, and after the Rome incident the sales of his book increased exponentially.[87] He made sure many of those who had supported him during the assault incident received signed copies of the work, including First Lady Eleanor Roosevelt.[88] Even the Baltimore-based *Afro-American* was among the papers which sent correspondents to Angelmo Farm to interview the tenor. It was almost as if the paper was doing penance for how he had been criticized by the biweekly publication 16 years earlier after his performance at the Lyric Theater.

In near total secrecy, Hayes returned to London as a musical ambassador on behalf of the US Army in September 1943 while World War II was raging around him. The plan was for him to be the featured soloist with a choral group of 200 African American soldiers accompanied by the London Symphony Orchestra. It was not until Hayes had landed in the United Kingdom and cleared all medical tests that he alerted a few back home of his travel to war-torn Europe. The US military press apparatus then announced his arrival in the country. The performance was advertised as "The United States Army (the European Theatre of Operations) in collaboration with the *Daily Express* presents a U.S. Army Negro Chorus of 200 Voices with Roland Hayes and the London Symphony Orchestra conducted by Technical Sergeant Hugo Weisgall."[89] Several of the singing soldiers had formal musical training and were thrilled at the opportunity to perform with the celebrated tenor.[90] The performances received widespread coverage, and Hayes remembered the "Power" and significance of being onstage with this 200+ group of polished African American soldiers.[91]

It is what happened to Hayes after his performances in the United Kingdom that had greater baring on his role in race relations in the US military at the time. Hayes was approached by the US ambassador when he arrived in

England, who asked if he would conduct a field investigation in the hope of preventing further racial outbreaks among the American enlisted ranks. As a special attaché for the U.S. military, he would investigate the complaints of racial discrimination registered by several African American soldiers stationed throughout the United Kingdom. Hayes's own high-profile Rome, Georgia, assault was well known and was, to be sure, a factor in him being invited by US military officials to England. Hayes was asked to stay behind after his engagements to speak to several groups of soldiers.[92]

At the heart of the African American soldiers' complaints was their resentment of the treatment they received by their white superior officers and countrymen, whom they called "Paddies."[93] Hayes spent more than ten days traveling throughout the country and meeting African American soldiers including stops in "Salzburg" (which in this case was being used as a code for an undisclosed geographical location in the United Kingdom), Bristol, Savranake, Plymouth, and of course, the greater London area. The soldier's comments were generic, but they were all too familiar to the tenor. While they found their contact with the British citizenry to be receptive, if not friendly regarding their presence in the country, the white American soldiers were quick to discourage any such contact and used all available military means to prevent it. If it meant humiliating the Black soldiers, perpetuating demeaning racial stereotypes (e.g., spreading falsehoods that Black men had tails like monkeys, that they had an instinct for violence, and that they were natural sexual predators, among others), using the military police inappropriately, or urging the white officers to restrict their liberties on trumped up charges or vague suspicions, it was done.

True to his "Jim Crow segregation leanings" (meaning his hesitancy to challenge the status quo), Hayes did not advocate for outright desegregation in the military ranks (which of course did not take place until the Truman administration), but simply argued that those rules that were in place should be enforced. In practical terms, the singer opined that since the soldiers knew there was segregation within the military, they should not resist it. However, he urged in his report that the military structure needed to be consistent with its existing regulations and not allow blatant instances of racial animus to go unchallenged. He further suggested that the military should place "handpicked" sensitivity officers on the bases where the African American soldiers could go to if they felt they had been aggrieved in some overt manner. It would be the role of these "trusted" officers to enforce military regulations when cases of abuse could be demonstrated. This "equal treatment" among the ranks, the tenor argued, would go a long way to softening the racial tensions that he observed throughout his investigation.[94]

As an added suggestion, Hayes proposed that the 200-voice African American chorus that he had recently performed with be kept in place by the military and allowed to perform throughout the United Kingdom. This, he felt, would be a gesture of good will and demonstrate to the British population and white American soldiers alike the accomplishments of the spit and polished Black soldiers. It likely never entered Hayes's mind that this particular suggestion (i.e., that Blacks be allowed to entertain whites, as they had throughout the history of the United States) was, in many ways, at the core of the African American soldier's complaint. Most white Americans saw their Black countrymen as "natural performers" and entertainers and thus it was an acceptable role for them. The Black soldiers, on the other hand, wanted respect, as men and in that situation, as fighting men. As watered down as they may have seemed, these were some of the suggestions that Hayes offered in his report to the ambassador and the military structure. To what extent they were acted on is not known.

Apparently unknown to the U.S. military structure based in Britain or the American embassy personnel, after his return to the United States, Hayes submitted a semi-anonymous letter from the African American soldiers directly to First Lady Eleanor Roosevelt at the White House. In his preface to the letter, he wrote the First Lady about his recent trip to Great Britain. Hayes reported on the success of his concerts and supported his assertion with thank-you letters that he received from the US ambassador and the military officers as well as the glowing reviews of his engagements. He then reported on his "invited" assignment to the First Lady and saw it as his "patriotic duty" to bring the situation to the attention of the president and to her.[95] In his meetings with Black and white officers, large and small groups, Red Cross workers in various locations throughout the United Kingdom, Hayes reported his observations.

The First Lady responded to Hayes's November 8 letter. In a written communication dated November 23, the First Lady expressed her concerns about the racial discrimination among the military ranks and said that she would report this directly to the president, General George Marshall (US military chief of staff), and a "Mr. McCloy." She also agreed with Hayes that it was the white people who needed to be educated, but acknowledged the difficulty of that challenge.[96] A month after receiving the response from Mrs. Roosevelt, Hayes wrote his friend Noël Sullivan in California reporting that he had "kept [his] pledge to our men in Arms to report their situation to men in the high places of our Nation."[97] This was Hayes at his racially conscious and patriotic height.

Fall 1947 marked a milestone in the tenor's career. It had been 30 years since he had taken the audacious action and rented Boston's Symphony Hall for a solo recital. Hayes highlighted the occasion with another recital and set out to identify several of the 1917 attendees, whom he believed took a chance on a young and unknown singer 30 years earlier. He received letters from several of these loyal patrons, who had since become steadfast supporters. Also marking the thirtieth anniversary milestone, *The Christian Science Monitor* did a feature story on the tenor. After summarizing his early experience in Georgia and Tennessee (including the obligatory information about his formerly enslaved mother), and his subsequent arrival to Boston more than 30 years earlier, Hayes addressed himself to issues of racial equality and parity. His statement to Laura Haddock seemed to summarize his long-held views on this delicate and controversial issue:

> I feel 95½ percent of the Negro-white problem is the responsibility of the Negro. It is not enough for the Negro to say, "I have certain gifts. Why am I not permitted to contribute and develop them to the full?" He must prove he has these gifts and that they are worthy of taking their place alongside the good and great contributors of all races. . . . I could have fought prejudice in words and actions all my way, but how far would it have gotten me? I had to prove myself and my art as being worthy of what I sought.
>
> Now I have the satisfaction of seeing that it has paved the way for others-four or five of my race who are fine artists.[98]

It was such statements (i.e., that African Americans needed to prove themselves "worthy" of the white man's respect) that caused Roland to drift again and again into troubled waters with many within the African American civil rights community at the time. When he had had the opportunity to stand up to Jim Crow in a forceful way, he did not, despite the level of protection his popularity would have given him. The idea of taking the blame from where it belonged and placing it with African Americans seemed backward to many civil rights activists.[99]

In the late 1940s, Hayes produced another volume titled *My Songs*. In it, he introduced the term "Aframerican." According to him the term, "Negro is a misnomer," and he believed "Aframerican" to better reflect those Africans transplanted to the United States.[100] In the late 1940s, not even the most progressive African American leaders (including Du Bois and the like) said such things. This was still a time when most Black Americans were still inclined to run away from their African ancestry because of the many negative stereotypes they had been fed throughout their experience in America.[101] Hayes had not even intimated such language in *Angel Mo'*.

It is worth noting that even though Hayes never made it to Africa (as his friend Robert Broadhurst had wished to see come about), he followed with great interest the independence movements on the African continent from the late 1950s into the 1960s. Although he repeatedly received invitations to visit newly independent West African countries including Ghana, Ivory Coast, and Nigeria, he never made it there. Hayes remained a lifelong admirer of Emperor Haile Selassie and often spoke of him as the ideal African leader right up until the time of the deposed Ethiopian monarch's death in the mid-1970s. Although it was carried out in total stealth, the tenor performed for the exiled Ethiopian leader when the later lived in Britain in the 1930s.

In short, an argument for Roland Hayes as an African American activist and supporter of the race could be easily made. However, during his lifetime many saw him as the antithesis of a "race" leader. He was not in the tradition of Du Bois, Garvey, and many well-known names, but his legacy has been preserved and is available for scrutiny by other scholars and interested readers.

Notes

1 These were most renowned orchestra conductors of the era. Leopold Stokowski, Eugene Ormandy, Bruno Walter, and Otto Klemperer became conducting legends.
2 Paul Robeson, Marian Anderson, Todd Duncan, and Dorothy Maynor were all groundbreaking African American vocal artist. Marian Anderson would be the first African American to sing a solo role at the Metropolitan Opera in 1955. Todd Duncan debuted the role of Porgy in Gershwin's opera *Porgy and Bess*. Dorothy Maynor also had a major career as a classical vocalist. She retired from her career and founded the Harlem School for the Arts in 1964.
3 MacKinley Helm, *Angel Mo' and Her Son Roland Hayes* (Boston: Little, Brown, 1942), 6.
4 Christopher A. Brooks and Robert Sims, *Roland Hayes: The Legacy of an American Tenor* (Bloomington: Indiana University Press, 2015), 13.
5 Brooks and Sims, *Roland Hayes*, 13.
6 Daisy Robinson Tapley (1882–1925) was a gifted keyboardist (piano and organ), but her claim to fame was as a celebrated contralto. In 1910 Tapley became the first African American women to record commercially. She also performed in Europe and established herself as a musical maven in New York between 1910s and the mid-1920s.
7 Christopher A. Brooks, "Love's Old Sweet Song: The Life and Times of Daisy Robinson Tapley" (manuscript completed and in review).
8 Brooks and Sims, *Roland Hayes*, 22.

9 Brooks and Sims, 34.
10 Brooks and Sims, 62. Hayes met many continental Africans.
11 Brooks and Sims, 58.
12 Brooks and Sims, 58.
13 Brooks and Sims, 59
14 Brooks and Sims, 58.
15 Brooks and Sims, 58.
16 "Amodu Tijani, Chief Oluwa of Lagos," National Portrait Gallery, accessed October 21, 2020, https://www.npg.org.uk/collections/search/person/mp51013/amodu-tijani-chief-oluwa-of-lagos?search=sas&sText=Amodu+Tijani%2C+Chief+Oluwa+of+Lagos
17 *Amodu Tijani v. The Secretary of the Southern Provinces* (1921).
18 Brooks and Sims, *Roland Hayes*, 62.
19 Jeffrey Green, "Alcindor, John," *Oxford Dictionary of National Biography* (online ed.). Born Ferdinand Lewis "Lou" Alcindor Jr., John Alcindor is the great-uncle of Kareem Abdul Jabbar.
20 African Progress Union, "The African Progress Union Annual Report, 1921–1922," 1922. W. E. B. Du Bois Papers (MS 312). Special Collections and University Archives, University of Massachusetts Amherst Libraries. Among the women admitted by 1922 were Alcindor's wife and the wives of other male members.
21 Hayes Papers, Detroit Public Library, letter dated October 28, 1920. See also Brooks and Sims, *Roland Hayes,* 63.
22 Brooks and Sims, 63.
23 By 1922, the organization had begun admitting women as committee members. There were at least eight women listed among the 20-member organization. Roland Hayes's friend, Robert Broadhurst had resigned and was replaced by a woman, Miss Emma Smith.
24 Brooks and Sims, *Roland Hayes,* 69.
25 Helm, *Angel Mo',* 136.
26 "African Progress Union Annual Report," 2.
27 Cengage, *Houghton Mifflin Company's History Companion.*
28 Cengage, *Houghton Mifflin.*
29 Helm, *Angel Mo',* 149. According to Hayes, he and Brown were staying at the Mont Thabor Hotel, which was centrally located near several tourist attractions. A white American couple saw Brown in the lobby and after realizing he was a guest demanded that the hotel put him and Hayes out. The hotel found them other accommodations and had their mail forwarded to them at the other facility.
30 Patrick Manning, *Francophone Sub-Saharan Africa: 1880–1985* (New York: Cambridge University Press, 1988).
31 Helm, *Angel Mo',* 35. The story of Hayes's West African great-grandfather had been passed along to him through family lore. After meeting Princes Tovalou and Oanilo in Paris in 1922, they informed him that the "Abá 'Ougi," was also from a royal clan in their country.
32 The French colonial practice of "mission civilisatrice" (civilizing missions) was the practice of converting colonized subjects and encouraging them to adapt the French way of life, including language and other practices.

33 Brooks and Sims, *Roland Hayes*, 129. Hayes would have kept such a meeting.
34 Sal Fradella, *Jack Johnson* (Boston: Branden, 1990).
35 Brooks and Sims, *Roland Hayes*, 140–143.
36 Hayes Papers.
37 Hayes's very favorable treatment by the paper had dated back for at least a decade by this time.
38 The exception to this rule, however, was those news organizations in the south. The African American papers in southern states tended to be more tepid about such issues, if not more accommodating of such practices. Many of them had to rely on white business advertising dollars.
39 *Washington Daily American*, January 6, 1926.
40 *Washington Tribune*, January 6, 1926.
41 *Washington Daily American*, January 6, 1926.
42 *Washington Tribune*, January 6, 1926.
43 Laura Wheatley was the president of Baltimore's Colored Parents Teachers Association at the time of the incident. She became somewhat of a concert promoter in her own right.
44 Helm, *Angel Mo'*, 201. Once again, the account in *Angel Mo'* contrasts with other version of these events. In Hayes's account, he arrived in Baltimore the day of the concert; however, in several others (i.e., newspaper accounts and other private correspondence), he arrived the day before and stayed in the Wheatley home. See also the account reported in the Baltimore *Afro-American*, January 9, 1926.
45 *Afro-American*, January 9, 1926.
46 *Afro-American*, January 9, 1926.
47 Helm, *AngelMo and Her Son*, 201. Also *Afro-American*, January 16, 1926. Other live accounts indicate that there was a disturbance inside the theater similar to that which Hayes experienced in the 1924 Berlin recital.
48 Brooks and Sims, *Roland Hayes*, 120–122.
49 *Afro-American*, January 9, 1926.
50 *Afro-American*, January 16. 1926.
51 Brooks and Sims, *Roland Hayes*, 149–151.
52 *Afro-American*, January 16, 1926. Despite what Laura Wheatley wrote in her editorial, she and Hayes were fully aware of the Jim Crow situation that he was going to confront at the Lyric Theater and for reasons that were not entirely clear chose to go forward with the recital.
53 *Washington Post*, April 27, 1930, A3. See also *Washington Post*, January 18, 1931, and January 25, 1931, respectively.
54 Alan Keiler, *Marian Anderson: A Singer's Journey* (Chicago: University of Chicago Press, 2002), 186. Keiler indicated that the Hampton choir was allowed to perform there, because it was an educational organization, and it was a benefit performance.
55 By this time, Hayes and William Lawrence had parted ways with some acrimony after the pianist informed the tenor that he would not travel with him to the Soviet Union at the last minute. Richard Percival Parham jumped at the chance to work with Hayes, and the two had a very fruitful professional relationship and friendship for twelve years. It only ended after Parham died in 1938. Hayes was totally left bereft at his friend and musical partner's death.

56 Patrick Hayes, "White Artists Only," *Washingtonian,* April 1989, 95–103. See also Raymond Arsenault, *The Sound of Freedom, Marian Anderson, the Lincoln Memorial, and the Concert that Awakened America* (New York: Bloomsbury Press), 92. It may be a different edition. Please use the one you found on Google.
57 Hayes, "White Artists Only."
58 Hayes, "White Artists Only."
59 "Negro Spirituals Win Hayes Praise," *Washington Post,* February 1, 1931, M12.
60 "Negro Spirituals Win Hayes Praise."
61 Arsenault, *Sound of Freedom,* 91.
62 See Keiler, *Marian Anderson,* 186–211, for a more detailed discussion of the events leading to the Marian Anderson incident.
63 Hayes's private papers, courtesy of A. Hayes Lambe. Among these papers was a large envelope that had once been sealed (which was opened before the author's receiving this material). On front of the large envelope was written in the handwriting of the elderly Roland Hayes, "This envelope is to be opened *ONLY* by *my—wife Helen Alzada Hayes*—Otherwise, it must be destroyed without being opened by anyone [signed] *Roland W. Hayes.* " As this envelope had been opened (and it cannot be ascertained whether it was done before or after Hayes's death) when it reached the author in spring 2008, the recipient, (presumably Alzada Hayes), apparently chose not to destroy its contents. The documents inside establish the birth and attempted "adoption" of Hayes and Bertha's daughter, Maya. It also documented how their daughter had been ruled as the illegitimate daughter of the Countess Colloredo-Mansfeld that she had had (though she was married to the count when the child was born) by a tribunal in Switzerland. Also found in the envelope were several letters written by Countess Bertha to Hayes and his representative attempting to conceal their relationship in the late 1920s, as it had begun to appear in news accounts in Europe and the United States.
64 In addition to hiring the New York–based numerologist and character specialist Blanche Watson, whom he consulted about his relationship with Alzada, Hayes consulted with specialists in this area. After Watson placed her name, "Helen Alzada Mann," in a numerical grid, she gave the tenor a written assessment of her character and pronounced her suitability as a mate. Hayes then moved forward to court and eventually to marry Alzada. In the late 1950s, Hayes sought out parapsychologist Karlis Osis at Duke University to arrange a séance at which Mother Fannie apparently appeared.
65 Brooks and Sims, *Roland Hayes,* 204.
66 On occasion, Hayes would accept an engagement for a "special" fee of $500 but did not encourage such a practice.
67 *Boston Chronicle,* January 20, 1934.
68 *Pittsburgh Courier,* January 20, 1934.
69 *New York Times,* July 17, 1942.
70 *Atlanta Daily Word,* July 15, 1942.
71 *New York Times,* July 17, 1942.
72 Brooks and Sims, *Roland Hayes,* 243.
73 A. H. Lambe, personal communication, April 2007.
74 A. H. Lambe.

75 A. H. Lambe.
76 Hayes Papers. See letter dated July 17, 1942.
77 Hayes Papers. See telegram dated July 18, 1942.
78 Hayes private papers, courtesy of Afrika H. Lambe.
79 Hayes Papers. See letter dated July 28, 1942.
80 *Time* (magazine), July 27, 1942. This article recounted the fundamental highlights of the story but prefaced it with information about two previous racial incidents before the Hayes assault.
81 Hayes Papers. See letter dated July 25, 1942.
82 There were several variations of his responses, but these were the main themes that he focused on in them. If Roland received negative mail, which certainly was a strong possibility, he seems to have discarded such communications.
83 Hayes Papers. See letter dated August 26, 1942.
84 Hayes Papers. See letter dated September 6, 1942.
85 Langston Hughes, "My America," *Journal of Educational Sociology* 16, no. 6, special issue: "United We Stand" (February 1943): 334–336.
86 Hughes, "My America,'" 335.
87 Brooks and Sims, *Roland Hayes*, 258–259.
88 Brooks and Sims, 258–259.
89 The Royal Albert Hall Playbill, September 28, 1943. After completing his service in the US Army, Weisgall became a celebrated conductor and composer in his own right.
90 Private First Class Kenneth Cantril, of Springfield, Missouri, who had a solo in one the works presented in the series of performances, had already sung with the St. Louis Municipal Opera Association and continued his vocal studies in Britain when time allowed. He was also a talented keyboardist as well.
91 "Coloured Soldiers Give a Concert at the Albert Hall," *Picture Post Magazine* 21, no. 3 (October 16, 1943): 18. Hiram Swain, a white soldier from Rome, Georgia, wrote Roland while he was in England with the nebulous but mandatory heading "Somewhere in England," attempting to explain to the tenor that they had met once before on his farm when he had to drive a bank cashier from Rome to Angelmo Farm some years earlier. Swain apologized for not being able to attend the singer's concert in London even though some of his fellow American soldiers were able to be there. Hayes also penned an essay titled "Power," to remember this transformative moment in his career.
92 Brooks and Sims, *Roland Hayes*, 264.
93 Hayes Papers. See letter to Ambassador Winant dated November 10, 1943.
94 Hayes Papers. See letter to Ambassador Winant dated November 10, 1943.
95 Hayes Papers. See letter to Eleanor Roosevelt dated November 8, 1943.
96 Hayes Papers.
97 Sullivan Papers at the Bancroft Collection, Berkeley. See letter dated December 18, 1943. In this letter to Sullivan, Hayes also described the destruction of the German bombing campaign for various parts of London and other parts of the country that he witnessed.
98 Laura Haddock, "My Song is Nothing! Roland Hayes Calls His Voice the Tool of a More Imperative Mission—Racial Harmony," *Christian Science Monitor*, November 22, 1947, 6.

99 Brooks and Sims, *Roland Hayes,* 270. Even as of this writing in 2022, the author finds these comments out of line with the political thinking of that era because they appear to blame those who were facing discrimination and segregation.
100 Hayes, "Foreword" to *My Songs, Aframerican Religious Folk Songs Arranged and Interpreted* (Boston: Little, Brown, 1948).
101 Brooks and Sims, *Roland Hayes,* 273.

CONTRIBUTORS

Jomills Henry Braddock II is professor of sociology at the University of Miami.

Christopher A. Brooks is professor of anthropology at Virginia Commonwealth University.

Matthew Buttermann is director of jazz studies at Fordham University.

Marvin Chiles is assistant professor of history at Old Dominion University.

Marvin P. Dawkins is professor of sociology at the University of Miami.

Bertis D. English is professor of history at Alabama State University.

Judson L. Jeffries is professor of African American and African Studies at The Ohio State University.

Kevin C. McDonald is is adjunct professor of applied jazz percussion at the Reva and Sid Dewberry Family School of Music at George Mason University.

Derryn Moten is professor and chair of the Department of History and Political Science at Alabama State University.

Waweise Schmidt is retired professor of biology at Palm Beach State College in Florida.

Arthur Smith is CEO of Arthur Smith Advising.

Theodore Walker Jr. is associate professor of ethics and society at the Perkins School of Theology at Southern Methodist University in Dallas, Texas.

INDEX

Abraham Lincoln Republic Club, 138
Academy of Morgan College, 9
Africa, xvii, 274
African Methodist Zion Church, 130
African Progress Union, 255
Alabama Christian Movement for Human Rights, 140, 149
Alabama State Board of Education, 91
Alabama State University, 57
Alabama Tribune, 147
Ali, Duse Muhammed, 253, 254, 256
Allee, W. C., 38, 39
Alpha Kappa Alpha, xix, 16
Alpha Kappa Nu, xix
Alpha Phi Alpha, xix, 10, 16, 18
Alston, Melvin, 108
Alston v. School Board of City of Norfolk (1939–1940) 132
American Chemical Society, 70, 71
American Federation of Musicians, 237
American Gold Classic, 169
Anderson, Rebecca J., 73, 74
Apollo Theatre, 216
Armstrong, Byron, 10, 220
Astrobiology, 46
Atlanta Daily World, 266
Augusta National Golf Club, 170
Austin Fellowship, 60

Bailey v. State of Alabama, xvii
Baldwin, Ruth Standish, xvi
Ball, Robert "Pat" 163
Baltimore, Maryland, 63
Baltimore Afro-American, 181, 259
Baraka, Amiri, 232
Bassette, Andrew W. E., 105
Bell, Derrick A., 143

Bennett, Tony, 218
Berlin Conference, 1884–1885, xviii
Bethune, Mary McLeod, 9, 252
Billingsley, Orzell, Jr., 143
Bioethics, 41
Biology of the Cell Surface, The (Just), 43
Birmingham News, 89, 128
Birmingham Post Herald, 142
Birmingham Reporter, 129, 144
Birth of a Nation, xiii
Birth of Bebop, The, 234
Black Caruso (Roland Hayes), 252
Black Wall Street, 11
Bloomfield Moore Fellowship, 63
Blue Devils (band), 208, 209
Boston Chronicle, 265
Boston Symphony Hall, 273
Boston University, 8
Botha, Louis, xi
Bowler v. Richmond (1941), 109
Braxter, Eugene O., 133
Browder v. Gayle, 82
Brown, Clifford, 228, 229, 236
Brown, Oscar, 239
Brown, Pete, 164, 169
Brown, S. N., 5
Brown v. Board of Education, 87, 95, 99, 139
Brown II (1955) 114, 115
Bryant, Ray, 226
Burg, Harvey M., 128
Burrough, Helen Nannie, 4

Cable, Francis L. Ross, 189
Camp Meade, 5
Campanis, Al, 159
Carnegie, Andrew, xv
Carver, George Washington, 252

Central Intercollegiate Athletic Association (CIAA) 179, 180, 181, 182, 185, 186, 187, 188, 189, 190, 191, 192, 193, 194, 195, 196
Cherry Blossom (club), 210
Chesapeake, Ohio & Southwestern Railroad v. Wells (1887), 111
Chicago Defender, 2
Chicago Tribune, 67
Christian Science Monitor, 273
Christian Street YMCA, 7
Citizen & Southern Bank, 7
Civil Rights Act of 1866, xii
Civil Rights Act of 1875, xii, 111
Civil Rights Act of 1964 241
Civil War, 1
Clark, Eural, 164
Clark University, 3
Cobb, William, 59, 60, 61, 68, 73, 74
Coleman, Frank, 6, 11, 12, 13, 14, 15, 20
Coltrane, John, 220
Colored Women's League, xv
Congress of Racial Equality, 115, 145
Connor, Eugene "Bull" 89
Cook, Helen Appo, xv
Cooper, Julia Anna Haywood, 4, 20
Cooper, Oscar James, 6, 7, 8, 10, 11, 12, 13, 14, 15
Count Basie Orchestra, 213
Crisis, The, 253
Crouch, Stanley, 224
Crummell, Alexander, xvii
Crump, Phyliss, 7
Cully v. Baltimore & Ohio R. R. (1876) 111
Czechoslovakia, 38

Daily News, 145
Dartmouth College, 11, 47, 50
Darwin, 43
Davis, Benjamin O., Sr., 4
Davis, Miles, 220, 223, 229, 233
Davis v. Board of School Commissioners of Mobile County (1963) 85, 86
Davis v. Prince Edward (1951) 114
Deans v. Richmond (1929) 107
DeFares, Jack, 188
Delta Sigma Theta, xix, 63
Department of Justice, 89
DePauw University, 58, 59, 60, 66

Dickerson, Mahala Ashley, 81
Diggs, Watson, 10
Dixon v. Alabama State Board of Education (1961) 84
Donald Byrd Dance Group, 235
Douglas, William O., 144
DownBeat, 242
Dr. Oscar J. Cooper Way, 7
Dreer, Herman, 8
Drew, Charles, 70
Drum Conversation, 229
Du Bois, W.E.B., xv, xvi, xvii, xxii, 1, 16, 17, 37, 130, 253
Dudley, Edward R., 133
Duke Ellington Orchestra, 204
Dumas, Alexandre, 12
Dunbar Theatre, 7
Durham, North Carolina, 182

E. E. Just Program and Symposium, 49
Eckstine, Billy, 218
Elks Club, 9
Ellington, Duke, 206, 207

Farmer, James, 115
Fauset, Jessie, 4
Fields, James A., 105
First Congregational Society, 2
Fisk University, 60, 135, 252, 253, 267
Fitzgerald, Ella, 214
Fleetwood, Christian, 4
Fletcher Henderson Orchestra, 203
Flower, Richmond, 91
Fortune, T. Thomas, xiii
Franklin v. Parker (1963), 84
Frazier, E. Franklin, 19
Freedom Sounds (Monson), 227
Freedom Suite (Sonny Rollins), 239
Freedomways, 240
Frontiers of America Club, 9
Ft. Des Moines, Iowa, 5, 8
Ft. Louis, 169
Ft. Meade, 5

Gamma Phi, xix
Gamma Psi, 130
Gaston, Arthur G., 132
General Education Board Fellowship, 61
Gibbs, William B., 109

Index · 285

Giddings, Paula, 20
Gil Evans Orchestra, 239
Giles v. Harris, xiii
Gill, Robert L., 8, 14
Gillespie, Dizzy, 215, 223
Gleaster, John, 169
Glidden Company, 65, 66, 67, 69
Gomillion v. Lightfoot (1960) 86, 87
Goodman, Benny, 212, 215
Grand Basileus, 14
Grand Keeper of Records, 6, 14
Grand Keeper of Seal, 6, 14
Greater Hartford Open, 170
Green v. Bridgeton (1879), 111
Greenberg, Jack, 143, 146, 150
Greer, Sonny, 205, 206
Grooms, Hobart, 92
Guatemala Julian Laboratories, 72

Hall, Peter, Sr., 143
Hall v. DeCuir (1868) 111
Hampton Institute, 18, 187
Harlan, Marshall, xiii
Harlem Globetrotters, 193
Harris, Alfred W., 105
Harris, B. F., 105
Harris, George Edmund, xvi
Harvard Law School, 102, 135
Harvard University, 60
Hastie, William Hastie, 100, 103, 113
Havana, Cuba, 207
Hawkins, Coleman, 225, 230, 243
Hayes, James H., 105
Heard v. Georgia (1888), 111
Henderson, Fletcher, 213
Highwarden, Ethel, 14, 36
Hodges v. United States, xiii
Holmes, Alfred "Tup" 165
Holmes v. Atlanta (1955), 165
Hood, David H., Sr., 133
Houston, Charles Hamilton, 81, 100, 103, 104, 105, 113
Howard, Oliver O., 2, 3
Howard, Perry Wilborn, Jr., 103
Howard Journal, 5, 10
Howard University, 1, 2, 3, 6, 12, 13, 16, 35, 38, 39, 48, 50, 61, 63
Howard University School of Law, 81, 102, 113, 131

Hudson, Polly, 143
Hughes, Langston, xviii, 252, 269
Hughes, Solomon, 164
Huntington, Collis P., xv
Hurley, Ruby, 83
Hurt, Eddie, 180, 182

Illustrious Omega Psi Phi Fraternity, Inc., xix, xxii, 3, 12, 14, 20, 23

James E. Walker Post 26 (American Legion), 6
Jim Crow, 158, 159, 184, 186, 195
Joe Louis Open, 168
John, Wilfred, 188
John Wesley United Methodist Church, 10
Johnson, Anna Roselle, 63
Johnson, Frank, Jr., 92
Johnson, George, 174
Johnson, Jack, 258
Johnson, Mordecai, 102
Joseph K. Brick Agricultural Industrial and Normal School, 5
Julian Associates, Inc., 73
Julian Laboratories, 69
Julian Research Institute, 73
Just, Ernest E., 6, 11, 12, 13, 14, 15

Kappa Alpha Psi, xix, 10
Kappa Sigma, 5
Kennedy, Robert F., 89
Kenton, Stan, 204
Kimball Union Academy, 12, 37
King, Martin Luther, Jr., 82, 84, 148
Knights of Labor, xiv
Knights of Pythias, xix
Kotick, Teddy, 226
Ku Klux Klan, 2

Lacy, Sam, 181
Langston, John Mercer, 102
Lee, Benjamin, 16
Lee v. Macon County Board of Education (1963) 84, 86, 89, 92, 94
Letter from Birmingham Jail (King), 84
Lightfoot, Phillip M., 86
Lincoln, Abraham, xxii
Logan, Rayford, 4, 18, 19
London Manifesto (Du Bois), 256
Long, Herman H., 111

Looby, Z. Alexander, 103
Louis, Joe, 164, 166
Love, Edgar Amos, 8, 9, 10, 11, 12, 14, 15, 20
Lucy, Autherine, 83, 143
Lyric Theater, 259, 261, 263

M Street High School, 4
Macon County Board of Education, 91, 94
Manning, Kenneth, 13
Manuel Arts High School, 168
Margold, Nathan Ross, 107
Marine Biology Laboratory (MBL) 35, 40, 48, 50
Marshall, Thurgood, 100, 113, 133, 134
Marshall, Louis, 106
Mason-Dixon line, xi, 1, 7
Masters Tournament, 165
Max Roach Industries, 238
McCabe v. Atchison, Topeka & Santa Fe Railway Company (1914), 108
McKinley, William, xiv
McLendon, John, 186, 187, 191, 193
Meharry Medical College, 3
Meuse-Argonne Offensive, 8
Mexico, 71
Miller, Kelly, 16, 70
Milma Publishing Company, 237
Mingus, Charles, 237
Missionary Society of the First Congregational Church, 1
Modern Drummer, 242
Modern Touch, The (Benny Golson Sextet), 229
Monk, Thelonious, 233
Monroe, Earl, 194, 195
Monsanto Open, 170
Monterey Jazz Festival, 231
Montgomery, Alabama, 57
Montgomery Advertiser, 81, 83
Moody, Orville, 169
Morehouse, Henry Lyman, xvii, 11
Moreland, Jesse E., 16
Morgan, Irene, 110
Morgan State University, 180, 181
Morrill Acts of 1862 and 1890, xix
Morrow, George, 226
Moten, Bennie, 209, 210, 211
"Mother To Son" (Hughes), xviii
Motley, Constance Baker, 94, 143
Mount Washington United Methodist Church, 8

Nabrit, James M. III, 143, 146
National Afro-American Council (NAACL), xiv
National Association for the Advancement of Colored People, xvi, 9, 19, 83, 84, 109, 139, 183
National Association of Colored Women, xv, xvi
National Association for Improving Negro Country Life, 267
National Congress of British West Africa, 257
National Public Links Golf Championship Tournament, 163
Nazis, 38
Negro Music Festival, 253
Negro spirituals, 252, 264
Newman, Stephen Morrell, 20
Newport Jazz Festival, 238
New York Post, 165
New York Times, 145
Niagara Movement, xv, xvi
Nicklaus, Jack, 166, 169
Norfolk Journal and Guide, 108
Norfolk State University, 108
North Carolina A & T University, 240
North Carolina College, 193
Notasulga High School, 90

Oakley, Charles, 194
Oak Park, 67, 68, 69
Ogden, Robert C., 18
Owens, Jesse, 37

Paine College, 174
Palmetto State (South Carolina), xi
Pan African Congresses, 19
Park, Robert, 183
Parker, Charlie, 204, 209, 215, 220, 223, 225, 237, 243
Parks, Rosa, 82, 109, 150
Pearl Harbor, 11
Pendergast, Tom, 208
Percussion Bitter Sweet (Max Roach), 240
PGA, 169
Philadelphia Club, 12
Phi Beta Kappa, 59, 64
Phi Beta Sigma, xix
Pi Gamma Omicron, xix
Pittsburgh Courier, 147, 265
Plessy v. Ferguson, xii, 81, 95, 108, 111, 113

Pollard, Joseph Roland, 105
Poll tax, 133
Powell, Richie, 243
Powell v. Alabama, 144
Pryor, Charles Caffey, 81

Quarles, Benjamin, 16

Radical New York Group, 107
Railroad Company v. Brown (1873), 111
Rainbow Gardens, 211
Randolph, A. Philip, 252
Reconstruction, 1
Reid, Thomas Harris, 105
Rhodes, Ted, 169, 171, 172
Richmond, Virginia, 98
Richmond Afro-American, 108
Ritchie, Albert, 9
Rives, Richard T., 92
Robinson, Jackie, 165
Robinson v. Memphis & Charleston Railroad (1883), 111
Rollins, Sonny, 226, 239
Rooney Rule, 160
Roosevelt, Theodore, xix
Rowan, Carl, 83

Savoy Ballroom, 213
Schnetzler, Hedwig, 36, 39
Schuh, Richard, 13
Shady Rest Golf and Country Club, 162
Shakespeare, 4
Shores, Arthur D., 81, 143
Sixteenth Street Baptist Church, 148
Shuttlesworth, Fred, 88, 140, 141, 150
Shuttlesworth v. Birmingham Board of Education, 88
Sifford, Charlie, 164, 171
Sigma, xi, 59
Sigma Gamma Rho, xix
Sinatra, Frank, 218
Sit Down and Listen: The Story of Max Roach (film), 233
Smith v. Allwright, 134
Smuts, Jan, xi
South African National Party, xi
Southern Christian Leadership Conference, 82
Southern Workman, 18

Spiller, Bill, 164
Spingarn, Arthur, 106
Spingarn Medal, 258
St. Louis Dispatch, 93
State ex rel. Abbott v. Hicks (1892), 111
Stell v. Savannah-Chatham Board of Education (1963), 84
"Stompin' at the Savoy" (Max Roach), 229
Storey, Moorfield, 106
Styles, Fitzhugh Lee, 104
Syntex Laboratories, 71

Taft, William Howard, xx
Talented Tenth, xvii
Talladega College, 130
Tate, Buddy, 215
Terry, Clark, 216, 218
Texas Western University, 194
Theatre Owners and Bookers Association, 207
Thirkield, Wilbur Patterson, 3, 15, 16, 17, 18, 19, 20
368th Infantry, 8
Till, Emmett, 139
Tour De Force (Sonny Rollins), 236
Trevino, Lee, 170
Trotter, William, xv, xvi, 17
Tubman, Harriet, xv
Tuskegee Civic Association, 86
Tuskegee High School, 86, 89, 90
Tuskegee Institute, xix
Tuskegee Institute Community Education Project, 86
Twelve Clouds of Joy (band), 209
Tyson, Edwin French, 4

Underground Railroad, 2
Union League Club, 67
United Negro College Fund, 111
United States Golf Association, 162, 163
United States v. Jefferson City Board of Education (1967), 87
United States of America vs. George Wallace, et al, Defendants, 90
Universal Negro Improvement Association and African Communities League, 252
University of Alabama, 83
University of Chicago, 5, 12, 36
University of Minnesota, 65

University of Mississippi, 82
University of Pennsylvania, 64

Vanguard Jazz Orchestra, 228
Vaughn, Sarah, 218
Voting Rights Act of 1965, 241

Wake Forest University, 192, 193
Walden, A. T., 103
Wallace, George, 83, 89, 92
Wallace, Lurleen, 93
Waller, Fats, 206, 207
Washington, Booker T., xv, xix, 16, 253
Washington Afro-American, 259, 260
Washington Daily American, 259, 260
Washington Post, 263
Webb, Chick, 210, 213, 214, 223–24, 230
West Virginia State College, 60

White, Charles B., 101
White, Walter, 252, 268
Wilder, L. Douglas, 115
Williams, Joe, 217
Wilson, Woodrow, xiv, xxii
Winston-Salem, 185
Winston-Salem Teachers College, 180, 182, 190, 189, 191, 196
Witkop, Bernard, 62, 73, 74
Woods, Tiger, 165, 166, 171
Woodson, Carter G., 4, 103
World Golf Hall of Fame, 166
World War I, 8

YMCA, 6
Young, Lester, 204, 209, 213

Zeta Phi Beta, xix

www.ingramcontent.com/pod-product-compliance
Lightning Source LLC
Chambersburg PA
CBHW030608230426
43661CB00053B/1890